Global Geopolitical Power and African Political and Economic Institutions

Global Geopolitical Power and African Political and Economic Institutions

When Elephants Fight

John James Quinn

LEXINGTON BOOKS
Lanham • Boulder • New York • London

Published by Lexington Books
An imprint of The Rowman & Littlefield Publishing Group, Inc.
4501 Forbes Boulevard, Suite 200, Lanham, Maryland 20706
www.rowman.com

Unit A, Whitacre Mews, 26-34 Stannary Street, London SE11 4AB

British Library Cataloguing in Publication Information Available

Library of Congress Cataloging-in-Publication Data Available

ISBN: 978-0-7391-9644-1 (cloth : alk. paper)
eISBN: 978-0-7391-9645-8 (electronic)

∞™ The paper used in this publication meets the minimum requirements of American National Standard for Information Sciences—Permanence of Paper for Printed Library Materials, ANSI/NISO Z39.48-1992.

Printed in the United States of America

For Renuka, Jack, and James

Contents

List of Figures

List of Tables

Acknowledgments

I would like to acknowledge the many people who have helped in the process of the writing of this book. Thanks especially to Dennis P. Quinn, Jr., my brother and friend, who has read several versions of this work through the years and offered much support. Thanks as well to Truman State University, where I teach and write, for assistance with several aspects of this project, including a much needed sabbatical release and financial and logistical support. Thanks also to my colleges and students (past and present) at Truman who have heard and engaged with many of my ideas, either in the hallway or classroom. I would also like to thank the faculty members and my former cohort at UCLA who helped shape much of my thinking: much of Chapters 2-4 are derived from parts of my dissertation. This goes especially for Mike Lofchie and Richard Sklar. I also owe a debt in general to Africanists and political scientists whose writings and ideas have informed my views and opinions; much of this book and my knowledge of international relations, political science, and Africa clearly depend upon secondary sources. I have tried to cite the sources most central to the paradigms, theories, or data I have relied upon, but inevitably I shall have forgotten to cite some important ones, though references to them might be in cited works. Also, thanks to Maura Parson, Rachel Anderson, and Nicholas Wehner for assistance in proofreading. Maura, especially, read the whole manuscript with a keen eye. Also, I would like to thank the anonymous reviewer for this manuscript, as well as those who saw earlier versions of the statistical chapter sent around as a possible article, for their valuable feedback and the time. I would also like to thank the various people at Lexington Books who have been involved in this process, beginning with Alissa Parra, who brought the manuscript in, as well as subsequent editors Justin Race and Joseph Parry. Thanks also to their assistants, including Kathryn Tafelski, Sarah Craig, Geoffrey Zokal, and Emily Roderick. Thanks also to Anita Singh for her work on the final production side. Also, thanks to Jacqueline Frances Brownstein who created the initial index. I would also like to thank my family, especially my wife, Renuka, and my sons, Jack and James (for whom this book is dedicated), for their forbearance, especially during the latter parts of this project [and for the pleasure that being with them brings when I am home]. Finally, responsibility for any errors (or omissions) in the text, including spelling, typos, or argument is mine.

Chapter 1

Geopolitics, International Relations, and Sub-Saharan Africa

"Tembo zikipigana huumia nyasi."   Swahili proverb
[When elephants fight, it's the grass that suffers.]

There is a tide in the affairs of men,
Which, taken at the flood, leads on to fortune;
Omitted, all the voyage of their life
Is bound in shallows and in miseries.
On such a full sea are we now afloat;
And we must take the current when it serves,
Or lose our ventures.   *Julius Caesar*, 4:3, 218–224

Scholars of sub-Saharan Africa generally acknowledge two widespread, relatively rapid, and significant periods of change in the fundamental political and economic institutional structures and practices of the region.[1] The first period witnessed the decolonization of most of the sub-continent between 1957 and 1966.[2] This comparatively quick process (historically speaking) was followed by the emergence of one-party or no-party (read military) political regimes in the region nearly everywhere. Although the hastily departing colonial countries had established parliamentary regimes to replace colonial political structures, only three of the region's ex-colonies maintained these bequeathed multiparty electoral systems for more than a decade.[3] In this context, most political power in the region became controlled by the elites of a single political party, or the military, within a decade of decolonization.

In this first period, the economic landscape of the region also would feature a significant change in structures and practices of economic power, resulting in the centralization of economic power into the hands of the political elites. On the one hand, the widespread adoption of moderately to strongly inward-oriented development policies greatly increased governmental control over

1

economic policies and flows. On the other hand, the rise of state-led investment and the nationalization of formerly foreign-owned economic sectors
increased the political elite's direct control of the economy. These trends
were strongest in Afro-Marxist and socialist states, though even nominally
capitalist states often featured majority state ownership of vital economic sectors. For example, in Nigeria the government nationalized its petroleum sector, and Zaire (now the Democratic Republic of the Congo) nationalized its
copper sector. Even the most paradigmatically capitalist states of Kenya and
Ivory Coast had substantial numbers of state-owned enterprises, though this
ownership did not extend to majority state ownership of most of its capital-
intensive firms or of a major mineral or oil exporting sector.[4]

The second region-wide change in political institutions and practices of
the sub-continent is often referred to as "the second wave" of liberation.[5]
What emerged was a relatively rapid, and nearly universal, change in the
major political institutions and practices: nearly every nation abandoned one-
party and no-party states and adopted multiparty electoral regimes. In fact,
between 1990 and 1997, all but six sub-Saharan African nations held some
form of multiparty election, though the attendant levels of political and civil
freedom varied greatly.[6] More recently, all but three have held such elections.
This was paralleled by similar region-wide changes in economic policies and
ownership patterns: most countries transitioned away from inward-oriented
economic development policies and most began to privatize many formerly
majority state-owned companies. Significantly more foreign direct investment (FDI) also began flowing into the region.

Therefore, the second period has witnessed, at least in outward institutional
form, a region-wide change of the major economic and political institutions
and practices of the region. It has also meant a partial fragmentation of both
political and economic power away from the political center. Nonetheless,
despite evidence of region-wide and massive changes in the formal institutions and practices in the region, significant political and economic power
still remains in the hands of political incumbents. However, these powerful
political elites wield significantly less political and economic power than they
did in the first period and are less secure in their tenure. In fact, some turnover
of political office is emerging, though incumbency rates remain high.

I intend to illustrate how these two important, region-wide shifts in African
political and economic institutions and policies are linked to two prior and
massive geopolitical shifts at the center of international power. I argue that
different leading states have significantly dissimilar views on how best to
manage the international system, especially vis-à-vis ideas and preferences
concerning free trade, types of economic policies, types of political systems,
alliance structures, and so forth. Therefore, the type of international system
which follows a global geopolitical transition is quite likely different from

the prior one. To underline the point, had either Nazi Germany or the Soviet Union become the hegemon following WWII, the world order would have been quite different from the one which emerged.[7]

With the new geopolitical equilibrium, new system leaders, or would-be leaders, try to create positive and negative incentives to secure allies (or ward off potential adversaries) in an attempt to cement into place their leadership in the international community. These incentives can be bilateral or multilateral: they can be in the forms of aid, investment, access to markets, access to technology, access to weapons, entrance into defense treaties or agreements, or in the denial of such things. They can even involve the use of coercion or military force where the benefits of such tactics are perceived. Moreover, a new geopolitical equilibrium can create an opportunity where newly arising and widely shared norms can be institutionalized (or attempted to become institutionalized) by the system leaders or would-be leaders. This can be tied to the above previously-discussed attempt to consolidate a position of leadership within the international system.

Also, with a significant geopolitical realignment, the "learning" about what caused the shift occurs and how power is pursued or is not pursued internationally can change radically, as learning is system wide. This has to do with any change in the legitimacy of particular practices and institutions throughout the system.[8] Approaches, ideas, and ideologies associated with the "losing" camp would be weakened in their legitimacy. Beyond learning, the power of particular ideas or ideologies themselves can change radically after a realignment for other, similar, reasons: first, the amount of resources placed behind them may change with the fortunes of their advocates, and second, newly ascendant ideas or ideologies can be adopted by institutions and enshrined into practice, which will likely result in increased economic, political, military, or diplomatic support for their continuation.

Moreover, changes in international norms about what is considered to be possible or permissible in the new system are often likewise radically altered: the perceived fairness and effectiveness of particular political, social, and economic institutions and policies are re-evaluated at such times, resulting in the adoption of new systems and practices. This can have been either out of a sense of change in perceived instrumental rationality or morality or from some combination of both.

This newly shaped set of incentives created by powerful states along with the new lessons drawn from recent geopolitical changes necessarily transforms the set of constraints and opportunities facing other leaders, especially those of weaker nations, such as those in sub-Saharan Africa.[9] Leaders of weaker states then have to respond to these significant geopolitical shifts in power, ideas, norms, and sets of incentives along with the newly drawn lessons associated with these changes in order to maximize their domestic power. These responses become reflected in the leaders' choices of domestic political and economic institutions, as well as in their economic and political foreign policies.

I hold that leaders of weaker nations are especially vulnerable and sensitive to changes in the international system and will respond in ways that they perceive would likely extend and deepen their own grasp on domestic economic and political power. Also, other pretenders to power in these states may reevaluate their chances of realigning domestic power given the change in constraints and opportunities in the new international environment: they may change the means by which they attempt to gain economic or political power within their own nations, which may or may not include access to resources from other countries. Hence, the ultimate link between the changes in the international community and changes in the political and economic institutions of African states is complex and multilayered. However, these changes reflect many incentives of many actors, so the more radical the change at the geopolitical center, the more radical the changes will be throughout the larger system.

INTERNATIONAL RELATIONS THEORY, HIERARCHY, AND AFRICA

Relations among and between powerful states may approximate realist, neorealist, or neoliberal positions of anarchic relations among autonomous states, but they are especially ill-adapted in describing the relations between advanced nations and weak ones. Hierarchical relations are likely a better description.[10] Quite clearly, the weakness of African states is hard to square directly with the assumption of a Hobbesian state of war among and between all states. To the contrary, countries in the region of sub-Saharan Africa have engaged in fewer interstate wars than countries in other regions. Lemke has gone so far as to suggest that Africa can be considered to be a "zone of peace"—at least where interstate wars were concerned.[11] Political elites in the region have tended to fear external invasion much less than domestic insurgencies. Foreign backed domestic rivals would be especially dangerous, however, because they are potential claimants to the throne with access to external resources with some domestic legitimacy.[12]

The normal realist view of a system based upon anarchy and self-help does not fit the region well; since independence, most of Africa's states have been characterized by weak military ability, underdeveloped economies, low levels of growth, and persistent current account imbalances. No sub-Saharan African country is a military threat to any of the great or super powers, and few of them have been real threats to their neighbors. In fact, only South Africa had a nuclear weapons program, though it was eliminated before 1990. Few of them even have an air force or navy worth mentioning. Some countries may have larger standing armies than others, but none of them can project power outside of their immediate region, let alone internationally.[13] For example, the Mobutu regime in Zaire (now the Democratic Republic of the Congo) was able to stay in power after the Shaba I and Shaba II uprisings only due to American, French and Belgian support.[14] However, once the Cold War ended, Mobutu's backing by the West also ended, and he was unable to quell a domestic uprising in the east following the Rwandan Genocide with only domestic resources at his disposal.[15]

Moreover, many African nations performed quite poorly economically and became heavily reliant upon official development assistance (ODA) (i.e., economic aid) from dominant powers as well as the most important multilateral intergovernmental organizations (IGOs), such as the World Bank and International Monetary Fund (IMF). Even with the support of these institutions or foreign donors, few African states were able to maintain fiscal balance, especially from the 1980s onwards.[16] With the policies of "conditionality" resulting in links between economic policy reform and continued aid, the de facto sovereignty of many developing nations in economic foreign policy has clearly diminished. Many African countries are also quite reliant upon access to advanced countries' markets—much more than these latter countries need access to African markets (let alone investments from them), and some are quite reliant upon first world military and diplomatic support to stay in power.[17] A partial exception to these trends may exist for major producers of strategic resources, such as oil or minerals: this may result in a stronger negotiating position vis-à-vis developed nations as oil or mineral exporting countries offer strategically important goods. Nonetheless, even these countries rely upon prevailing norms and external assistance to stay in power. The recent problems in Nigeria and their need for assistance with their insurgency in the North are particularly telling.[18] Most leaders of sub-Saharan African nations seek access to resources from an array of domestic, regional, and international sources. And these resources are often necessary to provide economic, military, and diplomatic security for themselves and their countries: all of this seems quite at odds with many key assumptions of realism.[19]

Many scholars of African International Relations have argued that neither realism nor neorealism reflects African realities.[20] Jackson and Rosberg write that "Black Africa challenges more than it supports some of the major postulates of international relations theory."[21] Importantly, and possibly ironically, many African leaders have chosen to undermine their own domestic capabilities in order to deny competitors a strong institutional base upon which to launch a competition for power.[22] Undermining one's own domestic power is in direct opposition to key realist predictions and assumptions. Others hold that the crucial distinctions between internal and external power, as well as legitimacy, are less important in Africa.[23] Others challenge the common IR assumption that the state is the most relevant unit of analysis for African foreign relations: Warlords, ethnic rivalries, the World Bank, the IMF, and non-governmental organizations (NGOs) all matter quite a bit in relation to African political and economic realities.[24]

Importantly, the quasi-state literature suggests that most states in sub-Saharan Africa exist only because of the internationally recognized norm of sovereignty: since weak nations cannot defend against direct challenges to their own sovereignty, they only exist as a result of this international norm.[25] Jackson argued that negative (de jure) sovereignty props up these weak states, which lack positive (de facto) sovereignty. The norm of sovereignty is so important to powerful international actors that it becomes extended to weaker states (at least in principle) for the benefit of the powerful.[26] Realizing their inherent weakness, Third World elites have jealously guarded the norm of sovereignty as it allows them access to international sources of money, prestige, and power needed to consolidate power domestically. In addition, these sources of power have allowed elites to rule over a postcolonial state which did not emerge "endogenously" or naturally from its past, except in a very few cases.[27] The norm of (de jure) sovereignty guards their security more effectively than a dozen divisions of tanks. Given this view of sovereignty and how African leaders maintain their domestic power, hierarchy is the better lens through which to view the relations of African states and powerful ones.

This view of hierarchy is consistent with East's empirical analysis of the foreign policy behavior of small (read weak) states. East suggests that small states' foreign policies can be characterized as such:

> (a) low levels of overall participation in world affairs; (b) high levels of activity in intergovernmental organizations; (c) high levels of support for international legal norms; (d) avoidance to the use of force as a technique of statecraft; (e) avoidance of behaviour and policies which tend to alienate the more powerful states in the system; (f) a narrow functional and geographic range of concern in foreign policy activities; (g) frequent utilization of moral and normative positions on international issues.[28]

These actions indicate a view of choices made under conditions of hierarchic power relations.

Nonetheless, even if some aspects of African foreign policy or international relations appear to be hierarchical (de facto), the principle of (de jure) sovereignty still organizes the larger international relations system, and sovereignty is still the prevailing norm in the wide system. As a result, a recalcitrant leader of a less powerful nation, such as Mugabe, can stand against the will of the international community for prolonged periods, though at great economic, military, and political cost to the nation and its citizens.[29] This is in part because Russia and China have been known to veto UN Security Council actions which would punish nations for issues that could be seen as undermining these countries' sovereignty—but they do so to protect a strong norm of sovereignty more for themselves than for the sake of the particular weaker nations. This underscores the irony and co-existence of hierarchy and sovereignty: weak states stand against international pressures at great harm to themselves, but for the potential benefit of a minority at the helm. Therefore, states in sub-Saharan Africa are still technically sovereign (de jure) vis-à-vis more powerful nations; however, even with sovereignty, should leaders of weak states go against the wishes of the great/super powers, they will likely find that they obtain fewer carrots and face more severe sticks in the international realm. They may also find themselves unable to develop or grow well under these circumstances. This may ultimately lead to the overthrow of the recalcitrant elite as the economies implode or stagnate. Great powers would not have this problem.

Why Should a Geopolitical Change Matter to the System?

Clearly, if the world is hierarchical, from the perspective of weaker nations in regards to major powers, then a significant geopolitical power shift would necessarily impact these weak state leaders tremendously. Such a shift results in a new system leader, new system leaders, or new would-be system leaders, and these new vying great powers likely have different views of how the international community should be arranged, or what foreign policy decision should be pre-eminent, or what political or economic arrangements are in its/ their self-interests compared to the prior system leader or leaders.[30] Once these new system leaders emerge or begin to lead (or the now more powerful system leaders assert their power), they are likely to work on changing international institutions, practices, and norms to deepen or reinforce their newfound power and to cement it internationally. This then changes the constraints and opportunities facing leaders of weaker nations; therefore, a change in leadership at the center greatly impacts the space and nature of choices at the periphery.

However, I argue that dominant powers or hegemons cannot merely set the rules or dictate their preferred norms for the new international order in a costless way: therefore, they need to draw allies by offering some international or regional public goods enjoyed by others who then would back and/or condone the ideologies and rules underpinning the rising order.[31] Therefore, the new system leaders, or would-be leaders, who choose to project power internationally, need to place real resources into the creation or changing of international institutions, regimes, or practices which best promote their interests—and which help bring new allies on board. These resources offered as incentives can be diplomatic, economic, or military, and they can be either positive or negative. They could be such things as access to markets, denial of access to markets, access to some seas or sea lanes, denial of some seas or sea lanes, protection from threats, membership in cooperative organizations, recognition, support in intergovernmental organizations, trade enriching deals, sanctions, economic or military aid, recognition of other countries' leaders, and so forth. Moreover, such resources could also be distributed bilaterally as well as multilaterally, depending on the power and access of the leaders or would-be leaders.

These new resources or potential resources affect the calculus of leaders of other nations seeking to ally with them, bandwagon with them, balance against them, or merely obtain resources from them. At the end of the day, however, the institutions, practices, or norms to which some incentives are attached are intended to bolster the leadership or prosperity or safety of the more powerful states promoting these international institutions, practices, or norms. These could be in the service of either short-term or long-term self-interests, depending on the time horizons of those promoting these ideas, institutions, and norms. Given the above, a change in the power of leaders of the geopolitical system should have a significant impact on the material resources backing particular institutions, practices, and norms embraced or propagated throughout the system as leaders and would-be leaders attempt to consolidate their position of power.

Not only do leaders or would-be leaders need to offer concrete material carrots and sticks to reward allies or punish adversaries, but they also need to justify their base of power through some claims of legitimacy[32]—unless the claims to leadership are only based upon coercion. Nearly every form of rule has a justifying ideology trying to wrest or obtain consent from the governed or ruled, whether through divine rights of kings, rule through combat, governing with the consent of the governed, nationalism and self-determination, economic efficiency, market efficiency, military security, or "bringing home the bacon."[33] This should be seen as true at the international level as well, though it would be leadership rather than rule, per se. Such a promotion of ideas which justify the international leadership's role in the system reduces the use of hard power needed to lead as soft power can help cement in place international positions of power or leadership.[34]

Part of this argument rests on the assumption that the power of ideas depends partially on the material (military, economic, and diplomatic) power or resources of those advocating for them: ideas and ideologies necessarily become stronger or weaker accordingly to the power of their backers (at least in the short term). When backers of (prior) status quo ideas lose power internationally, their preferred ideas, ideologies, institutions, and norms become less legitimate, weaker, or even discredited.[35] By contrast, as the backers of competing ideas gain relative power internationally, their preferred ideas, ideologies, institutions, and norms become more ascendant, more legitimate, and more credible. And as rewards (or punishments) for certain behaviors change, so do behaviors, especially for less powerful states.

Importantly, when there is a significant shift in power among players, especially a rapid one, a policy window opens through which new ideas, ideologies, regimes, and institutions are more easily adopted or institutionalized in the international system. This may translate to lower costs for would-be hegemons to implement or change institutions, norms, and practices than at other times. Therefore, many things are likely to change dramatically following a relatively rapid geopolitical realignment.

Linking these parts of the argument, system leaders who are interested in consolidating their new power positions are likely to push the ideas or ideologies which promote their power, both as a means to wield international influence and as a means to increase their own domestic resources and power. Ultimately, they hope that their preferred ideas, ideologies, regimes, or points of view become institutionalized in practice or "normal procedure" in the international community. Therefore, new system leaders with ideas strongly at odds with those of the prior system leaders are likely to push for institutions and quite different norms and practices than the prior ones, and these changes should be more in line with their (then) perceived self-interests.[36] These changes are likely to emerge, at least in certain spheres, as the newly powerful nations are then better able to translate preferred ideas into norms and institutions as a reflection of their increased military, economic, diplomatic, and political power—given the previously mentioned assumption that the power of ideas is bolstered by the resources placed behind them.[37]

However, once these norms, ideologies, and or ideas are institutionalized or become seen as "normal" or "acceptable international behavior," they become even more powerful than before.[38] On the one hand, institutions tend to create their own public and private constituents who organize to defend their newfound assets and positions.[39] On the other hand, once ideas are formalized into institutional practices and IGOs and other multilateral or bilateral treaties, political inertia prevails and the costs associated with changing or reversing them are considerably higher than during the transitional period of the establishment of new institutions or regimes.[40] For example, according to Hall, challenging ideas within the context of pre-existing institutionalized ideas required significant real political power to pursue a new agenda as attempts at reform can be blocked by office holders who adhere to a competing orthodoxy, world view, or set of ideas.[41] Therefore, ideas enshrined in institutions become more powerful with actors inside and out defending the new status quo.

Moreover, this story is not completely a story about material power of great powers and their distribution of international resources or ideas only having power when backed by powerful actors. Another reason we should expect significant changes in international norms and institutions following a geopolitical realignment is that such shifts are usually associated with "learning" or "updating" concerning the causes and consequences of the recent shift. These lessons should impact all leaders' assessments of what is possible as well as how to obtain what is possible. That is to say ideas about politics and economics in the international community sometimes have independent power (or effects) not reducible to the power of the actors backing them or institutions enshrining them.

Importantly, the weight of consensus behind ideas is likely to be greatly impacted (or perceived to have been impacted) right after a major geopolitical shift, because a geopolitical shift usually comes with intellectual lessons "explaining" the shift. These quick lessons show others how to be powerful (or not) in the political, military, diplomatic, and economic arenas, though the lessons often evolve with time. The ensuing rising consensus discredits or weakens old ideas or norms that had been backed by the declining camp both as a result of fewer resources behind the ideas and by a weakening in the belief or a discrediting of the very ideas that had underpinned the prior arrangements.[42]

This is not to say, however, that all ideas whose champions have lost on the battlefield or in the marketplace are destined for the "dustbin of history." Rather, it is to suggest that defeat carries interpretations that usually weaken them. Part of the strength of these rising or falling ideas in consensus comes from interpretations of events drawn from near history, though the lessons from history can be revised over time or strongly contested. Sometimes, though, early lessons drawn have a consensus and are thereby stronger.

Moreover, and similar to the idea of learning, I believe that ideas (or principles) also have a particularly strong and independent impact when they affect the very calculus by which elites and others attempt to maximize their power.[43] That is to say ideas matter more when they are held to be "true" in a scientific, social-scientific, or quasi-social scientific view, to the point where important actors use these ideas to guide how they achieve ends: that is, when they are perceived to be useful instrumentally. This is particularly true for choices of political or economic institutions that are held to lead to particular socially beneficial outcomes. For example, the backers of democracy during a time when democracy is seen as leading to economic growth and prosperity are in a stronger position in comparison with a period when democracy is proposed merely as a "fair" or "just" political system, but one which suffers from economic malaise. As such, backers of particular economic systems are stronger when empirical evidence appears to show that these systems produce more or better fruit than competing ones.[44]

Similarly, such ideas can be stronger when backed by members of the academy or other think tanks, as these academic circles can affect how widely consensuses are held. Therefore, an evolving, and partially independent, world of ideas exists in which debates about how best to govern and run countries and economies occur that informs, and is informed by, past and current economic and political systems and their attendant successes and failures. As one scholar wrote, "[t]he economics of every period and place reflects not only contemporary political demands but crucial professional interpretations of the actual development of the recent past."[45] This could be extended to political systems as well.

Another way ideas can impact how society accepts or does not accept types of political rule (or economic ideologies) exists on a moral level; a change here can clearly have an impact on the decision-making constraints and opportunity of elites. As will be discussed later, the rise of African nationalism in the wake of WWII led to more protests and violence on behalf of emerging nationalist leaders, and these nationalist leaders could count on followers participating in such acts even though such action might result in arrest, prison, or worse. As ideas diffuse throughout society, and old forms of legitimacy are discredited, the formerly justifying ideology becomes no longer tenable. Therefore, the power of ideas, norms, or ideologies vis-à-vis economic and political systems are found in a mix of presumed truth values and the amount of resources placed behind them by the supporters (or opponents) as well as their potential basis of moral support within the larger society (or legitimacy). Some of this shift in power can be learning, but some could be emulation, as imitation may be a shorthand form of learning.

In sum, a change in the economic, military, and political power of the advocates of certain ideas (which occurs with a geopolitical shift) has the potential to change the importance or relevance of many ideas, ideologies, and norms. More scholars have included ideas as possible sources of power beyond that springing from the material power and self-interests of actors and states.[46] The spread or diffusion of ideas matters, and this arises from a mixture of coercion, compellence, persuasion, and "learning" from past circumstance or even changing norms over fairness or justice.[47] Famously, Marx contradicted Hegel in asserting the material power of classes over the independent role of ideas. More likely one source of power can bolster the other, or one source may weaken the other, depending on the relationships between particular ideas and particular self-interests and widely held beliefs about causation, especially in the high stake games of military defense, economic development, and diplomacy. With a rapid shift in geopolitical power, the change in perceived power is great in a short period, and the opportunity for changing or creating new institutions (or collapsing old ones) is much greater. Such a period is also a time when would-be reforms can take advantage of a policy window to affect change before a new equilibrium is established.

The "mutual constitution" of interests between and among actors and the international system, which constructivists hold to be true, is likely "truest" soon after a significant geopolitical shift occurs and during the transitional period.[48] First, new lessons and learning impinge and impact the strategy and tactics of actors seeking to maximize their interests and power. Second, during such a shift, a period of institutional and power uncertainty arises, where means-end calculations pertaining to how to maximize power occurs in a shifting and evolving circumstance, where information costs are high and views of the near future are in doubt.[49] Some material sources of power may remain relatively untouched during these periods of transition, but how, where, and when to use power to achieve ends always rests on judgments about their effectiveness in any particular context and within particular shifting coalitions of ideas and power.

Thus, after shifts of geopolitical power, the type of economic and political systems of the more powerful side are likely to be emulated or adopted out of a mixture of believing that these institutions promote the power and authority of the nation and its leaders as well as in the hope of reward from leading nations. Leaders of weaker states may want to appear to be seen as natural allies by the system leader(s).

Why Such a Change Should Matter to African States in Particular

When a relatively rapid geopolitical shift in power occurs, a changed structure of hierarchy necessarily results, and the new leaders or would-be leaders often have different interests in significant issues important for leaders of weaker states (as discussed before). Importantly, the weakest nations (e.g., economically, politically, and militarily) are likely to be among the most sensitive and vulnerable to such changes in the center of power. As the leaders and would-be leaders place economic, military, political, and diplomatic power behind these new multilateral as well as bilateral institutions, norms, and expectations, they impact weaker states most directly, given their sensitivity and vulnerability. The newly changed incentives and expectations should involve high cost to weaker nations should they oppose or ignore the preferences of the stronger states, in the forms of compellence, deterrence, neglect, or even ridicule.[50]

Although weaker states could gain strength through collective action and try to challenge the leaders in the hierarchy or to improve their position within it, this is unlikely. First, leaders of minor power nations may or may not have sufficient common interests with other leaders of minor powers vis-à-vis the powerful nations in the system to work toward collective action. Second, even when interests align, leaders of these countries have a hard time overcoming collective action problems in the pursuit of these common goals.[51] The costs and problems associated with collective action are well known in domestic spheres,[52] and they are even higher in the international arena when stakes can be higher and the cast of key characters more ambiguous.[53] Third, since leaders of developing nations often seek resources from the international community to develop or stay in power,[54] powerful states could use a "divide and rule" strategy to break apart such blocs.[55] Therefore, we should expect weaker nations to be unable, on average, to strongly or effectively challenge the rising new norms of the emerging international geopolitical order, and its associated changes in the regimes, ideologies, and institutions advocated by more powerful nations.

These impact of these changes should be particularly strong in sub-Saharan Africa, as it is the region containing so many of the weakest and poorest states in the world; if international shifts in power are to affect Third World nations, they should most clearly affect sub-Saharan African nations.[56] In fact, some have argued that African nations, in particular, have been nearly completely dependent upon the international system and its norms to maintain themselves in power.[57] As discussed above, some scholars in the quasi-state literature hold that many states in Africa could not even exist if it were not for the norms of *uti possidetus* and external sovereignty, as they do not have effective control over much of their own territory, or de facto (or positive) sovereignty. Countries whose regimes require external funding or foreign troops to remain in power are obvious examples. Weak or failing states must be (nearly always) price takers in such systems.[58]

Beyond a description of the relative weakness of African nations, most of the political regimes that emerged in the early post-independence period can be described as being built upon a neo-patrimonial foundation—which makes them particularly potentially vulnerable to changes in external support. In this form of rule, "the chief executive maintains authority through personal patronage, rather than through ideology or rule of law."[59] Thus, parties tend not to have ideological followers as much as clients who support the political status quo because it delivers to them some form of patronage. Should the access to patronage disappear, many argue that such systems collapse. In fact, many scholars of African politics argued that the primary glue of the political systems following independence was patronage and not ideology.[60] African leaders maintain access to rule and patronage through a mixture of domestic, regional, and international resources available to them, including justifying ideologies.

As such, to the degree that African leaders are reliant upon international resources (e.g., economic aid, military aid, access to markets, access to funding) for the funding of patronage, they are dependent upon the preferences of the leaders of the international system. A shift in geopolitical leadership can clearly have an impact on how the leaders of such nations access, or attempt to access, resources from the international sphere, and these can change the likely success of divergent approaches to maintaining political power.

Should international power brokers signal that they care about the domestic institutions or practices of other nations, weak nations would become more likely to adopt or implement reforms aligned with these preferences. Leaders of weak states are likely to do so to obtain resources or curry favor with the powerful states—at least up to the point where leaders of weaker states find that their power is more threatened by doing so than enhanced by doing so.

Therefore, the ability of African leaders to maintain power is premised upon the political and economic arrangements within the nation, their access to internationally or regionally available resources, and the basis of legitimacy of their rule, domestically, regionally, and internationally. As a result, regimes based primarily upon neo-patrimonial rule that lose access to patronage are quite likely to collapse—especially under stress—as no ideological or institutional legacies would endure in the absence of these reciprocal ties. Therefore, African leaders of such systems are exceptionally vulnerable to changing constraints and opportunities for obtaining resources internationally.

I contend that African leaders and would-be leaders are not merely passive agents in their responses to these changes; rather, they are agents in a system where their relative economic, military, and diplomatic powers have been meager as they search for both domestic and international sources of power, wealth, and security to ensure their political longevity. The assumption is that the leaders of sub-Saharan nations are mainly rational actors pursuing continued rule within their own political systems, but they maximize their domestic political and economic resources across domestic, regional, and international contexts.[61] Moreover, the power of African leaders or nations at the international level depends much on the constellation of international power. It also depends on whether or not weak states can influence events by bandwagoning or balancing—even if only in the exercise of voting at the United Nations (UN) or in other IGOs. For example, as will be discussed in later chapters, during the Cold War, the American foreign policy of containment, in conjunction with the domino theory, allowed weak states more leverage than they probably would have had otherwise.

The Two Geopolitical Shifts

The two global geopolitical shifts under study are these: first, the move from the European dominated multipolar system, which ended with World War II and led to the bipolar Cold War period; second, the move from the bipolar Cold War system to the post-Cold War period marked by US primacy. These are well-established global geopolitical shifts according to mainstream international relations scholars. In fact, according to Gaddis, the end of the Cold War brought about nothing less than the collapse of an international system, something that has happened in modern history only once before—if one accepts structuralism's emphasis on the shift from multi-polarity to bipolarity at the end of World War II.[62]

With the end of each period, significant changes in poles and players can be seen. In the first period, one sees the shift from European dominance in military, economic, and political domains, which had supported a colonial system in sub-Saharan Africa and elsewhere, to the rise of anticolonial US and USSR, with their nuclear power.[63] With the second change in the international structure, we see the economic, military, and political power of the US rise relative to the rest of the world with given the rapid collapse of the second pole. This quick fall of the USSR left the US without a significant rival or set of rivals, though some have discussed Europe, Japan, or China as possible counterweights. However, in this new period, none of these powers pose a similarly significant threat to US interests as the Soviet Union did, and Europe and Japan are clear allies of the US. As a result, many suggest that the world became unipolar.[64]

Although some forces for change in economic and political institutions (both material and intellectual) were evident in Africa before these international transformations, the geopolitical shifts (and their attendant "lessons" and changes in world views) accelerated and consolidated the push for these changes in important ways.

PLAN OF BOOK

The book discusses the basic contours of the two geopolitical shifts, along with the changes in ideas and interests of the rising system leader(s), as well as broader changes in international norms and ideas associated with the learning in light of system change. Then, it discusses the way in which these shifts in geopolitical power and their attendant changes in perceived self-interests and norms changed common practices or led to new ways in which international resources were distributed. Then the book explores how these changes in resources and ideas at the center have impacted African leaders and societies, which have then led to later significant changes, in the shape and contour of political and economic institutions and practices in the region.

The book argues that the timing of these significant, region-wide changes, as well as the particular institutions that emerged in the region, were consistent with the interests of one or more of the (rising) great powers of the time, the prevailing ideas of what constituted proper political or economic order (both normatively in instrumentally), and the interests of the political entrepreneurs within Africa given their domestic, regional, and international constraints and opportunities. These constraints and opportunities had a mix of material, intellectual, and ideological sources. Thus, the book shows how the institutions that emerged in Africa were a mix of actors' incentives, prevailing ideas at the time, and international, regional, and domestic constraints upon actors. Although the argument is that the international system underwent two significant transformations, it holds that the primary goal, as per the rational choice assumptions discussed before, of most African political leaders was the maximization of political power as well as the maintenance of this political power—and it argues that this primary goal remained constant through both geopolitical shifts. However, it also assumes that the individual perceptions of leaders mattered as much as reality did in the decision making choices of leaders on how to act politically within their own environment.

The bulk of the book and its argument is "case illustrative" in methodology, though Chapter 8 employs regression analysis to draw conclusions. It attempts to show that in the wake of two global geopolitical shifts, African political and economic institutions have also undergone two major shifts soon thereafter. This approach is similar to some of Gourevitch's work examining a common exogenous shock through a system and then tracing out the results.[65] It cannot prove, per se, that geopolitical shifts in power and attendant ideas resulted in the significant changes witnessed in sub-Saharan Africa. However, the book shows how events in Africa during two major periods were clearly consistent with the prevailing thesis of this work, including the timing of these changes. The book also describes the prevailing political and economic institutions of sub-Saharan Africa that have emerged in the wake of these two geopolitical shifts. It also describes some of the variation in the level of reforms and types of institutions adopted in each period.

Therefore, the work sets out a strongly descriptive analysis of the major political and economic institutions of sub-Saharan Africa from decolonization to the present set within the context of changing international ideas and material power. It also describes and explains their genesis and change. Moreover, Chapter 8 tests more directly the proposition that the political elites, who were most beholden to external resources to remain in power, were the most vulnerable to international pressure and were, therefore, the most likely to undertake political reforms that actually increased levels of political and civil rights in these states. The conclusion speculates about the likely future of current arrangements. Therefore, the book is a bit of a hybrid: it makes an argument about change and endurance between changes as well as attempting to describe in broad terms the prevailing political and economic institutions and practices for the two periods.

The hope is that this book provides a strong basis for the introduction and overview of the history of the political economy of sub-Saharan Africa from the end of the Second World War until the recent present for students within a strong international relations context, as well as for undergraduate, graduate students, or others interested in African political economy or African international relations. It places this study within an overview of changing power relations and changing intellectual climates. It should provide a nice organizing principle for the learning of the details of African political and economic institutions, why they came into being, and why they have changed twice relatively rapidly, and under what conditions they might likely change again.

CONTRIBUTION OF THE BOOK

Other scholars of international relations have focused on how significant changes in the structure of the international system can help explain later significant and widespread changes within the system, such as in the levels of economic trade, the levels of conflict, or the frequency of great wars.[66] However, most of these analyses of changes in geopolitical structure have centered upon their effects upon "great" powers. In fact, Waltz has famously penned that the study of "international politics is written in terms of the great powers of an era."[67] Mearsheimer (2002) similarly argued that realism primarily interests itself in wars among or between the great powers.[68] By implication, such approaches ignore or underemphasize the impacts of significant geopolitical changes upon the weakest nations. In this work, by contrast, the region of sub-Saharan Africa is examined to illustrate the links between these two particular geopolitical changes and later changes in regional economic and political institutions and practices. Outside of a dependency approach, most international relations (IR) scholars do not examine directly or systematically the impact of structural changes at the center of power upon periphery nations: this allows for a possible contribution for this book.[69]

Moreover, the book can weigh in on the relative strength of international and domestic influences on the changes in institutional forms and practices of the major economic and political regimes in the region in the two periods. For example, one of the most notable books on African democratization or liberalization at the end of the Cold War argued that external forces had little impact on the movements to reforms.[70] For example, Bratton and van de Walle wrote:

> international factors, like change in the international balance of power, . . . cannot on their own account for regime change, let alone the installation and consolidation of democracy. Instead, the trajectory of political transitions is most directly affected by the domestic factors such as the relative strength and cohesion of incumbent and opposition forces.[71]

It is clear that the domestic forces pushed for reform and played a key role facilitating changes. It is also clear that international explanations were not singularly at work: however, part of the ability of these domestic forces to be effective was partially determined by the material and ideological changes associated with the geopolitical shift. These changes affected domestic elites in the new circumstances and the changed perception of the likely success for a struggle for reform by both reformers and status quo politicians.[72] Therefore, international changes, including in the legitimacy of ideas and availability of international resources, affected the very thing Bratton and van de Walle say matters the most: the relative strength and cohesion of incumbent and opposition forces. This is because international forces and changes in material and ideological power and norms impact domestic African social forces and not just the centers of the system or the elites in Africa. Moreover, the ability of elites to be strong and unified is dependent upon flows from the system.[73] Mobutu, in particular, lost tremendous amount of support with the end of the Cold War, even being cut off from World Bank and IMF monies. Therefore, those pushing for reforms may have had external assistance with the associated changes of ideas, flows, and legitimacy with the geopolitical shift.[74]

In this work, I do not argue that international changes dictate change in Africa; rather, these two shifts changed the constraints and opportunities facing political elites in the system. These leaders, in turn, adjusted their behavior in attempting to maintain themselves in power. In the first period, African leaders seemed less constrained by the international community and were better able to pursue policies that consolidated their power. Those who came to control most of their economies seemed to have even more autonomy, and they followed more inward-oriented development policies and were more authoritarian, *ceteris paribus*.[75] However, in the second period, these nations were more dependent upon, and constrained by, the international system. The most constrained countries, therefore, were the most likely to adopt multiparty electoral regimes with increased levels of political and civil rights, adopt more liberal economic policies, and to sell off state enterprises (though not mining or oil exporting giants). This is not to say that most African nations became democratic, capitalist nations, but the reforms adopted were in the direction of liberal reforms. The destination is yet to be attained. Nations may yet take different paths or turn around, depending on their perceived self-interests in light of the combination of domestic and international constraints of doing so.

NOTES

1. The term Africa refers to sub-Saharan Africa, unless otherwise specified, though both are used.

2. However, the former Portuguese colonies achieved independence by 1975. See Chapters 2 and 3 for full references to the literature of this period. (South) Rhodesia (1965) and South Africa (1934) were independent from direct European rule, but with white minority governments until much later.

3. Importantly, the colonial governments were newcomers to democracy in Africa as the colonial structures were authoritarian in nature, especially before 1945. See Crawford Young, *The African Colonial State in Comparative Perspective* (New Haven: Yale University Press, 1994).

4. For which states had majority state ownership in the region, and its impacts on economic development policies, see John James Quinn, *The Road oft Traveled: Development Policies and Majority State Ownership of Industry in Africa* (Westport, CT: Praeger, 2002); for extent of nationalizations, see Leslie L. Rood, "Nationalisation and Indigenisation in Africa," *Journal of Modern African Studies* 14, 2 (1976): 427–447.

5. Or as Huntington's third wave arriving to African shores, see Samuel P. Huntington, *The Third Wave: Democratization in the Late Twentieth Century* (Norman, OK: University of Oklahoma Press 1991). For ties to ideology, see Crawford Young, *Ideology and Development in Africa* (New Haven: Yale University Press, 1982).

6. See Chapters 5 and 6 for full references relating to this period.

7. This point was nicely made by John Gerard Ruggie, "Multilateralism: The Anatomy of an Institution," *International Organization* 46 (1992): 561–598; see also John Gerard Ruggie, "The Past as Prologue? Interests, Identity, and American Foreign Policy," *International Security* 21 (1997): 89–125.

8. The learning may or may not be correct or the lessons can change over time, but the lessons are probably the strongest influence while new institutions and practices are being established to account for perceived failures of the prior institutions and practices.

9. For theme of constraints and opportunities and role in international relations, see David Kinsella, Bruce Russett, and Harvey Starr, *World Politics: The Menu for Choice* (Boston: Wadsworth, 2013).

10. However, it could be that during some periods, relations among some of the great powers are better described as anarchic (such as during non-polarized, multipolar systems, while in others, hierarchy may be a better description (such as in a bipolar (with hierarchy in each pole but with some non-alignment but attempts at balancing between the poles) or in unipolar system). For overview of neoliberalism and neorealism see, for example, David Allen Baldwin, ed. *Neorealism and Neoliberalism: the Contemporary Debate* (New York, Columbia University Press, 1993). Many of these ideas about hierarchy may also be consistent with Organski's view of hierarchies of states rather than anarchy (power transition theory), though I do not characterize the relations among and between the major powers, only that of African regimes and great or super powers. See A. F. K. Organski, *World Politics* (New York: Knopf, 1958). For application of power transition theory to Africa, see Douglas Lemke, *Regions of War and Peace* (Cambridge: Cambridge University Press, 2002). For hierarchy in Africa see Mohammed Ayoob, "Inequality and Theorizing in International Relations: The Case for Subaltern Realism." *International Studies Review*, Vol. 4, No. 3 (Autumn

2002), pp. 27–48; Mohammed Ayoob, *The Third World Security Predicament* (Boulder, CO: Lynne Rienner Publishers, 1995). For hierarchy in Latin America, see David Lake, "Escape the State of Nature: Authority and Hierarchy in World Politics," *International Security* 32, 1 (2007): 47–79.

11. Lemke, *Regions of War and Peace*. However, Herbst argues that African international relations (as understood more by realism) began with the Congolese war, see Jeffery Herbst, "Western and African Peacekeepers: Motives and Opportunities," in John W. Harbeson and Donald Rothchild, eds., *Africa in World Politics: The African State System in Flux* (Boulder: Westview, 2000): 308–323.

12. Many think of Africa as prone to war, disease, and starvation, but the wars tend to be civil and not interstate. However, if one thinks of sub-state actors as state-like, then the frequency of war among these actors may be equal or greater than in other regions. For this view, see William Reno, "Africa's Weak States, Non-state Actors, and the Privatization of Interstate Relations." *Africa in World Politics: the African State System in Flux* (Boulder: West View Press, 2000): 286–307.

13. Jeffrey Herbst, *States and Power in Africa: Comparative Lessons in Authority and Control* (Princeton: Princeton University Press, 2000).

14. Crawford Young and Thomas Turner, *The Rise and Decline of the Zairian State* (Madison, WI: University of Wisconsin Press, 1985).

15. For the overthrow of Mobutu from a regional as well as international relations perspective, see John James Quinn, "Diffusion and escalation in the Great Lakes Region: the Rwandan genocide, the rebellion in Zaire, and Mobutu's Overthrow," in Steven E. Lobell and Philip Mauceri, eds., *Ethnic Conflict and International Politics: Explaining Diffusion and Escalation* (New York: Palgrave Macmillan, 2004): 111–132.

16. See, for example, Thomas M. Callaghy, and John Ravenhill, eds., *Hemmed In: Responses to Africa's Economic Decline* (New York: Columbia University Press, 1993); Carol Lancaster, *Foreign aid: Diplomacy, Development, Domestic Politics* (Chicago: University of Chicago Press, 2008); Carol Lancaster, *Aid to Africa So Much To Do, So Little Done* (Chicago: University of Chicago Press, 1999); also David Williams, "Aid and sovereignty: quasi-states and the international financial institutions." *Review of International Studies* 26, 4 (2000): 557–573. For a review of some views of the state of the state in Africa, see John James Quinn, "W(h)ither the State (System)?" *International Politics* 38, no. 3 (2001): 437–446.

17. This analysis is also sympathetic to David Lake's views of hierarchy: that is, that some countries, with juridical sovereignty, actually are dependent upon stronger states or recognize the authority of some stronger states and enter into a hierarchical relationship. See David Lake "Leadership, Hegemony, and the International Economy" *International Studies Quarterly* 37 (Winter 1993–94): 459–489. This relationship takes place out of the purported Hobbesian anarchic world, and the subordinate states abdicate some sovereignty to a more dominant state (Lakes analyses from this from the perspective of the US and Latin America). This comes with some recognition that the stronger state provides something in return (e.g., military protection, access to markets, protection from other predatory states, development assistance). For Lake, military security is the key to these relationships more than trade (inter)dependence.

18. Adam Nossiter, "Nigerian Army Noticeably Absent in town Taken from Boko Haram." *New York Times* (March 20, 2015): Africa. http://www.nytimes.com/

2015/03/21/world/africa/nigerian-army-noticeably-absent-in-town-taken-from-boko-haram.html?_r=0

19. Christopher Clapham, *Africa and the International System: The Politics of State Survival* (Cambridge: Cambridge University Press, 1996); see also Hans J. Morgenthau, *Politics Among Nations: The Struggle for Power and Peace*, Fifth Edition, Revised, (New York: Alfred A. Knopf, 1978), especially: 4–15.

20. I. William Zartman, "Africa as a Subordinate State System in International Relations," *International Organization* 21, 3 (1967): 545–564; Kevin C. Dunn and Timothy M. Shaw, *Africa's Challenge to International Relations Theory* (Palgrave Macmillan, 2001); Douglas Lemke, "African Lessons for International Relations Research." *World Politics* 56, 1 (2003): 114–138. For African foreign policies, see Stephen Wright, ed., *African Foreign Policies* (Boulder: Westview, 1999); and Gilbert Khadiagala and Terrence Lyons, eds., *African Foreign Policies: Power and Process* (Lynne Rienner Publishers, 2001); for an overview of comparative foreign policy in Africa, see John James Quinn, "African Foreign Policies," in Robert Denemark et al., eds., *The International Studies Compendium Project* (Oxford: Wiley-Blackwell, 2010): 24–46.

21. Robert H. Jackson and Carl G. Rosberg, "Why Africa's Weak States Persist: The Empirical and the Juridical in Statehood," *World Politics* 35, 1 (Oct., 1982): 1–24, p. 24.

22. Ibid; Clapham *Africa and the International System*; William Reno, *Warlord Politics* (Boulder, CO: Lynne Rienner Publishers, 1998); Thomas M. Callaghy, *The State-Society Struggle: Zaire in Comparative Perspective* (New York: Columbia University Press, 1984).

23. Kevin C. Dunn, "Tales from the Dark Side: Africa's Challenge to International Relations Theory." *Journal of Third World Studies* 17 (2000): 61–90; Clapham *Africa*; and Quinn, "W(h)ither the State." These works discusses two possible spheres of legitimacy for African states as much as revenues.

24. Dunn and Shaw *Africa's Challenge*; Lemke, "African Lessons;" and Reno, *Warlord Politics* all argue that the relevant units of analysis for Africa are non-state and sub-state levels. See also, William Reno, "Africa's Weak States, Nonstate Actors, and the Privatization of Interstate Relations," in John Harbeson and Donald Rothschild, eds., *Africa in World Politics: the African State System in Flux* (Boulder: West View Press, 2000).

25. See especially, Robert H. Jackson, *Quasi-states: Sovereignty, International Relations, and the Third World* (Cambridge: Cambridge University Press, 1990); also Jackson and Rosberg, "Why Africa's Weak States Persis; also, Ibid.

26. China and Russia both seem to be the most interested in defending the norm of sovereignty in the post-cold war era, though it has not been through hard balancing, see Thazha V. Paul, "Soft balancing in the age of US primacy," *International Security* 30, 1 (2005): 46–71.

27. Pierre Englebert, *State Legitimacy and Development in Africa* (Boulder: Lynne Rienner, 2000). He argues that endogenous states has strong ties to pre-colonial cultures and structures or ones that reflect the culture of a new majority as in a majority settler colony.

28. Maurice A. East, "Size and Foreign Policy Behavior: A Test of Two Models," *World Politics* 25, 4 (1973): 556–576, p. 557.

29. It is unclear if ZANU-PF will long survive intact in post Mugabe era, though he appears to be making a way for his wife to stay in power after he is gone. See "Zimbabwe's ruling ZANU-PF confirms Mugabe's wife as women's head" *Reuters* (Sat Dec 6, 2014). http://www.reuters.com/article/2014/12/06/us-zimbabwe-politics-idUSKBN0JK0IQ20141206

30. This view of the world is necessarily at odds with a neorealist view that all states have similar interests when they face similar constraints. For this view, see Kenneth Waltz, *Theory of International Relations* (Reading, MA: Addison-Wesley Publishing Company, 1979).

31. Hegemonic stability theory offers the distinction between coercive and benign hegemons. For an overview of this literature see Stephan Haggard and Beth Simmons, "International Regimes," *International Organization* 41 (Summer 1987); see also G. John Ikenberry, "Rethinking the Origins of American Hegemony," *Political Science Quarterly*, Vol. 104, No. 3 (Autumn 1989), pp. 375–400. For a nice overview of regimes and the regime literature, see Robert Gilpin, *Global Political Economy: Understanding the International Economic Order* (Princeton: Princeton University Press, 2001), Chapter 4. Also, this view may be closer to Young's de facto imposition of regimes where a mix of incentives, power and leadership requires / allows regimes to operate—though regimes can change or be created through other means, such as arising from a negotiation or even or spontaneously. His second view of regime change is very similar to this one: changes in underlying structure of power. See Oran R. Young, "Regime dynamics: the rise and fall of international regimes," *International Organization* 36, 2 (1982): 277–297. Also, Lake argues that dominant powers provide some public goods, and weaker states enter into a sort of social contract whereby they abdicate some sovereignty over some issues in return for protection. See Lake, "Escape the State of Nature."

32. Jackson, *Quasi-states*. Also, this is taught as a stylized fact in Introduction to Political Science classes.

33. Weber defines the state as the organization with the monopoly of legitimate use of violence, which then begs the question of what is legitimate. He then outlines traditional sources, charisma, and legal-rational as the basis of legitimate rule. Max Weber, "The Three Types of Legitimate Rule" *Berkeley Publications in Society and Institutions*, 4, 1 (1958): 1–11. Translated by Hans Gerth.

34. For soft power, see Joseph S. Nye, "Soft power," *Foreign policy* 80 (1990): 153–171.

35. See for example, Stephen D. Krasner, "Sovereignty: An Institutional Perspective," *Comparative Political Studies* 21, 1 (1988): 66–94.

36. Unless specified more precisely, institution is used to refer to the formation of IGOs, and norms relative to expectations and established practices. The term "regimes" is used when these terms are more blurred and practices are embedded in habit or institutions. Technically, these terms can be used interchangeable, though a slight distinction is implied in this analysis. For definitions of norms, regimes, and institutions see, Stephen D. Krasner, "Structural causes and regime consequences: regimes as intervening variables," in Stephen D. Krasner, ed., *International Regimes* (Ithaca: Cornell University Press): 1–21; see also Robert O. Keohane and Joseph S. Nye, *Power and Interdependence* (Boston: Little, Brown, 1977).

37. Here, by ideas, the I mean prevailing beliefs about cause and effect as well as beliefs about ends and means which can condition, or channel, the means through which one seeks one's self-interest. See Ernst B. Haas, *When Knowledge is Power: Three Models of Change in International Organizations* (Berkeley and Los Angeles: University of California Press, 1990). These can also be called "principles" which are "belief(s) about facts, causation, and rectitude." See, Krasner, "Structural causes" p. 2. Ideology refers to a system of though which attempts to justify a social, economic, or political status quo or recommend an alternative one based upon prevailing views of what is right, wrong, natural, effective, or "true" human nature, or some mix thereof. It is intended for mass mobilization or for the masses to support or condone a system (depending if it justifies an alternative arraignment or the current status). For discussion of ideologies and competing terms and views of them, see Leon P. Baradat, *Political Ideologies: Their origins and Impact, 9th edition* (Upper Saddle river: Pearson Education, 2009). Norms are considered to be common means of interaction in the international community, many of which are cultural or historic practices, though many emerged or are created with the institutionalization of behavior in multilateral or bilateral institutions and treaties. Institutions refer to formal organization governed by rules or bylaws or well understood procedures which distribute resources of one type or another (see above). For a definition and theory of norms, as well as a review of the literature, see Martha Finnemore and Kathryn Sikkink, "International norm dynamics and political change," *International Organization* 52, 4 (1998): 887–917.

38. Judith Goldstein, "Ideas, Institutions, and American Trade Policy," in G. John Ikenberry, David A Lake, and Michael Mastanduno, eds., *The State and American Foreign Economic Policy* (Ithaca, NY: Cornell University Press, 1988): 179–218.

39. Anne O. Krueger, "Virtuous and Vicious Circles in Economic Development," *American Economic Review* 83, 1–2 (May 1993): 351–355.

40. Douglass C. North, *Institutions, Institutional Change and Economic Performance* (Cambridge: Cambridge University Press, 1990); Douglass C. North, *Structure and Change in Economic History* (New York: W. W. Norton & Co., 1981); Oliver E. Williamson, *The Economic Institutions of Capitalism: Firms, Markets, Relational Contracting* (New York: The Free Press, 1985); James E. Alt and Kenneth A. Shepsle, *Perspectives on Positive Political Economy* (Cambridge: Cambridge University Press, 1990); Peter Gourevitch, *Politics in Hard Times: Comparative Responses to International Economic Crises* (Ithaca, NY: Cornell University Press, 1986).

41. Peter Hall, "Policy Paradigms, Social Learning, and the State: The Case of Economic Policymaking in Britain," *Comparative Politics*, Vol.25, No.3 (1993): 275–96.

42. Ikenberry suggests that new policy ideas proceed most quickly following a crisis which discredits the old policy ideas. This creates openings for new ideas. Moreover, leaders of social forces are likely to back the ideas which serve their self-interests or internal needs. See G. John Ikenberry, "The International Spread of Privatization," in Ezra N. Suleiman and John Waterbury, eds., *The Political Economy of Public Sector Reform and Privatization* (Boulder, CO: Westview Press, 1990): 88–110.

43. For example, Keynesian economics has significantly changed how policy makers see their economic world, both normatively and empirically. See, for example,

Peter A. Hall, ed., *The Political Power of Economic Ideas: Keynesianism across Nations* (Princeton: Princeton University Press, 1989). Also, See Ikenberry, "The International Spread of Privatization;" See also, Young, "Regime dynamics."

44. Shively calls this legitimacy by results. See, W. Phillips Shively, *Power and Choice: An Introduction to Political Science* 14th edition (New York: McGraw-Hill Education, 2014), Chapter 1.

45. Gerald M. Meier, "The Formative Period," in Gerald M. Meier and Dudley Seers, eds., *Pioneers in Development* (Washington D.C.: Oxford University Press for World Bank, 1984), p. 11.

46. See for example, in mainstream literature, Judith Goldstein and Robert O. Keohane, eds., *Ideas and Foreign Policy* (Ithaca, NY: Cornell University Press, 1993); for a review of constructivism and role of ideas and actors, see Ted Hopf, "The Promise of Constructivism in International Relations Theory *International Security* 23, 1 (Summer, 1998): 171–200; for a review essay, see Jeffrey T. Checkel, "The Constructivist Turn in International Relation Theory," *World Politics* 50, 2 (Jan. 1998); 324–348; for a seminal work on constructivism see, Alexander Wendt, "Anarchy Is What States Make of It: The Social Construction of Power Politics" *International Organization* 46, 2 (Spring 1992): 391–425; also see overview essay by John Gerard Ruggie, "What Makes the World Hang Together? Neoutilitarianism and the Social Constructivist Challenge." *International Organization*, 52 (1998): 855–885 doi:10.1162/002081898550770.

47. Perhaps the best known argument for diffusion is by Huntington, *The Third Wave*; for an empirical exploration of democratic diffusion, see Harvey Starr "Democratic Dominoes: Diffusion Approaches to the Spread of Democracy in the International System." *The Journal of Conflict Resolution*, Vol. 35, No. 2 (Jun., 1991), pp. 356–381; and Daniel Brinks and Michael Coppedge, "Diffusion Is No Illusion: Neighbor Emulation in the Third Wave of Democracy," *Comparative Political Studies* 39, 4 (May 2006): 463–489, 464. For another empirical treatment of diffusion of ideas more generally, see Dennis P. Quinn, and A. Maria Toyoda. "Ideology and Voter Preferences as Determinants of Financial Globalization." *American Journal of Political Science* 51, 2 (2007): 344–363.

48. For a reviews and expositions of constructivism see Hopf, "The Promise of Constructivism;" Checkel, "The Constructivist Turn;" Wendt, "Anarchy Is What States Make of It," Ruggie, "What Makes the World Hang Together;" Haas, *When Knowledge is Power*.

49. For competing explanations of causes of change or continuance of institutional within competing paradigms, see Peter Hall and Rosemary C.R. Taylor, "Political Science and the three Institutionalisms," *Political Studies* XLIV (1996): 936–957. This analysis is a hybrid of the three pure types, as recommended by the authors, but it is closer to rational choice and historic institutionalism but with some emphasis on the role of ideas in shaping interests—especially as it impacts mean-ends attainment of goals.

50. For praise or ridicule, see Waltz *Theory of International Relations*, pp. 75–76. He also mentions emulation.

51. In the case of sub-Saharan Africa, there were clearly some common problems facing African nations: Nearly every sub-Saharan African country experienced

European colonization which shaped their boundaries and economies, most became independent within a decade of each other, most have had similar levels of development, most had similarly low levels of human capital, especially during the period of decolonization, and most fought against colonialism and white rule wherever it was seen. However, even if problems facing Africa were common, the response was not always. For an overview of African foreign policies see Wright, ed., *African Foreign Policies*; Gilbert Khadiagala and Terrence Lyons, "Foreign Policy Making in Africa: An Introduction," in Khadiagala and Lyons, eds., *African Foreign* Policies, pp. 1–13; Quinn, "African Foreign Policies."

52. Mancur Olson, *The Logic of Collective Action: Public Goods and the Theory of Groups* (Cambridge: Harvard University Press, 1965).

53. For example, see Philip G. Cerny, "Globalization and the Changing Logic of Collective Action," *International Organization* Vol. 49, No. 4 (Autumn 1995): 595–625; Robert D. Putnam, "Diplomacy and Domestic Politics: The Logic of Two-Level Games," *International Organization* Vol. 42, No. 3 (Summer 1988): 427–460.

54. See Clapham, *Africa and the International System*; Also, Jackson and Rosberg, "Why Africa's Weak States Persist;" Jackson, *Quasi-states*; Reno, "Africa's Weak States."

55. For example, the inability for nations to form a debtor's cartel in the 1980s is often given as such an example. For overview of debt crisis see Thomas D. Lairson and David Skidmore, *International Political Economy: The Struggle for Power and Wealth, 2nd Edition* (Belmont, CA: Thomson-Wadsworth): 325–362.

56. For Africa's place in international system, see Clapham, *Africa and the International System*; Jackson and Rosberg, "Why Africa's Weak States Persist;" Jackson, *Quasi-states*; Reno, "Africa's Weak States."

57. Lake would argue that they give up some sovereignty and enter into a hierarchical relationship with more powerful nations for increased security or access to some other public good. See Lake, "Escape the State of Nature." (However, he writes mostly about countries in the US sphere of influence).

58. For idea of weak state, see Jackson and Rosberg, "Why Africa's Weak States Persist; Jackson, *Quasi-states*; Reno, "Africa's Weak States."

59. Michael Bratton and Nicolas van de Walle, *Democratic Experiments in Africa: Regime Transitions in Comparative Perspective* (Cambridge: Cambridge University Press, 1997), p. 458.

60. Bates, Robert H., "The Impulse to Reform in Africa." in Jennifer A. Widner, ed., *Economic Change and Political Liberalization in sub-Saharan Africa*. Baltimore: The Johns Hopkins University Press, 1994: 13–28; Callaghy, *The State-Society Struggle*; Clapham, *African and the International System*; Englebert, *State Legitimacy*; Goran Hyden, *African Politics in Comparative Perspective* (Cambridge: Cambridge University Press 2006); Richard Sandbrook, *The Politics of Africa's Economic Recovery* (Cambridge: Cambridge University Press, 1993); Quinn, *The Road oft Traveled*; Roger Tangri, *The Politics of Patronage in Africa: Parastatals, Privatization, and Private Enterprise* (Trenton, NJ: Africa World Press, Inc., 1999); Nicolas van de Walle, "Neopatrimonialism and Democracy in Africa, with an Illustration from Cameroon." in Jennifer A. Widner, ed., *Economic Change and Political Liberalization in sub-Saharan Africa* (Baltimore: The Johns Hopkins University Press, 1999): 129–157;

Crawford Young, "The Third Wave of Democratization in Africa: Ambiguities and Contradictions," in Richard Joseph., ed., *State, Conflict, and Democracy in Africa* (Boulder, CO: Lynne Rienner Publishers, 1999): 15–38. Most scholars tend to apply it to all of Africa equally, at least implicitly. However, some new research suggests that neo-patrimonialism was quite varied in Africa; see Anne Pitcher, Mary H. Moran, and Michael Johnston. "Rethinking Patrimonialism and Neopatrimonialism in Africa." *African Studies Review* Volume 52, Number 1 (April 2009): 125–156. Clearly, most states have been neo-patrimonial, but those with majority state ownership were more neo-patrimonial than others; the incentives associated with it led politicians to weaken domestic institutions and increasing corruption. See John James Quinn, "The Effects of Majority State Ownership of Significant Economic Sectors on Corruption: A Cross-Regional Comparison," *International Interactions* 34, 1 (2008): 81–128.

61. For this view of African leaders, see John James Quinn, *The Road oft Traveled*; Clapham, *Africa and the International System*, among others. It is a rational choice assumption, but I hold it to be bounded by ideas, institutions, and information costs. As mentioned above, this analysis is a hybrid of the three pure types, but it is closer to rational choice and historic institutionalism, though but with some emphasis on the role of ideas in shaping interests—especially as it impacts mean-ends attainment of goals and shifts in moral compasses. See, Hall and Taylor, "Political Science and the Three New Institutionalisms. For assumptions of rational choice, see Margaret Levi, "A Model, A Method, and A Map: Rational Choice in Comparative and Historical Analysis," in Mark Irving Lichbach and Alan S. Zuckerman, eds., *Comparative Politics: Rationality, Culture, and Structure* (Cambridge Studies in Comparative Politics, 1997); Barbara Geddes, "How the Approach You Choose Affects the Answers You Get: Rational Choice and its Uses in Comparative Politics," *Paradigms and Sand Castles: Theory Building and Research Design in Comparative Politics* (University of Michigan Press, 2003): Chapter 5.

62. John Lewis Gaddis, "International Relations Theory and the End of the Cold War," *International Security* (1992): 5–58, p. 53.

63. Clearly colonialism impacted Africa as much, although this aspect is not elaborated upon herein. The rise of Europe rise and its justifying ideologies in the later 1800s do not gainsay the theories set forth within; rather they are quite consistent with them.

64. William C. Wohlforth, "The stability of a unipolar world." *International Security* 24, no. 1 (1999): 5–41. As some readers may note, the slow rise of China, at least as a commercial and diplomatic rival to the US, could represent an emerging third change in geopolitical power. However, the rise of China as an economic rival, and even Russia as a more bellicose actor in its sphere of influence, will unlikely lead to rapid geopolitical shift, at least in the short term. However, their slow rise might change some of the international options for resources and ideologies for some African leaders. These changes are slower, less sure, and still evolving. Nonetheless, China, in particular, can shelter some African nations from other international pressures, though it cannot yet now do so for the whole region. Some nations which have had natural resources or were stronger markets for China may be partially sheltered from the new norms emerging from the US and its allies. Though China has not represented a significant military threat beyond its own borders as of yet. Nonetheless,

some initial speculations of the likely impact of this emerging trend are addressed, especially in the conclusions.

65. Peter Alexis Gourevitch, "Breaking with Orthodoxy: the Politics of Economic Policy Responses to the Depression of the 1930s," *International Organization* 38, no. 01 (1984): 95–129.

66. For some seminal works see, Waltz, *Theory of International Relations*; Organski, *World Politics*; A.F.K. Organski and J. Kugler, *The War Ledger* (Chicago: University of Chicago Press, 1980); Charles Kindleberger, *The World in Depression, 1929–39* (Berkeley, CA: University of California Press, 1973); Robert Gilpin *The Political Economy of International Relations* (Princeton, NJ: Princeton University Press, 1987); Lake "Leadership, Hegemony, and the International Economy."

67. Waltz, *Theory of International Relations*, p. 72.

68. John J. Mearsheimer, "Realism, the Real World, and the Academy," *Realism and Institutionalism in International Studies* (2002): 23–33.

69. One exception is a very recent publication linking the rise and fall of the diffusion of democracy to hegemonic shocks. See Seva Gunitsky, "From Shocks to Waves: Hegemonic Transitions and Democratization in the Twentieth Century," *International Organization* 68, 3 (June 2014): 1–37.

70. Bratton and van de Walle, *Democratic Experiments in Africa*, esp. pp. 30–33.

71. Ibid., p. 33.

72. For a formal model speculating when and where different parts of African society or different leaders might have the self-interest to push for political and/ or economic reforms, see Quinn, *The Road Oft Traveled*, Chapter 9.

73. For role of elites to resist reform, see Huntington, *The Third Wave*, also Theda Skocpol, *States and Social Revolutions: A Comparative Analysis of France, Russia and China* (Cambridge University Press, 1979).

74. For a similar argument, though looking more at aid and pressure, see John W. Harbeson, "Externally Assisted Democratization: Theoretical Issues and African Realities," in John W. Harbeson and Donald Rothchild, eds., *Africa in World Politics: The African State System in Flux* (Boulder, CO: Westview Press, 2000): 235–262.

75. See John J. Quinn, "Economic Accountability: Are Constraints on Economic Decision Making a Blessing or a Curse?" *Scandinavian Journal of Development Alternatives and Area Studies* 19, 4 (December 2000): 131–169; also John J. Quinn, "The Managerial Bourgeoisie: Capital Accumulation, Development and Democracy," in David G. Becker and Richard L. Sklar, eds., *Postimperialism and World Politics*. Westport, CT: Praeger, 1999: 219–252.

Chapter 2

The First International Geopolitical Shift

African Decolonization in International and Regional Contexts

One of the most historic and impactful milestones for sub-Saharan Africa was the relatively rapid decolonization of the region. The events unfolded so quickly that from 1957 to 1966, nearly all the former French, British, and Belgian colonies in the region gained political independence.[1] The Portuguese colonies would have to wait until the mid-1970s to gain theirs, though few doubted the eventual outcome given the decolonization of so many other countries in the region.[2] When and how the continent became independent would have significant and lasting effects on the types of political and economic institutions and practices that would later arise. The speed of the decolonization would mean that new institutions and practices were emerging and developing in a common intellectual climate and under a similar set of social, political, and economic circumstances.

The speed and nature of the decolonization in sub-Saharan Africa must be viewed from an even larger perspective. By the time decolonization began in sub-Saharan Africa, it was already a worldwide trend. Many former colonies in the Far East, the Near East, the Middle East, and North Africa had obtained their political autonomy beginning soon after the end of World War II.[3] In fact, "[b]etween 1945 and 1960, no less than forty countries with a population of eight hundred million—more than a quarter of the world's inhabitants—revolted against colonialism and won their independence."[4] As such, the decolonization of Black Africa represented only one aspect, yet quite an important one, of a larger movement.

Moreover, this worldwide shift in decolonization can be linked to the new geopolitical structure that emerged after WWII. The interstate system had been multipolar before the war, and the major powers at the time (circa 1938) included the US, Germany, the Soviet Union, and the UK as well as Japan, France, and Italy, though the first four were clearly among the most powerful.[5] In Europe, there appeared to be a balance among several great powers: Britain and France were balancing against Germany, though the Fascist nations of Spain, Portugal, Italy, and Japan were aligned with Germany. The Soviet Union (apparently) was on the sidelines and did not appear to be an expansionistic power. In the Far East, the British and French as well as the Dutch and the Americans had significant influence through their colonial possessions.[6] Japan was becoming a more important military presence in the region, in part as a result of inheriting former German colonies in the region; however, China was seen as a partial balance to Japan, though it was clearly struggling in the war. The colonial powers of France and England dominated the regions of North Africa, sub-Saharan Africa, and the Middle East, while the US maintained its sphere of influence in Latin America.

With the end of the Second World War, and the emergence of the two nuclear superpowers, a major geopolitical shift was evident. Much of war-torn Europe was destroyed, and Germany and Japan were occupied. Much of Eastern Europe was occupied by the Soviet Union. As leaders of their respective spheres, the US and USSR were significantly more powerful than other prior great powers. For example, these two countries were by far the largest spenders on their militaries: England and France were only spending 16% and 10%, respectively, as much on their militaries as was the US.[7] Moreover, the formers' economies were only 35% and 15% of America's, respectively. The US and the Soviet Union were the highest ranked military powers in the aftermath of WWII. The later duopoly of nuclear weapons by the US and USSR added to this disproportionate power, though other nations (including France and the UK) would later join the nuclear club.

Despite discussions of bipolarity, many scholars see the rise of America as a form of hegemony, where America was the preponderant power, at least economically. To reconcile bipolarity and American hegemony, some views of a hierarchy, at least among the allies of each pole, has to be considered. Though America's European allies could cut loose from any arrangements with America as the leader, the departing country might find itself isolated in dealing with a closer and potentially more hostile Soviet Union. America, however, would not easily jettison potentially valuable allies in its balance against the Soviet Union, so this arrangement would have to be carefully managed, with all seeing benefits to American leadership in the Western sphere. The same logic could be applied to US allies in the Pacific in the wake of the Chinese Revolution of 1949 and emergence of the communist regime there. The provision of the nuclear umbrella, Marshall Fund monies, access to American markets and investment, and the funding and managing of the Bretton Woods institutions which would help rebuild Europe and much of the rest of the world was just the ticket.[8]

INTERNATIONAL TRENDS AND
AFRICAN DECOLONIZATION

Many important international factors contributed to the rapid shift in colonial status for most of sub-Saharan Africa following World War II: the change in international norms relating to colonialism, the weakening of the colonial European states relative to the new superpowers, the free trade aims of the US, the anticolonial foreign policy of the USSR, and the logic of the domino theory evident during the Cold War. Moreover, French, British, and Belgian willingness to abandon formal administration in the region also stemmed partially from the changes in costs and benefits from their colonial holdings in light of the changing international and regional environments.

End of WWII and Changing International Norms

Of these above-mentioned factors, perhaps the most striking was the rapid worldwide deterioration of the international legitimacy of colonialism in the wake of the Second World War (WWII). Among the more important events, ideas, or announcements which helped undermine colonial legitimacy leading up to this point included the following: Wilson's Fourteen Points, Lloyd George's 1918 declaration of self-determination for the colonial possessions and for occupied Europe, Lenin's castigation of imperialism, and Russian revolutionaries' declaration that any group in Czarist Russia was free to secede; these ideas carried much weight and began to undermine any remaining moral claims supporting colonial rule.[9] These declarations stood in stark contrast to the older ideas upon which colonialism was based, such as the "civilizing mission," the "white man's burden," or the three C's espoused by Livingstone (Christianity, Civilization, and Commerce).[10] As these old values fell into disrepute, the notion of self-determination and indigenous rule became paramount, if not sacrosanct.

The juxtaposition of this clash of ideas was seen most clearly in the light of the anti-Nazi propaganda espoused by the allies during WWII. The wartime propaganda and rhetoric favoring national self-determination and racial and ethnic equality were antithetical to prior justifications of colonialism. Soon after the war, "European colonialism became illegitimate, and the unqualified right of all colonial peoples to self-government became a basic norm of the international community."[11] In fact, these new norms of self-government were so powerful that countries in sub-Saharan Africa were granted independence despite their level of state capacity. The older, prevailing norm of European stewardship to prepare colonies for the mantle of self-government was cast aside and impatience with foreign imposed rule grew–however "unprepared" the new nations were for self-government.[12]

This waning legitimacy of colonialism was not only apparent in international discourse, but it was also evident within sub-Saharan Africa. African soldiers drafted into the European armies were exposed to such ideas and helped transform the social and political landscape of the region upon their return: they brought back with them ideas such as racial equality, democracy, and self-determination. Moreover, African troops had seen for themselves the vulnerability of Europeans, having fought with and against them. The myth of European invincibility was also partially undermined with the Japanese victories in the Russo-Japanese War of 1905 as well as repeated Japanese victories over the French, British, and Dutch in the Pacific theater during the early years of WWII. Moreover, as might be expected, the above mentioned anti-fascist ideas promulgated during the war years were taken seriously by Africans wishing to remove the yoke of colonialism.

Perhaps more importantly, these new norms found incorporation in the agenda of international organizations, especially within the United Nations (UN).[13] As former colonial nations joined the UN, the zeal for ending colonization grew among its membership. Moreover, in its charter, Article 73 addresses issues concerning members "which have or assume responsibilities for the administration of territories whose peoples have not yet attained a full measure of self-government." Subsumed under Article 73 are norms of behavior, including responsibilities for providing, "political, economic, social, and educational advancement," development toward self-government, peace, and security, and reporting occasionally to the UN vis-à-vis these norms.[14] In fact, the UN often became the major official avenue for the expression of self-determination for the various colonial subjects. Through this international body, the issues and procedures for the eventual independence of the trust territories of Togoland, Cameroon, Tanganyika, and Ruanda-Urundi were discussed and established.[15] In fact, the UN set deadlines for colonial governments to demonstrate reasonable progress toward self-rule within these protectorate territories.

The importance of UN supervision of trust territories far exceeded its direct influence: the moves toward independence in the trustees' territories had a demonstration (or diffusion) effect on Africans in other colonies that influenced expectations for the timetables set for independence.[16] The argument supporting continued colonial rule in one country was not as defensible while its neighbor was given political independence. By December 1960, after much of the region had decolonized, the UN passed resolution 1514(xv), the Declaration on the Granting of Independence to Colonial Countries and Peoples. "This resolution brought about a new interpretation of the international principle of self-determination according to which colonial tension could only be resolved by transferring sovereignty to the territories previously defined by the European overseas expansion."[17]

Rise of AntiColonial US, USSR in Context of Cold War

The rapid rise in power of the United States of America, relative to colonial European powers, following WWII also influenced and reinforced these changes. America emerged from the war with nearly uncontested military and economic might. Barring the attack on Pearl Harbor, its homeland was nearly completely unscathed, with a booming economy. Since the war was fought mainly in Europe, Asia, and Africa, the US emerged with its industrial infrastructure intact and soon assumed the mantle of the world's hegemon.[18] With its preponderant economic and military power, its role as a stabilizer for the international community, as the leader of the North Atlantic Treaty Organization (NATO), and as the dispenser of Marshall Funds, the US was in a position to influence the shape of the new international system. Moreover, at the end of the day, America was the guarantor of Western European security vis-à-vis the Soviet Union. Through these institutions, and with its role as security anchor, the US would distribute significant resources to shape the post-war international system into one which served its long-term interests. The US had long opposed colonial empires, from Latin America to China, but it was never before so able to hasten their end. The US's rise in international power would help it bring about what was seen as both right and in its self-interest.

Although the Soviet Union also rose to the rank of a superpower, it cannot be considered a hegemon for two reasons. First, its claim to this superpower status was based purely upon its military, rather than its economic, might— much of which had been destroyed during the war. Second, the USSR had no preferences for a free trade system, and this is part of the normal definition of a "hegemon" in political economy. As per Kindleberger, a hegemon is a single leader willing to assume responsibility for (a) maintaining a relatively open market for distress goods; (b) providing counter-cyclical long-term lending; and (c) discounting in a crisis.[19] Therefore, although the USSR dominated in its sphere of influence, it cannot be considered a "hegemon" as understood in the political science literature. Notwithstanding the lack of title, it was one of the two poles of the bipolar system.

The shift in the balance of international military and economic power toward America and the Soviet Union and away from Britain and France had direct consequences for Africa. Even before WWII, America had not supported colonial rule which discriminated against American economic involvement in such markets—especially within the British Commonwealth. With the geopolitical shift in its favor, America began to use its new-found power to undermine the colonial system, in general, and the British Commonwealth, in particular. In fact, during the war and at the height of British dependence on America, Roosevelt convinced Churchill to enter into the Atlantic Charter on August 1941. The document embodied these ideals:

renunciation of territorial aggrandizement; opposition to territorial changes made against the wishes of the people concerned; *restoration of sovereign rights and self-government to those forcibly deprived of them; access to raw materials for all nations of the world and easing of trade restrictions*; world cooperation to secure improved economic and social conditions for all; freedom from fear and want; freedom of the seas; and abandonment of the use of force, as well as disarmament of aggressor nations. [Italics added][20]

Signatory countries of the United Nations pledged allegiance to this charter on January 1, 1942 which brought the main metropolitan countries into a commitment straightforwardly contrary to the spirit of colonialism.[21] Although Roosevelt and Churchill would disagree over the precise meaning of this document (Roosevelt considered it to apply to the whole world, while Churchill only envisioned it to apply to occupied Europe), the future implications of the charter were apparent even then.[22] Thus, the US had forced upon a dependent UK an agreement which would shape the postwar world and which promoted American interests in free trade at the expense of the former's empire. This helped set the stage for the eventual African decolonization.

American Pressure to Decolonize

Furthermore, American foreign policy interests, both corporate and national, were institutionalized at this time through the creation of the Bretton Woods system.[23] The institutions created were the International Monetary Fund (IMF), the International Bank for Reconstruction and Development (IRBD or the World Bank), and the General Agreements on Tariffs and Trade (GATT). These institutions were associated with the United Nations, which had been created to replace the League of Nations. Although GATT fell short of many American corporations' desires for a more comprehensive free trade treaty (which would have been realized through the International Trade Organization (ITO)), these new international institutions helped open these formerly protected colonial markets to US corporations.[24] This Bretton Woods system established international money management practices as well as trade and tariff agreements which were consistent with American corporate and political interests in freer trade. The Bretton Woods system reflected and reinforced American trade preferences, which were generally inconsistent with colonial interests.

Not only were American transnational corporate and trading interests served by the decolonization of Africa, but Cold War logic also compelled American foreign policy goals to push its allies in that direction as well. The Cold War pitted American and Soviet power and influence against each other in an ideological war—with much of the Third World as its battlefield.

Victories were registered by either conversion to, or away from, "Marxist" or "capitalist" governments. American policy was centered on the containment of communism as both a system and an idea.

In this context, American foreign policy favored a controlled decolonization for two reasons. First, America's interests in expanding free trade and capitalism were consistent with its prior foreign policy goals: each was seen as right and in America's self-interest in promoting a free trade regime. Second, and more instrumentally, American policymakers at the time believed that independence in the Third World was inevitable for all colonies and that any opposition to decolonization could alienate future leaders of these emerging nations. By pressing its allies toward the rapid decolonization of their colonies, America hoped to stave-off communist penetration by avoiding alienating the rising Third World leaders and pushing them into a Soviet embrace.[25] Therefore, American diplomats pressed their allies into allowing a moderate (non-communist) political class to argue for independence and come to assume leadership with the end of colonial rule.

Because of the then-dominant idea of "the domino theory," American foreign policymakers became even more concerned with the makeup of potential post-colonial regimes.[26] To preempt Soviet-backed nationalist movements from gaining control of newly emerging countries, America felt that rapid decolonization was more important than ever. America's quick withdrawal from the Philippines, as well as its successful transfer of power to a moderate post-colonial government, illustrated American action beyond American rhetoric. In pursuit of the policy of universal decolonization, the US used both diplomacy and direct material incentives to compel its allies to take significant steps toward the political independence of their colonies. America also promoted decolonization by making Marshall Aid contingent on steady progress toward this goal. One example of this type of coercion is evident with America's treatment of the Netherlands over Indonesian independence. US policymakers believed that the Dutch government had not made sufficient concessions to Indonesian nationalists and that this would drive the nationalists firmly into the rival communist camp. Thus, in December 1948, the US suspended five million dollars of Marshall Aid designated for the Netherlands East Indies.[27] This action helped lead to a reversal of Dutch policy in Indonesia. This American gesture was surely not lost on the British and French, both of whom were heavily reliant on Marshall Fund money for the reconstruction of their domestic economies.

Although America had great influence on its allies through its role as the leading force in the North Atlantic Treaty Organization, as the leading force behind the Bretton Woods institutions, and as the source of Marshall Funds, its direct control over the colonial policies of its allies was occasionally limited. The United States often had to rely exclusively on diplomatic activity to achieve its goals concerning decolonization, as its actions regarding British Libya and French North Africa in the late 1940s suggest.[28] American influence was especially constrained in cases where large colonial settler populations existed, whether French or British. Under such circumstances, the European leaders were much more vulnerable politically to settler and domestic demands than to American ones.

In fact, where white settlers were concerned, the transition to independence was nearly always longer and more complex.[29] The plight of settlers had a major influence on domestic politics within the metropoles, and the governments had less free rein in this arena. The decolonization of both North and South Rhodesia, the problems with "Mau-Mau" in Kenya, and the French-Algerian conflict display cases where significant amounts of force and material were brought to bear in order to maintain political control, though without success. In fact, these situations were potentially destabilizing for the ruling parties in the metropole—as the case of Algeria indicates. In fact, this crisis precipitated the downfall of the French Fourth Republic. These would also create clear lessons for colonizers everywhere about the costs of trying to defeat an entrenched nationalist movement demanding self-rule.

In two other situations, America did not actively press its allies to quit their colonies more quickly: (1) where a good faith effort and progress was being made toward the goal of decolonization; or (2) when the inheritors of power were likely to be communists. Examples of American quiescence in both cases are evident. On the one hand, the abstention by the United States concerning the Algerian debate in the United Nations displayed American satisfaction with French progress after French officials conceded on the principle of self-determination.[30] On the other hand, US support for French efforts to maintain their colony in Vietnam as well as American opposition to the transfer of power to Marxist nationalists in Indonesia both revealed the reversal of American policy in the face of perceived communist involvement.[31]

Rise of the Left in Europe

Not only was colonization becoming more costly and its international legitimacy in decline, but also many political parties were gaining seats and power within the metropolitan countries which were less committed to colonization than prior ruling parties. Left leaning parties were winning more seats in European capitals, and sometimes gaining a majority. They were clearly more liberal in regards to their colonial subjects; however, their "liberalness" was initially manifest in the support for more development rather than quick decolonization. In fact, "the Fourth Republic, like the British Labour Party, gave high priority to the advancement of African welfare through *équipement social*."[32] Many leaders, even on the left, saw the rebuilding of their war-torn countries to be of a higher priority than African decolonization. Those who exercised real responsibility often moderated their views further. In fact, upon assuming power, the Labour Party "watered down a radical 'Charter of Freedom for Colonial People' in favor of a policy statement which, by subordinating self-government to long-term economic and social planning and local government reform, reflecting the newly emerging liberal imperialist consensus."[33]

Nonetheless, the independence of India had been carried out under Labour Party rule, and this helped set a precedent for decolonization elsewhere. Attlee's was more dispassionate about African independence than Indian, and the former's decolonization would be subordinated to British national (pragmatic) self-interest. Interestingly, it would be the Conservative Party at the helm when Ghana became independent in 1957. In the French case, "leading figures in all the main parties believed it was essential for France to maintain its empire."[34] This included most left parties in France. They too would increase funding for their colonies, which would increase financial pressures for later decolonization.

Rising Norm of Nationalism and its Impact on Empire

Although international factors strongly influenced the waning European power to leave their colonies, more was necessary to convince them to relinquish their African holdings. Other factors shaped the choices taken by the metropoles concerning these colonies. Nonetheless, since several of the colonial countries had colonies elsewhere and Africa was at the trailing edge of decolonization, the colonial powers had discovered elsewhere the very high cost, in both lives and material, of maintaining political control in the face of a determined nationalist movement. For example, the initial French reaction in Algeria and Vietnam was to use military force. Through force of arms, the French Fourth Republic tried to re-impose colonial status in both places. These campaigns proved to be costly and misguided, as would be displayed in Vietnam with the defeat at Dien Bien Phu. Moreover, French attempts to forestall decolonization in Algeria resulted in its independence as well as the collapse of the Fourth Republic itself.

Although the British had not fought any large-scale wars to keep their colonies after WWII, they had used force against rising nationalist demands. For example, the British faced the significant Mau Mau uprisings in the early 1950s over land alienation. The British "won" in their efforts to crush the Mau Mau movement, though this victory came only after British promises to concede the principle of multiracial parity between Europeans and non-Europeans within Kenya.[35] By acceding to its most popular demand, the British could isolate the Mau Mau movement and keep it from becoming a truly nationalist movement. Interestingly, the person it jailed as the leader of the Mau Mau would become the first president of Kenya.

Although the Belgians did not have a direct experience with decolonization outside of sub-Saharan Africa, they were witnesses of the problems experienced by the French, British, and the Dutch.[36] Their closest neighbors, the Dutch, tried to reestablish their colony in Indonesia—despite Sukarno's unilateral declaration of independence right after cessation of the war. The Dutch, who were nearer to Belgium in economic and military capability than were either Britain or France, fought for four years until a peace was finally brokered by the United Nations. The lesson from the Dutch experience in trying to impose its political or military domination over a unified and determined nationalist movement was the same as that learned by the French—it did not work. The goal of independence from foreign rule was one that Third World nationals around the world were dedicating their lives and treasure to achieve.

The Portuguese also had not experienced the process of decolonization outside sub-Saharan Africa. This lack of experience elsewhere might go some distance in explaining why they followed policies similar to those the Dutch and French initially followed.[37] Unlike the other colonial powers, however, Portugal was under military rule and domestic discontent with foreign policies was less of a concern among the ruling elites. The Portuguese waged a military campaign against the nationalists from 1961 to 1974 and tried to quell all indigenous attempts to organize for independence.[38] Only the coup against Caetano and the resulting democracy led to Portugal's decision to withdraw from its colonies. Severe repression of indigenous political organizations by the Portuguese had facilitated the radicalization of the insurgency, which adopted Marxism as its banner. With Portugal's withdrawal, most of their former colonies became Afro-Marxist, Socialist, and/or allied with the Soviet Union (as per American fears).[39]

In sum, European colonial powers knew that a determined nationalist movement which would use force of arms to achieve its ends would be costly, if not impossible, to end—short of independence or the use of massive violence on their part.

The Rubicon Already Crossed

Beyond military lessons from elsewhere in the colonial empires, the European powers had set important precedents for decolonization elsewhere. The intellectual foundations for the granting of independence to sub-Saharan Africa were first established in Asia. Ironically, the first major decolonization after WWII involved a traditionally non-colonial power: the United States. As early as 1935, the American government had promised to grant independence to the Philippines within ten years. Even with the intrusion of WWII, independence was achieved by July 4, 1946—only one year off schedule. The British, for their part, had crossed their ideological Rubicon concerning decolonization with India in 1947.[40] Britain initially tried to use a combination of coercion and co-optation to keep their "jewel in the crown." Nonetheless, the UK eventually lowered its goal to that of maintaining trade relations and keeping India in the Commonwealth. The choice to allow Indian independence followed only after a determined independence movement greatly increased the costs of colonization. The determination and style of Gandhi's nationalism drew ever increasing numbers into resistance to British rule and proved to be quite effective. Although the nationalist party would later divide into the Congress Party and the Muslim League, they were united enough to press for independence at critical junctures.

Moreover, in Asia, the Middle East, and North Africa, the former European colonial powers discovered that they could maintain strong economic ties with former colonies without bearing the costs of direct rule. England retained its influence in Egypt, and it kept India in the Commonwealth—long after each achieved self-rule. Although France had lost most economic ties in Asia after decolonization, its economic links to Morocco and Tunisia were retained.[41] In fact, all of these countries would go on to become some the of largest trade partners of some of their former African colonial countries after the latter achieved independence.[42]

Rising African Nationalism

African nationalism was unlike other types of nationalism in that it did not emerge or revolve around ethnicity or language Per Se.[43] Rather, it tended to be rooted in the new political parties and trade unions which emerged throughout French and British Africa after WWII. When nationalism that resembled European style nationalism emerged in sub-Saharan Africa, it was considered illegitimate by most political leaders. This type of nationalism was perceived as a threat to the territorial integrity of the colony, as with Biafra and Katanga. It was often called "tribalism" or sub-nationalism. One scholar says of African nationalism:

> [It was] different in this one and single respect: whereas in Europe nationalism began the concept of naturally united people seeking to mark out an appropriate political state, in Africa nationalists took state boundaries as given and attempted to wrest its control on behalf of the variety of peoples who had, by chance, been located within those boundaries.[44]

Thus, instead of being a movement for nationhood for a people united by blood, language, or culture, African nationalism was an attempt to expand economic, social, and political access for Africans in the face of the near monopolization of such power by Europeans. This is also in the context of near universal discrimination against most African politically and economically during colonization. As such, African nationalism was about race and subjugation, for it had been along racial lines that subjugation had been practiced. The newly emerging indigenous elites found their professional and business possibilities greatly restrained under the colonial system. Few Africans held posts in the upper levels of the colonial bureaucratic structures, government, or the armed forces. African nationalism was therefore primarily antiracist and anticolonial in character.[45] As a result, it would encourage a united resistance movement toward overthrowing colonization as opposed to dividing into the various "sub-national" groups based on ethnicity and language. This would have a significant effect on the type of organization that would arise to resist colonization as well as the type of organizations that would come to rule independent sub-Saharan Africa.

Although the nationalist movements would become best known for their demands for independence, the early nationalist movements sought African inclusion in the colonial institutions, rather than their overthrow.[46] Though the lack of advancement for colonial subjects was evident everywhere, more advancement for French subjects existed than for British, at least in principle. In the French colonies, there was an early fiction that an *évolué*, an educated African who accepted French culture, could be assimilated into French cultural, political, and economic life. The British never really promoted this idea of the incorporation of Africans into British life and culture. The elites in the French colonies could, by contrast, even become a member of the National Assembly of France.[47] This was mostly symbolic given the limited access to educational or career opportunities for locals. The case of the Belgian colonies was even more restrictive than the British—although they promoted the same symbolic idea of the incorporation of *évolués*. The Belgians restricted the level of either educational attainment or colonial positions of most Congolese. In the Belgian Congo, there were only sixteen university graduates in any field at the time of independence.[48] Advancement for Congolese was also quite restricted in the ranks of administration, the army, and political organs. Congolese never achieved the highest rank in any of these structures, being limited to only the lowest ranks in each.[49] Despite some variation, real opportunities for career or educational advancement under the various colonial systems were quite restricted overall.

Nationalist political parties emerged and grew in strength soon after World War II. The first major nationalistic political parties usually began as congresses interested in promoting the interests of the middle class individuals who filled their ranks. In general, a congress:

claimed to represent "all the people"; it had a loosely-knit, often federal structure comprising a number of affiliated associations and pressed its claim to eventual self-rule or (in the French case) to equality of political and social rights by petitions and deputations, supplemented (when these did not succeed) by mass demonstration, national boycotts and general strikes.[50]

Among the more notable early congresses included: the National Council of Nigeria and the Cameroon (NCNC); the Rassemblement Démocratique Africain (RDA); the United Gold Coast Convention (UGCC); and the Northern Rhodesian African Congress.[51] The NCNC of Nigeria, which was formed in 1944, began as a truly nationalist party; however, it would later become identified by many as a regional party based on Ibo aspirations.[52] The RDA was formed by African deputies of the French Assembly in an inter-party meeting in Bamako in 1946.[53] This group attempted to unite members across nations to work toward African emancipation. This organization was originally affiliated with the French Communists, but several years later its President, Houphouët-Boigny, led his group into a cooperative association with the French metropole.

Over time, these congresses evolved into a nationalist independence parties, most of whom would go on to lead in the post-independence period, though sometimes they would split into regional or competing parties, one of which would almost always come to dominate.[54] One of the first splits occurred when the UGCC of Ghana had a strong disagreement with a powerful member: Kwame Nkrumah. Nkrumah founded the rival Convention People's Party (CPP) in 1949, which would be the first to argue for the independence of Ghana and go on to lead after independence. The NCNC of Nigeria became considered more of a regional party when Azikiwe accepted the premiership of the Eastern region, which in turn led to its partial regionalization. After the passage of the *loi cadre* of 1956, which gutted the bureaucracies of the two federal units, the French colonies shifted toward promoting territorial autonomy. French administration in Africa had consisted of two large territories: the French West African Federation (AOF)—with the capital in Dakar, and the French Equatorial African Federation (AEF)—with its capital in Brazzaville. Togo and Cameroon were treated separately as they were United Nations Trust Territories.[55] Because of the divisions of the former French colonies, the RDA itself divided along similar lines. The RDA wing in Cote d'Ivoire became the Parti Démocratique de Côte d'Ivoire (PDCI) and the wing in Guinea became the Parti Démocratique de Guinée (PDG), for example.

The first nationalist political parties in French Africa had platforms which favored reform instead of independence. In the early years, these postwar political parties sought to secure for Africans equality of rights as French citizens, rather than full independence.[56] In fact, the discussions held in the meeting of African administrators in Brazzaville in early 1944 centered on the reform of the system and not its eradication.[57] The assembled leaders endorsed the end of forced labor, an expansion of the educational system, a limited participation in elections, and the extension of the voice of Africans in the administration of the colonies.[58] Although most of those who attended were colonial administrators, the results of this conference were embraced warmly by the *"cercles des évolués."*[59]

Growing Cost/Declining Returns on African Colonies

Another factor which impacted European choices about continued colonization had to do with the returns and costs to colonization in Africa in the face of this growing nationalism.[60] Demands by Africans for economic and political inclusion increased throughout the post-WWII period. A scarcity of good jobs for Africans was exacerbated by the return of the WWII veterans. In combination with high levels of inflation, low levels of employment helped foster an environment of protest in most colonies.[61] Moreover, with the change in ideology concerning colonization, the rise of left parties in both the British and French, both of these nations began to allow for the formation of labor unions and political parties as a way to address demands for African empowerment. Thus, the doors for regular and legitimate avenues of expressing dissatisfaction opened just as reasons for popular discontent increased.

African nationalists also began to argue for increased spending for both schools and hospitals, beyond greater inclusion in the colonial ranks of power. Partially in anticipation of, and partially in response to, nationalist demands, Great Britain passed the Colonial Development and Welfare Acts of 1945. These acts (and similar initiatives in France) provided the legislative framework for redressing some of the economic neglect from which most of the imperial possessions had suffered. But this "positive" imperialism put an impossible strain on administrative structures.[62] To appease the growing demands of emerging nationalist movements—especially the demands for independence:

> the African colonies [had to be kept at] an acceptable level of affluence; [however] it was beyond the economic capacity of either Britain or France, both seriously weakened by the war, to transfer sufficient real resources to the colonies to enable them to modernize their economies quickly, and so pre-empt the claim of most nationalist leaders that affluence would begin with independence. . . . The only way out of their self-created dilemma was to substitute rapid political advance for rapid economic advance: to give independence and then be free to restrict the flow of aid to manageable levels on the reasonable grounds that independent states did not have the same claims as colonies.[63]

The Belgians, too, increased social spending in their colonies after WWII. Funding for schools, hospitals, and clinics was greatly expanded: "In 1939 outlays for the operating and investment budgets totalled only 788 million Congo francs, while by 1950 these outlays had risen to 11,473 million, a fifteen-fold increase in eleven years."[64] Moreover, the spending in the last decade of colonization tripled—with government expenditure hovering around 30% of GNP.[65] All these things required money from colonial budgets which were less and less able to raise the same level of funding. Although none of the colonial powers decolonized their holdings for purely economic reasons, by the late 1950s, Britain and France began to realize that the costs of their autarkic economic systems now exceeded their marginal benefits and—barring another calculus—decolonization was in order.[66]

Partly as a result of these increased costs, economic returns to colonial ventures were in decline during this period. According to D. K. Fieldhouse, by the time decolonization came about, the metropolitan countries felt less of a need to hold on to their colonies. By 1952, as the Korean War boom ended, most of the British colonies had begun "to run a deficit with the dollar area."[67] In fact, the British colonies had begun to become a drag on the empire or threaten some strong interests: colonial demands on credit markets were increasing interest rates; many British firms feared unfair competition emerging from the colonies; and the cost of aid was escalating.[68] In terms of the French-held colonies, France began to subsidize enormous deficits in the balance of trade. This was in spite of "not unfavorable terms of trade for colonial export and the artificially high prices paid for selected colonial staples in France."[69] Fieldhouse argues that "with the exception of intense international commodity shortages between 1945 and 1950, the French economy as a whole obtained little benefit from the 'resource base' notionally offered by the colonies."[70]

In the French case, the commercial support for colonization was split, but it was edging toward decolonization. Several industries clearly relied on the protected colonial markets for their well-being and lobbied for the continuation of this policy. Perhaps the best example is the cotton textile industry which employed over 220,000 French workers in the early 1950s and sent more than 35% of its exports to colonial markets.[71] Fieldhouse argues, however, that industries heavily reliant upon the colonial markets were declining ones, and the rising sectors were either neutral or opposed to colonial rule.[72]

Lack of European Resort to Violence

Prior to the effective American enforcement of the Monroe Doctrine and its rise to hegemony after the Second World War, military power had often been used by the great powers to defend their property in the colonial and

semi-colonial regions of the world. European powers had routinely relied
upon "gunboat" diplomacy to achieve such ends. In fact,

> [a]t various times, Britain had blockaded Nicaragua, Argentina, and El Salvador.
> In 1897 German gunboats had threatened Port-au-Prince, Haiti; in 1900 the
> French had moved against Santo Domingo in the Dominican Republic; in 1901
> Britain France Germany, Belgium, and Italy prepared to occupy Guatamanlan
> ports; and in 1902–1903 Germany and Britain blockaded Venezuela.[73]

With the emergence of American hegemony, its crusade to halt the spread
of Communism, and its ability to influence its allies' behavior, these practices nearly came to an abrupt end. America was concerned about the possible radicalization of Third World leaders, and it tried to influence how her
French, British, and Belgian allies interacted with their former colonies as
part of larger geopolitical and strategic considerations. America feared that
too strong a reaction to nationalist demands would radicalize Third World
leaders who would then join the Soviet orbit. The US favored military intervention only to counter communist penetration, or other significant geopolitical threats.

The British and French, however, did test American leadership and resolve
when they used military force to reverse the nationalization of the Suez
Canal. Egypt's Nassar nationalized the Suez Canal Company on July 26,
1956.[74] Fearing that a closure of the canal could jeopardize the flow of oil to
Europe, as well as the associated loss of control and revenues, England and
France attempted to recapture the canal militarily. Along with Israel, they
devised a scheme which provided for an Israeli attack against Egypt, which
would prompt England and France to deploy troops at the canal site to serve
as a buffer between Egypt and Israel. This plan was designed without prior
US knowledge or approval and was to provide plausible deniability about
English and French intentions—that is, retaking the canal while avoiding
international sanctions.

Unfortunately for the conspirators, American as well as world opinion was
strongly against this action: the attempt to retake the Canal Zone by force
was strongly condemned by the General Assembly of the United Nations.[75]
More importantly, with the recent invasion of Hungary and a potential Soviet
nuclear threat in the background,[76] the US not only backed the UN measure to
censure these actions, but it also cut off oil supplies to England and France.[77]
Within hours of having the Canal Zone secured, the British French governments agreed to a cease fire and withdrew their forces. In Britain, at least,
this event signaled the end of the British policy of military intervention and
the move to the "grand strategy of nonintervention and . . . conciliation . . .
[towards] . . . the moderate nationalists."[78] Given this shift in geopolitical

power, the relative abundance of foreign corporations operating in developing nations, and the rise in economic nationalism, the nationalization of foreign-owned companies became common throughout the Third World by the 1960s and 1970s. Moreover, the Suez Crisis is often seen as a symbolic turning point in geopolitical power away from European leaders to US and USSR leadership of their respective spheres.

Therefore, American foreign policy from WWII onwards encouraged cooperation with moderate leaders to forestall the establishment of pro-Soviet regimes. Overt actions involving the use of military force in their former colonies jeopardized these well-articulated American interests. Importantly for Africa, the Suez crisis, the French loss of Vietnam and Algeria, the enforcement of the Atlantic Charter upon the British, and the logic of the Cold War, all set the stage for a peaceful and quick transfer of power from European countries to indigenous leaders in most of sub-Saharan Africa, especially after episodes of violence.

Violence in Africa as Trigger

Nationalist anti-colonial actions were central to the timing of independence for the first state to be decolonized in sub-Saharan Africa: Ghana in 1957. According to one source, the pivotal event in the decolonization of Ghana took place in February 1948 with the outbreak of riots that left twenty-nine dead.[79] Because of this incident, the British decided to take the initiative and proceed with the decolonization of both the Gold Coast and Nigeria.[80] Thus, mass action used against the metropole was particularly effective. Although violence sometimes played an important role in the timing of decolonization, especially in other parts of British Africa, the process of decolonization through the mid- to late-1960s was relatively free of violence.

Nationalist disturbances were also central to the timing of the decision to decolonize in the Belgian Congo.[81] In fact, the Belgians had no effective plans for decolonizing the Congo in the early 1950s. The first mention of decolonization occurred in 1955 when Professor Val Bilsen published a book in Belgium suggesting the need for eventual decolonization, giving a timetable of thirty years for completion. This proposal was well received in many *évolué* circles in the Belgian Congo.[82] It was strongly condemned by one of Congo's most notable nationalist movements, the Alliance des Bakongo (ABAKO). Although Lumumba's Mouvement National Congolaise (MNC) did not endorse the thirty-year timetable, it did not call for immediate decolonization.

ABAKO, however, began a campaign of civil disobedience to put pressure on the Belgians and demanded immediate independence. In fact, the event which would change Belgium's schedule for decolonization occurred on January 4, 1959. In the capital, Leopoldville (now Kinshasa), the colonial administration tried to disperse a crowd which had gathered for an ABAKO meeting. The crowd reacted strongly to this show of force, and, for three days, assaulted symbolic artifacts of the colonial system: they attacked social centers, administrative buildings, Catholic missions, and Portuguese stores.[83] With the outbreak of riots and looting in Leopoldville, the Belgian government acted swiftly. In January of 1960, Belgium invited the representatives of the Congolese nationalist movements to a round table to discuss decolonization. By the end of the conference, a decision was taken to set the date of independence for 30 June of that very year. The shortness of the proposed transitional period shocked all involved. In fact, the announcement was met with "minutes of silence instead of an outburst of joy."[84]

One scholar gave four primary reasons for this seemingly disproportionate and quick response to one violent episode in the Congo: first, the Belgians felt themselves above the problems faced by the other metropolitan countries and resolved to face decolonization through negotiation; second, indigenous articulations of such demands were late in coming; third, the Belgians felt unable to use force to slow nationalist demands for rapid independence given domestic public opinion and particular Belgian political dynamics; fourth, the three principal apologists for colonization were silent or politically impotent: the church, the colonial administration, and Belgian companies.[85]

In the French colonies, the timing of independence was much more in concert across countries, with most of its colonies in the region becoming independent in 1960.[86] Late in the colonial period, all of the newly forming states were given a choice between continued French ties with a slow process of decolonization and immediate independence without French aid. Guinea, in 1958, chose the latter option of immediate independence against much French opposition. It was the only former French colony to do so. Nearly all other chose the former. Moreover, in sub-Saharan Africa, very little violence occurred aside from in Cameroon. Nevertheless, the independence of former French colonies in sub-Saharan Africa can be said to have been won partially by bloodshed—though it was blood spent in Algeria and Vietnam.[87]

Rising Economic Nationalism Internationally

Another rising international trend, though chiefly among former colonial countries, emerged during the Cold War period. Beginning especially in the 1960s, Third World nations were nationalizing foreign-owned companies involved in industry as well as mining and oil production. Its rise was facilitated by the logic of the Cold War, American foreign policy preferences, the pressure for restraint that American leaders would place on their allies vis-à-vis Third World nations, and the rising economic nationalism throughout the

Third World. Even post-independence, America remained concerned about the possible radicalization of African leaders.

As will be seen in the Chapter 4, the nationalization of capital-intensive industries and oil or mining sectors swept through much of the region and consolidated significant levels of economic power into the hands of the political elites. Nationalization refers to the confiscation of all, or part, of private businesses or property on the part of the state, with or without compensation for seized property.[88] Connotatively, it implies that the state itself has become the at least the majority shareholder of these companies or businesses, often up to 100% ownership. The term was first used as a legal concept in the constitution of Mexico and the first decrees of the USSR after 1917.[89] Nationalizations of foreign companies in the Third World tended to coincide with the emerging nationalism evident in countries that were newly independent, or that had undergone a social revolution.

As discussed in the discussion on resort to force, European nations had defended their property using gunboat diplomacy prior to WWII. America was more concerned with the geopolitics of the Third World during the Cold War than the protection of any particular corporation's losses. Therefore, should American corporate property be nationalized by a non-communist state, the US would take no action to reverse it. Moreover, it wanted its allies to adopt a similar policy—unless the nationalization country was aligned with the Soviet Union (like Cuba). For example, the US did nothing the post-1950 cases of the nationalization of American companies for fear of triggering Communist expansion.[90] In fact, the US policy toward nationalization was accommodationist: it "has never denied that foreign states had the right to take over property, but has held that such actions must be pursued in nondiscriminatory ways, undertaken for public purposes, and accompanied by prompt and adequate compensation."[91] Even when American companies faced nationalization in Venezuela, Nicaragua, Mexico, Iran, Guatemala, Bolivia, Cuba, Peru, and Cuba, the United State government was very reluctant to use force to reverse these nationalizations.[92]

As a result of American pressure, its allies also became disinclined to use military force to reverse nationalizations—despite huge economic losses. For example, the British had a significant number of large multinational corporations (MNCs) overseas which faced the losses of oil rights and production IN Iran (1951) as well as the loss of the Suez Canal (1956)—all through nationalizations. The stake of British interests Iran was quite large, accounting for of the Anglo-Iran oil company.[93] In these latter cases, the British government officially denied the right of these countries to nationalize foreign property. However, given the problems in Europe at the time of the Iranian action, Britain was wary of using military force in these cases. In fact, the British were notified that America strongly opposed the use of force in the case of

Iran—barring three unique instances: a Russian invasion, invitation from the Iranian government, or to facilitate the evacuation of British nationals.[94]

The more pragmatic approach to Third World nationalizations by the US and her allies would create an environment in which it would become more widespread. In fact, the worldwide wave of nationalizations also washed through much of sub-Saharan Africa in the late 1960s and through the 1970s. The nationalization of industries prior to the 1960s was relatively rare—though there were some important cases. For example, two American asphalt companies had been taken over in 1904 and 1905; however, the motivation for these particular acts appears to have had more to do with the personal enrichment of the dictator than it did with economic nationalism.[95] A rising number of nationalizations occurred in the 1960s; but an even more dramatic increase occurred in the 1970s. Using American-owned raw material firms as an example, this trend can be illustrated. Between 1900 and 1950—a fifty-year period—only six takeovers occurred. From 1951 to 1965, an additional three more were undertaken; but from 1965 to 1974 the frequency jumped to thirty-four—ten of which happened in Africa.[96] Expanding the analysis to include all such businesses, 455 foreign companies were nationalized in one degree or another worldwide between 1960 and 1969. This number increased again in the 1970s, with 914 nationalizations from 1970 to 1976—over double the number of takeovers for the second period.[97] Therefore, the trends of nationalizations that would sweep much of Africa were part of a larger international trend, facilitated by US condoning such actions in the light of rising political and economic nationalism and America's fears of pushing Third World leaders into the Soviet camp.

CONCLUSIONS

The rapid decolonization of most of the countries of sub-Saharan Africa resulted from several converging and historically proximate reasons linked with the new geopolitical alignment following WWII. The geopolitical shift in power away from the European nations with colonial empires toward a bipolar system led to two anticolonial powers militated for a quick decolonization of most of the Third World, with sub-Saharan Africa at the trailing edge. Moreover, the war effort as well as the interests of the US and USSR in free trade or communism deepened and accelerated the shift in worldwide ideologies and norms delegitimizing colonialism. These shifts in norms and ideology were bolstered by American and Soviet self-interest and power, through international organizations such as the United Nations as well as the structure of the bipolar world order. The weakened and collapsing institutions of colonialism were then faced with confident and growing nationalist movements throughout the subcontinent. These latter forces were fed by changes in ideology backed by the rising powers. These newly powerful ideologies further delegitimized colonization and its associated views of racial hierarchy. These views were too closely associated with Nazi propaganda for comfort. These nationalist movements in sub-Saharan Africa were also fueled by previously successful independence movements, such as those in India, Algeria, and Indonesia, and diffused throughout the Third World. Also, the clear military and economic ascendency of the United States and the USSR placed real constraints on the use of military power by European nations in the Third World. Moreover, pressure from a free-trade America, as well as the diminishing economic returns on holding a colony, convinced the metropoles to hasten their departures.

In this context, the indigenous groups that led the fight for independence did not have to create strong and cohesive organizations to convince the colonial powers to leave, as was the case in regions which fought colonization earlier. As such, even the leading nationalist movements tended to be relatively weak in organization and discipline—especially in comparison with those that had struggled longer for independence. Nonetheless, in sub-Saharan Africa, the newly emerging nationalist groups would contend for power amid few economic constraints on their power, and they faced even fewer political ones. The context in which Africa decolonized set the foundation for the types of political and economic institutions and practices which would emerge, given the mix of strengths and weakness of the groups who would rule over the quickly abandoned colonial bureaucracies, their preferred ideologies vis-à-vis the best political or economic structures to achieve development, as well as the relative autonomy granted Third World leaders in the emerging Cold War competition. These institutions and practices consolidate economic and political power into the hands of those who held the political reins of power. This is what we turn to next.

NOTES

1. D. K. Fieldhouse, "Arrested Development in Anglophone Black Africa?" in Prosser Gifford and Wm. Roger Louis, eds., *Decolonization and African Independence: The Transfer of Power, 1960–1980* (New Haven: Yale University Press, 1988), p. 138; for general reference on decolonization, see John D. Hargreaves, *Decolonization in Africa* (New York: Longman, 1988); for other treatments of relative rapid decolonization on state strength, see Christopher Clapham, *African and the International System: The Politics of State Survival* (Cambridge: Cambridge University Press, 1996); also Robert H. Jackson and Carl G. Rosberg, "Why Africa's Weak States Persist: The Empirical and the Juridical in Statehood," *World Politics* Vol. 35, No. 1 (Oct., 1982): 1–24; for overview of colonial matters, see Crawford Young,

The African Colonial State in Comparative Perspective (New Haven: Yale University Press, 1994). Spain's colony in sub-Saharan Africa became independent in 1968. The remaining British colonies (and their dates of independence) were these: Mauritius (1968), Swaziland (1968), the Seychelles (1976), and Zimbabwe (Rhodesia) (1980). The remaining French colonies were these: Comoros (1975), Djibouti (1977). Spain relinquished Equatorial Guinea in 1968 and Western Sahara in 1976. South Africa decolonized Namibia in 1990.

2. Some might argue that the white minority led countries of Rhodesia and South Africa were not independent while under minority rule, though Rhodesia declared itself independent in 1965, it did not official become decolonized from the UK until 1980.

3. Latin America was decolonized much earlier and is not considered part of this wave. Most of this region had gained independence before 1825.

4. Geoffrey Barraclough, *An Introduction to Contemporary History* (New York: Penguin Books, 1978), p. 153.

5. According to CINC scores of the correlates of war database, the power rankings of these countries (with rounding) in 1938 were these: US (0.17), Germany (0.15), USSR (0.16), UK (0.078), China (0.09), Japan (0.06), France (0.055), and Italy (0.03). See National Material Capabilities, 4.0 http://cow.la.psu.edu/COW2%20 Data/Capabilities/nmc4.htm. China was not considered by all to be a great power. Cites in David J. Singer, Stuart Bremer, and John Stuckey, "Capability Distribution, Uncertainty, and Major Power War, 1820–1965." in Bruce Russett, ed., *Peace, War, and Numbers* (Beverly Hills: Sage, 1972): 19–48. Also, discussed in David J. Singer, "Reconstructing the Correlates of War Dataset on Material Capabilities of States, 1816–1985," *International Interactions* 14 (1987): 115–32.

6. For this section, see especially, Stephen Ambrose and Douglas G. Brinkley, *Rise to Globalism: American Foreign Policy Since 1938* (New York: Penguin Books, 1997): 1–2.

7. Unless stated otherwise, data from this section is taken from tables in William C. Wohlforth, "The Stability of a Unipolar World" *International Security* 24, 1 (Summer, 1999): 5–41. The index set the hegemon's spending at 100% (the US).

8. See Chapter 1 for references on hegemonic stability theory and hierarchy.

9. Barraclough, *Contemporary History*, p. 156.

10. For prior justification of colonization, see Young, *The African Colonial State*, esp. 165–71.

11. Robert H. Jackson and Carl G. Rosberg, "The Marginality of African States," in Gwendolen M. Carter and Patrick O'Meara, eds., *African Independence: The First Twenty-Five Years* (Bloomington: Indiana University Press, 1986), p. 45.

12. Ibid., pp. 45–70.

13. For a good overview of the UN's role in decolonization, see Donald F. McHenry, "The United Nations: Its Role in Decolonization," in Carter and O'Meara, eds., *African Independence*, pp. 31–44.

14. See UN Charter, Chapter XI, Article 73, http://www.un.org/en/documents/charter/chapter11.shtml

15. Trust territories were ones that had been taken away from Germany and Turkey, placed under UN supervision, but then farmed out to a traditional colonial

government to rule, though officially the UN supervised from a distance. For an in depth analysis of colonial rule linked to UN, see Rupert Emerson, "Colonialism, Political Development, and the UN," *International Organization* 19, 3 (Summer 1965): 484–503.

16. The diffusion argument was more made during the third wave and applied to democratization. It can easily be applied to the regional anticolonial sweep. See, Samuel Huntington, *The Third Wave* (Oklahoma University Press, 1990); for an empirical exploration of democratic diffusion, see Harvey Starr "Democratic Dominoes: Diffusion Approaches to the Spread of Democracy in the International System *The Journal of Conflict Resolution*, Vol. 35, No. 2 (Jun., 1991), pp. 356–381; and Daniel Brinks and Michael Coppedge, "Diffusion Is No Illusion: Neighbor Emulation in the Third Wave of Democracy," *Comparative Political Studies* 39, 4 (May 2006): 463–489, 464. For an empirical treatment of the diffusion of ideas, see Dennis P. Quinn and Maria A. Toyoda, "Global Ideology and Voter Sentiment as Determinants of International Financial Liberalization," in Beth Simmons, Frank Dobbin, and Geoff Garrett, eds., *The Diffusion of Neoliberalism* (Cambridge University Press, 2007).

17. Alicia Campos, "The Decolonization of Equatorial Guinea: The Relevance of the International Factor," *The Journal of African History*, 44, 1 (2003): 95–116, p. 99.

18. For views on hegemony see Robert Gilpin, *U.S. Power and the Multinational Corporation: The Political Economy of Foreign Direct Investment* (New York: Basic Books, 1975); Stephen D. Krasner, "State Power and the Structure of Foreign Trade," *World Politics* 28 (April 1976): 317–47; for an overview see Robert O. Keohane, *After Hegemony: Cooperation and Discord in the World Political Economy* (Princeton, NJ: Princeton University Press, 1984), esp. Chapter 3; for a critique see Duncan Snidal, "Limits of Hegemonic Stability Theory," *International Organization* 39 (August 1985): 579–614.

19. Charles P. Kindleberger, *The World in Depression, 1929–1939* (Berkeley: University of California Press, 1973), p. 292; for an expanded definition see Charles P. Kindleberger, "Dominance and Leadership in the International Economy: Exploitation, Public Goods, and Free Rides," *International Studies Quarterly* 25 (June 1981), 247; for other definitions see Robert Gilpin, *U.S. Power and the Multinational Corporation: The Political Economy of Foreign Direct Investment* (New York: Basic Books, 1975); and David A. Lake, *Power Protection, and Free Trade: International Sources of U.S. Commercial Strategy, 1887–1939* (Ithaca, NY: Cornell University Press, 1988).

20. *Columbia Encyclopedia* Fifth Edition (New York: Columbia University Press, 1993): S.V. "Atlantic Charter."

21. On the one hand, the idea of self-autonomy is self-evidently contradictory to colonialism. On the other hand, free trade would open their colonies' markets to world competition.

22. For a good overview on American pressure to do away with the colonies of its allies, see William Roger Louis and Ronald Robinson, "The United States and the Liquidation of British Empire in Tropical Africa, 1941–1951," in Prosser Gifford and Wm. Roger Louis, eds., *The Transfer of Power in Africa: Decolonization 1940–1960* (New Haven: Yale University Press, 1982): 31–56.

23. For an overview of Bretton Woods, see Joan E. Spero and Jeffrey A. Hart, *The Politics of International Economic Relations* 7rd Ed., (Stamford, CT: Cengage, 2003); for its role in establishing a trading system see Richard Rosecrance, *The Rise of the Trading State: Commerce and Conquest in the Modern World* (New York: Basic Books, 1986), Chapter 7; for the institutionalization of free trade ideas in the Bretton Woods system see Judith Goldstein, "Ideas, institutions, and American Trade Policy," in G. John Ikenberry, David A Lake, and Michael Mastanduno, eds., *The State and American Foreign Economic Policy* (Ithaca, NY: Cornell University Press, 1988): 179–218.

24. Actually, it was not instituted because American Senate did not ratify it, not due to a lack of American influence over other countries.

25. Louis and Robinson, "Liquidation of the British Empire," pp. 44–45.

26. For analysis of containment, see Deborah Welch Larson, *Origins of Containment: A Psychological Explanation* (Princeton: Princeton University Press, 1989).

27. Louis and Robinson, "Liquidation of the British Empire," pp. 44–45.

28. William Roger Louis, "Libyan Independence, 1951: The Creation of a Client State," in Gifford and Louis, eds., *Decolonization and African Independence*, pp. 168–69.

29. Edmond Keller, "Decolonization, Independence and Beyond," in Phyllis M. Martin and Patrick O'Meara, eds., *Africa* 2nd Ed., (Bloomington, IN: Indiana University Press, 1986), p. 145.

30. Keith Panther-Brick, "Independence, French Style," in Gifford and Louis, eds., *Decolonization and African Independence*, pp. 94–95.

31. Tony Smith, "A Comparative Study of French and British Decolonization," in Gifford and Louis, eds., *The Transfer of Power in Africa*, p. 94.

32. Hargreaves, *Decolonization*, p. 95.

33. Ibid., p. 87.

34. Tony Chafer, *The End of Empire in French West Africa: France's Successful Decolonization?* (New York : Berg, 2002), p. 86. Aside from the French Communists. For an in depth view of French Socialist and British Labour views on decolonization, see Miles Kahler, *Decolonization in Britain and France: The Domestic Consequences of International Relations* (Princeton: Princeton University Press, 1984), esp., Chapter III.

35. Bethwell A. Ogot and Tiyambe Zeleza, "Kenya: The Road to Independence and After," in Gifford and Louis, eds., *Decolonization and African Independence*, p. 408.

36. Hargreaves, *Decolonization*, p. 178; Jean Stengers, "Precipitous Decolonization: The Belgian Congo," in Prosser Gifford and Wm. Roger Louis, eds., *The Transfer of Power in Africa: Decolonization 1940–1960* (New Haven: Yale University Press, 1982), p. 332.

37. Hargreaves, *Decolonization*, pp. 212–218; Aquino de Bragança with Basil Davidson, "Independence without Decolonization: Mozambique," in Gifford and Louis, *Decolonization*, pp. 427–44.

38. John A. Marcum, "The People's Republic of Angola: a Radical Vision Frustrated," in Edmond J. Keller and Donald Rothchild, *Afro-Marxist Regimes:*

Ideology and Public Policy (Boulder, CO: Lynne Rienner Publisher, 1987), esp. pp. 68–71.

39. For several descriptions of former Portuguese colonies see Keller and Rothchild, *Afro-Marxist Regimes.*

40. Arguably one could look to South Africa and Ireland as previous examples of decolonization since they had achieved formal independence in 1910 and 1922, respectively. These and the earlier decolonization in North America, however, were distant historically and probably had little bearing on the present cases, especially since few African leaders drew on these examples for inspiration.

41. For an account of Tunisian and Moroccan independence see Keith Panther-Brick, "Independence, French Style," in Gifford and Louis, eds., *Decolonization and African Independence*, pp. 78–92.

42. For example, France remained the largest trading partner of Côte d'Ivoire until the 1980s, and she was also the most important trading partner for Senegal throughout the 1970s. Great Britain remained Kenya's largest trading partner through 1981, and she was the largest exporter to Ghana. Belgium was Zaire and Rwanda's largest trading partner in through 1980. See *Africa South of the Sahara 1987*, S.V. Various Countries.

43. For an overview of early African Nationalism, see Thomas Hodgkin, *Nationalism in Colonial Africa* (New York: New York University Press, 1957).

44. Richard Hodder-Williams, *An Introduction to the Politics of Tropical Africa* (London: George Allen & Unwin, 1984), p. 71.

45. Basil Davidson, *The Black Man's Burden: Africa and the Curse of the Nation-State* (New York: Times Books, 1992), p. 165.

46. Hodder-Williams, *Politics of Tropical Africa*, p. 69.

47. Ibid.

48. Stengers, "Precipitous Decolonization," p. 307.

49. Ibid., p. 331.

50. Richard Sandbrook, "Patrons, Clients and Factions: New Dimensions of Conflict Analysis in Africa," *Canadian Journal of Political Science* Vol. V, No 1 (March 1972), cited in Tordoff, *Governments and Politics*, p. 63.

51. Tordoff, *Governments and Politics*, p. 63.

52. See James S. Coleman, *Nigeria: Background to Nationalism* (Berkeley & Los Angeles: University of California Press, 1958); J. F. Ade, Ajayi and A. E. Ekoko, "Transfer of Power in Nigeria: Its Origins and Consequences," in *Decolonization and African Independence*, pp. 245–69. However, Sklar has argued that the NCNC retained its pan-tribal character throughout the period. See Richard L. Sklar, *Nigerian Political Power: Power in an Emergent African Nation* (Princeton: Princeton University Press, 1963); Richard L. Sklar and C.S. Whitaker, Jr., "Nigeria," in James S. Coleman and Carl G. Rosberg *Political Parties and National Integration in Tropical Africa* (Berkeley: University of California Press, 1964): 597–654.

53. Ruth Schachter Morgenthau, *Political Parties in French-Speaking West Africa* (Oxford: Clarendon Press, 1964), p. 88.

54. For synopsis of African Political Parties at time of independence, see Tordoff, *Government and Politics.*

55. For overview of French colonies, see Ruth Schachter Morgenthau and Lucy Creevey Behrman, "French-Speaking Tropical Africa," in Michael Crowder, ed., *The Cambridge History of Africa Vol. 8 from c. 1940 to c. 1975* (Cambridge: Cambridge University Press, 1984), p. 615.

56. Tordoff, *Government and Politics*, p. 66.

57. Yves Person, "French West Africa and Decolonization," in Gifford and Louis, eds., *The Transfer of Power in Africa*, p. 144.

58. Ibid., p. 144.

59. Elikia M'Bokolo, "French Colonial Policy in Equatorial Africa," in Gifford and Louis (eds.), *The Transfer of Power in Africa*, p. 192.

60. For an overview of the development of intellectual nationalism in Africa see Richard L. Sklar, "The Colonial Imprint on African Political Thought," in Carter and O'Meara, eds., *African Independence*, pp. 1–31.

61. William Tordoff, *Government and Politics in Africa* (Bloomington: Indiana University Press, 1984), p. 51.

62. See Anthony Low, "The End of British Empire in Africa," in Prosser Gifford and W.M. Roger Louis, eds., *Decolonization and African Independence: The Transfer of Power in Africa 1960–1980* (New Haven: Yale University Press, 1988), pp. 38–39.

63. Fieldhouse, *Black Africa*, p. 23.

64. Crawford Young and Thomas Turner, *The Rise and Decline of the Zairian State* (Madison, WI: The University of Wisconsin Press, 1985), p. 39.

65. Ibid., p. 39.

66. Fieldhouse, *Black Africa*, p. 21.

67. Ibid., p. 7.

68. Ibid.

69. Ibid., p. 14.

70. Ibid., p. 15.

71. Ibid., p. 17.

72. Ibid.

73. Stephen D. Krasner, *Defending the National Interest: Raw Materials Investments and U.S. Foreign Policy* (Princeton: Princeton University Press, 1978), p. 162.

74. For accounts of the Suez crisis see Stephen E. Ambrose, *Rise to Globalism: American Foreign Policy, 1938–1976* (New York: Penguin Books, 1971/ Revised 1976); Hargreaves, *Decolonization in Africa*, pp. 156–58; Low, "The End of the British Empire in Africa," p. 51.

75. Ambrose, *Rise to Globalism*, pp. 251–53.

76. Ibid. Khrushchev threatened to destroy each nation with nuclear war if they did not withdraw.

77. Ibid.

78. Low, "End of British Empire," p. 51.

79. Anthony Low, "The End of the British Empire in Africa." in Gifford and Louis, eds., *Decolonization and African Independence*, p. 39.

80. Ibid.

81. For accounts of the effects of nationalism on Belgian decolonization, see Hargreaves, *Decolonization in Africa*, pp. 175–83; Ilunga Kabongo, "The Catastrophe

of Belgian Decolonization," in Gifford and Louis, eds., *Decolonization and African Independence;* Crawford Young, *Politics in the Congo: Decolonization and Independence* (Princeton: Princeton University Press, 1965); Crawford Young, "Zaire, Rwanda and Burundi," in Michael Crowder, ed., *The Cambridge History of Africa*, Vol. 8 1940–1975 (Cambridge: Cambridge University Press, 1984): 698–754; and Stengers, "Precipitous Decolonization," pp. 305–36.

82. Kabongo, "Belgian Decolonization," in Gifford and Louis, eds., *Decolonization and African Independence*, p. 384.

83. Young, "Zaire, Rwanda and Burundi," in Crowder, ed., *The Cambridge History of Africa*, p. 709.

84. Kabongo, "Belgian Decolonization," p. 381.

85. Stengers, "Precipitous Decolonization."

86. In sub-Saharan Africa, Guinea became independent in 1958, Comoros in 1975, Djibouti in 1977, and all the rest in 1960.

87. Morgenthau and Behrman, "French-Speaking Tropical Africa," p. 616; However, there was a serious, yet unsuccessful, revolt in Madagascar in 1948 with anywhere from 11,000—90,000 deaths reported. See Bonar A. Gow, "Madagascar," in Michael Crowder, *The Cambridge History of Africa* Vol. 8, 1940–1975 (Cambridge: Cambridge University Press, 1984): 674–697, and especially p. 678.

88. Leslie L. Rood, "Nationalisation and Indigenisation in Africa," *Journal of Modern African Studies* 14, 2 (1976):427–447, p. 429. Rood contrasts the term to "expropriation" which implies the taking of individual pieces of property, which has a negative connotation. Nationalization, he considers to have a positive connotation. For the contrast between classical and actual conceptions of nationalization see Abd-el-Kader Boye, *L'acte de nationalisation* (Daker: Édition Berger-Levrault, 1979): 12–24. For American view as well as international laws concerning it see Kenneth A. Rodman, *Sanctity Versus Sovereignty: The United States and the Nationalization of Natural Resource Investments* (New York: Columbia University Press, 1988).

89. Dianne Bolton, *Nationalization—A Road to Socialism?: The Lessons of Tanzania* (London: Zed Books Ltd., 1985), p. 2.

90. Stephen D. Krasner, *Defending the National Interest: Raw Materials Investments and U.S. Foreign Policy* (Princeton: Princeton University Press, 1978).

91. Ibid., p. 148.

92. Ibid., pp. 144–46.

93. Ibid., pp. 120, 121, and 148.

94. Dean Acheson, *Present at the Creation* (New York: Norton, 1969), pp. 503, 506; cited in Ibid., p. 122.

95. Krasner, *Defending the National Interest*, pp. 139–40.

96. Ibid., p. 218.

97. Stephen D. Krasner, *Structural Conflict: The Third World Against Global Liberalism* (Berkeley & Los Angeles: University of California Press, 1985), Table 7.3, p. 184.

Chapter 3

The Consolidation of
Political Power in Africa

The Rise of One- and No-Party States

With the decision to decolonize the region so quickly, the departing powers had to establish some sort of system of self-governance in their colonies to replace colonial structures in anticipation of self-rule. Most British, French, and Belgium territories had a version of a multiparty electoral system established for them in the late colonial period, usually with at least one election undertaken before independence.[1] The first set of elections tended to be won in a landslide by the party that was most associated with the goal of independence, with some exceptions. The large victories usually awarded to these parties reflected the national collective will for independence. The victorious parties became ensconced in power and would be able to dominate their societies for at least a generation, unless they were displaced by a military coup. But even successful coup leaders would later come to dominate the new political landscape, often transforming the regime into a new one-party, personalist regime.[2]

Few countries maintained the multiparty systems created for them in the late colonial period. In fact, within less than a decade, nearly all competitive electoral systems were displaced by one- or no-party systems.[3] Of the fifteen former French colonies, fourteen former British colonies, and three former Belgian colonies, only the former British colonies of the Gambia, Botswana, and Mauritius maintained multiparty polities through 1989.[4] All the rest would become controlled by a single political party or a military regime. Unsurprisingly, none of the Portuguese colonies inherited multiparty electoral institutions. The Portuguese militarized response to domestic pressures for political and economic liberalization led to the very Afro-Marxist regimes the US had feared. These also resulted in one-party regimes. Both one-party regimes (where only one party has seats in the legislature) and no-party regimes (where there is no legislature and rule by the military) clearly consolidate significant political power into a narrow elite. Thus, as a result of domestic, regional, and international contexts, and ultimately the geopolitical shift following WWII, political power in sub-Saharan Africa would be concentrated in the hands of the political or military elite.

RELATIVE ADVANTAGES OF FIRST NATIONALIST PARTIES IN CONTEXT OF WEAK CIVIL SOCIETY

Perhaps the most important reason for the latter consolidation of political power by one party lay with the peculiar advantages enjoyed by the first truly identifiable, national, anticolonial movement and its ability to transform itself into a major political party. Within the power vacuum created by the rapidly departing metropoles, these organizations accrued several advantages over other potential movements vying for postcolonial political power: (1) the tendency for other groups to have already joined these movements in the run up to independence; (2) their therefore higher average levels of organizational and institutional experience; (3) their national name recognition and legitimacy as the first anticolonial parties and leaders; and (4) colonial recognition as the principal negotiators for decolonization, which translated into national prominence and access to significant political and economic resources. Furthermore, once these parties gained victories in the first elections—and they usually did so by substantial majorities—they used the political and economic levers of the state to further reinforce and deepen their rule. Whatever party won the first election gained nearly complete access to the distribution of state patronage as well as control over the levers of state coercion. Also, if their majorities were large enough, these parties could simply change the rules of the game to obtain a monopoly over, or create clear disadvantages for, potential opponents. Finally, since the new ruling party controlled so much power and had unaccountable sway over state resources, members of small parties would "cross the floor" and join the majority party, although this trend was evident in pre-independence elections as well as post-independence elections.

Pre-independence Bandwagoning

The first nationalist parties with a major organizational structure in place and which opposed colonialism often become known as "the" nationalist party and tended to gain a significant political advantage over other parties or movements. In fact, the leaders who were the first "to establish a relationship between individuals and an organization gave them a great advantage over those who came later, since the latter had either to try to reach individuals who were less reachable or to undo what the initial organization had done."[5]

Not only did preexisting groups have the advantage by recruiting the low hanging fruit, but competing groups or parties would also have to prove why forming a new political party or movement would strengthen, rather than weaken, the goal of independence—a difficult argument to make. In addition, other influential groups such as trade unions, student groups, youth groups, church groups, and women's movements tended to ally themselves with the largest and most visible nationalist movements rather than create competing organizations. Thus, the first national movement to argue for independence was immediately able to attract other groups that pursued the same goals— thereby greatly increasing its power. Since no cause was seen to be as legitimate as political independence from colonization, most individuals who had special skills or headed organizations usually lent their support to the most visible preexisting independence movements. Also, as Olson would argue, this group had already overcome its collective action costs, while potential rival organizations still faced them.[6]

The trend of indigenous organizations jumping on the bandwagon of political independence was reinforced by the colonial practice of recognizing one official representative of the African people within their colonies. Oftentimes, such an organization could only gain this status if it could prove that it enjoyed overwhelming popular support. Potential rival organizations would then choose to join the umbrella of the independence movement—the dominant strategy of creating one large and powerful organization to negotiate a speedy decolonization. Thus, most groups would not dare challenge the power and influence of the preeminent nationalist parties until after gaining independence from the colonial powers; however, by then a grassroots challenge to compete against this movement became almost organizationally impossible.

Organizational Advantage

The nationalist movement enjoyed another distinct advantage in the electoral process: they nearly always held a comparative advantage in organizational ability. Colonization was associated with active discrimination against Africans in employment, and few resources were dedicated to lead Africans to self-government, especially prior to World War II. In addition, few independent, indigenous economic, political, or civil organizations existed before WWII. Therefore, not many Africans had accumulated experience in creating, managing, and promoting modern organizations. Not only did the leaders and cadres of the nationalist movements acquire such experience in building these movements, but—by being the umbrella group for national independence—they also acted like a magnet and attracted individuals with such abilities and talents. As a result, their initial relative advantage in human capital of leadership was greatly reinforced.

The scarcity of leaders with organizational capacity was further exacerbated by the low levels of literacy in the region. In 1965, just a few years after independence, the average number of Africans enrolled in primary, secondary, and tertiary schools was 52%, 4%, and 0%, respectively.[7] Organizations need leaders and workers who can carry out complex organizational tasks such as enrolling members, raising money, establishing platforms, and so on. With the shortage of educated locals, few alternate institutions to rival the first anticolonial movement could have emerged. Thus, the "organizational capital" within the society that is required to create new groups was relatively low.

National Name Recognition

One of the greatest advantages held by the first national independence parties was national name recognition. In the region, any party that became renown in the country as the primary vehicle for independence obtained a national prominence which was difficult to match. In addition, since few channels of mass communication existed at the time of independence, any early lead in popularity was difficult to overcome. Newspapers rarely reached outside the capital; radios were scarce; and television sets remained a thing of the future for most in the region. Even where these channels of communication existed, the low levels of education (especially in the official, national tongue) diminished their impact. Therefore, the first party that was able to achieve the reputation of being the key player in the struggle for independence had a great advantage and strong "brand recognition" that was not easily overcome or equaled.

Sometimes, however, a party's reputation was established for them through the fame of a leader, and not vice versa. African leaders who held high positions in the few pre-independence political associations could lend their name to a party to the great benefit of both. For example, Félix Houphouët-Boigny had been elected to the French National Assembly during the colonial period and claimed credit for sponsoring the law that abolished the much-hated practice of forced labor.[8] These accomplishments elevated Houphouët-Boigny to the level of hero and liberator. Houphouët-Boigny's followers took that opportunity to build a strong national party structure around his personage. Léopold Sénghor, who also had been a member of the French National Assembly, founded the broadly based Union Progressiste Sénégalais (UPS) and led Senegal to independence as its first president. In East Africa, Julius Nyerere parlayed national prominence from the colonial period into postcolonial power for his party as well as for himself. As president of the Tanganyika African Association Party, he gained significant national and international exposure. Tanganyika was a UN protectorate, and Nyerere had several opportunities to address this international body, which "kept Tanganyika before the eyes of the world and Nyerere before the eyes of Tanganyikans."[9] From this platform, he built the Tanganyika African National Union (TANU), which went on to sweep the first national elections.

Colonial Recognition

Another important means of increasing the power and preeminence of a "nationalist party" vis-à-vis other would-be rivals was, ironically, through official recognition by colonial authorities. To simplify the task of negotiating with the various representatives for unorganized protests, colonial authorities would often recognize one group as the official representative of "the" resident African population. Colonial officials felt that "there had to be a spokesman for the African collectivity. With relatively few exceptions, the leaders of troublesome mass-oriented organizations were accepted in this role of *interlocuteur valable*."[10] The colonial leaders had to accept a negotiating partner that had strong legitimacy among the domestic population. The recognition of one group aided the metropole by creating a leadership that could be held responsible for the actions of the liberation moments. Once a group became known as the official channel for indigenous discontent, other leaders could only address the colonial administration through the new interlocutor. This was a form of access and ultimately control that gave great advantage to the early leaders of such movements.

Although such recognition was not an unqualified blessing (the official negotiator often was imprisoned), colonial recognition in the form of imprisonment could give the "colonially appointed national leader" prominence as a martyr. Thus, such leaders often became the focus of nationalist aspirations and gave the leaders the national name recognition they so craved. For example, when Nkrumah was brought out of prison to negotiate the decolonization of Ghana, his organization (the Convention People's Party [CPP]) became the official representative of the will of the Ghanaian people. Other leaders, first imprisoned, then elevated to the status of the official representative of African nationalists have included Dr. Hastings Banda (leader of the Malawi Congress Party [MCP]), Jomo Kenyatta (leader of the Kenyan African National Union [KANU]), and Kenneth Kaunda (leader of the United National Independence Party [UNIP]).[11] The parties of all these individuals convincingly swept the elections in their respective countries.[12]

Exceptions to First Single Nationalist Party

Perhaps the most notable exception to the advantage of the first nationalist party can be seen in Guinea, where the Parti démocratique de Guinée (PDG) was formed in 1947 as a regional wing of the Rassemblement Démocratique Africain (RDA), but a well-organized Socialist party had already been established.[13] The RDA was launched by Madeira Keita, and its territorial section in Guinea headed by Sékou Touré. A major component of this party consisted of the postal workers' union. Given the prior organization of the Socialist party, the PDG did not have the advantage of operating in an organizational vacuum. In fact, when French authorities moved against the RDA throughout its territories, the PDG almost disappeared from 1948 to 1951—except in trade union strongholds. As a result, in the first pre-independence elections in Guinea, no single party emerged as dominant. The Socialist party captured 30.4% of the vote; the PDG polled only 14%. Touré then actively worked to increase the profile of the party as well as union membership: the latter rose from 2,600 to over 39,000. Also, between elections, the untimely death of the leader of the Socialist party left it rudderless and weakened. The combination of the invigoration of the PDG and the weakening of the Socialist party resulted in the PDG landslide victory in the 1957 election, winning all but four seats in the Territorial Assembly. They were hence in control of the reins of power when independence was declared, and they went on to be the single party of Guinea until 1984.

GENERAL WEAKNESS OF ALTERNATIVE POTENTIAL ORGANIZATIONS

Not only were there significant advantages accrued to the first well-organized independence party, but significant hurdles also existed for those who might wish to create competing political parties in the independence period. In fact, few organizations existed that could have mounted an effective national political campaign against an already established and large independence party— even if they had wanted to do so. Apart from umbrella nationalist congresses or parties, the most visible organizations that could form competing political parties (e.g., traditional or ethnic leaders, church groups, labor unions, youth groups, business groups) faced significant constraints or barriers to becoming a rival political movement or party. Many were too weak, too new, too urban, or too parochial in interests to offer (or want to offer) real competition to existing nationally organized nationalist parties.[14]

Perhaps the most obvious indigenous foundation upon which to launch a national organization as an alternative to the major nationalist party lay with the traditional leaders. These leaders, however, had a limited potential for achieving national political power for several reasons. First, their power had been severely circumscribed under colonialism. In French Africa, the policy of direct rule denied traditional leaders almost all power outside of purely cultural or traditional domains. Under this system, traditional leaders did not have their own local institutional or practices to administer, such as police, prisons, or schools. Thus, few were very well organized, and those that were, usually found themselves with few resources with which to wage a campaign for political power.[15] Although these leaders often had control over access to land, compared to the resources available to those in active management of the state, these resources would be meager.

Traditional leaders fared only marginally better under Belgian rule, which consisted of aspects of both direct and indirect rule. Although traditional authorities had more access to patronage under this system, their unique position in this scheme provided both a floor and ceiling to their power within these new institutions. On the one hand, Belgian policy could be considered a diluted version of indirect rule because traditional organizations were respected and chiefs were incorporated into the colonial ladder.[16] On the other hand, these leaders were included at the lowest rung of the administrative ladder and only over one administrative area, even if their traditional area was much larger. So, if the domain of a traditional ruler was large, his (or her) formal power would be associated with the small colonial area, thereby weakening the particular chief. Moreover, the limited access of these leaders to local forms of patronage was greatly overshadowed by the intensity of Belgian rule: "in relation to populations, there were more white officials, more paramilitary forces, more agricultural officers enforcing more drastic programs of compulsory cultivation, than elsewhere in tropical Africa."[17] This form of rule was highly centralized as well as paternalistic and rested on three main pillars: the state, the Roman Catholic Church, and big business, such as Union Minière du Haut-Katanga (UMHK) in Congo.[18]

In British Africa, with the practice of indirect colonial rule, traditional leaders had the most access to local resources;[19] this fact has been held to be significant in the partial fragmentation of the political elite in these colonies. But the power of these traditional leaders under indirect rule should not be overestimated. Even though most of the traditional authorities were stronger than their counterparts in French or Belgian colonies, few of them controlled the most important modern sectors or industries or had power that extended beyond the district or regional level. The power of the traditional leaders must be understood relatively and in comparison with the leaders of the first nationalist parties. The latter had organizations with a national reach, and they had stronger ties to the modern export sectors, the army, the police, and the bureaucracy. Most of the power of the traditional elites rested in their relationship to local government or traditional sources of wealth.

Finally, whether traditional elites had independent political power because of colonial patterns of rule or not, their legitimacy to rule was in doubt everywhere because to "a greater or lesser extent, they owed their titles and access to power more to the colonial rules than to traditional rights, [and] generally operated within the traditional milieu. [Second, s]ince every country . . . consisted of more than one traditional state, kingdom, or ethnic group, the traditional elite were handicapped in competing with politicians for power at the national levels."[20]

Thus, traditional leaders were often seen as collaborators with colonial administrators, which decreased their legitimacy. Also, unless traditional leaders were the leader of a majority ethnic group within the country in question, fellow citizens from other ethnic or linguistic groups would hardly back them for national office based upon their traditional leadership of an alternative ethnic or linguistic group; their legitimacy was usually limited to their particular group. This gave traditional leaders a great initial advantage in overcoming collective action costs, but it also established a ceiling for most leaders because their coethnic supporters would be less than a majority in the nation. In sum, as a result of their lack of access to modern sources of wealth or patronage, their affiliation with colonial rule, and their identification with particular ethnic groups, traditional rulers could not generally mount effective national campaigns.

Beyond traditional leaders, other more modern organizations were equally ill-suited to be the foundation for a competing national political party. Although indigenous political and economic associations were able to organize in French and British Africa after WWII (or by 1957 in the Belgian Congo), they were few in number and relatively inexperienced at the time of independence. The groups or their leaders were also usually considered too parochial or regional to launch national organizations. Labor unions rarely extended their reach beyond their immediate urban sectors; students' groups had little influence outside the campus or capital and rarely had access to economic resources; and youth and women's organizations also tended to be urban and localized. Finally, though religious institutions could have nationwide organizations and ties, few had direct designs on capturing political power. Thus, there was a scarcity of such groups that had the possibility, inclination, or desire to orga-nize most of the rural peasants and farmers into a political party that had not already been mobilized for the main independence party.

Finally, the prior dominance of European personnel in the top positions within business, administration, and the military also helps explain the relative paucity of African professional organizations.[21] African professional groups representing lawyers, teachers, civil servants, and doctors were uncommon. Those that did exist tended to have mostly expatriate constituents. Thus, any indigenous professional organizations created in the post-WWII era tended to be small and relatively powerless compared to the new elites of the nationalist party. As mentioned above, the groups under discussion often joined the first vibrant independence party and already had their position within it.

ROLE OF ELECTORAL INSTITUTIONS
AND STATE STRUCTURES

The type of state structure and electoral arrangements devised by the departing colonial powers often had mixed effects in how much power the new elites consolidated, or at least how quickly. Institutional arrangements shape the ability of groups to gain and maintain access to office, and their strategies to do so.[22] Nearly every African independent country emerged with a unitary system of government. This greatly increased the political control of those winning national election by eliminating competing, autonomous institutions that could share power. With no autonomous regional government, losing parties could not retreat into a state or provincial government and try to regroup later. By contrast, a federal system might allow parties losing at the national level some regional source of patronage to hold themselves over until the next set of elections. Only Nigeria was considered to have had any deep experience with federalism,[23] though in Congo (Zaire) regional governments had significant de facto power during the First Republic.[24]

In addition, several other institutional mechanisms associated with voting and elections reinforced the ability of one party to consolidate power within the region. The most important ones included election procedures using proportional representation (PR), unusually large PR constituencies, balloting which included party lists, and more pre-independence elections under the above conditions.

By contrast, some institutional structures brought with them forces of fragmentation, especially in the former British colonies, such as these: elections held under "first-past-the-post" schemes; electoral roles that listed the name of the individual, and not the party; constitutions that gave exaggerated levels of power to some entrenched minorities; and regionally concentrated power in conjunction with a first-past-the-post system or some version of federalism. In these cases, the pre-independence elections did not reinforce tendencies toward complete one-party rule; to the contrary, it seemed to add to the number of post-independence elections with several competing parties.

French Colonies

The concentration of political power in the form of one-party rule was quite predictable in the former French colonies.[25] First, the constitutions that were created for French Africa were patterned after the French Fifth Republic, which had provided for a strong executive, a weak legislature, and a unitary system. The earlier, discredited French Fourth Republic experienced significant parliamentary gridlock, for which the powerful legislative assembly received blame. The "lesson" drawn from this experience resulted in De Gaulle and Debré designing a constitution that allowed for executive autonomy to resolve constitutional impasses. This preference for a strong executive to cope with legislative deadlock was included in French colonial political institutions.

The makeup of voting constituencies in French Africa also added to a speedy one-party outcome. These electoral institutions usually had "multi-member list systems in which lists were identified by party name, and the voters chose a party rather than an individual candidate."[26] Thus, voters chose by party, not by candidate, in a multi-member district. Moreover, many countries also included an American style "winner-take-all" approach (as in the Electoral College), within multimember voting constituencies. The result was that "[r]egardless of the distribution of the vote, this system insures that all seats will go to the victorious party."[27] [That is to say the one with a plurality.] Exaggerated showings for strong parties along with either an underrepresentation or an elimination of weaker parties usually followed. Furthermore, in some countries, the political elites enlarged constituency size to exaggerate the effect of this "winner-take-all" voting system. For example, the Côte d'Ivoire "moved from 60 assembly seats and 19 constituencies in 1957, to 100 seats and 4 constituencies in 1959, and finally to 70 seats and a single constituency in 1960."[28] This helped ensure that the PDCI would gain all the legislative seats.

In addition, prior to independence, French colonies had several elections conducted under these institutional arrangements, which, in turn, deepened the concentration of political power. This effect was to allow the strongest parties to gain additional seats before independence through repeated exposure to these institutions. In fact, there were seven territory-wide elections before the introduction of universal suffrage as well as two pre-independence elections with universal suffrage.[29] The average period between the first territory-wide election (but prior to universal franchise voting) and independence was relatively long in these colonies, with eleven years as the average.[30]

The combination of these institutional variables unique to the former colonies of France, in addition to the above mentioned advantages to the leading party, virtually guaranteed a "super" majority to the leading nationalist party. When parties did win by a convincing majority, smaller parties often found it in their interest to bandwagon with the winning party, making unnecessary the use of coercion to form a one-party state. In fact, in Ivory Coast, Senegal, Guinea, and Mali, one party controlled all the seats of the legislature at the time of independence.[31]

British Colonies

The electoral systems put in place in the former British colonies did not have the same overwhelming tendency to concentrate power in one party, and legislative monopolies were normally established only after independence. But even here, one-party dominance was the rule and not the exception. In fact, the British introduced electoral systems that tended to reinforce fragmentary pressures and thus maintain electoral competition. Most were based on the British Westminster model with executive accountability to the legislature: a simple vote of no confidence could dismiss the prime minister and dissolve the legislature, and new elections would be held. Also, electoral districts tended to be based on single member districts as well as the first-past-the-post system where the names of the individual candidate, and not the parties, were on the ballot.[32] This arrangement reinforced the potential power of regional candidates and smaller opposition parties.[33] As long as rival parties had large concentrations in some electoral districts, they could win a few seats—even if they were badly outvoted in the nation as a whole. This allowed some pockets of regional or ethnically dominant parties to retain seats, even if they could not become a significant opposition party in the legislature. Moreover, several former British colonies inherited constitutions that gave exaggerated levels of power to some entrenched minorities—as in Kenya and Zimbabwe.[34] Finally, Nigeria was decolonized with a federal system that vested authority in states, though most former British colonies did not decolonize under federalism.

As a result of these institutional attributes that fragmented power, fewer "natural" one-party systems emerged within the former British colonies for several reasons. On the one hand, as we saw earlier, the British colonial policy of indirect rule ensured that local government was more vibrant than in the other colonies. On the other hand, the electoral institutions of the former British colonies reinforced fragmentation and thus extended franchise: more elections did not always reinforce centralized rule.

Even with these political institutions that encouraged some fragmentation of party power, the other pressures described previously usually resulted in a one-party dominant system. In fact, strong parties of national prominence arose in almost all countries—Nigeria and Uganda being the prime exceptions.[35] Of all the former British colonies, only Malawi and Tanzania formed one-party systems by merger or election.[36] In Kenya, a de facto one-party system existed from 1969 to 1982; however, the one-party state was only complete after Kenyatta's government imposed a ban on the Kenya's People Union (KPU).[37] A comprehensive ban on opposition parties was not passed until the early 1980s.

Belgian Colonies

The Belgian colonial administrations devised indirect electoral institutions that were intended to reinforce geographic and ethnic division. However, given the ethnic heterogeneity of the Congo, and the bicommunal nature of

Burundi and Rwanda, the results for these three were quite different from most former British and French colonies. In the Belgian Congo, for example, the first elections of 1957 involved a two-tier, indirect system to elect urban officials.[38] The directly elected lower tier of communal councils elected the urban council, which comprised the upper tier. Just before the 1959 election, one year before independence, Belgium added a third tier to the system, which was also indirectly elected. Therefore, voters only cast ballots for candidates running for the lowest levels of government: the Circonscription Council, Territorial Council, and a Communal Council. From this first tier, the second tier (Provincial Council) was elected; the third tier was elected indirectly by a combination of the second tier, the Belgian Parliament, the king, and a Government Council.[39] The elections of 1960 were also three tiered, but a change called for the direct election of the House of Representatives, while the indirect election of the Senate continued.[40] Similarly, indirect electoral systems were also instituted in Ruanda-Urundi (later Rwanda and Burundi).

Of these three, the Belgian Congo was the least prepared for independence because it had experienced the fewest number of pre-independence elections.[41] The Belgians had not even seriously considered decolonizing the Congo until one year before its actual independence, thus giving the Belgian colonies the shortest transition periods, apart from the Portuguese.[42] By contrast, since Belgium's Rwanda and Burundi had been trust territories of the United Nations, elections involving universal suffrage were held in Ruanda-Urundi five years before independence.[43]

The effects of this quick transition on the strength of parties in the Belgian Congo were clear: given their tendency to reinforce ethnic or regional differences combined with the absence of one ethnic group having a majority in the country and no time for a national independence movement to arise, no single dominant party emerged with first elections; rather, several parties that reflected deep regional and ethnic differences emerged to compete for power. In fact, the time was so short that only two parties made any serious efforts to organize nationally: Lumumba's Mouvement National Congolais (MNC/L) and the Parti National du Progrès (PNP). Other large parties were more clearly aligned with the specific areas; for example, the Alliance des Bakango (ABAKO) and the Confédération des Associations Tribales du Katanga (Conakat) were associated with the capital (and the Kongo people) and with Katanga, respectively.[44] The fragmentation of political power was so great in the Congo that the three largest parties only had a bare majority (69) of the 137 seats in the Chamber of Deputies.[45] With no clear leadership, civil war later resulted. The crisis was resolved with a coup under the leadership of then Colonel Joseph Mobutu. There were, in fact, two military coups, with the second (1965) resulting in the rule of Mobutu until 1997.

In both Burundi and Rwanda, the bicommunal nature of the societies would come to overwhelm any electoral institutions set in place. In each society, one ethnic group comprised approximately 85% of the population (the Hutu), and the politics tended to be divisionary and strong. In each, the result was one party dominating the political landscape. [46] For example, while Belgium was preoccupied with the "crisis in the Congo," an emerging Hutu elite in Rwanda declared itself sovereign in the "coup of Gitarama" in January 1961. Internal self-rule was granted in 1961, and full independence came on July 1, 1962. Grégoire Kayibanda, leader of the Mouvement démocratique républicain (MDR), became the first president, and his party (Parti de l'émancipation du people Hutu [Parmehutu]) won all 47 assembly seats.[47] A purge of Tutsis followed, with many fleeing to neighboring countries, sowing the seeds of later violence.

Burundi seemed to temporarily overcome the ethnic division in the first set of elections. In fact, the Union Pour le Progreès National (UPRONA) bridged the gap between Hutu and Tutsi populations, and it emerged with a significant majority, winning 58 of the 64 seats. But with the death of Prince Louis Rwagasore, leader of UPRONA, distrust between Hutu and Tutsi became apparent. Moreover, with the abolition of the monarchy in 1966, UPRONA came to be seen as representing Tutsi power, and its legitimacy among the Hutus was greatly compromised as a result. Because of a combination of a short transition period in the Congo and the peculiar ethnic composition of the other two countries, all three Belgian colonies experienced great post-independence chaos, which eventually resulted in the consolidation of power through one- or no-party rule.

Portuguese Colonies

No pre-independence elections were held in the Portuguese colonies in preparation for decolonization. This fact, however, should not be surprising as Portugal itself was ruled by a military dictatorship during most of this period. The initial attempts to repress indigenous organizations in combination with the unparalleled speed with which the Portuguese decolonization occurred virtually guaranteed that authoritarian regimes would assume power. The Portuguese government had not been interested in granting political independence to its colonies and more radical and militant nationalist pressures emerged; armed resistance began in 1961 in Angola, in 1963 in Guinea-Bissau, and in 1964 in Mozambique.[48] Attempts to suppress rebellion came at a very high cost for Portugal. It stationed over 40,000 men in Guinea-Bissau, and 60,000 men in Angola and Mozambique.[49] Also, military expenditures rose from 4.55% of GNP in 1960 to 8.3% in 1971; this latter figure represented 45.9% of government expenditures. Finally, Portugal lost over 7,674 soldiers in fourteen years.[50] On April 25, 1974, a military coup d'etat changed the ruling structure in Portugal. Then the new junta, under General Spinola, took immediate steps to stop the war and moved rapidly toward granting independence to these colonies. All would be independent by the end of the following year.

Following the coup in Portugal, and its quick departure from Africa, Marxist-Leninist resistant groups instituted Leninist one-party regimes. In Guinea-Bissau, the Partido Africano da Indepêndencia da Guiné e Cabo Verde (PAIGC) assumed power as a one-party Marxist-Leninist regime in September 1974. Mozambique became ruled by the Frente de Libertação de Moçambique [FRELIMO]) at independence in June 1975. In Angola, the Portuguese would not leave the colony until November 1975. But three different and contending military forces fought for ultimate control of the country, which began a civil war that raged until after the end of the Cold War. However, the Movimento Popular de Libertação de Angola (MPLA), which was Marxist-Leninist in outlook, was considered the official government for years.[51]

ADVANTAGES TO PARTY IN WINNING INITIAL ELECTIONS

Winners of the first pre-independence elections would usually go on to win every subsequent election. But for a small subset of countries, another party might displace them at a later pre-independence election. In French Africa, parties that won a majority in the 1957 elections in Congo-Brazzaville, Dahomey, and Niger would be defeated at the polls in the subsequent pre-independence elections (i.e., 1959).[52] Nonetheless, whichever party had a significant majority in the last election before independence was nearly always able to consolidate power at independence. Through the use of patronage, coercion, or co-optation, parties that won the last pre-independence elections or gained the reins of power were almost everywhere able to consolidate their power after decolonization. Part of the advantage in consolidating rule was clearly traceable to the winner's access to resources for distributing patronage as well as the tools of co-optation and coercion.

The Role of Patronage

Many groups that would later contend with these nationalist parties for political power once independence was achieved found themselves at a great disadvantage. Not only was the ruling party more mature and better organized, but it also gained access to the power and resources of the state that were used to undergird their power. Alternate parties were no longer running against novices and equals in the quest for power; they were running against the heroes of political independence who also controlled state patronage and access to nearly all formal sector employment. And to the degree that the state controlled more of the economy, a greater amount of patronage was available to be dispensed politically.[53]

The use of patronage to secure office was widespread throughout the region. In Nigeria, for example, each of the regional powers used state patronage to reinforce local rule. The most dominant regional party in the west, Action Group, "won popular support by providing a wide range of services including free primary education, medical facilities, tarred roads, and water supplies."[54] The use of patronage was so widespread that an internal investigation found the ruling party had "siphoned off some £6 million of public money into its own coffers, thus enabling it to strengthen its organization and further reward its supporters."[55] Governments typically used commercial patronage to reward political loyalty and punish political disobedience; the forms of this patronage included "government loans, marketing board licensing, and government contracting . . . . In all regions, these agencies serve[d] the political interests of the government only."[56]

Another example can be seen in Zambia where state patronage helped to secure the United National Independence Party's (UNIP) advantage over the United Progressive Party (UPP) in post-independence elections. When the UPP formed to challenge the power of UNIP, the latter's reaction was "to tighten its ranks, replace those officials who joined the new party, and institute an intense card-checking campaign to assert its control. The party also reaffirmed its control over patronage and distribution, so that the appearance of the UPP was followed by threats to withdraw licenses, evict council householders, and dismiss employees who were found not to support the ruling party."[57]

These policies and practices clearly had the intended political effects throughout most of the region. Smaller parties often voluntarily chose to merge with the ruling party since they knew that "government patronage was too important to be forgone and . . . that governments rewarded their friends and punished their enemies."[58] As such, very strong economic incentives were created to defect from a losing party. In fact, the steady attrition of politicians from losing to winning parties was one of several clear and important developments during the first years of independence.

In addition, as will be discussed in detail in the next chapter, African political leaders would come to have direct control over significant sectors of their domestic economies: as a result of inward-oriented economic development policies, policies of state-led industrialization, the existence of monopsonistic agricultural marketing boards, an overvalued currency with rationing, the nationalization of capital-intensive industries and/or significant mining or oil exporting sectors, and most formal sector employment distributed by the state, political control over economic policies and economic sectors was as great here as any other region of the developing world, if not more so.[59] Political control over economic sectors and government jobs clearly increased the power of these elites.[60]

Co-optation

In addition to patronage, many countries made moves to co-opt or incorporate previously autonomous groups into the structure of the ruling party. An African version of corporatism placed women's groups, students' groups, and labor unions within a wing of the dominant political party. Under Nyerere, for example, youth groups or women's associations became wings of the Tanganyika African National Union (TANU).[61] In Ghana, "the CPP (Convention People's Party) under Nkrumah . . . attempted to monopolize the press, radio, education, and all other forms of communication in the new state."[62] In Togo, under Eyadéma, almost all social groups were incorporated into the single party Rassemblement du Peuple Togolais (RPT).[63] Zaire had perhaps the most corporatist structures of all the sub-Saharan African countries. The trade unions became ancillary of the single party the Mouvement Populaire de la Révolution (MPR).[64] In 1969, all independent youth groups were placed under the control of the Jeunesse du Mouvement Populaire de la Révolution (JMPR).[65] Although students resisted these moves and held strikes and protests, they were eventually subdued, and in one instance, dissenting students were drafted into the army.[66]

Even states with strong labor unions soon found the power of such organizations curtailed by the new governments, especially when the state became the owner of significant sectors. Unions soon found that their autonomy was greatly limited, and they were often denied the right to strike. For example, the formidable Mineworkers Union of Zambia knew that the government would not tolerate a strike in the copper industry.[67] In Zaire, the three major trade unions were fused into a single labor ancillary of the MPR.

Rule Changes, Coercion, and Repression

In addition to patronage and co-optation, state elites often changed the institutional rules for elections. They also resorted to both coercion and repression of opponents to consolidate their rule after independence. The first real extension of power of these parties was usually through legislative means. For example, soon after independence, most former British colonies jettisoned their inherited Westminster model of constitution in favor of strong executive presidencies.[68] This had the effect of increasing the power of the chief executive, and by extension, the ruling elite aligned with the chief executive.

Ghana was the first (1960) to transform itself into a republic with a powerful president. Zambia, too, became a republic in 1964, with Kaunda bearing the title of president. Although Tanzania named Nyerere president as early as 1962, he did not begin acting independently of his cabinet until 1964.[69] Other former British countries that began with executive prime ministers and later moved to presidential (or military) systems include these: the Gambia, Kenya, Nigeria, and Uganda.[70] Only Botswana and Mauritius maintained their Parliamentary systems from independence until the early 1990s—though the executive in Botswana does carry the title president and Mauritius became a republic in 1992. Presidential systems with fixed terms of office and without formal accountability to elected assemblies shifted significant power to these new presidents and away from the legislatures, especially in the environment of one-party control of both branches.

Even in French Africa, with electoral systems that already favored one party over others, rule changes were often an integral part of the formation of a one-party regime. After the first elections, the winning party often used "gerrymandering, a change of electoral law to increase the distortion of percentage of seats relative to percentage of votes, and sometimes even the arrest of opposition leaders."[71] Such practices continued after independence as well. In Togo and Benin, a change in the election law after independence created a national single constituency that virtually assured one-party dominance.[72]

The most usual means of one-party formation was through the formal banning of opposition parties or the repression of their members. According to a twenty-six country study from independence to 1975, twelve one-party regimes were created through these mechanisms of coercion, compared to six by elections and three by mergers.[73] Banning parties was far more common in British Africa, where only two one-party regimes had evolved through elections, none by merger (although the Kenya African National Union [KANU] and the Kenya African Democratic Union [KADU] did have a one-party de facto regime for a period), and four by bans. Ghana, Uganda, Zambia, and Kenya all finally banned opposition parties—though most had made life difficult for opposition leaders prior to their outright banning and all had become one-party dominant states. Within the former French colonies of Central African Republic (CAR), Niger, Upper Volta (now Burkina Faso), Benin, Gabon, Togo, and Congo, the banning of opposition parties or a military coup was necessary before opposition parties were completely eliminated.[74]

Although the formal banning of opposition parties was needed to achieve complete one-party rule in most of British Africa, the majority parties had already won significant power electorally in most cases and dominated politics within their societies. Kenya, Zambia, and Ghana all had competitive systems for several years following independence, but one party had a clear-cut majority in each case. For example, the merger between KANU and

KADU in November 1964 came only after KANU had convincingly swept the elections the year before.[75] KANU had won 83 of 124 seats (about 67%).[76] Also, Nkrumah's Convention People's Party (CPP) of Ghana had won more than 72 of 104 seats (almost 70%) before it began its policies of co-optation and harassment of opposition party members.[77] Finally, Zambia's UNIP party won 81 seats to the African National Congress's 23 (over 77% of the seats).[78] These super majorities of 2/3 or greater were maintained until the banning of opposition parties in later years. Thus, even in the countries where a minority party existed, the smaller parties wielded little real power and were routinely excluded from significant decisions.

One party usually had a clear legislative majority in the former French colonies as well. In both Upper Volta and Niger, the party that would impose one-party rule had already won an overwhelming majority in pre-independence elections.[79] In the Central African Republic (CAR), one party won all of the seats in the assembly. With the death of Barthélemy Boganda, however, this unity was destroyed and the party split in two soon after the election. After Dacko's party prevailed, he banned all other political parties.

Even with supermajorities, coercion was often used to facilitate a monopoly of power into one party. Both before and after the banning of rival parties, governments would often arrest and harass opposition members who appeared to threaten the party's rule. For example, Ghana had a long record of arrests, and threats of arrests, of opposition members.[80] In Togo, the suppression of the opposition in the elections of 1961 was so extensive that it was cited as the chief reason for the coup d'état in 1963.[81] The army in Ghana made a similar claim when it moved against Nkrumah in 1966. When the ruling party in Zambia (UNIP) was faced with an electoral threat from UPP, the government responded with such force and coercion that only Kap-wepwe, the leader of UPP, was able to stand for office in one by-election.[82] The complete banning of UPP came the following year. But this situation was not unique to Zambia: all countries in the region used some combination of coercion, co-optation, and patronage to consolidate their rule, even though the incumbent political elites already had nearly complete control of the political institutions already.

The Post-independence Bandwagon Effect

In sub-Saharan Africa, many members of minority parties often "voluntarily" crossed the floor to become members of the majority party. This phenomenon was due in part because, as minority members of legislatures in a system where political support depends upon the distribution of patronage, opposi-tion politicians faced diminished access to national resources and increased threat of coercion. Given the near "zero-sum" view of politics in postcolonial

Africa, this is not surprising. As Hodder-Williams states, "One of the clearest developments of the first years of independence is the steady attrition of opposition party representation and the continuous trickle of parliamentarians across the floor. Self-interest lay behind this; but it was also a self-interest fostered by the pressures from their constituents."[83] This trend was most noticeable in countries where one-party dominant states existed, such as in Senegal and Kenya—though it clearly happened in other countries as well. Within six years of independence, and after being effectively denied access to state resources, the opposition parties in Senegal fused with Senghor's new ruling party, the Union Progressive Sénégalaise (UPS). In Kenya as well, the Kenyan African Democratic Union (KADU) dissolved itself by joining the Kenya African National Union (KANU). Members of the parliament in a political system based upon patron-client ties found they could not reside in a permanent minority and hope to hold on to their constituents.

ROLE OF IDEAS AND IDEOLOGY IN THE CONCENTRATION OF POWER

Ideology also played an important role in the creation and maintenance of one-party states in sub-Saharan Africa. There were two primary pillars to the legitimacy of this type of rule: socialist and African one-party ideologies. By the early 1960s, socialist ideology had captured the attention of many African intellectuals.[84] Countries that attempted to follow a Marxist-Leninist approach to development believed in the one-party form of rule as a matter of doctrine.[85] Lenin had argued for a centralized, disciplined party led by professional revolutionaries that would act as the vanguard of the proletariat. This self-selected vanguard party would lead the workers who suffered from "false consciousness" during the initial stages of revolution. The vanguard party, which understood the "true" workings of the world, would make decisions for the immature, or even missing, proletariat until scientific socialism could take hold. This party was assumed to have complete dominion over the state in order to complete the economic and political revolution. Even Karl Marx had called for "a revolutionary dictatorship of the proletariat" during the revolutionary transformation from a capitalist to a communist society—which is ideologically consistent with one-party rule.[86] Countries in Africa that have, or have had, self-proclaimed Marxist-Leninist regimes include these: Angola, Mozambique, Ethiopia, Somalia, Congo, Benin, Zimbabwe, and Madagascar.

Even regimes that were not avowedly Marxist-Leninist were favorably inclined toward the idea of one-party rule. African Socialism, or Populist Socialism as it is often called, had several recurrent themes. First, there "was the stress upon the idea of the common interests of the entire population.

African societies were held to be relatively homogenous, without sharply demarcated social classes; the social enemy was external, in the form of Western imperial structures. The doctrine of class struggle, accordingly, was held to be alien to socialism in Africa."[87]

Thus, the idea of the one-party state was logically compatible with this the African version of ideology. Populist socialist countries included Tanzania, Senegal, Ghana, Guinea, Guinea-Bissau, and Mali.[88] Zambia's official ideology, known as "humanism," was explicitly anti-capitalist and pro-Socialist. Even countries that were not explicitly Socialist tended to be sympathetic to it, at least in general terms. For example, even in Kenya, the Kenyatta regime espoused a form of socialism—although Kenya is renowned for having followed a capitalist path.

The other great legitimizing ideology for the African one-party state is what Zolberg calls one-party ideology.[89] This creed was similar to—and was partially derived from—African socialist ideas, and it reflected the dilemma of African identity. Since (as noted elsewhere) African nationalism did not correspond neatly to ethnic, linguistic, or cultural boundaries, the question of who was Ghanaian, Guinean, Nigerian, Zairian, Togolese, or Senegalese took on particular importance. The nationalism of the colonial period was marked by membership to a group that opposed colonialism within the territorial boundary. Once the common enemy was absent, and with the advent of political independence, there remained no common *volk*, language, mythology, or ethnicity to unite those who remained behind in this territorial/political unit. Their unity rested on the common effort to oppose colonialism; but that pillar—the nationalist movement—was removed by its very success.

In place of unity through opposition, unity within the victorious party—under a unitary system—was substituted. The party no longer represented a group reflecting aggregate electoral preferences; rather, it became the new source of nationalism. The case of Guinea offers a good example: "To the extent that nationalism must define a membership unit in which the participants share a political fate, it not surprising to find the Guineans stressing the widest, best-known membership group, the party . . . Support for the party and its ideas is a way of entering into a social contract, of participating in a community that is in the process of becoming."[90]

Zolberg outlines five key elements of what he calls one-party ideology, which he compressed from speeches by Sékou Touré. Apparently, Touré believed the following concerning African unity:

(1) there is a natural trend towards "unity"; (2) African societies *are* divided; (3) these divisions are not to be viewed, as an American thinker might, as healthy "pluralism," but rather in a negative way as "internal contradictions" (a Marxist borrowing); (4) unity is manifest in support for the dominant party.

A corollary follows naturally from these four. Sékou Touré pointed out that the unity of Guinea was demonstrated in 1957 in spite of attempts by "enemies" to "sabotage" it. Hence we may add: (5) the failure of unity can stem only from the actions of men who willfully interfere with the natural course of history.[91]

These themes were soon picked up by other African leaders. Julius Nyerere argued that democracy was possible without the existence of an opposition party; Ghanaian newspapers questioned the need for an opposition party to have a democracy; Senghor belabored the distinction between single and unified parties, implying that the latter were more representative; Keita argued that since the party was the true reflection of the will of the people, there was no reason for it to be out of step with society.[92]

With the aid of socialist and one-party ideology, the dominant parties or military elites that emerged from the anticolonial struggle found themselves in charge of new nations. They had to make the transition from the politics of opposition to the politics of management. The increased demands placed upon them by the heightened expectations of the emerging groups, as well as the need to staff new bureaucracies, strained the administrative ability of the new ruling elites to near its breaking point. Had these groups formed cohesive organizations in a longer struggle to obtain independence, their organizational strength might have been greater. No matter how weak these new groups were, they were relatively strong compared to other domestic organizations.

THE SELF-INTEREST OF THE RULING ELITE

Finally, it was in the apparent self-interest of political elites to establish one-party states. This facilitated their ability to maintain power and personal wealth. Only those outside the party might challenge it. In addition, African leaders faced significant challenges in managing issues of governance, development, and nation building. These ideas could easily be seen as conducive to the national interests as well as their own. The pull of self-interest in conjunction with ideas concerning development (see next chapter) reinforced the tendencies to promote a single party rule.[93]

MILITARY COUPS AND THE CONSOLIDATION OF POLITICAL POWER

Military coups also achieved the result of consolidating political power into the hands of elites in much of the region. In fact, coups were relatively common in the Third World from World War II onwards. Between 1945 and 1960, there were thirty-three successful and nineteen attempted coups world-wide.[94] Of these, Latin America experienced 58% of the successful coups as well as 53% of the unsuccessful ones. North Africa and the Middle East were at the second highest rates of successful coups, with 21%. Sub-Saharan Africa had only one successful coup (3%) and two attempted coups (11%): all were in Sudan.

Other African countries began having coups with the onset of independence, beginning with the Belgian Congo in 1960. Ethiopia, Ghana, and Guinea also had early coups, as did Dahomey (Benin) and Togo in 1963. But this form of incorporating power into the state did not become prevalent until well after independence because they were relatively uncommon at first. Beginning in 1966, five more coups took place, and by 1975 this number increased to thirty, in sixteen countries. Looking at a longer period, we see that from January 1, 1956, to April 30, 1984, over fifty-six coups in forty-five sub-Saharan countries took place.[95] Even these surprising numbers cannot capture the pervasive role of the military in the politics in Africa. During the same period, an additional sixty-five *attempted* coups took place as well.

In fact, in a worldwide context, sub-Saharan Africa experienced 41% (60) of all successful coups and 45% (77) of all attempted coups between 1960 and 1989. Latin America experienced 26% (38) of all successful coups and 18% (30) of all attempted coups during the same period. North Africa and the Middle East had 12% (18) of all successful coups and 14% (24) of all attempted ones.[96] Part of the reason for such African percentages is discussed below, though we must first remember that sub-Saharan Africa also constituted about a quarter of the countries of the world.[97] Moreover, coups are more likely to occur in Third World nations, and between 1960 and 1989, sub-Saharan Africa did indeed represent a very large share of all low- and middle-income nations.

Although many competing explanations for the spate of coups in sub-Saharan Africa during this period have been set forth, the key element appears to have been the weakness of economic and political institutions throughout the region.[98] Where most of the organizations, institutions, or groups within a society are relatively strong, the military's ability to take over is more circumscribed; however, where they are weak, the military features prominently in the political landscape.[99] In fact, according to one scholar, "*these variations occurred within a relatively narrow range.*"[100] What triggered these coups would vary from country to country; however, the underlying precondition for coups was met in virtually every African country at the time: the weakness of the ruling parties that inherited power. These weaknesses were exploited by military leaders for several reasons. First, these countries were vulnerable to coups by small military forces.[101] Second, with near absolute governmental power vested in the hands of an unaccountable few, corruption was a normal consequence. Thus, an army (whether self-serving or nationally minded) often had a facile excuse for overturning such a regime: to serve the national interest.[102] Third, the army was one of the few alternate institutions of power in the region with strong internal cohesiveness and organizational capacity.[103] With a monopoly of coercive force, and great cohesiveness and organization, armies were often able to supplant the first leaders. Finally, when the rulers of one-party states relied too heavily upon coercion to maintain their power, they were already weakening their legitimacy, and they became more and more vulnerable to military coups.[104] In fact, Collier found that one-party regimes formed through coercion were more susceptible to coups than were those formed by mergers.[105]

Although one-party rule was vulnerable to military coups, ironically, countries that did not have a majority ruling party or coalition emerge were even more likely to fall to military takeovers. In Uganda, Zaire, and Nigeria, no single party had a clear legislative majority at the time of independence and each had weak coalition governments. Initially, the parties of these countries were mainly regionally or ethnically based—and all eventually succumbed to civil strife and ultimately military coups. Thus, the concentration of power by a single party or the establishment of a ruling majority party may have forestalled some of them.

The above overview of factors leading to the general pattern of coups in sub-Saharan Africa is not intended to be exhaustive; rather, the explanations were general to the region as a whole. They do not describe what in particular triggered each coup. Multiple causes for coups have been put forth,[106] not all of which are unique to Africa.[107] Additionally important and often cited reasons for these coups are the following: (1) class, regional or corporate interests of the military;[108] (2) personal interests, fears, or ambitions of those in the military;[109] (3) the demonstration effect of the success of earlier coups; and (4) the role of international forces.[110]

It also seems likely that poorly institutionalized countries are more likely to have coups, especially where their legitimacy is in question.[111] Englebert has argued that countries that had governments with an endogenous claim on legitimacy were more stable than those that did not, and most African countries did not. Moreover, nearly all African countries emerged as quickly from colonialism and the same dynamics that would lead to a one-party state would also militate in favor of countries ripe for successful coups. Many explanations for the region-wide expansion of military power have been offered. Notwithstanding the various reasons, this analysis holds that military coups have reinforced other, preexisting factors contributing toward the consolidation of political power in the region.

Nonetheless, the inheritors of political power in the early independence period of sub-Saharan Africa had monopoly control, or tantamount to monopoly control, over the formal political institutions of these new nations, and they would use this political power to gain similar levels of control over economic policies, as well as key aspects of their economies and employment opportunities within their nations that would increase their political power—at least in the short to medium term. This is the issue to which our attention now turns.

NOTES

1. For details on pre-independence and early post-independence elections, see Ruth Berins Collier, *Regimes in Tropical Africa: Changing Forms of Supremacy, 1945–1975* (Berkeley: University of California Press, 1982): 44, Table 2. Congo had two, in 1957 and 1959, though the first was no for national office. It is often called a military regime. Nonetheless, this was only three years or one year before independence (Ibid., 42–43). Those countries under Portuguese rule had no pre-independence elections, but Portugal itself was authoritarian until the coup in 1974.

2. See, for example, Robert H. Jackson and Carl G. Rosberg, *Personal Rule in Black Africa: Prince, Autocrat, Prophet, Tyrant* (Los Angeles: University of California Press, 1982); also, Victor T. Le Vine, "African Patrimonial Regimes in Comparative Perspective," *The Journal of Modern African Studies* 18, 4 (Dec., 1980): 657–73.

3. A one-party state has a monopoly (or effective monopoly) on the control of the legislature, whereas a no-party regime has not legislature. It is often called a military regime. For definition, see Collier, *Regimes in Tropical Africa*. Also see John James Quinn, *The Road oft Traveled: Development Policies and Majority State Ownership of Industry in Africa* (Westport, CT: Praeger, 2002), p. 8, endnote 3.

4. The Gambia's multiparty regime was toppled in a military coup on 23 July 1994. Unlike the last coup d'etat in Gambia (1981), Senegal did not intervene to reverse it.

5. Aristide Zolberg, *Creating Political Order: The Party-States of West Africa* (Chicago: Rand McNally & Company, 1966), p. 15.

6. Mancur Olson, *The Logic of Collective Action: Public Goods and the Theory of Groups* (Cambridge, MA: Harvard University Press, 1965); for an application of these ideas to Africa, See Robert H. Bates, *Markets and States in Tropical Africa: the Political Basis of Agricultural Policies* (Los Angeles: University of California Press, 1981).

7. World Bank, *Sub-Saharan Africa: From Crisis to Sustainable Growth* (Washington, D.C.: The World Bank., 1989) Table 32, pp. 274–275. The zero percentage represents a negligible amount of college educated Africans—not an absolute lack of them.

8. Ruth Schachter Morgenthau, *Political Parties in French-Speaking West Africa* (Oxford: Clarendon Press, 1964), p. 181.

9. John D. Hargreaves, *Decolonization in Africa* (New York: Longman, 1988), p. 132.

10. Zolberg, *Creating Political Order*, p. 17 (Italics in original).

11. Hargreaves, *Decolonization*, pp. 186–203.

12. This parallel is even evident in the more modern example of Nelson Mandela and the African National Congress (ANC).

13. Unless states otherwise, data and information from this section are from Zolberg, *Creating Political Order*, p. 28–30.

14. For an overview of these groups see Immanuel Wallerstein, "Voluntary Associations," in James S. Coleman and Carl G. Rosberg, Jr., eds., *Political Parties and National Integration* (Berkeley: University of California Press, 1964): 318–39; also Elliot J. Berg and Jeffrey Butler, "Trade Unions," in Coleman and Rosberg, eds., *Political Parties*, pp. 340–81; and William John Hanna, "Students," in Coleman and Rosberg, eds., *Political Parties*, pp. 413–43.

15. Collier, *Regimes in Tropical Africa*, pp. 84–87; though the Marabouts in Senegal were strong, they backed parties as opposed to forming any.

16. Crawford Young, *Politics in the Congo: Decolonization and Independence* (Princeton: Princeton University Press, 1965), p. 131.

17. Hargreaves, *Decolonization*, p. 176.

18. William Tordoff, *Governments and Politics in Africa* 2nd Edition (Bloomington: Indiana University Press, 1993), p. 31.

19. Tony Smith, "Patterns in the Transfer of Power: A Comparative Study of French and British Decolonization," in Prosser Gifford and Wm. Roger Louis, eds., *The Transfer of Power in Africa: Decolonization 1940–1960* (New Haven: Yale University Press, 1982), pp. 87–116; Hargreaves, *Decolonization*.

20. J. F. Ade Ajayi, "Expectations of Independence," in "Black Africa: A Generation After Independence," *Daedalus: Journal of the American Academy of Arts and Sciences* (Spring 1982), p. 3.

21. Paul Kennedy, *African Capitalism: The Struggle for Ascendancy* (Cambridge: Cambridge University Press, 1988), especially pp. 28–59.

22. For the importance of institutions see Douglass C. North, *Institutions, Institutional Change and Economic Performance* (Cambridge: Cambridge University Press, 1990); Douglass C. North, *Structure and Change in Economic History* (New York: W. W. Norton & Co., 1981); Oliver E. Williamson, *The Economic Institutions of Capitalism: Firms, Markets, Relational Contracting* (New York: The Free Press, 1985); James E. Alt and Kenneth A. Shepsle, *Perspectives on Positive Political Economy* (Cambridge: Cambridge University Press, 1990); Peter Gourevitch, *Politics in Hard Times: Comparative Responses to International Economic Crises* (Ithaca, NY: Cornell University Press, 1986); and, of course, Collier, *Regimes in Tropical Africa*.

23. See, for example, Richard L. Sklar, "Developmental Democracy," *Comparative Studies in Society and History* 29, 4 (October 1987): 686–714.

24. Crawford Young and Thomas Turner, *The Rise and Decline of the Zairian State* (Madison, WI: University of Wisconsin Press, 1985), p. 31–42.

25. See Keith Panter-Brick, "Independence, French Style," in Prosser Gifford and Wm. Roger Louis, eds., *Decolonization and African Independence: The Transfer of Power, 1960–1980* (New Haven: Yale University Press, 1988): 73–104; Morgenthau, *Political Parties*; Zolberg, *Creating Political Order*, p. 107; also Collier, *Regimes in Tropical Africa*, pp. 80–94.

26. Collier, *Regimes in Tropical Africa*, pp. 80–81.

27. Zolberg, *Creating Political Order*, p. 80.

28. Ibid.

29. Collier, *Regimes in Tropical Africa*, p. 44.

30. Ibid., p. 45.

31. William Tordoff, *Government and Politics in Africa* (Bloomington: Indiana University Press, 1984), p. 74; Zolberg, *Creating Political Order*, pp. 79–81; and Collier, *Regimes in Tropical Africa*, p. 105. In Côte d'Ivoire, the de facto party was formed before independence.

32. Zolberg, *Creating Political Order*, pp. 80–81.

33. It is a well-known stylized fact that a SMDP system tends to lead to a two party system, though regional concentration could allow other parties to maintain a presence. In Africa, during the first period, it seems that small parties remained until banned, but the larger parties had merged into a majority. For general effects of electoral system on seat allocation, see Arend Lijphart, "Electoral Systems: Majority and Plurality Method Versus Proportional Representation," *Patterns of Democracy: Government Forms and Performance in Thirty-Six Democracies 2nd Edition* (New Haven: Yale University Press, 1999): 130–57.

34. Richard Hodder-Williams, *An Introduction to the Politics of Tropical Africa* (London: George Allen & Unwin, 1984), p. 81.

35. There is some question as to whether any of the Nigerian parties were national or regional in nature. See James S. Coleman, *Nigeria: Background to Nationalism* (Los Angeles: University of California Press, 1958); also J. F. Ade Ajayi and A. E. Ekoko, "Transfer of Power in Nigeria: Its Origins and Consequences," in Gifford and Louis, eds., *Decolonization and African Independence*, pp. 245–269. Richard Sklar has argued that the NCNC retained a pan-tribal character throughout the period, which would qualify it as a national party. See Richard L. Sklar, *Nigerian Political Power: Power in an Emergent African Nation* (Princeton: Princeton University Press, 1963); also Richard L. Sklar and C.S. Whitaker, Jr., "Nigeria," in Coleman and Rosberg, *Political Parties*: 597–654.

36. Collier, *Regimes in Tropical Africa*, p. 105.

37. Tordoff, *Government and Politics*, p. 103.

38. Collier, *Regimes in Tropical Africa*, pp. 42–44; also Crawford Young, *Ideology and Development in Africa* (New Haven: Yale University Press, 1982), pp. 162–78.

39. Young, *Politics in the Congo*, p. 168.

40. Collier, *Regimes in Tropical Africa*, p. 43.

41. For accounts of the effects of nationalism on Belgian decolonization, see Hargreaves, *Decolonization*, pp. 175–183; Ilunga Kabongo, "The Catastrophe of Belgian Decolonization," in Gifford and Louis, eds., *Decolonization and African Independence*, pp. 381–400; Crawford Young, *Politics in the Congo*; Crawford Young, "Zaire, Rwanda and Burundi," in Michael Crowder, ed., *The Cambridge History of Africa*, Vol 8, 1940–1975 (Cambridge: Cambridge University Press, 1984): 698–754; and Jean Stengers, "Precipitous Decolonization: The Belgian Congo." in Gifford and Louis, eds., *The Transfer of Power in Africa*, pp. 305–36.

42. Collier, *Regimes in Tropical Africa*, pp. 42–44.

43. Ibid.

44. Young, *Politics in the Congo*, pp. 298–306.

45. Ibid., p. 302.

46. For discussion of bicommunalism, see David E. Schmitt, "Bicommunalism in Northern Ireland," *Publius: The Journal of Federalism* 18 (Spring 1988), 33: 33–46. R. S. Milne, *Politics in Ethnically Bipolar States: Guyana, Malaysia, Fiji* (Vancouver: University of British Columbia Press, 1981). For bicommunalism in Africa, see John James Quinn, "Diffusion and Escalation in the Great Lakes Region: The Rwandan Genocide, the Rebellion in Zaire, and Mobutu's Overthrow," in Steven E. Lobell and Philip Mauceri, eds., *The Internationalization of Ethnic Conflict: Explaining Diffusion and Escalation* (New York: Palgrave Macmillan, 2004): 111–132, also John James Quinn, "The Nexus of the Domestic and Regional within an International Context: The Rwandan Genocide and Mobutu's Ouster," in Amy L. Freedman, ed., *Threatening the State: the Internationalization of Internal Conflicts*, (Oxford: Routledge): 39–74. For a similar idea, "Ethnic dominance," see Paul Collier and Anke Hoeffler, "On the Incidence of Civil War in Africa," *The Journal of Conflict Resolution* 46, 1 (February 2002): 13–28.

47. *Africa South of the Sahara 1987* (London; Europa Publications Limited, 1986), S. V. Rwanda.

48. Basil Davidson, "Independence of Portuguese Africa: Background and Emergence to 1974, in *Africa South of the Sahara 1987*: 30–33, p. 31.

49. Hargreaves, *Decolonization*, p. 216.

50. Davidson, "Independence of Portuguese Africa," p. 31.

51. For an overview of Portuguese policy in Angola see Gerald J. Bender, *Angola under the Portuguese: The Myth and the Reality* (Los Angeles: University of California Press, 1978).

52. Collier, *Regimes in Tropical Africa*, p. 67. Guinea is not included as no party had a majority in the first round.

53. John J. Quinn, "The Managerial Bourgeoisie: Capital Accumulation, Development and Democracy," in David G. Becker and Richard L. Sklar, eds., *Postimperialism and World Politics* (Westport, CT: Praeger, 1999): 219–52.

54. Tordoff, *Government and Politics* 2nd ed., p. 107.

55. Ibid.

56. Sklar, *Nigeria*, p. 452; also see Ibid., pp. 447–53, generally.

57. Cherry Gertzel and Morris Szeftel, "Politics in an African Urban Setting: the Role of the Copperbelt in the Transition to the One-Party State 1964–1973," in Cherry Gertzel, Carolyn Baylies, and Morris Szeftel, eds., *The Dynamics of the One-Party State in Zambia* (Manchester: Manchester University Press, 1984), p. 135.

58. Hodder-Williams, *Politics of Tropical Africa*, p. 121.

59. Quinn, *The Road oft Traveled*; Roger Tangri, *The Politics of Patronage in Africa: Parastatals, Privatization, & Private Enterprise* (Trenton, NJ: Africa World Press, 1999).

60. See, Quinn, "The Managerial Bourgeoisie"; Bates, *Market and States*; Tangri, *The Politics of Patronage*; John J. Quinn, "The Impact of State Ownership

of Resources on Economic and Political Development in Sub-Saharan Africa," *Ufahamu* Vol. XXI, No 1and 2 (Winter/Spring 1993): 60–79. For state employment, see Peter S. Heller and Alan A. Tait, "Government Employment and Pay: Some International Comparisons." *Occasional Paper* 24 (Washington, D.C.: International Monetary Fund, October 1983); also World Bank, *Bureaucrats in Business: The Economics and Politics of Government Ownership* (Washington, D.C.: World Bank, 1995).

61. J. Gus Liebenow, *African Politics: Crises and Challenges* (Bloomington: Indiana University Press, 1986), p. 234.

62. Ibid.

63. John Heilbrunn, "Authority, Property, and Politics in Benin and Togo," (PhD Dissertation, UCLA, 1994), p. 510.

64. Young and Turner, *The Rise and Decline*, p. 62.

65. When I lived in Zaire, I was told by the local boy scouts that they were part of the JMPR. Personal observations, 1983–1984.

66. For a story concerning this event see Jan Vansina, "Mwasi's Trials," in "Black Africa," special issue *Daedalus*, pp. 49–70.

67. Richard L. Sklar, *Corporate Power in an African State: The Political Impact of Multinational Mining Companies in Zambia* (Los Angeles: University of California Press, 1975), p. 123.

68. Tordoff, *Government and Politics*, 2nd ed., p. 60.

69. Ibid.

70. See Alfred Stepan and Cindy Skach, "Constitutional Frameworks and Democratic Consolidation: Parliamentarianism versus Presidentialism," *World Politics* 46 (October 1993):1–22; also *Africa South of the Sahara* S.V. various countries.

71. Collier, *Regimes in Tropical Africa*, p. 67.

72. Ibid., p. 106. However, as noted elsewhere, they were not fully one-party states until the opposition was banned.

73. Ibid., pp. 98–102.

74. Ibid., p. 105.

75. Bethwell A. Ogot and Tiyambe Zeleza, "Kenya: The Road to Independence and After," in Gifford and Louis, *Decolonization and African Independence*, p. 416.

76. See African Elections Database, SV Kenya, 1963. http://africanelections. tripod.com/ke.html

77. Zolberg, *Creating Political Order*, p. 81.

78. Sklar, *Corporate Power*, p. 21. Also, an independent won one seat. Also, see African Elections Database, SV Zambia, 1968. http://africanelections.tripod.com/ zm.html

79. Collier, *Regimes in Tropical Africa*, p. 109.

80. Zolberg, *Creating Political Order*, p. 81.

81. Collier, *Regimes in Tropical Africa*, p. 107.

82. Cherry Gertzel, Carolyn Baylies and Morris Szeftel, "Introduction: The Making of the One-Party State," in Gertzel et al., eds., *One-Party State*, p. 16.

83. Hodder-Williams, *Tropical Africa*, p. 121.

84. See for example Paul E. Sigmund, ed., *The Ideologies of the Developing Nations* 2nd Edition (New York: Praeger Publishers, 1972); also Young, *Ideology and Development*.

85. See Edmond J. Keller & Donald Rothchild, *Afro-Marxist Regimes: Ideology and Public Policy* (Boulder: Lynne Rienner Publisher, 1987).

86. Karl Marx, "Critique of the Gotha Program," in Robert C. Tucker, ed., *The Marx-Engels Reader* 2nd Edition (New York: W.W. Norton & Company, 1978), p. 538.

87. Young, *Ideology and Development*, p. 98.

88. Ibid., pp. 97–182.

89. Zolberg, *Creating Political Order*, Chapter 2.

90. Ibid., p. 46.

91. Ibid., p. 45 (Italics in original).

92. Ibid., pp. 48–63.

93. Also, this is consistent with the assumptions of the rational choice assumptions vis-à-vis politicians: African political leader maximize their political power. See Chapter 1 for elaboration and citations.

94. Data for this section on coups comes from Coups d'état events, 1946–2009. Monty G. Marshall and Donna Ramsey Marshall, Center for Systemic Peace, July 30, 2010. http://www.systemicpeace.org/inscr/inscr.htm

95. Pat McGowan and Thomas H. Johnson, "Military Coups d'État and Underdevelopment," *Journal of Modern African Studies* 22, 4 (1984), p. 638.

96. Coup events, 1946–2009. Marshall and Marshall.

97. World Bank, *World Development Report 1989* (Washington, DC: World Bank, 1989). One hundred and twenty are listed, with another 10 listed as non-reporting. See front matter, and adding in countries with more than 500,000 people. See page 230.

98. See Liebenow, *African Politics*, p. 240; also, Liebenow, "The Military Factor in African Politics: A Twenty-Five-Year Perspective," in Gwendolyn M. Carter and Patrick O'Meara, eds., *African Independence: The First Twenty Five Years* (Bloomington: Indiana University Press, 1986): 126–59; and especially Aristide Zolberg, "Military Intervention in the New States of Tropical Africa: Elements of Comparative Analysis," in Henry Bienen, ed., *The Military Intervenes: Case Studies in Political Development* (New York: Russell Sage Foundation, 1968): 71–102.

99. See Samuel Huntington, *Political Order in Changing Societies* (New Haven: Yale University Press, 1968).

100. Zolberg, "Military Intervention," p. 74 (Italics in original).

101. Liebenow, "Military Factor," p. 129.

102. S. E. Finer, *Man on Horseback: The Role of the Military in Politics* (New York: Frederick A. Praeger Publishers, 1962), pp. 35–47.

103. See for example Ibid., esp. Chapter 2; also Ruth First, *Power in Africa* (New York: Pantheon Books, 1970); Zolberg, "Military Intervention."

104. Finer, *Man on Horseback*, pp. 72–75; Liebenow, *African Politics*, pp. 247–49.

105. Collier, *Regimes in Tropical Africa*, p. 103.

106. Claude E. Welch Jr., *Soldier and State in Africa* (Evanston, IL: Northwestern University Press, 1970); also Welch, "The African Military and Political Development," in Henry Bienen, ed., *The Military and Modernization* (Chicago: Aldine, Atherton, 1971); for a taxonomy of reasons, see Robin Luckham, "The Military,

Militarization and Democratization in Africa: A Survey of Literature and Issues," *African Studies Review* 37, 2 (September 1994): 13–76; also Liebenow, "The Military Factor."

107. For example see John J. Johnson, ed., *The Role of the Military in Underdeveloped Countries* (Princeton: Princeton University Press, 1962).

108. Michael Lofchie, "The Uganda Coup—Class Action by the Military," *Journal of Modern African Studies* 10 (1972): 19–35; Finer, *Man on Horseback*, pp. 47–56.

109. Samuel Decalo, *Coups and Army Rule in Africa* (New Haven: Yale University Press, 1976); Finer, *Man on Horseback*, pp. 56–60.

110. Robin Luckham, "French Militarism in Africa," *Review of African Political Economy* 24 (May-August, 1982): 55–84; Aristide Zolberg, "The Military Decade in Africa," *World Politics* 25, 2, pp. 309–31; and Rene Lemarchand, "The CIA in Africa: How Central, How Intelligent?" *Journal of Modern African Studies* 14, 3 (1976): 401–26.

111. Pierre Englebert. *State Legitimacy and Development in Africa* (Boulder, CO: Lynne Rienner Publishers, 2000).

Chapter 4

The Consolidation of Economic Power in Africa

Inward-Oriented Development and Majority State Ownership

Not only were the new political elites of sub-Saharan Africa able to consolidate political power within one- or no-party systems in nearly every state, but they also expanded their control over their formal economies in nearly all states, though some exercised much greater control than others. Their desire to have done so stemmed from several mutually compatible goals at the time: to de-link their economies from that of the former colonizers, to shift more economic control into the hands of their citizens, to promote rapid economic development through a developmental state, and, finally, to consolidate their party's (or group's) hold over political power. As the intellectual climate of the time was quite favorably disposed toward most of these goals, many of the normal tradeoffs usually associated with establishing policy appeared to have been missing. As such, the pursuit of state control over the economy had significant legitimacy associated with it: it was seen as the faster means of promoting national economic independence as well as economic development.

The programs or approaches used to promote social and economic development, and which also allowed government leaders to concentrate more power into their own hands (directly or indirectly), were these: (1) an expansion of the "traditional" functions of the state; (2) the implementation of programs of nationalization, indigenization, and Africanization; (3) programs of state-led industrialization; and (4) the adoption of inward-oriented development policies.

THE RAPID EXPANSION OF THE STATE

Even in the early period, the expansion of the state in its traditional functions was evident throughout the continent. The post-colonial governments dramatically increased spending for social services, including education and health care, as well as for the traditional civil service. In Nigeria, for example, within "five years of independence, Nigeria's civil service increased by one-half again, and some ministries quadrupled in size."[1] The growth of government was so great that it had become the employer of 62% of all wage employment by 1970—with 300,000 people working for the Nigerian government.[2] Ghana, as well, had great increases in the size of the government: state employment accounted for over 55% of 60,000 trained professionals.[3] Moreover, judging by expenditures, the size of the administration in Guinea increased by 80% from 1959 to 1962; and in Mali, the increase was 60% for the same period.[4]

The case of Zaire, in particular, illustrates the dramatic increases in the levels of state expansion as the number of public employees increased from 167,900 in 1960 to 340,700 in 1975—representing over a two-fold increase.[5] Of these numbers, the following breakdowns are available: the number of civil service employees nearly doubled: from 11,500 to 21,500; contract personnel increased from 96,000 to 105,800 (an increase of 10%); teachers increased from 37,300 to 143,400 (nearly a four-fold increase); and the military increased from 23,100 to 70,000 (over a three-fold increase).[6] To add to these amazing increases, the number of teachers would later rise to 230,100 by 1978.

By the 1980s, the percentage of workers in the formal sector working for the state was quite high in Africa, at 59.7%, though this included traditional civil society as well as employment in state-owned enterprises.[7] In Tanzania, for example, combining these two categories, state employment represented more than three quarters of public sector workers in the 1980s.[8] According to one study, the "normal" state workers, such as teachers, postal workers, bureaucrats, and so forth, made up about 42% of state workers in societies where the government could control up to 75% of formal employment (so "traditional" civil service jobs could be upwards of 30 of all formal wage employment).[9] Therefore, the government control over formal sector employment continued to grow from independence until the mid- to late-1980s.

Nationalization

As discussed in the second chapter, a wave of nationalization washed through much of sub-Saharan Africa in the late 1960s and through the 1970s. According to the United Nations, of a documented 875 cases of nationalization from 1960–1974, 340 (or 39%) were in Black Africa.[10] Therefore, Africa was a leading part of this worldwide movement. In fact, outside of the petroleum sector, sub-Saharan Africa led all other regions in the "instances of nationalisation of mining, agriculture, manufacturing, trade, public utilities, banking and insurance."[11]

One of the earliest and largest nationalizations occurred in Zaire (now the Democratic Republic of the Congo) in 1967, with the nationalization of the Belgian copper company, the Union Minière du Haut Katanga (UMHK). The UMHK earnings and exports represented 50% of Zairian revenues and 70% of its foreign exchange earnings.[12] On January 1, 1967, Mobutu unilaterally declared a 60% share ownership, though it was later raised to a 100% share when no foreign co-investment became available.[13] The result was the creation of the new Zairian parastatal, Gécamines (Générale des Carrières et de Mines).[14]

Zambia also nationalized its copper industry, which routinely accounted for 90% or more of its exports. The importance of copper to Zambia cannot be overstated. Money from the copper industry supplied about 60% of all government revenues for the first five years of independence.[15] The copper sector was nationalized in 1970 when the government acquired 51% of all mining equity.[16] This transfer of property was taken one step further in 1979, when the government increased its share of equity from 51% to just over 60%.[17]

In Nigeria, also, the state assumed effective control and ownership of its oil sector with the enactment of the Nigerian Enterprises Promotion Decree of February 1972.[18] The government owned 55% of the domestic petroleum industry by 1974; and with a similar decree in 1977, its share of ownership jumped to 60% by 1979.[19] This sector was particularly important for the Nigerian economy, accounting for 69% of GDP and 90% of government revenue from 1970 to 1989.[20]

Indigenization and Africanization

The instruments of indigenization and Africanization also greatly increased the political power of the ruling elites (as well as their personal wealth). Indigenization is "the process by which a government limits participation in a particular industry to citizens of the country, thus forcing alien owners to sell."[21] Here, the property is transferred to its citizens rather than the state. Schatz wrote that "[i]ndigenization in the private sector is a policy of extending Nigerian ownership and control by government fiat or pressure."[22] With such programs, governments acquired new powers of regulation as well as new clients grateful to have access to new property. Importantly, indigenization disproportionately benefitted individual members of the ruling elite or party.

Indigenization targets were usually limited to small- or medium-sized firms, which the government believed local owners could manage without alien personnel or where foreigners were perceived to have gained property unfairly during colonization. Usually such an act required foreign owners of enterprises to sell all, most, or part of these businesses to locals in the equivalent of a fire sale. Countries which pursued such policies included Zaire, Nigeria, Ghana, Uganda, Kenya, Zambia, and Malawi.[23] Where the socialist countries introduced such acts, small- and medium-sized firms were more likely seized by the state as these actions were driven more by socialist ideology than by African economic nationalism. Therefore, the prohibition was against private property, and not only that of aliens. Tanzania and Guinea both fall into this latter category of countries.[24]

One important African example of indigenization occurred in Nigeria. The above-mentioned Nigerian Enterprises Promotion Decree (the Indigenization Decree) of February 1972 acted as sources of both nationalization as well as indigenization, and it was comprised of two separate schedules.[25] Schedule I set aside over twenty activities in small-scale industry, services, and retail trade exclusively for Nigerian citizens.[26] This required foreign owners to sell 100% of their interests to Nigerian citizens or to liquidate them. In Schedule II, usually involving more capital-intensive activities, owners were required to either quit the enterprise completely or to sell at least 40% of their equity shares to Nigerians.[27] Not all firms were subject to these laws, and not all property went to Nigerian private citizens. Very large firms were exempted from Schedule I, as were the large import and wholesale trade sectors.[28] In addition, not all industries were bought by private citizens; many firms had shares purchased by the Nigerian state itself. In fact, the government obtained stakes equaling over 50% of the oil producing companies, 40% of banking, and between 40% and 49% of insurance firms.[29]

A later decree in 1977 stiffened these two schedules and added a third. Under the new decree, "all enterprises were included in three schedules covering full (100%), majority (60%), and minority Nigerian ownership (40%). In general, areas of higher technology and management were classified under Schedule III, permitting foreign capital to hold up to 60% of the equity."[30] By contrast, medium-sized firms could only keep 40% equity shares for foreigners, while the smallest businesses could keep up to 60%.[31] The 1972 and 1977 Nigerian Decrees combined resulted in the "sale of stock valued at ₦200m and ₦331m and affected about 611 and 1000 companies, respectively."[32]

Perhaps the most well-known indigenization programs occurred in Zaire (now the DRC): Zairianization (1973) and Radicalization (1974). The first decree, Zairianization, transferred the ownership of most commerce, most plantations, many small industries, construction firms, transportation, and property-holding enterprises from foreigners to citizens—all without compensation.[33] The largest sectors, the plantations and "strategic" companies, were transferred to the public sector. Many particular plantations and most large commercial businesses actually went to the politicians or their support-ers.[34] Between 1,500 and 2,000 enterprises were transferred from non-Zairian owners and given "to the political aristocracy" or their allies.[35] The new owners, known as *acquéreurs*, were chosen on the basis of their political allegiance to Mobutu rather than for their business acumen. One year later, in 1974, "Radicalization" extended this process to affect approximately 120 companies established before independence (thus exempting American busi-nesses). These included textile mills, breweries, cigarette factories, cement works, and construction firms among others.[36] This program applied mostly to larger businesses, which proved to be mostly Belgian-owned ones that had not been seized under Zairianization.[37]

Even "capitalist" Kenya had programs of indigenization. In 1976, the Trade Licensing Act prohibited non-citizens from trading in rural areas or in the periphery of urban areas.[38] Moreover, the Kenyan state transferred large amounts of land to black Kenyan citizens with significant land. For example, the Ol Kalou Settlement Scheme settled 2,000 families on 56,000 hectares; the Haraka Settlement Scheme moved 14,000 families to about 105,000 hectares; and the Shirika Settlement Schemes was to move over 19,300 families onto 192,000 hectares.[39] The Kenyan government also cre-ated the Industrial and Commercial Development Corporation (ICDC) and the Industrial Development Bank (IDB) which provided loans or entered into joint ventures agreements with private firms to create large commercial and industrial projects.[40]

Finally, most countries in sub-Saharan Africa pursued some degree of Africanization. This is the process of replacing foreign employees with indigenous Africans, resulting in a transfer of jobs.[41] This was usually a governmental requirement that industries limit the number of foreigners they employed to a designated number. Although Africanization of the civil service was a top priority for almost all nations, due to the lack of trained manpower, the implementation of Africanization encountered many bottle-necks and setbacks. For example, Tanzania was only able to fill 26.1% of its senior and middle grade posts with its citizens; Zambia was only able to provide citizens for 38 of 848 top administrative positions and only 26% of Division I and II sectors.[42] Ghana was slightly more successful in African-izing its administration, with 60% of the senior post held by Ghanaians.[43] Senegal, too, was able to replace foreigners at a relatively high rate in the lower levels of industry (7% foreign) and commerce (10% foreign).[44] Even there, however, "only 27% of employers and upper management and 18 per cent of technicians and officials were Senegalese."[45]

Despite the incompleteness of these Africanization programs, the numbers involved were enormous: "it is believed that the exercise involved training for some 100,000 to 200,000 expatriate-held posts which were Africanized between 1958 and 1968."[46] Extensive Africanization programs were followed in most countries, with the exceptions of the Ivory Coast, Malawi (for the army), and Botswana.[47] In Botswana, for example, the middle-management positions had the same percentage of indigenes in the late 1980s as in the early 1970s.[48] Even in the "super-scale" grade, expatriates filled 22% of the top 183 administrative positions.[49]

State Investment in Industry

African states also grew in size though investment in new industries.[50] In fact, the annual average growth of the industrial sectors was 13.8% for the years of 1965–1973.[51] Manufacturing, often considered the most dynamic subsection of industry, increased at an average annual rate of 10.1% for the same period.[52] Although not all of this investment in industry was public, such investment did constitute the largest share. In Côte d'Ivoire, for example, through an active program in investment in industry, the state went from "owning 10% of total industrial capital in 1967 to 53% in 1980."[53] But in this case, the state did not usually hold a majority of the shares of these companies.

Botswana, too, had some state ownership of industries and was active in promoting development. Unlike most other mineral exporting countries, Botswana did not demand majority ownership of its mining industry, but it did demand between 15% and 25% of the total shares of stock, with an option to buy up to 50% of all shares.[54] Moreover, Botswana invested vertically, and it obtained 5.27% of De Beers Consolidated Mines in 1988, through its subsidiary Debswana.[55] Botswana's public sector only comprised 7.3% of GDP at factor cost in 1978 and only constituted 7.7% of gross fixed capital formation.[56]

As a result of the above-described expansion of state industries, state takeovers, and state investment, by the late 1980s, "some three thousand financial and nonfinancial African PEs [public enterprises], [were] fully or partially controlled by governments."[57] Also, these public enterprises comprised an average of 35.3% of domestic capital and 27% of fixed capital formation.[58] For example, in the late 1970s and early 1980s, the share of these public enterprises of GDP at factor cost were as high as 37.8% for Zambia, 25% for Guinea, and 19.9% for Senegal.[59] During the same time frame, their share of gross fixed capital formation could also be quite high: 61.2% for Zambia, 39.5% for Côte d'Ivoire, 37.9% for Gambia, and 32.7% for Tanzania.[60] Furthermore, control of wage employment held by the state became significant for almost all of the countries in the region. Overall, the average percentage of wage employment through the state was 35.9% by the late 1980s.[61] Where states controlled most of their industries or export producing sectors, the share of state wage employment was 70.85%; this compares to an average of 37.27% for the other countries.[62]

Inward-Oriented Development Policies

The final salient means of the political elite to consolidate their control over the economic domain was through the implementation of inward-oriented development policies. Inward-oriented policies (moderate or strong) are those which result in incentive structures which are biased toward, or distinctly favor, production for the domestic market. Their average rate of effective protection is medium to high and is fairly widespread, direct import controls and licenses are present and may be pervasive, and the exchange rate favors imports over exports.[63] The most common inward-orientated policies which added greatly to government power were tariffs, non-tariff barriers, currency overvaluation, and export taxation.

Each of these policies associated with inward-oriented development helped consolidate economic and political power in the hands of the political elite: the creation or extension of tariffs, non-tariff barriers (NTBs), and currency overvaluation created rents which could be allocated to political supporters in return for loyalty.[64] For example, tariffs or non-tariff barriers create rents through higher profits, that can be distributed as patronage. Loyalty can be partially ensured with the threat of the removal or reduction of a tariff or NTB (e.g., an import license) for disloyal supporters. Also, currency-overvaluation means that those who are given access to hard currency and import items gain the value of the difference between official rates and market rates as well as any profits from the market (including rents from protection). Thus, importers were subsidized by exporters, and the then higher demanded foreign currency was rationed or distributed through authority and not the market. The former became a significant source of support for the elites, or they themselves would prosper individually with side businesses for themselves, their families, or their inner circle. Such policies were used to keep the political elite unified and wealthy.

In addition, these policies created constituents on their own, who in turn became independent forces for their continuation—even should politicians wish to reverse them later. For example, many of the enterprises or importers which emerged in the region after the establishment of inward-oriented policies, either state or private, could not survive without continued protection or access to cheap hard currency. Therefore, those associated with the new enterprises, including both workers and management, became strong defenders of, and pressure groups for, inward-oriented development and state ownership of industry.[65]

Most countries in sub-Saharan Africa, from the 1960 until the 1980s, had highly protected markets, whether through tariffs or NTBs.[66] For example, the trade-weighted average of tariffs for eighteen sub-Saharan countries in 1987 was 27.78%.[67] In the same year, Burkina Faso had a weighted tariff level of

52.8%, Kenya's average tariff level was 35%. Benin, Burundi, Ghana, and Senegal had average tariff levels near 30%. But it must be kept in mind that although tariff numbers reflect real levels of protection, they are an average, and effective protection levels for non-agricultural goods were usually much higher. These countries would often also use NTBs to reduce economic competition. Using an index for the level of NTBs, which runs from 0% to 100%, where 100% is completely closed, eighteen countries in the region had an average of 69%—though the range for this number in the region ran from 14.9% to 100%. Countries such as Benin, Congo, Sierra Leone, Tanzania, Zambia, and Zimbabwe featured NTBs of 100%—usually because of currency rationing.

Beyond relatively high levels of tariff protection, the levels of currency overvaluation were usually very high and added another dimension to inward-oriented policies.[68] African countries (outside the French Franc Zone [CFA]) had an average of 91% currency overvaluation from 1966 to 1986.[69] Although this number is high enough, some countries experienced, such astronomical rates that it is hard to believe that individuals paid in domestic currency could find exporting profitable at all. For example, Nigeria had an average level of overvaluation of 146%, with a peak of 1,065 in 1986. Zaire, too, has had high levels of overvaluation: its average level was 131% for this period and reached a high of 4,000% in 1977. Finally, Ghana had an average level of currency overvaluation of 423%, with a high of 4,264% in 1982!

The use of high and systematic taxation of agricultural exports was also a prominent feature on the economic map of inward-orientation. The taxation of exports changes the relative benefits to that sector, and producers may shift away from exporting sectors to ones which produce for the domestic market, making it inward-oriented. Also, the popularity of these taxes stemmed from their simplicity, ability to collect and enforce, and the political weakness of the taxed groups. These exports were usually shipped through a single port, the governments had monopsonies so they could set producer prices, and, finally, farmers have been among the most difficult to organize politically.[70]

The average level of taxation for agricultural exports in Africa was fairly high, at 66% for this period, though there was much variation.[71] The rates of such taxation ranged from 98% to *minus* 80% (where a negative number represented a subsidy). It should be noted, however, that subsidies were the exception to the rule; the mode was 80–90% (using increments of 10%), and the median tax rate was 70.6%. Perhaps the highest average level of taxation of agricultural exports for any country for this period was in the Republic of the Congo, which had an average level of 94%! Benin, too, had a high level of taxation on agricultural exports at 83%. Finally, Mauritius taxed its farmers an average of 93% of the world price for tea.[72] By contrast, the lower levels of taxation tended to hover between 10% and 50%. Kenya, for example, had an average level of taxation at 12.7%. Zimbabwe, too, was relatively low at 35%. Even Ivory Coast, which has been more outward-oriented than most, had an average level of taxation on agricultural exports of 59% for this period.

In sum, with the rapid expansion of the state immediately following independence, the power of the new state elites over both the political and economic life of the country was greatly enhanced and consolidated. They could control who gained access to the state through their control over the programs of nationalization, indigenization, and Africanization. The state grew also with an increase in traditional state functions as well as inward-oriented development policies. Both increased state investment and inward-oriented policies—all within the context of one- or no-party states—greatly increased their purview over economic power within their countries.

MATERIAL INTERESTS AND THE CONSOLIDATION OF ECONOMIC POWER

The non-ideological explanations of state expansion into the economic domain fall into two principal groups. On the one hand, political groups and organizations which might have been expected to oppose the state's expansion into economic endeavors were weak at the time, and, as discussed in the prior chapter, the rising political elite was relatively strong when compared to civil society. Importantly, the indigenous bourgeoisie was either weak or non-existent, the power of the international business class was de-linked from state power, and the right of foreign ownership of domestic resources had been de-legitimized. As explained previously, economic nationalism cut into the inviolability of (foreign) private property, especially when it was obtained through oppression.

Weakness of the Indigenous Bourgeoisie at Independence

The rapid and significant consolidation of so much economic power in the hands of the new ruling parties occurred partially due to the absence of a powerful indigenous, capital-owning bourgeoisie which could have blocked such a significant intrusion into this domain.[73] During the colonial period, large-scale capital accumulation on the part of Africans was nearly impossible for two basic reasons:

> One stemmed from the attitudes of colonial officials. This varied from indifference or a marked reluctance to provide assistance to downright hostility and discrimination in dealing with indigenous interests. The second obstacle was the

superior competition offered by foreign capital, a competition which Africans were normally ill equipped to cope and against which they received little or no protection.[74]

In addition, Africans had been regularly barred from most of the trading houses and from ownership of natural resources during the colonial period, which were usually controlled by European companies. Thus, most of the mining, oil, or industrial capital in Africa at the time of independence was foreign or state-owned. For example, in the case of the Belgian Congo (now the DRC) in 1958, just two years before independence, the colonial minority owned 95% of all capital assets and 82% of all enterprises; also they were responsible for 70% of all material output and 58% of all marketed agricultural output.[75] In terms of access to wealth through wages, the colonial minority who only represented 2% of all wage earners controlled over 45% of all wages.[76]

In Kenya, indigenous Africans had been alienated from certain lands and certain trades during colonization. The best farmlands were the "white highlands" which comprised of approximately 7.3 million acres farmed by about 4,000 settlers.[77] Moreover, whites had a monopoly on the most profitable crops, such as coffee, until the mid-1950s.[78] This state of affairs changed slowly, even with independence. By 1977, over 57.5% of the "large farms" had been transferred to black Kenyans, "and these transactions involved some 18,000 hectares of land worth K,18 million."[79]

Despite land reform, the Kenyan non-agricultural capital remained firmly in the hands of foreign owners for many years after. In fact,

[f]oreign dominance of the private non-agricultural sector of the economy was virtually complete at independence; [even by] 1970 . . . foreigners still overwhelmingly controlled this sector. Public ownership . . . was about 25%. [Even] in the service sector, . . . where the most serious efforts were being made to install Africans in business, in 1966 roughly 58 per cent of the turnover was accounted for by firms wholly or mainly owned by non-citizens, which a substantial proportion of the remaining 42 per cent was accounted for by firms owned by non-African citizens, both European and Asian.[80]

In Ivory Coast, the ascendancy of foreign capital was equally quite clear. With independence, the state began to foster local investment, which comprised most of the indigenous industrial investment capital right in the early years after independence. By 1967, the state's share of total industrial capital was only 10%—and this figure greatly eclipsed the capital held by Ivoirian citizens![81] With plantations, however, African planters were more numerous and prosperous as a class—unlike most countries in Eastern and Southern Africa.

In Nigeria, as well, foreign companies controlled most of the investments near the time of independence. In 1963, for example, the percentage of manufacturing which was foreign owned was calculated to be 88.7%.[82] This percentage only fell to 84.8% by 1965.[83] In Senegal, too, foreign capital was dominant at the time of independence. Over 95% of the most modern industrial sector was owned by French firms.[84] These consisted of groundnut processing plants and light industry directed at the local market. With independence, the monopoly of the import/export trade was assumed by the state, and not by private companies.

The indigenous bourgeois class that had begun to emerge during the colonial period was quite limited when compared to either international capital or the new political elites acting through government. This class in sub-Saharan Africa was most often dependent on the new states for its continued accumulation of wealth. It required access to credit, international contacts and some forms of protection to compete—especially given the low level of business experience. The indigenous, capital-owning bourgeoisie, which may have opposed the consolidation of economic power by the new government, was usually in no position to make strong demands against the new political elite.

Weakened Foreign Bourgeoisie, Especially European MNCs and Businesses

As we have indicated above, a large and vibrant foreign bourgeoisie did exist in the region at the time of independence; indeed, it was a strong force for the economic status quo. Even with the clear ascendancy of foreign over local capital, the former operated from a relatively weakened political position immediately after African independence. In fact, they were especially vulnerable to the demands for nationalization and indigenization that were sweeping the subcontinent as well as the rest of the developing world.

The explanation for the rise of nationalization in the Third World following the decade of the 1960s had to do with the decline of colonial control of much of the world, the rise of economic nationalism, and the rise of American hegemony. As we saw earlier, before effective American enforcement of the Monroe Doctrine after the Second World War, European nations often employed gunboat diplomacy to defend their property and profits in colonies and semi-colonies.[85]

With the enhanced geopolitical power of America in the wake of WWII, and its Cold War goals of halting the spread of Communism, these practices were ended. Although America also wanted to protect its overseas investments, geopolitical concerns trumped such narrow mercantilist concerns of its allies. As American policy was to forestall radical anti-American or pro-Communist leaderships, it feared that coercive diplomacy would radicalize the new leadership and could lead them into the Soviet orbit. In fact, the US policy towards nationalization was accommodationist; it did not deny that new nations had the right to nationalize property, especially property taken during colonial conquest. Nonetheless, the US held that these takings should be undertaken in "nondiscriminatory ways, undertaken for public purposes, and accompanied by prompt and adequate compensation."[86] The US itself was reluctant to pursue force when US companies were nationalized throughout much of Latin America.[87]

Also, MNCs at the time were reluctant to push their power to the limit within newly independent Africa. First, most of these companies usually owed their economic positions to the foreign-imposed, colonial governments—which had barred Africans from certain economic spheres. The legitimacy of these companies was, therefore, suspect—which limited their ability to maneuver. Their legitimacy was especially cast in doubt when they owned non-renewable natural resources which had been acquired through colonization. They also owned a fixed asset which could not exit and which clearly was part of the African soil. Such companies were able to elicit little sympathy once independence arrived, and they were usually quite vulnerable to nationalist demands. The nationalizations of mining industries in Zaire, Zambia, and Togo illustrate this view. It is also supported by the example of Botswana which demanded less than majority state ownership, but which did not have a vibrant mining sector until well after the colonial period.

The second reason that MNCs did not usually press their power to its full advantage was that the share of any one company's holdings in the region tended to be small as a percentage of its total worldwide assets. Therefore, companies often came to view these assets as expendable in light of potential future profits which could be earned through adoption of a conciliatory stance towards nationalization. Companies which had only one source of revenue, however, tended to use every avenue open to them to reverse nationalizations. For example, the nationalized UMHK in Zaire was able, through its own power and that of the Belgian government, to negotiate a management contract which actually increased its profits when compared to its operations pre-nationalization.[88] Third, these companies often obtained loans, tax breaks, or insurance through their own government to stave off the worst effects of nationalization. For example, the American companies which were nationalized in the 1960s and 1970s were compensated by the Overseas Private Investment Company (OPIC) or could write off such losses against their American tax liabilities.[89] Combining the last two points, we can see that it often made little economic sense to expend much political or economic capital to recapture these assets—by efforts in either Africa or the metropolitan political center.

Finally, Richard Sklar has argued that MNCs were policy-takers, instead of policy-setters. He suggested that MNCs follow a "doctrine of domicile" which results in local subsidiaries of MNCs following local laws or practices—even if they conflict with the corporate policies of their parent companies.[90] Subsidiaries of a MNC may have to follow very different practices and laws than other subsidiaries of the same MNC. These local subsidiaries of MNCs adapt to local political conditions where they can make money and abandon those where they cannot. In neither case do they seek to challenge a government's authority. This doctrine was described as the "basis of corporate planning for a prolonged relationship between the international mining companies and Zambia."[91] Corporate behavior at the time appeared to be in accord with this idea which was prevalent during this period. Sklar states that the doctrine of domicile is "an ideological notion, relevant to the value premises of multinational corporations. It affirms that the individual subsidiaries of an international business group do operate in accordance with the requirements of divergent and conflicting state policies."[92] As such, the doctrine of domicile would suggest that MNCs operating in the Third World would not act directly to oppose the attempts by the ruling elites to consolidate economic power, if they can find another avenue to gain profits. This would play to their greatest strength at the time, the promise of future investment or the threat of withdrawal of investment or expertise into or out of each country.[93]

Thus, foreign companies were at a distinct disadvantage in affecting the trade regimes of the post-independence African nations—especially when it came to the protection of "their" property rights in former colonies. Their mother countries were unlikely to create a diplomatic break with the new nations—let alone engage in military force to reverse these policies, and no international law existed which would do so. Although nationalization and indigenization did not become national policy in every country, they were region-wide trends. Even in states with little nationalization, a domestic capital-owning bourgeoisie and foreign businesses which had been associated with colonial rule remained weak in the early independence period. Neither was able to stand in the way of the trend of the economic centralization of power throughout Africa.

The Self-Interest of the Ruling Elite

Finally, the self-interest of political elites to establish the policies of expanding the size of the state, investing in industries, beginning programs of nationalization, indigenization and Africanization, and following inward-oriented economic policies cannot be ignored. As shown in the section on patronage vis-à-vis political consolidation, the first parties to gain a legislative majority self-consciously used the resources of the state to secure later political monopolies. With this greatly inflated state system, the leaders of the new states had tremendous control over the many public enterprises and wage employment.

With state ownership or control of industries or export sectors, the political elite could appoint managers with exorbitant salaries to the top posts in the new state bureaucracies. They could also designate who obtained business opportunities created under indigenization programs through the allocation of credit or simple designation. Inward-oriented development policies also brought great economic resources to the political elites—which could be translated into political support. These policies, by their nature, created scarcities since they ignored international prices. For example, an overvalued currency creates an exaggerated demand for both imports and the currency with which to import them. These imbalances lead to import restrictions, currency rationing, and higher tariffs. Each of these increases the domestic price of the good. We discussed above, whoever is given access to the currency of the import license reaps the difference between the international price for the good and its domestic price—as well as the difference in value between official and unofficial exchange rates.

In sub-Saharan Africa, being awarded either highly sought after import licenses or access to hard currency associated with inward-oriented policies was a road to rapid wealth. The distribution of now-scarce commodities created a relationship of dependency between businesspeople and politicians: these revenues were available only to members of political important clients, the state enterprises themselves, or the political elite.[94] Any acts to oppose the political elite or the leader would result in the forfeiture of this access, if not worse consequences.

In addition to the lure of easy access to greater patronage, many leaders in the region actually believed that the policies would work. As will be discussed later, sound economic analysis seemed to indicate that rapid growth would result from these policies. This growth would reinforce their rule: leaders that follow sound practices are more likely to remain in power. With the state-ownership of industries and its role in planning, the ruling elites thought that they could claim credit for the rapid development that everyone thought was going to ensue.

Also, these policies could easily have the effect of denying would-be competitors access to financial resources with which to launch campaigns of opposition. Politics in sub-Saharan Africa is based on patron-client ties and requires massive amounts of resources to compete. Therefore, the near monopolization of economic resources by the ruling elites powerfully reinforced their overall dominance since they controlled access to both wealth and jobs. This greatly consolidated the hold on power for two major reasons: first, the incumbents in the government party are able to outspend competing parties in any election; second, under these conditions, few wealthy enterprises or entrepreneurs existed under these conditions to bankroll an opposition movement. Thus, an independent and wealthy business class, which could finance such a movement or which might oppose inward-oriented policies, was unlikely to emerge with the state consolidation of economic power.

Furthermore, with so much of the wealth of the society flowing through the hands of the state, it made no sense to oppose the ruling party and lose. A simple logic emerges: since a party which obtains 51% of the popular vote could control 100% of state-controlled patronage available to state elites where most economic opportunities are through the state, politicians cannot lose an election and maintain their base of support. And as discussed in the prior chapter, elections were not usually so close that one could challenge and get anywhere near the 50% mark. This meant that contenders must win the election at all costs. With so much of the economy controlled by state elites, the political stakes involved were even higher. Politicians who lose an election have no powerful economic sanctuaries or bases to which to retreat and remount the next campaign. Rampant corruption was the usual result since the loss of an election entailed both political and economic catastrophes.[95] Thus, the consolidation of access to economic wealth by the ruling elite was altogether politically rational, if not economically so.

In addition, these policies created constituencies for their continuation as well as protection of the incumbent political elites. The expansion of state power over much of the economic wealth of these new nations not only allowed for patron-client relationships to continue, but it allowed them to flourish and to become entrenched.[96] The policies of expanding the size of state bureaucracies, nationalization of foreign-owned industries, Africanization, indigenization, and inward-oriented trade policies created thousands of jobs to be filled, and millions and millions of dollars worth of assets to be distributed—all by the ruling party.[97] Those aligned with these sectors would become threatened by their reversal, and they would become supporters of the new status quo. Since the ability of the political elite and their supporters to reap rents was based on protected markets or access to scarce commodities, the liberalization of these statist policies would directly threaten the interests of the political elites and their clients. Thus, policies created constituencies who defended the policies; this is what Krueger called a vicious cycle of policy.[98]

Finally, these policies allowed for massive amounts of rent-seeking that could enrich the individual members of the ruling elite and their clients, apart from the political support they could garner. The implementation of policies such as inward-oriented development or state-owned industrialization created vast streams of wealth which flowed directly through the collective hands of the ruling party. Not only could this wealth be used for the development of the nation, but it could also be redirected into the pockets of individual members of the ruling elite and their supporters. These policies made many members of the ruling elite, as well as their friends, quite wealthy.[99]

The access to state economic and political power has permitted the ruling elites to enrich themselves and their class in the process. According to Richard L. Sklar, a "managerial bourgeoisie" emerged in Africa, defined primarily by its relationship to power.[100] He observed that "class interests are likely to prevail when they are promoted in the name of national aspirations."[101] Clearly the ideology of the time in conjunction with economic nationalism provided this condition. Sklar argues that class consolidation took two forms: "support for indigenous enterprise, including the transfer of foreign assets to local owners; and nationalization or state participation in the ownership of productive property and natural resources."[102] Thus, the self-interest of the dominant class is clear in these policies.

Larry Diamond, too, has argued that the African state has been the basis of dominant-class formation, and he has specified four pathways though which it can occur . . .

> through its legitimate employment and expenditures; through its development plans and strategy; through the manipulation of patronage and ethnic ties to inhibit the development of lower-class consciousness and organizations; and finally, through the illegitimate accumulation of public wealth, that is, political corruption.[103]

Thus, class interests as a whole were promoted by these policies; the interests of the ruling party and the managerial bourgeoisie were the same.

Beyond promoting class interests, many individual leaders among the political elite became enormously wealthy because of these policies. Often the rulers became so powerful both politically and economically, that one-party or military rule often collapsed into personal rule. "Personal rule is a system of relations linking rulers not with the 'rubric' or even with the ruled (at least not directly), but with patrons, associates, clients, supporter, and rivals, who constitute the 'system.'"[104] Perhaps the most notable example is Mobutu Sese Seko of Zaire, who by his own estimate, may have been the second richest man in the world at one time, with over $8 billion in a Swiss bank account.[105] In fact, Callaghy compared him to Louis XIV since neither saw sharp dividing lines between the property of the nation and the property of the ruling elites; between 17% and 22% of the national budget is devoted to Mobutu's personal use.[106] He also ruled over governing political elites who were dependent on Mobutu for wealth.[107] Many elected members of the MPR became large farmers, ranchers, and planters.[108]

In Nigeria, during the boom years of high oil prices and production, the state either spent or exported most its earned capital.[109] During the second Republic, for example, it is estimated that between $5 and $7 billion of hard currency was exported by top government officials.[110] In 1977, over $25 million a day was transferred by corrupt politicians.[111] Even the governors of most states were able to amass comparable fortunes; a commission found that ten of twelve governors were guilty of corruption and misuse of funds to the tune of sixteen million naira in the mid-1970s.

Even leaders of countries with less access to their domestic economies were able to garner huge fortunes during their rule. For example, Houphouët-Boigny accrued a vast fortune and was personally financing construction of the Basilica at Yamassoukro at a cost of over $360 million.[112] Dr. Hastings Banda, as well, was enormously wealthy and owned a diverse portfolio including: "breweries, distilleries, food processing industries, textiles and metal products manufacturing, tourism and hotels and wholesaling and retailing."[113]

IDEOLOGICAL JUSTIFICATIONS FOR THE CONSOLIDATION OF ECONOMIC POWER

Ideological justification for the expansion of state power into the sphere of economics came from many sources. This drive for greater control over the economies of the region was far more than merely a naked power grab by the new ruling elites: they had ideological cover for these actions. In fact, many views of development at the time were either compatible with, or directly called for, the state ownership or industries, state-led development, and inward-oriented development policies

Economic Nationalism

The underlying ideological foundation for the intrusion of the African state into the economies of this region was very similar for the ideological justification of political independence—nationalism.[114] In fact,

> African nationalism, like other nationalisms, is in part a revolt against an inferior economic status . . . [which] includes demands for higher prices for farmers; for higher wage and salary levels for manual and clerical workers, for a large share in international and foreign trade for African merchants (as against European, Lebanese or Indian firms); for the nationalization, or profit-squeezing for foreign concessions; for more rapid industrial development; and (in countries of European settlement) for the breaking up of European estates and their redistribution among African peasants.[115]

This tap root of economic nationalism also led to the "Africanization" of managerial and bureaucratic positions throughout the continent as well as to the moves to nationalize and "indigenize" foreign companies.[116] The only institutions thought capable of bringing about the appropriate economic transformations demanded by this nationalism were the new post-colonial states; thus, economic nationalism helped propel these nations in the direction of the concentration of economic power in the hands of the ruling elites.

Enthusiasm for increasing these new governments' control over their economies to provide Africans with greater access to wealth was greatly enhanced by the perceptions of an unjust economic hierarchy created during the colonial period. There was, in fact, abundant evidence for this perception.

> [T]he economy of a typical black African state consisted of three levels: Europeans and Americans at the top holding the large industries, Asians in the middle doing much of the wholesale and retail trading, and Africans at the bottom continuing in farming, market trading, and rudimentary services.[117]

The results of economic discrimination during the colonial period against African indigenous capital, and all Africans in general, were plain for all to see. Since the colonial governments had caused many of the imbalances, it was believed that the post-colonial government could make amends.

Unlike the impetus for political nationalism, which had political independence as its final goal, economic nationalism sought control—either through management or ownership—of the institutions of economic power. Nonetheless, these two trends reinforced each other and led to the growing trend of the worldwide creation of state-owned industries as well as the nationalization of the domestic assets of MNCs.

Belief in Planning

The desire of leaders in Africa to extend political control over their economies was supported by an optimistic view of the effects of widespread economic planning. F.X. Sutton argued that the leaders of the new nations in sub-Saharan Africa believed deeply in rationally planned development. In fact, most countries in the region followed an approach which was

> distinguished by its faith in governmental leadership and planning, by its faith in the competence and potential helpfulness of the developed countries, and by a comprehensive appreciation of the need for human development and social change. In goals and methods, it is a vision of rationalization. In contrast the laissez-faire doctrines of Western tradition, it shows little trust in the mere freeing of indigenous propensities to truck, barter, and to put one thing together with another.[118]

The "background influences" which helped to create this confidence in planning included experiences with Soviet planning, national economic management during the Great Depression, the wartime mobilization of resources carried out by several countries, and the postwar Marshall Plan for the recovery of Western Europe. The planning undertaken in the Soviet Union had appeared to have resulted in a massive transformation of the agrarian country into an industrialized country.[119] At that time, the costs in repression and human lives were little-known outside the USSR.

The Great Depression and the ensuing war effort both affected the views of economic development and planning in several ways. First, export pessimism prevailed as the price for the goods exported by most underdeveloped countries declined. There was, in fact, a decline in the terms of trade against such resources and crops. This led many Third World countries, especially in Latin America, to begin domestic industrialization projects as avenues for growth. This trend was greatly reinforced by the disruption of the Atlantic trade with the Nazi war effort. Second, the depression also coincided with the rise of Keynesian analysis.[120] Perhaps the most important aspect of Keynesianism to Third World development was not its application as a means of resolving unemployment, but rather its attack on classical economics and its emphasis on state intervention in the economy. By casting the government as the ultimate guardian of the economy, Keynesianism could be used to justify discretionary national economic management.[121]

Finally, the American Marshall Plan, which provided much necessary capital to reconstruct Western Europe, proved to be a great economic and political success. Not only was Communism discouraged from gaining a foothold politically, but most of these economies also rebounded quite nicely. Each of these apparent successes gave more credence to planning economic growth.

Development Economists

Not only did the norms concerning colonial rule undergo a transformation immediately after WWII, but so also did the ideas concerning national economic development. The eradication of poverty and the development of nations became a central focus for economics, and a new cadre of economists—called development economists—emerged.[122] These new thinkers explored the difficulties of eradicating poverty in Asia, Africa, and Latin America and in achieving sustainable, rapid economic growth.

In the study of the persistence of poverty in the Third World, these development economists departed from two primary assumptions of classical economics: (1) that all economies function in very similar manners and respond similarly to economic incentives; and (2) that the interaction between advanced and less advanced economies *within an open trading system* results in mutual economic benefits and growth.[123] The assumption that Third World nations were different from others vis-à-vis development was given some support by the zeitgeist and prevalence of Keynesian economic thought: the proposition that there were "special cases" which deviated from "normal" economies seemed to be a logical distinction that could be applied elsewhere.[124]

Development economists asserted that most developing nations suffered from the problem of under investment (stemming in part from rural under-employment, as opposed to the urban unemployment noted by Keynes). Most of these theorists perceived the crux of the problem of development to be associated with a fundamental lack of capital or investment to fuel growth.[125] They claimed that as latecomers to industrialization, Third World nations faced constraints to growth that were different from those of the early modernizers.[126] Inherent to these countries were "special" circumstances which kept investments at levels below those necessary to escape poverty. Given the lateness of industrialization, other structural constraints for development had presented themselves which had not interfered with earlier development.[127]

Some of the first development economists argued that poverty itself was a structural difficulty which inhibited economic progress: it established a vicious cycle in which poverty begot more poverty. For example, Ragnar Nurske argued that countries with a small market with a low per capita income could not generate a sufficient level of investment to free themselves from low levels of poverty.[128] Harvey Leibenstein added to this idea his notion of a low level equilibrium trap which Tony Killick characterizes as "a vicious circle similar to Nurske's, [containing] a neo-Malthusian hypothesis."[129] Thus, Leibenstein believed that any economic growth would be overtaken by population growth rates in low-income countries.

Other eminent development economists of the time advanced explanations for poverty that were quite compatible with these arguments. Simon Kuznets showed that most developing countries were struggling to modernize and industrialize with only one-half or one-third the levels of per capita incomes of the previous industrializers.[130] Gunner Myrdal espoused the idea that unmitigated market forces reinforced international inequalities.[131] W. W. Rostow asserted that the low level of technology or science available to these countries created a ceiling on per capita output, which in turn would depress growth.[132]

Most of these economists rejected the orthodox belief that export-led growth was a means of achieving the necessary capital and investment for development. Nurske, for example, held that the growth of world markets for primary commodities would be too slow to gain sufficient investment capital or development (oil-exporting countries being the prime exception).[133] A scholar of the period argued that the "decline in export prices, the low price elasticities and income elasticities of demand for primary products, and unstable foreign exchange receipts—all these adverse characteristics led to export pessimism."[134] The Prebisch-Singer view of a secular decline of the terms of trade of primary products encouraged other approaches to development. In addition, since these thinkers believed there would be a lack of investment due to inherent poverty, they turned to new approaches for achieving economic progress.[135]

The solution to these problems was, therefore, state intervention to bring about a sufficient level of investment to lead these countries out of poverty. Most of the development economists at the time believed in two views which justified their optimism with respect to state intervention in the economy: (1) the complementary view of investment decisions and (2) the view that import substitution industrialization (ISI) would lead to dynamic gains to investment in industries by generating mutually reinforcing forward and backward economic linkages.

The complementary view of investment, which was widely held at the time, was quite optimistic about state involvement in the economy because it assumed that "a single act of investment will tend to produce a stream of benefits in excess of the private returns to the investor, by expanding the size of the market and thus tending to induce further capital formation by others. Hence the social value of an act of investment exceeds its private value."[136] As a result, markets which were small, or in which levels of savings were low, could be "kick-started" with strategic investing. With planning, a state or social investment could bring about much more investment than would be the case in a capitalist, or export-oriented, approach.

The second common view of investment was that although an export-led approach had the advantage of allocating resources to their most efficient use, this would only have marginal effects on long term increases in growth. This approach was seen as "static," since it only led to a one-time increase in welfare. By contrast, an approach which favored ISI, and which utilized forward and backward linkages in the economy, was believed to be "dynamic."[137] Hirschman, for example, argued that these linkages could lead to more sustained growth and development.

Combining these two ideas, the economists believed that the state could choose more dynamic investment policies than would market-based investors. State investments in certain sectors (i.e., industry) would lead to dynamic gains that far outweighed gains from free trade. Moreover, these investments would attract much more additional investment than the private returns would show.

In order for these rapid development to be realized, most scholars at the time felt that a strong state was needed in order to create the capital necessary to break out of the poverty traps or to provide a "big push." Furthermore, since it was assumed that there was a lack of entrepreneurial capital and skill in the region, many felt that state intervention was necessary to provide leadership in creating the industrialization that was so very vital to development.[138]

Despite great areas of consensus, one area of great disagreement among these economists existed: whether or not the state should become the owner of factories, farms, and banks. Most development economists saw an active role for the state to promote savings, providing protection for industries, and to provide the capital necessary for economic development—in addition to providing infrastructure and social services.[139] Although there was a split in opinion as to whether or not the owners should be private or public, the ideas and solutions provided by these thinkers greatly legitimized the concentration of power of vast parts of the economy by the state.

Expectations at Independence

At the time of independence, most thinkers had an abundance of enthusiasm about the prospect of rapid economic growth. The widespread belief that the relatively "backwardness" of African economies was due primarily to colonial obstacles implied that political freedom would result in economic development for its denizens. It was widely believed that the new governments could quickly improve the material lives of most Africans. As mentioned above, the perceived "successes" of the Soviet and Chinese models of development reinforced such views.[140] The colonial state had been perceived (correctly) as inhibiting Africans from obtaining a large degree of wealth and accumulation. It was widely believed that with the transfer of significant resources from foreign companies to the new states would translate into a rapid transfer of wealth to local citizens.

The degree of the optimism concerning economic growth was based on a faith in planning and the theories of development economists which greatly exceeded all past experience. As one scholar notes,

Ten newly independent African countries were among the eighteen UN delegates that persuaded the General Assembly to declare the goal of the UN Development Decade to be the attainment in each less developed country of a substantial increase in the rate of growth, with each country setting its own target, taking as the objective a *minimum* annual rate of growth of aggregate national income of 5% at the end of the decade.[141] [Italics in original.]

These anticipated growth rates far overshot the historic achievement of other industrialized countries: Britain never reached above a 2% average growth level from 1853 to 1913; and Germany's rate of growth was below 5% before WWII.[142] In fact, "the wealth of Western Europe and North America had been accumulated over a long period . . . [and] took a century or more of relatively slow growth before these countries achieved comparative affluence . . . Moreover, . . . Latin America provided a depressing case study in post-colonial poverty."[143]

Neo-Marxist Theories

Other ideas which were persuasive at the time justified the rejection of capitalist development policies and reinforced the tendencies toward the concentration of economic power by the new states. Neo-Marxist theories, like the ideas of the development economists, also held that the economies of less-developed countries were structurally different than were more advanced economies. Importantly, these theories postulated that the economic interaction between advanced and less advanced countries always took place to the detriment of the latter; this would necessarily create an argument against development based upon comparative advantage and toward one of state-led inward-oriented development.

Although this line of thought can be traced to Marx and Lenin, Paul Baran is often considered to be the father of contemporary dependency theory.[144] With *Political Economy of Growth* in 1957, Baran argued that capitalism would not lead to the development of the former colonial countries as held by classical Marxism.[145] To the contrary, he argued that metropolitan countries drained the surplus out of these countries and that development could not then occur. The surpluses generated by capitalist expansion were withdrawn from the region instead of being reinvested domestically or being consumed in conjunction with locally produced goods—as the bourgeoisie had done in Europe. Two mechanisms ensured that the surplus would not remain in underdeveloped regions: foreign monopoly in international commodity markets and foreign monopoly in industrial technology.[146] Following from these premises, he held that economic growth under capitalist auspices was impossible; and that only socialist economic planning offered a rational solution to the problem of underdevelopment.[147]

Baran's argument was extended by other dependency theorists, who argued that newly emergent economies were tied into the world capitalist system in ways which would keep them permanently in a state of dependence. In brief, this approach emphasized the tendency of capitalism to promote a permanent international division of skills and labor in which advanced countries controlled the high value industries and the newly developing countries would only participate in low value productions and actions.[148] The first industrializers constituted the "core" countries of the international capitalist system; they had control over decisions concerning investment and finance, while a large "periphery" would be subservient to the core countries, providing unskilled labor and raw materials. In addition to the "freezing in place" of these divisions of labor, these thinkers agreed with Baran that economic surpluses created in the periphery were removed to the core. The overall effect of these two forces kept the latter in a permanent state of "underdevelopment." The first group of dependency theorists held that there would be growth without development, and that workers in the Third World would remain the "hewers of wood and drawers of water" for the world economic system.[149]

These arguments include three interwoven processes of thought:

(1) the drain of surplus from the periphery to centre; (2) the creation of self-reinforcing international division of labour whose effects are to generate further self-reinforcing structural imbalances in the colonial economy; (3) the conservation of precapitalist modes of production in such a way as to arrest the advance of the productive forces.[150]

Later evidence would indicate that industrialization was in fact occurring in much of the periphery, but rapid development was not.[151] These types of arguments would emerge and strengthen in the late 1970s and early 1980s. This dependent development was held to be limited to an enclave of capitalist development. Although some earlier modifications of dependence theory would show that interaction of advanced and less advanced economies thus resulted in a "dual economy," which in turn resulted in severe social degradation and distorted forms of development.[152]

A contemporaneous intellectual position known as neocolonialism emerged in Africa; it was first espoused by Kwame Nkrumah and thereafter associated with the idea of dependency theory. This theory held that the class structures which formed in the Third World were such that the local emerging bourgeois class was dependent on the international capitalist class and had primarily non-nationalist allegiances.[153] According to the All-African People's Conference held in Cairo in 1961, neocolonialism is

[t]he survival of the colonial system in spite of the formal recognition of the political independence in emerging countries which become the victims of an indirect and subtle form of domination by political economic, social, military, or technical means.[154]

The core idea is that the ruling elites in developing countries were "comprador" or puppet governments which did the will of the international corporate class, to the detriment of their nationals. According to Nkrumah, "[t]he result of neo-colonialism is that foreign capital is used for the exploitation rather than for the development of the less developed parts of the world."[155] He felt that neocolonialism could be battled as long as countries followed non-alignment polices, such as those of Ghana. Foreign investment could have a beneficial effect as long as it was "invested in accordance with a national plan drawn up by the government of the non-aligned State with its own interests in mind."[156]

The ideas proffered by development economists and neo-Marxist/ dependency thinkers helped discredit capitalism in many African intellectual circles by minimizing its potential to produce either sustained economic development or eventual economic autonomy. They also were ideas which dovetailed with the ideas and personal interests of many members of the new ruling elite in sub-Saharan Africa. The past injustices of the colonial system which had established strong economic businesses owned by metropolitan citizens or countries made their nationalization even more palatable, and it also meant that no strong domestic bourgeois class would oppose this agenda. The citizens of these countries believed that their states, led by fellow citizens, bolstered with the domestic or state ownership of industries, and bequeathed the power of planning, would lead them to economic prosperity and political freedom. All the signs pointed in the same direction.

CONCLUSIONS FOR CHAPTERS 3 AND 4

Political elites in most countries of sub-Saharan Africa consolidated significant amounts of political power into their own hands. Furthermore, most countries had extended the state's control over economic matters to a significant degree—all by the late-1970s. By then, most of the one-party states had been formed, the first wave of military coups had swept through the region, and the nationalization of large industries, if they had taken place, had been mostly completed. The ability of the first truly identifiable independence party to capture and consolidate power resulted from several factors: (1) the relative power vacuum in which the first elections were held; (2) the advantages that accrued to the first national anticolonial movement to form an effective political party; (3) the relative weakness of alternative political parties; (4) the nature of the electoral institutions created by the colonial powers—within unitary systems; and (5) ideologies which supported the consolidation of power. Once the party won office, they had several means of tightening their grip on power including: (1) control over state patronage; and (2) use of the coercive arms of the state. Once these parties were in place, their power was such that a military coup was usually required to bring about a change in rule. It should be remembered, however, that coups also served as a means for consolidating power where no party was able to do so.

The rapid extension of state control over the economic sphere was achieved through the following factors: (1) the rapid expansion of state agencies; (2) programs of nationalization, indigenization, and Africanization; (3) programs of state-sponsored industrialization; (4) an international climate which checked Western powers from reversing these new programs by military force; (5) the weakness of domestic and foreign bourgeois classes; (6) the influence of development economists; (7) ideologies which undermined capitalism and advocated state-centered development policies; and

(8) the self-interests of political elites and their class interests. In sum, most material, ideological, and structural variables all pointed in the direction of power consolidation in sub-Saharan Africa from the 1960s to the late 1980s.

Although the degree of consolidation of either economic or political power differed slightly from country to country, most had one-party states or military governments and most were unitary. Although most countries had inward-oriented development policies, Ivory Coast, Kenya, Senegal, Malawi, Mauritius, Cameroon, and Botswana were more outward-oriented than others.[157] Furthermore, although almost all states in the region exhibited some level of state-ownership of the economy, significant differences in the degree of state-ownership in the economy could be seen. This difference in the degree of state ownership in the economy was pivotal and accounted for most of the differences in the degree of inward-oriented development—which in turn would have important implications for incomes in the region.[158] States with majority state ownership of most of their capital-intensive industries or of major oil or mineral export sectors were more inward-oriented. Nonetheless, many of the differences across countries concerning the level of political and economic power in the hands of the political elites were a question of degree.

NOTES

1. *Statistics of Sanctioned Posts in the Public Services of Nigeria,* prepared by the Chief Statistician, Lagos. Comparative Tables 1960–1961 to 1965–1966; cited in Ruth First, *Power in Africa* (New York: Pantheon Books, 1970), p. 106.

2. Ibid.

3. Ibid. Calculated from text.

4. Ibid., p. 110.

5. Crawford Young and Thomas Turner, *The Rise and Decline of the Zairian State* (Madison, WI: University of Wisconsin Press, 1985), p. 86.

6. Ibid. The military numbers do not include police.

7. Taken from Peter S. Heller and Alan A. Tait, "Government Employment and Pay: Some International Comparisons," *Occasional Paper 24* (Washington, D.C.: International Monetary Fund, October 1983).

8. Peter R. Fallon and Luiz A. Pereira da Silva, in David L. Lindauer and Barbara Nunberg, eds., *Rehabilitating government: pay and employment reform in Africa* (Washington, DC: World Bank, 1994): 82–102, p. 86–87.

9. Calculated from Ibid.

10. U.N. Secretary General, *Permanent Sovereignty Over Natural Resource,* A/9716 (Supplement to E/5425), 20 September 1974; cited in Leslie L. Rood, "Nationalisation and Indigenisation in Africa," *Journal of Modern African Studies* 14, 2 (1976): 427–47, p. 431.The sample was of 62 nations.

11. Ibid.

12. Young and Turner, *Rise and Decline*, p. 289.

13. For details see Ibid., pp. 288–96; also Michael Schatzberg, "Zaire," in Timothy Shaw and Olajide Aluko, eds., *The Political Economy of African Foreign Policy* (Aldershot, UK: Gower, 1984): 283–318.

14. Young and Turner, *Rise and Decline*, p. 288.

15. Richard L. Sklar, *Corporate Power in an African State* (Los Angeles: University of California Press, 1975), p. 52.

16. James H. Cobbe, *Governments and Mining Companies in Developing Countries* (Boulder: Westview Press, 1979), p. 245; also Sklar, *Corporate Power*, p. 34.

17. Marian Radetzki, *State Mineral Enterprises: An Investigation into Their Impact on International Mineral Markets* (Washington, D.C.: Resources for the Future, 1985), p. 113.

18. See especially Sayre Schatz, *Nigerian Capitalism* (Berkeley: University of California Press, 1977); Thomas J. Biersteker, *Multinationals, the State and Control of the Nigerian Economy* (Princeton, NJ: Princeton University Press, 1987); Claude Ake, ed., *Political Economy of Nigeria* (London: Longman, 1985); and Emeka Ezeife, "Nigeria," in Adebayo Adedeji, ed., *Indigenization of African Economies* (London: Hutchinson & Co. Ltd, 1981): 164–185; also for general political economy of Nigeria see I. William Zartman, *The Political Economy of Nigeria* (New York: Praeger Publishers, 1983), includes bibliography.

19. Cliff Edogun, "The Structure of State Capitalism in the Nigerian Petroleum Industry," in Claude Ake, ed., *Political Economy of Nigeria* (London: Longman, 1985), p. 94.

20. Tom Forrest, *Politics and Economic Development in Nigeria* (Boulder, CO: Westview Press, 1993), p. 134. Computed from Table 7.1.

21. Rood, "Nationalisation and Indigenisation, p. 430.

22. Schatz, *Nigerian Capitalism*, p. 58.

23. Rood, "Nationalisation and Indigenisation," pp. 432–33.

24. Ibid.

25. For overview see Ezeife, "Nigeria," pp. 164–86.

26. Schatz, *Nigerian Capitalism*, p. 59; also Thomas J. Biersteker, "Indigenization and the Nigerian Bourgeoisie: Dependent Development in an African Context," in Paul M. Lubeck, ed., *The African Bourgeoisie: Capitalist Development in Nigeria, Kenya, and the Ivory Coast* (Boulder, CO: Lynne Rienner Publishers, 1987): 255–62; Forrest, *Nigeria*, pp. 153–57.

27. Paul Kennedy, *African Capitalism: The Struggle for Ascendancy* (Cambridge: Cambridge University Press, 1988), p. 62.

28. Forrest, *Nigeria*, p. 154.

29. Schatz, *Nigerian Capitalism*, p. 59.

30. Forrest, *Nigeria*, p. 155.

31. Kennedy, African Capitalism, p. 62.

32. Paul Collins, "The State and Industrial Capitalism in West Africa," *Development and Change* 14, 3 (July 1983), p. 407.

33. Young and Turner, *Rise and Decline*, pp. 326–62.

34. Jean-François Bayart, *The State in Africa: The Politics of the Belly* translated by Mary Harper et al. (New York: Longman, 1993), p. 84; Young and Turner, *Rise and Decline*, p. 335.

35. Thomas M. Callaghy, *The State-Society Struggle: Zaire in Comparative Perspective* (New York: Columbia University Press, 1984), p. 191.

36. Young and Turner, *Rise and Decline*, p. 356.

37. Ibid., p. 354.

38. Claude Ake, "Kenya," in Adedeji, ed., *Indigenization of African Economies*, pp. 187–203, p. 195.

39. Ibid., pp. 188–90.

40. David Himbara, *Kenyan Capitalist, the State, and Development* (Boulder, CO: Lynne Rienner Publishers, 1994), p. 135.

41. Rood, "Nationalisation and Indigenisation," p. 430.

42. William Tordoff, *Government and Politics in Africa 2nd Edition* (Bloomington: Indiana University Press, 1993), p. 130.

43. Ibid., p. 129.

44. D.K. Fieldhouse, *Black Africa 1945–1980: Economic Decolonization & Arrested Development* (Boston: Unwin Hyman, 1986), p. 226.

45. Ibid.

46. Adebayo Adedeji, "The raison d'être of indigenization," part 1 of Chapter 2: "Historical and theoretical background," in Adedeji, ed., *Indigenization of African Economies*, p. 30.

47. Tordoff, *Government and Politics*, p. 130; John Holm, "Botswana: A Paternalistic Democracy," in Larry Diamond et al., eds., *Democracy in Developing Countries: Africa Vol 2* (Boulder, CO: Lynne Rienner Publishers, 1988), p. 203.

48. Holm, "Botswana," p. 203.

49. Ibid.

50. For an overview of industrialization in Africa see Martin Fransman, ed., *Industry and Accumulation in Africa* (London: Heinemann, 1982); and Gerald M. Meier and William F. Steel, *Industrial Adjustment in Sub-Saharan Africa* (London: Oxford University Press, 1989).

51. World Bank, *Sub-Saharan Africa: From Crisis to Sustainable Growth* (Washington, DC: World Bank, 1989), p. 222.

52. Ibid.

53. John Rapley, *Ivoirien Capitalism: African Entrepreneurs in Côte d'Ivoire* (Boulder, CO: Lynne Rienner Publishers, 1993), p. 71.

54. Cobbe, *Governments and Mining Companies*, pp. 192 and 208.

55. "Carats as Carrots in Botswana," *The Southern African Economist* (February/March 1988), p. 44.

56. John R. Nellis, "Public Enterprises in Sub-Saharan Africa," in Barbara Grosh and Rwekaza S. Mukandala, eds., *State-Owned Enterprises in Africa* (Boulder, CO: Lynne Rienner Publishers, 1994), pp. 6–7.

57. Ibid., p. 3.

58. Ibid., pp. 5–8, but the categories for majority state owned from John James Quinn. Using majority state ownership as the relevant criteria and 24 countries African

nations only. See John James Quinn, *The Road oft Traveled: Development Policies Majority State Ownership of Industry in Africa* (Westport, CT: Praeger, 2002).

59. Nellis, "Public Enterprises in Sub-Saharan Africa," p. 6.

60. Ibid., p. 7.

61. Taken from Heller and Tait, "Government Employment and Pay; see also Quinn *Road oft Traveled.*

62. Quinn, *Road oft Traveled*, p. 39.

63. World Bank, *World Bank Development Report 1987* (Washington, D.C., 1987), p. 82.

64. For discussion of the political rational for economic policy see Robert H. Bates, *Market and States in Tropical Africa: The Political Basis of Agricultural Policies* (Berkeley and Los Angeles: University of California, 1981).

65. Anne O. Krueger, "Virtuous and Vicious Circles in Economic Development," *American Economic Review* 83, no. 1–2 (May 1993): 351–55.

66. Although tariffs and non-tariff barriers are the usual indices of protection, they are problematic for several reasons. First, they do not necessarily capture all forms of protection. Second, such things as smuggling and black-marketeering remain uncaptured in such a measure. Third, tariffs are not uniformly applied in the Third World. In fact, one researcher calls into question the ability of scholars to measure outward orientation at all. See Lant Prichett, "Measuring Outward Orientation in Developing Countries: Can it be Done?" *World Bank Working Paper* (Washington, D.C.: The World Bank, 1991).

67. The tariff and non-tariff numbers in this section were compiled from the *Handbook of Trade Control Measures of Developing Countries: A Statistical Analysis of Trade Control Measures of Developing Countries 1987* (Geneva: United Nations Conference on Trade and Development, 1987).

68. Currency overvaluation was in effect a tax on exports and a subsidy for imports. Tariffs helped offset a blanket decrease of subsidies for imports by making particular imports more expensive. For logic and prevalence of currency overvaluation, see especially Bates, *Market and States*; and World Bank, *From Crisis to Sustainable Growth*; also Quinn *Road oft Traveled.*

69. All numbers on overvaluation are determined by taking the difference between the official and black market rates for domestic currency (valued in the dollar) and dividing by the official level. These numbers were taken from *Pick's Currency Yearbook* (New York: Pick Publication Corporation, Various years) and *World Currency Yearbook* (Brooklyn, NY: International Currency Analysis, Inc., Various years). Moreover, since most of the former Francophone countries belonged to the West African Monetary Union (WAMU) [now it is the West African Economic and Monetary Union] where their collective exchange rate was pegged to the French Franc, currency overvaluation was not been the same problem for them as for the other countries, since it was the French treasury, and not their own, that made up any shortfalls (by this measure it did not exist). It was more prevalent in other countries during the first period.

70. Bates, *Market and States.* For collective action costs and analysis see Mancur Olson, *The Logic of Collective Action: Public Goods and the Theory of Groups* (Cambridge, MA: Harvard University Press, 1965).

71. The tax rate (nominal protection coefficient) is measured by the difference between producer prices in domestic currency (converted to dollars) and world prices divided by world prices. This includes only the taxation rates for the major export crop of a country. For sources, see Quinn, *Road oft Traveled*. Since part of the valuation of these figures comes from prices in hard currency, currency valuation is partially responsible for the shape of these numbers.

72. Although sugar was its largest export, finding adequate numbers which would render a representative tax rate for the calculation was problematic.

73. For relative strength of African bourgeoisie at the time of decolonization, see Kennedy, *African Capitalism*; also Lubeck, ed., *The African Bourgeoisie*. For the effect of bourgeoisie on government policy, see Charles E. Lindblom, *Politics and Markets: The World's Political-Economic Systems* (New York: Basic Books, Inc., 1977); for a critique of his work, see Dennis P. Quinn, Jr., *Restructuring the Automobile Industry: A Study of Firms and States in Modern Capitalism* (New York: Columbia University Press, 1988).

74. Kennedy, *African Capitalism*, p. 28.

75. Jean-Philippe Peemans, "Accumulation and Underdevelopment in Zaire: General Aspects in Relation to the Evolution of the Agrarian Crisis," in Nzongola-Ntalaja, eds., *The Crisis in Zaire: Myths and Realities* (Trenton, NJ: Africa World Press, Inc., 1986), p. 75.

76. Ibid.

77. Colin Leys, *Underdevelopment in Kenya: The Political Economy of Neo-Colonialism 1964–1971* (Los Angeles: University of California Press, 1975), p. 29.

78. Ibid., p. 34.

79. Nicola Swainson, "Indigenous Capitalism in Postcolonial Kenya," in Lubeck, ed., *The African Bourgeoisie*, p. 142.

80. Ibid., p. 148.

81. Rapley, *Ivoirien Capitalism*, p. 71. However, as mentioned above, the state-owned share of would overtake foreign industrial capital by 1980, with a 53% share.

82. Schatz, *Nigerian Capitalism*, p. 122.

83. Ibid.

84. Catherine Boone, "Accumulating Wealth, Consolidating Power: Rentierism in Senegal," in Bruce J. Berman and Colin Leys, eds., *African Capitalists in African Development* (Boulder, CO: Lynne Rienner Publishers, 1994), p. 170.

85. Stephen D. Krasner, *Defending the National Interest: Raw Materials Investments and U.S. Foreign Policy* (Princeton: Princeton University Press, 1978), p. 162.

86. Ibid., p. 148.

87. Ibid., pp. 144–46.

88. Young and Turner, *Rise and Decline*, pp. 288–96.

89. Krasner, *National Interest*, pp. 300–14, p. 331.

90. Sklar, *Corporate Power*, pp 182–88.

91. Ibid., p. 184.

92. Ibid., p. 186.

93. For theory of strategies, see Albert O. Hirschman, *Exit, Voice, and Loyalty: Responses to Decline in Firms, Organizations, and States* (Cambridge: Harvard University Press, 1970).

94. And, as Barrington Moore has demonstrated, a dependent bourgeois class does not push for democracy. See, Barrington Moore, *Social Origins of Dictatorship and Democracy: Lord and Peasant in the Making of the Modern World* (Boston: Beacon Press, 1966).

95. Larry Diamond, "Nigeria: Pluralism, Statism, and the Struggle for Democracy," in Diamond et al., eds., *Democracy in Developing Countries*, pp. 33–92; Also, see J. Gus Liebenow, *African Politics: Crises and Challenges* (Bloomington: Indiana University Press, 1986).

96. For explanation of clientism see Robert H. Jackson & Carl G. Rosberg, *Personal Rule in Black Africa: Prince, Autocrat, Prophet, Tyrant* (Berkeley: University of California Press, 1982), esp. pp. 38–47; Richard Sandbrook, "Patrons, clients, and Factions: New Dimensions of Conflict Analysis in Africa," *Canadian Journal of Political Science* 5, 1 (March 1972): 104–19; also Naomi Chazan et al., *Politics and Society in Contemporary Africa* (Boulder, CO: Lynne Rienner Publishers, 1988), pp. 172–177; and Robert Fatton Jr., *Predatory Rule: State and Civil Society in Africa* (Boulder, CO: Lynne Rienner Publishers, 1992), pp. 53–65. For effects of entrench interest groups on economic outcomes, even in a democracy, see Mancur Olson, *The Rise and Decline of Nations: Economic Growth, Stagflation, and Social Rigidities* (New Haven, CT: Yale University Press, 1984).

97. For example of patronage and power see Larry Diamond, "Class Formation and the Swollen State," *The Journal of Modern African Studies* 25, 4 (1987): 567–90; Sayre P. Schatz, "Pirate Capitalism and the Inert Economy of Nigeria," *The Journal of Modern African Studies* 22, 1 (1984): 45–57; Bayart, *The State in Africa*; Bates, *Market and States*; Anne O. Krueger, "The Political Economy of the Rent-Seeking Society," *The American Economic Review*, 60, 3 (June 1974): 291–303.

98. Krueger, "Virtuous and Vicious Circles."

99. Fatton, *Predatory Rule*, pp. 58–65; Jackson and Rosberg, *Personal Rule*, pp. 44–46; Larry Diamond, "Class Formation;" and Callaghy, *The State-Society Struggle*, pp. 185–94.

100. Others have tended to define the dominant class "as one whose members own and control the means of economic production." Sklar argued that power, and hence class formation, can flow from sources other than economic ones. Richard L. Sklar, "The Nature of Class Domination in Africa," *The Journal of Modern African Studies* 17, 4 (1979), p. 531.

101. Ibid., p. 538.

102. Ibid.

103. Diamond, "Class Formation," p. 569.

104. See Jackson and Rosberg, *Personal Rule*, p. 19.

105. From an interview with "60 Minutes," cited in George B. N. Ayittey, *Africa Betrayed*, forward by Makaziwe Mandela (New York: St. Martin's Press, 1992), p. 254.

106. Callaghy, *The State-Society Struggle*, p. 179.

107. Kennedy, *African Capitalism*, p. 69; see also Young and Turner, *Rise and Decline*, pp. 326–62.

108. Guy Gran, *Zaire: The Political Economy of Underdevelopment* (New York: Praeger, 1979), p. 251. This was a result of the Zairianization and Radicalization schemes discussed above.

109. Schatz, "Pirate Capitalism," p. 47.

110. Ayittey, *Africa Betrayed*, p. 252.

111. Ibid.

112. Ibid., p. 242.

113. Ibid., p. 248.

114. For an overview of the various meanings of this term, see Samir Amin, "Nationalism," in John Eatwell et al., eds., *The New Palgrave: Economic Development* (New York: W.W. Norton, 1989): 247–51.

115. Thomas Hodgkin, *Nationalism in Colonial Africa* (New York: New York University Press, 1957), p. 115.

116. For analysis of effects of nationalism on economics see Harry G. Johnson, "A Theoretical Model of Economic Nationalism in New and Developing State," *Political Science Quarterly* 80, 2 (June 1965): 169–85.

117. Rood, "Nationalisation and Indigenisation," p. 428.

118. F. X. Sutton, "Planning and Rationality in the Newly Independent State in Africa," *Economic and Cultural Change* 10 (Oct-July 1961–62), p. 45.

119. For the debate on Soviet planning, see Michael Lipton, *Why Poor People Stay Poor: Urban Bias in World Development* (Cambridge, MA: Harvard University Press, 1976): 121–30; Amiya Kumar Bagchi, "Development Planning," in Eatwell et al., eds., *New Palgrave*, pp. 98–108.

120. Charles E. Stanley, *A History of Economic Thought: From Aristotle to Arrow* (Cambridge, MA: Blackwell, 1989): 222–40; Deepak Lal, *The Poverty of Development Economics* (Cambridge Mass.: Harvard University Press, 1985), pp. 7–10; see also See, for example, Peter A. Hall, ed., *The Political Power of Economic Ideas: Keynesianism Across Nations* (Princeton: Princeton University Press, 1989).

121. Gerald M. Meier, "The Formative Period," in Gerald M. Meier and Dudley Seers, eds., *Pioneers in Development* (Washington D.C.: Oxford University Press for World Bank, 1984).

Meier, "The Formative Period," p. 14.

122. See especially I. M. D. Little, *Economic Development: Theory Policy and International Relations* (New York: Basic Books, 1982); Tony Killick, *Development Economics in Actions: A Study of Economic Policies in Ghana* (London: Heinemann, 1978): esp. Chapter 2; H. W. Arndt, *Economic Development: The History of an Idea* (Chicago: University of Chicago Press, 1987), pp. 115–47; Fieldhouse, *Black Africa*, esp. pp. 85–90; Meier and Seers, eds., *Pioneers in Development*; Michael F. Lofchie, "The New Political Economy in Africa." in David E. Apter and Carl G. Rosberg, eds., *Political Development and the New Realism in Sub-Saharan Africa* (Charlottesville: University of Virginia Press, 1994), pp. 160–65; Albert O. Hirschman, *Essays in Trespassing: Economics to Politics and Beyond* (Cambridge: Cambridge University Press, 1981); and Lal, *Poverty of Development Economics*.

123. However, Hirschman holds that some development economists believed in the mutual benefit of trade. Hirschman, *Essays in Trespassing*, esp. pp. 1–24;

124. Ibid., p. 6.

125. Meier, "The Formative Period," p. 16.

126. Ibid., p. 7.

127. Alexander Gerschenkron, *Economic Backwardness in Historical Perspective* (Cambridge, MA: Harvard University Press, 1962); Albert O. Hirschman, *The Strategies of Economic Development* (New Haven, 1958).

128. This was argued in Ragnar Nurske, *Problems of Capital Formation in Underdeveloped Countries* (Oxford: Blackwell, 1953).

129. Harvey Leibenstein, *Economic Backwardness and Economic Growth* (New York: Wiley, 1957); Killick, *Development Economics in Action*, p. 13.

130. Simon Kuznets, *Postwar Economic Growth* (Cambridge, MA: Harvard University Press, 1964).

131. Gunner Myrdal, *Economic Theory and Under-Developed Regimes* (London: Methuen, 1957).

132. W. W. Rostow, *The Stages of Economic Growth* (Cambridge: Cambridge University Press, 1960).

133. Killick, *Development Economists in Action*, p. 13.

134. Meier, "The Formative Period," p. 14.

135. See R. Prebisch, *The Economic Development of Latin America and its Principal Problems* (New York: United Nations, 1950); and H. Singer, "The distribution of gains between investing and borrowing countries," *American Economic Review* 40 (May 1950): 473–85.

136. Killick, *Development Economics in Action*, p. 13.

137. Hollis Chenery, "Comparative Advantage and Development Policy," *American Economic Review* 51, 1 (March 1961): 18–51.

138. Lofchie, "Political Economy in Africa," pp. 164–65; also Kennedy, *African Capitalism*.

139. Fieldhouse, *Black Africa*, p. 89.

140. For the debate on the Soviet approach to development see Lipton, *Urban Bias*, pp. 121–30; also see Chandler Morse, "The Economics of African Socialism," in William H. Friedland and Carl G. Rosberg, eds., *African Socialism* (Stanford, CA: Stanford University Press, 1964): 35–52.

141. *Yearbook of the United Nations 1961*, p. 229, italics added by Leys. Quoted in Colin Leys, "African Economic Development in Theory and Practice," in "Black Africa," Special Issue of Dædalus, p. 99.

142. Ibid., p. 100.

143. Fieldhouse, *Black Africa*, p. 85.

144. Tordoff, *Government and Politics*, p. 17–18.

145. Paul A. Baran, *Political Economy of Growth* (New York: Monthly Review Press, 1957).

146. Leys, *Underdevelopment*, p. 11.

147. Arndt, *Economic Development*, p. 118.

148. For examples of this viewpoint, see Immanuel Wallerstein, *The Modern World System* (New York: Academic Press, 1974); André Gunder Frank, *Capitalism*

and Underdevelopment in Latin America (New York: Monthly Review Press, 1967); Samir Amin, *Accumulation on a World Scale 2 Vol* (New York: Monthly Review Press, 1974); Theotonio Dos Santos, "The Structure of Dependence," in K.T. Fann and Donald C. Hodges, eds., *Readings in U.S. Imperialism* (Boston: Porter Sargent, 1971): 225–36. For critical overviews of dependency theory see Michael Lofchie, *The Policy Factor: Agricultural Performance in Kenya and Tanzania* (Boulder, CO: Lynne Rienner Publishers, 1989), pp. 21–35; also Bill Warren, *Imperialism: Pioneer of Capitalism* (London: Verso, 1980), pp. 139–52; for sympathetic overviews see Vicky Randall and Robin Theobald, *Political Change and Underdevelopment: A Critical Introduction to Third World Politics* (Durham, NC: Duke University Press, 1985), pp. 99–136; Colin Leys, *Underdevelopment in Kenya: The Political Economy of Neo-Colonialism 1964–1971* (Berkeley and Los Angeles, University of California Press, 1975), pp. 1–27; and for a neutral review see H.W. Arndt, *Economic Development: The History of an Idea* (Chicago: University of Chicago Press, 1987), pp. 115–47.

149. For an overview see Tony Smith, "Requiem or New Agenda for Third World Studies?" World Politics 37, 4 (July 1985) 532–61; The phrase "hewers of wood and drawers of water" originated in Joshua 9: 21–27. King James Version of the Bible.

150. Warren, *Imperialism*, p. 140.

151. Peter Evens, *Dependent Development: The Alliance of Multinational, State, and Local Capital in Brazil* (Princeton: Princeton University Press, 1979), p. 32.

152. Fernando Henrique Cardoso and Enzo Faletto, *Dependency and Development in Latin America*, Translated by Marjorie Mattingly Urquidi (Los Angeles: University of California Press, 1971); Evens, *Dependent Development*.

153. Kwame Nkrumah, *Neo-Colonialism: The Last Stage of Imperialism* (New York: International Publishers, 1965); Leys, *Underdevelopment*. For contrary views on the nature of local class formation see Richard L. Sklar, "Postimperialism: A Class Analysis of Multinational Corporate Expansion," in Becker et al., eds., *Postimperialism*, pp. 19–40; also Becker and Sklar "Why Postimperialism?" in Becker et al., eds., *Postimperialism*, pp. 1–18.

154. Cited in Leys, *Underdevelopment*, p. 26.

155. Nkrumah, *Neo-Colonialism*, p. x.

156. Ibid.

157. Quinn, *Road oft Traveled*.

158. Ibid; also John J. Quinn, "The Managerial Bourgeoisie: Capital Accumulation, Development and Democracy," in David G. Becker and Richard L. Sklar, eds., *Postimperialism and World Politics* (Westport, CT: Praeger, 1999): 219–52.

Chapter 5

The Second Geopolitical Shift

African Political and Economic Reforms in International and Regional Contexts

In the second period, sub-Saharan Africa again experienced significant and region-wide reforms and restructurings of their fundamental economic and political institutions and practices beginning in the late 1980s and early 1990s. These events transpired relatively quickly by historic standards, just as in the wake of the prior geopolitical shift. In the political sphere, nearly every nation in sub-Saharan Africa abandoned one-party or no-party (read military) regimes and formally adopted multiparty electoral regimes within a short period. Before 1989, most nations had featured de jure one-party regimes; however, by 1994, no de jure African one-party regimes were still in place.[1]

In the economic sphere, as well, a marked change in the institutions and practices of the region was evident. Although a liberalization of economic policies had begun in the mid- to late-1980s, the pace and scope of these reforms quickened and deepened after the Cold War.[2] At one end of the spectrum, nearly all African nations rejected Afro-Marxism as their official developmental ideology by 1993.[3] Most African socialist countries also abandoned this approach, though this trend began earlier.[4] Moreover, the rise of conditionality linking multilateral economic aid to economic liberalization was so extensive that the vast majority of African nations had come under some form of structural adjustment lending programs. Finally, the privatization of many majority state-owned firms in the region also began slowly during the late Cold War period, which accelerated thereafter.

The major transformations of the regional institutions and practices were quickened by both regional and international changes associated with the second geopolitical shift. On the one hand, the emergence of common African political and economic institutions and practices were constructed upon the common regional social, political, economic, and intellectual foundations established in the wake of the prior geopolitical shift. Most countries had

121

been ruled by one-or no-party authoritarian regimes; most had had mildly to strongly inward-oriented development policies; most had had industrial policies of import substitution industrialization (ISI), most had faced rising levels of debt, most had had economies overly reliant upon a primary export commodity, most had experienced overall poor economic performance, and most had extended few political and civil rights to their citizens. African societies had experienced weak, corrupt, and inefficient states as well as declining incomes during most of the Cold War period.

On the other hand, clearly part of the explanation for the region-wide shift, as well as its timing, rested on non-African political, military, economic, and intellectual foundations, which were associated with the second geopolitical shift. Worldwide shifts in political and economic liberalization were underway and increased in the wake of the geopolitical shift, though Africa was a trailing part. Communist or socialist nations lost their most visible socialist champions with the fall of the Soviet Union and China's slow embrace of more liberal economic reforms. Beyond symbolism, followers of Marxism-Leninist could no longer find sources of international aid for adhering to such ideologies. Moreover, a reinvigorated America pushed for more liberalization of economic and political structures by linking aid to such changes, both bilaterally and through its influence in the World Bank, the IMF, and GATT (later the WTO).

Moreover, intellectual forces and voices critical of one-party and no-party states as well as inward-oriented development practices had become had become more dominant worldwide; in fact, neoliberal ideas of deregulation, free trade, and good governance (AKA democracy) were forming a new consensus in Western-led international financial institutions (IFIs).[5] The emergence of the norm of good governance and its adoption by aid agencies emerged right around 1989 and 1990, simultaneously with the end of the Cold War.[6] Given this rising consensus, America and her Western allies began tying the initiation of political and economic reforms to the continued flow of development aid. The material rewards or punishments reinforced perceived rising views on the best routes to growth, development, sound governance, and the reduction of corruption.

Since so many nations were reforming simultaneously, the overhaul of prevailing political and economic institutions and practices was undertaken during a relatively common intellectual climate and geopolitical environment. Therefore, the institutions and practices which emerged did so as a result of the interplay of both external and internal factors—consisting of both ideological and material forces. Despite the environment of change at the time, the self-interest of regional leaders did not change in this new period; they still wanted to maximize their political power and their chances of reelection; however, implementing many of these reforms was undermining to their patronage systems and was therefore a potential political threat to them.[7] Thus, unlike in the first period, not all the vectors went in the same direction; many were pointing in opposite directions and the outcomes were somewhat uneven as a result. Undertaking political and economic reforms was often seen as undermining the power of domestic elites, and they were often undertaken quite reluctantly.[8]

THE SECOND GEOPOLITICAL SHIFT

The second geopolitical shift witnessed the rapid decline and disintegration of one of the two poles of the bipolar period and the emergence of the "primacy" of the remaining pole, the United States. The speed of the shift was sudden: very few thinkers realized that the Soviet Union was about to fall, even though it was widely recognized that significant reforms had to be enacted to keep the Soviet Union viable, economically and militarily. According to one scholar, "[t]he possibility of precipitous Soviet decline seemed so remote and so speculative up until 1989 that little analytical energy was devoted to working through scenarios involving a declining challenger in the context of a prolonged great-power rivalry."[9] When Gorbachev embarked on his attempts to reform the Soviet Union, few knew that the ideological foundation upon which the edifice was built would soon crack and crumble.

The time between Gorbachev's initiation of reforms until the collapse of the Soviet Union was a mere six years. His first announcement for economic reform of the Soviet Union came in 1985. His call for openness (political reform or *glasnost*) was only three years later in 1988. This announcement came the same year as the end of the Brezhnev Doctrine, leading to the withdrawal of Soviet troops from Eastern Europe. This step removed the Soviet military backstop for the authoritarian regimes in the region, many of which would soon transition away from one-party socialist systems to multiparty democracies. The fall of the Berlin Wall was just one year later, in 1989. The subsequent regional changes were rapid: most authoritarian regimes supported by the Soviet Union were overthrown the same year. The two Germanys were united also in 1990. By 1991, the Soviet Union itself had dissolved into Russia and fourteen others.[10]

This collapse of the Soviet Union, and the Warsaw Pact with it, took the world by surprise. It left a potentially militarily super dominant America at the helm of North Atlantic Treaty Organization (NATO) with no corresponding military balance against them. In 1990, President George H. W. Bush announced that a new world order was in place as the US led a worldwide coalition to reverse Iraq's invasion of Kuwait. Analysts debated whether the world system had become unipolar, with the US as hegemon, or if it was uni-multipolar (with the US as superpower surrounded by several great powers).[11] The former French Foreign Minister Hubart Vedrine famously called the US a hyperpower (*hyperpuissance* in French), instead of a superpower. American was a hegemon without rival—militarily.[12] According to Nye:

> The American Navy was equal in size to the next 17 navies, American forces had air superiority, the United States took the lead in space and cyber space, and the US military budget represented nearly half the global total . . . No other state in modern history has had such military preponderance as the United States.[13]

This is stated with the caveat that Russia still maintained a vast nuclear arsenal (with second strike ability) that did not disappear with the geopolitical shift.

With the unification of so much of Western Europe in the European Union, the economic development of Japan, and the growing manufacturing base of China, the US did not have the same disproportionate economic power as in the wake of WWII, though it remained the largest single economy in the world by most measures.[14] The European Union (with twenty-five members) matched the US in economic output in 2004 (both were near $11 trillion and with about 20% of world GDP).[15] As of 2013, the estimated GDP of the EU was just slightly under the US at $15.83 trillion in 2013 compared to $16.72 trillion, respectively.[16] Nonetheless, the North American Free Trade Area (NAFTA) had a combined economy that was larger than Europe's, and scholars expect America (and NAFTA with it) to grow faster than Europe.[17] So Europe and Japan together could be seen as a balance, economically, against North America. Regardless of potential goals and conflicts over the balance of power, American and European goals in terms of free trade, democracy, and capitalism are largely in harmony, though coordination is required for alignment to occur.

Although China is recently discussed as a rising economic rival to the US, in 1990, close to the time of the shift, China's GDP was $0.4B, while the US's was $5.4B.[18] Moreover, their per capita GDPs were $370 and $21,970, respectively. Thus, at the time of the geopolitical shift, China was not as much on the radar screen as it would be later.

Layne, in analyzing arguments about US in the two decades following the end of the Cold War, stated: "It is beyond dispute, however, that the United States still enjoys a commanding preponderance of power over its nearest rivals."[19] Moreover, in another example of increasing Western power, the US-led North Atlantic Treaty Organization has extended itself deep into what used to be the Soviet sphere of influence. Just before the end of the Cold War, NATO had sixteen members. Beginning with the reunification of Germany (with bringing former East Germany into NATO), it expanded

Eastward. It came to include Poland, Hungary, the Czech Republic in 1999, and then Bulgaria, Estonia, Latvia, Lithuania, Romania, Slovakia, and Slovenia in 2004, and then Albania and Croatia in 2009.[20] NATO now stands at 28 members. This means that NATO has a potential of over four million active duty soldiers to call upon in case of an attack.[21] In addition, the US invaded Afghanistan and Iraq, both of which would have been unthinkable in the Cold War period. This combination of power has no rival, aside from its possible limits of use in asymmetrical warfare. It is only recently with Russia's apparent annexation of the Crimea (and prior invasion of Georgia) that we have seen a strong push back against American and Western expansion into what had been the Soviet heartland.[22] With this event, Russia was unceremoniously disinvited to the G8 economic summit.

Finally, with the fall of the Berlin Wall, the United States began using its increased power to promote the goals that have been at the heart of the Cold War contest. It "declared that free-market democracy is the world's only viable model for political and economic development, having fostered an open, globalized international economic system based on the 'Washington consensus' and multilateral institutions."[23] One prominent intellectual, Francis Fukuyama, argued in 1992 that the end of the Cold War coincided with the end of human political and economic evolution (in the Hegelian sense) with liberal democracy.[24] Some of the triumphalism may be less loudly trumpeted with the recent downturn in the US market due to lack of regulation of (or deep information concerning) derivatives, and their leveraging may have damaged the ascendant legitimacy of the Washington consensus. Despite the 2008 recession, the World Bank, International Monetary Fund (IMF), and United States Agency for International Development (USAID) are unlikely to change policy course regarding development policies in the developing world as a result (at least not in the short term).[25]

Thus, from 1985 until 1991, the Soviet Union unraveled, and America lost the only real counter-weight in economic, political, and military power from any other single state. As far as Europe is concerned, it could be a counter weight economically, though it was already democratic and was moving more toward private markets at the time. In fact, Europe has also signed on to the new liberal world view, in part or whole. As we will be discussed later, the worldwide movement toward the privatization of state-owned industries, often attributed to the Washington Consensus, was actually begun in the UK under Thatcher, and it spread first to the other states of Europe. Therefore, a rising Europe would be an unlikely challenger to status quo American core values or perceived self-interests in free trade and democracy. So, even more so than in the first period, the US would have significant influence and power to help shape the post-Cold War period, especially vis-à-vis political and economic liberalism. Moreover, especially in the two decades following the end of the Cold War, when countries were reacting to the new international geopolitical power structure which was emerging, few clear contenders were in view.

Worldwide Trends in Democratization

Aside from the Middle East, North Africa, and Eastern Europe, much of the larger international community outside of Africa appears to have already been on a path to increased democratization, or increases in political and civil rights, at the end of the Cold War, both as an empirical movement and an increasing normatively preferred form of government. That the movement for increased rights and more democracy was part of a global phenomenon is perhaps best known through the work of Samuel Huntington.[26] He suggested that democracy spreads internationally for a variety of reasons, including diffusion. Given that democracy diffuses or "snowballs," he suggested that democracy comes in waves (both forward and reverse since reverse waves are possible). He dated the third wave of democracy to 1974/5 when Portugal and Spain transitioned to democracy. It spread to Latin American in the late 1970s and the 1980s, and Asia in the late 1980s. Then following publication of his book, it spread (unevenly) to both Eastern Europe and Africa post-1989. Similar movements for economic liberalization began in the late 1980s, which have increased in scale and scope since the fall of the Berlin Wall.

At the beginning of the wave, in 1974, 29% of countries were ranked as "free" by Freedom House, and this number increased to 36% by 1989.[27] The number of "not free" countries fell from 46% in 1974 to 37% in 1989. By 2000, a decade after the end of the Cold War, 45% of all countries were coded as free and only 25% of the world's countries were ranked as not free. Therefore, the number of not free has fallen in this extension of the third wave from 46% to 25%, which is nearly a halving, while the number of free countries increased by 55% (29% to 45%). These trends may not be revolutionary, but they show steady progress toward greater increases in world levels of political and civil rights.

Comparing the levels of democracy by region, we see significant variation. Western Europe had nearly completely democratized following the Second World War, and the remaining countries liberalized in the 1970s. Most of Western Europe had therefore already democratized by the end of the Cold War, save for Turkey, which was ranked as partly free.[28]

In the Americas, most formerly authoritarian countries had already transitioned to democracy by 1989.[29] Countries such as Argentina, Brazil, Bolivia, Chile, Ecuador, El Salvador, Granada, Guatemala, Honduras, Nicaragua, Peru, and Uruguay had moved away from authoritarianism during the 1970s and 1980s.[30] In 1988/89, 25 countries were deemed to be free, six to be partially free, and four to be not free. Ten years later, in 1998/99, 24 countries were free, 10 partially free, and one not free. Twenty years later, in 2009, we see that 25 countries are listed as free, nine partly free, and only one as not free.

In Eastern Europe (listed as Central and Eastern Europe/Former Soviet Union (CEE and FSU)) and just before the end of the Cold War, no countries were ranked as free, and only two of the eight were listed as partly free. Ten years following the fall of the Berlin Wall, ten countries were coded as free, 11 were coded partly free, and six were not free. Twenty years later, 13 countries are coded as free, eight are listed as partly free, and seven as not free.

In Asia, (listed as Asia Pacific) in 1988/89, only 10 countries were coded as free, 14 partly free, and 10 were coded not free. Ten years later, 19 such countries were coded as free, nine partly free, and 10 not free. Twenty years later, 16 countries were listed as free, 15 partly free, and eight not free.

Finally (aside from sub-Saharan Africa), the Middle East and North Africa saw little movement in political liberalization until the "Jasmine revolution" of 2011; it began in Tunisia and spread to Egypt. Protests then spread to Syria, Libya, and Yemen. This particular wave has yet to be completed and its effects as of yet unknown: the civil war in Syria is particularly bloody and destabilizing and the American invasion of Iraq has also led to a state in continued conflict. Prior to the end of the Cold War, the region had one country listed as free, seven were coded as partly free, and ten were listed as not free. Ten years later, again only one country was listed as free, three were partly free, and 14 were coded as not free. In 2015, we see that two countries are considered to be free, three are partly free, and the rest (13) are not free.[31]

So, aside from some particular regions, the movement toward democracy or greater democratization was well underway prior to the end of the Cold War. The end of the Cold War would greatly impact regime change in Eastern Europe and sub-Saharan Africa and quickly.

Worldwide Trend in Economic Liberalization/Globalization

With the end of the Cold War, the world trading system got its largest overhaul since the creation of the Bretton Woods institutions with the creation of the World Trade Organization (WTO). This intergovernmental organization (IGO) replaced the General Agreement on Tariffs and Trade (GATT) in 1995. Also, and importantly, the GATT had successfully reduced average tariffs on world trade through a series of rounds, from 40% in 1940 to 5% in 1990. Despite these reductions in tariff levels, GATT did not have real power to impose sanctions nor did it cover things like services, property rights, or agriculture until the Uruguay Round (1986–1994), which created the WTO.[32] The new WTO has addressed key elements of concern for trade-related

aspects of intellectual property rights (TRIPs), but agricultural agreements
have proven, so far, to be beyond reach. Moreover, WTO rules have become
more binding than GATT rules were; the change from the GATT to the
WTO represents a movement away from political processes to more legal
ones. According to Gilpin, "the WTO is a full-fledged international organization rather than merely an international secretariat (like the GATT)."[33]
It also reduced or eliminated many important subsidies, "voluntary" export
restraints, non-Tariff Barriers (NTBs), and other diversions from free trade.

Not only was the WTO a stronger mechanism than the GATT, but more
countries also joined the GATT over the duration of the Cold War, with many
more nations joining the WTO. Over 128 members belonged to GATT, and
of these 29 joined after 1990, though six had joined between 1986 and 1990.[34]
In total, 153 members belong to the WTO, with an additional 29 countries
as observers. Since observers must commit to joining the WTO within five
years, about 80% of all countries will soon belong to this IGO.[35] Moreover,
most of the regions of the world are well represented in the WTO, save for
some Central and Eastern Europe/ Former Soviet countries and some North
African and Middle Eastern countries. Eleven countries from Eastern Europe
and seven from North Africa and the Middle East remain outside of this
regime, though many of them do have observer status.

The decrease in tariffs, in conjunction with the creation of the GATT and
then WTO, has promoted globalization dramatically during the Cold War as
well as after. As we can see in Figure 5.1, worldwide economic globalization

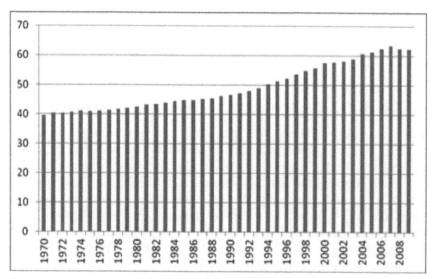

Figure 5.1   Economic Globalization: World Index 1970–2009.

had been on a slow increase during the Cold War, though it saw a very strong upswing following the end of the Cold War.[36] Using a weighted index of trade flows and trade restrictions, we see that the aggregate index of global economic globalization in 1970 was 40.19 (where 0 is autarky and 100 is pure free trade). This increased to 46.32 in 1989. By 1998, economic globalization had increased to 55.67, and in 2007, it was recorded at 64.23. Importantly, the creation of the WTO was in American economic interests, as well as its transnational corporations, though the GATT was also begun with strong American (and British) influence. As America has become more of an exporter of services and high tech industries, GATT no longer served American (perceived) interests as well as before.[37]

Rise of Bilateral Investment Treaties

One of the key elements of globalization not addressed by the Bretton Woods institutions was international property rights for investment. The spate of nationalizations worldwide from the late 1960s through the early 1980s testifies to this.[38] With the end of the Cold War, a proliferation of bilateral investment treaties (BITs) have sprouted that codify actions allowed to foreign companies and countries which have lost property.[39] These types of treaties make foreign direct investment (FDI) safer, should these treaties be honored. These treaties are held to lead to credible commitment. Although BITs began in the 1950s, they really "took off" after 1990. In one study explaining the rise of BITs, the end of the Cold War was significantly linked to their rise.[40] The rise of competitive exporting associated with the rise of globalization also was positively linked with their rise as well, and more BITs are held to lead to more FDI, as investors will chose to invest in countries with BITs over others, *ceteris paribus*. This also may have a diffusion element as well.

The frequencies reflected in these trends are such that, prior to 1989, there were 20 BITs worldwide signed per year as a high point in 1985 (though mostly there were 10 or fewer prior to 1985). Beginning in 1989, there were around 25 new treaties, and this climbed strongly nearly every year (in 1992, over 100 were signed), until 1996 when there were over 200.[41] These numbers trail downwards to just around 125 in 1999. So clearly, there was an explosion of these with the end of the Cold War.

International Trends in Privatization

Also, the movement toward economic liberalization and globalization, reflected in the selling of state owned assets, was also part of a larger international trend. Although many who follow emerging economies may think of privatization as stemming primarily from economic conditionality on the part of the World Bank and IMF, the recent worldwide wave of privatizations began in the United Kingdom following the election of Margaret Thatcher, and this was well before the end of the Cold War and not due to economic conditionality.[42] In fact, between 1980 and 2004, over a trillion dollars worth of state-owned firms were privatized worldwide, including over 8,000 acts of privatization.[43] Interestingly, the earliest privatizations within this wave came from OECD countries; this is also where most of the revenue was made.[44] Nonetheless, it was after the end of the Cold War that most of the privatizations in low- and middle-income countries occurred, and this trend accelerated until 1998 and beyond.[45] In fact, one author suggests the real question about privatization in the developing world is "how—not whether—to transfer state firms to private hands."[46] Worldwide, it was estimated that state owned enterprises' (SOE) share of global GDP fell from around 10% in 1979 to around 6% in 2001.[47]

Several measures of privatization are available, though revenue raised and acts of privatization are the two most common. Looking at the amount of revenue raised and number of privatization transactions by region (prior to 2004), North America and Europe together raised the most money with privatizations, $552 billion (1985), representing 871 individual sales.[48] East Asia and the Pacific saw the next highest revenue obtained from privatizations, at $318 billion, with 831 transactions. Latin America followed with revenues amounting to $197 billion, with 1,601 transactions. Eastern Europe and Central Asia followed in revenue raises, at $23.3 billion, though with the highest number of transactions at 2,453.[49] The Middle East and North Africa saw $19.9 billion raised, with 419 transactions. South East Asia was able to raise over $11 billion from such sales, with the fewest number of transactions at 335. Finally, sub-Saharan Africa raised the least amount of revenue, obtaining $9.5 billion, though it represented the second highest frequency of sales, with 1,662 transactions (just ahead of Latin America).

From another source, and with slightly different regional aggregations, a similar story can be seen from 1988 to 1998: Western Europe accounted for 52% of all such revenues, while Asia and Pacific accounted for 23%, Latin America had 15%, Eastern Europe and Former USSR had 4%, North American and Caribbean had 3%, and the Middle East and Africa (together) had 3%.[50] Much of this *initial* movement toward privatization occurred during the Cold War. In Europe, the UK, France, Turkey, Spain, West Germany, and even then socialist-led Italy had begun or had announced major privatizations in the 1980s. By contrast, before the end of the Cold War, very few communist countries had begun to dabble with privatization, though—importantly—China, Cuba, Hungary, and the Soviet Union were implementing *partial* privatization in order to reform and streamline their economies.[51] At the end of the Cold War, privatization in Africa seemed slower than in other regions, though the momentum was gaining.[52] Nellis suggests that Africa has privatized a smaller percentage of its state-owned enterprises (SOEs) than did other developing regions, especially when compared with Latin America: African countries had divested about 40% of their shares of SOEs by 2001.[53]

Why this International Trend towards Political and Economic Liberalization?

Increase in Relative Power of US and Europe

As we saw with the end of the Second World War, America had to compromise on several of its views concerning democracy and capitalism in order to keep allies during the Cold War period. With the change in international leadership away from a bipolar world with a liberal champion and a state socialist champion to one with a remaining pro-capitalism and pro-democracy hegemon, however, we should expect to see changes in the rules and norms of the international community to reflect the self-interests (and perceived self-interests) of the hegemon. Through a combination of "learning" and increasing influence at IGOs, the United States now can exert more influence on other countries' foreign policies, whether though economic, political, or military avenues.

Also, the United States, along with its allies in Europe and Japan, accounted for over half of the world's GDP in 2009.[54] These countries also have majority share voting in the World Bank and IMF and have achieved a consensus on linking political and economic liberalization through most bilateral aid as well as "good governance" and economic liberalization through multilateral aid. This gave the large, free market economies more say in the World Bank and IMF and drove many of these countries to distribute aid through them, instead of through the general assembly of the United Nations where one nation, one vote was the norm.

Within the European Union, there are twenty-eight countries, usually comprising the wealthiest countries outside of the US, Australia, Canada, and Japan. There are also five additional candidate countries. Therefore, America and its allies seem to have material and ideological control of the IGOs of the World Bank, IMF, and WTO. In the United Nations, clearly Russia, as the successor to the Soviet Union, is diminished in power, and China is only rising in power and not a balancer against the West yet, though both can exercise vetoes on the United Nations' Security Council. Therefore, American control of all IGOs is clearly bounded, though its power in the free trade organizations is clear.

Moreover, many of the countries which had been in the Soviet sphere of influence are now firmly aligned with "the West" in general, and NATO in particular. As mentioned above, Eastern Germany reunified with West Germany, and NATO came to include Albania, Bulgaria, Croatia, the Czech Republic, Estonia, Hungary, Latvia, Lithuania, Poland, Romania, Slovakia, and Slovenia.[55] NATO now has 28 members. These are the traditional European members, along with the US and Canada. This increases the relative power of capitalism as more countries are within the European Union and or NATO, which are all tied to America as hegemon and supporter of both democracy and free trade, at least rhetorically.

Decrease in Relative Power of Backers of State Socialism

This collapse of the Soviet Union also necessarily diminished the relative military, economic, and diplomatic power of non-democracies, and especially state socialist systems. This would mean that Russia no longer was using bilateral and multilateral ties to promote the spread of state socialism or to oppose liberal capitalism. Internationally, gone were the subsidies or military support for Marxist regimes throughout the world.[56] Also importantly, the withdrawal of Soviet troops from Eastern Europe took important military support away from these regimes, and they soon collapsed from popular protests.

Moreover, America and her allies no longer had to align with countries with poor human rights records just to keep them from joining the Soviet camp. Their departure from center stage of international power meant that normally marginalized developing countries no longer had a threat to defect to the socialist camp as part of their arsenal. Nonetheless, China is still authoritarian and wants to protect its sovereignty, though it no longer actively promotes Marxist-Leninism. China is in the odd position of defending the Leninist one-party system while (slowly) removing majority state control of the commanding heights of their economy, aside from "strategic" areas.

Also, neither the Russia nor China continues to advance a state-socialist or communist cause through their voting patterns in IGOs, such as the United Nations or its security council. Moreover, they would no longer cultivate allies in this competition or support those who remain in the battle. Nonetheless, these two countries still occasionally vigorously defend the norm of sovereignty by shielding non-democratic nations or those with poor human rights records.

Expanding European Union (EU)

The expansion of the EU could also be seen as helping deepen commitment for democracy and reliance upon capitalist markets by its example and regional norms. For example, any country wishing to join the European Union has to be a democracy; this is a political precondition of joining.[57] Therefore, some have argued that countries like Spain and Greece had to become stronger democracies to first join, and then to remain, in the European Union. Also, to be in the EU, members also have to have a market economy, though this clearly does not prohibit some state ownership (e.g., France, UK). It seems likely, however, that many of the early privatization in England and elsewhere in Europe were related to increasing European integration. Since there was to be free movement of goods, services, and people across borders, any state-owned firms which could not survive in the larger market would weigh down government budgets with increased subsidies. Despite some privatizations being linked to efficiency, clearly part of this trend is related to Margaret Thatcher's political views as well, though that would not explain the larger regional effects, aside from maybe an imitation or diffusion effect.

Role of Ideas: The Rising Legitimacy of Democracy and Capitalism

The collapse of the Soviet Union was taken by many, at least initially, as prima facie evidence that democracy and capitalist relations were superior to state-directed economic systems. Even the adoption of some democratic reforms within the Soviet Union signaled that entrenched political/bureaucratic interests could stall economic reform, so political reform had become a means to economic reform. In fact, both the Soviet Union and China adopted significant reforms of bureaucratic, state-directed economies in order to harness the power of markets for developmental reasons, though China has not adopted sweeping political reforms despite the tipping point almost presented by Tiananmen Square.

Moreover, the poor economic performance of countries which pursued state-led, inward-oriented development in the Near East, Latin America, and Africa was also seen as additional evidence that such approaches for development were inherently flawed.[58] By contrast, the rising strength of the Newly Industrializing Countries (NICs) was used as evidence that markets were superior to state direction (despite available evidence of significant state orchestration involved in this exporting approach).[59] The early successes of this model were often attributed to trade policies, though later malaise was chalked up to state dirigisme. (They were state-led, but outward oriented.)

Although many former communist countries are not democracies, those that are not have not endeavored to build their legitimacy of rule upon an anti-capitalist or anti-democratic foundation. Also, the finding from the democratic peace literature that democracies do not tend to go to war with one another gave added weight to the notion as more countries became democratic, the safer other democracies would be.[60] In fact, President George W. Bush cited this as a partial justifying reason for the invasion of Iraq: to remake the Middle East by fostering a new democracy.[61] Famously, Samuel Huntington as well as Fukuyama discussed the heightened universal appeals of democracy at this point in time.[62] Fukuyama, in particular, argued that the progression of human history as a dialectic struggle between ideologies was largely over and that the world would settle on liberal democracy with the end of the Cold War. He argued for the twin triumphs of political and economic liberalism.

Democracy, by itself, was also gaining grounds as a superior political system as well as a way to overcome the governance problems of many developing nations. The initial support for democracy came with bilateral aid agencies; in fact, the World Bank was initially not allowed to take the type of political institution into account for lending purposes during the Cold War.[63] By contrast, around 1989 the World Bank came to realize, or believe, that "good governance" was required for aid to developing nations to be effective.[64] Several studies have shown that good governance or a good policy regime (or the lack of corruption) was required for aid to be used effectively.[65] Therefore, good governance could become a Trojan horse to help bring about fundamental elements of accountability, participation, predictability, and transparency (e.g., the normal goals of democracy), which should reduce corruption and lead to better policy adopting and implementation.

Learning and the Failure of State-led Development/
Failure of State Socialism

Not only did the champions for state socialism quit the field, but the main ideological pillars supporting state-owned industries have also been nearly universally discredited. Most people feel that state-led inward-oriented development models for rapid and sustained development have failed, especially in the developing world, but also in Europe and Asia. Moreover, significant empirical evidence mounted during the Cold War period showed that inward-oriented development strategies and government control of industries were inefficient methods for attaining rapid and sustainable development.[66] In addition, the belief that one-party or no-party states are best for rapid economic development has also been undermined in most quarters.[67]

In fact, most of Eastern Europe, the states of the former Soviet Union, and Communist China have abandoned strict state socialism and adopted policies that are more capitalist in nature. The inherent problems of state socialism—such as the high cost and difficulty of central planning, the personal incentives for lower productivity, and the industrial incentives to hide difficulties—have become more widely recognized, even among scholars who are sympathetic to theories of social justice.[68]

The collapse of the Soviet Union also helped undermine the last major symbol of state socialism and facilitated learning about its failure. So socialism was reduced as an idea, per se, while its major supporters have either weakened or disappeared. Some argue that Marxism/Socialism as ideas or ideals remains strong, but most have to acknowledge that these ideas are on the defensive because they were both intellectual traditions and political movements, and in the latter sense they are greatly weakened.[69]

Not only has the state socialist path to development been largely discredited, but a growing consensus has also emerged that outward-oriented policies (laissez-faire according to some) are the best routes to development. The theories that underpin an outward-oriented development approach are well articulated, are gaining wide acceptance, and are being promoted by several international organizations.

The Bretton Woods international financial institutions, namely the World Bank and the International Monetary Fund (IMF), provide ideological support for these policies, and those who support such views tend to get promoted from within. For example, the World Bank researches and publishes economic analyses that strongly advocate the adoption of outward-oriented policies in Africa. Beginning with *Accelerated Development in Sub-Saharan Africa: An Agenda for Action*, (1981) continuing with *Sub-Saharan Africa: From Crisis to Sustainable Growth* (1989), and with *Adjustment in Africa: Reforms, Results, and the Road Ahead* (2001), the bank has attempted to gain the intellectual high ground and to refute the ideas set forth by the development economists and socialist thinkers. These works argue that economic advantages flow from simultaneously adopting outward-oriented economic policies and instituting smaller governments. They find that countries which pursued inward-oriented paths and/or with large state sectors had the worst economic experiences in the region. Other scholars outside of the bank have found similar results.[70]

In fact, the delegitimization of state socialism and inward-oriented policies has been so complete that economic debates tend to revolve around the question of how best to implement programs of economic restructuring, rather than entertaining the debates as to whether or not countries ought to do so.[71] Even among scholars on the left, less-popular voices that have long argued that capitalism can lead to development are now given more recognition.[72]

African countries, as well as some from Latin America, were seen as economic stragglers due to their developmental approaches of inward-oriented policies, import substitution industrialization, and authoritarianism. By contrast, the Asian tigers were seen as clear evidence that markets worked and that state directed economies did not–despite the fact that Asian success had a strong government hand in leadership and direction.[73] Even those who would argue that state-led export promotion is the best path to development, nearly all would agree that inward-oriented, import substitution development plans were a failure.[74] The development economists and their consensus have been abandoned.[75]

These ideas culminated in what would be called the "Washington Consensus."[76] This was an intellectual convergence of economic policy ideas that could be found within key American and IFIs in 1989. According to Williamson (who is said to have coined the term), "the Washington Consensus consists of the set of policies endorsed by the principal economic institutions located in Washington: the U.S. Treasury, the Federal Reserve Board, the International Monetary Fund, and the World Bank." [77] The term was meant to capture a real consensus of what worked and what did not in the immediate post-Reagan, post-Cold War period concerning Latin America—not to become synonymous for market fundamentalism, neoliberals, or market laissez-faire Reaganomics which set out to bash the state and to trust markets *über alles*.[78] According to Williamson, the key components of this consensus were these: (1) fiscal discipline, (2) a redirection of public expenditure priorities toward fields offering both high economic returns and the potential to improve income distribution, such as primary health care, primary education, and infrastructure, (3) tax reform (to lower marginal rates and broaden the tax base), (4) interest rate liberalization, (5) a competitive exchange rate, (6) trade liberalization, (7) liberalization of inflows of foreign direct investment, (8) privatization, 9) deregulation (to abolish barriers to entry and exit), and (10) secure property rights.[79]

Williamson has argued that his term has been misused as he only wished to portray a rising consensus, as mentioned previously, and not to recommend a set of policies to be imposed as orthodoxy upon other countries. Even though he intended the term to be descriptive, it has gained power as a result of the power of its backers and the consensus that emerged around it. When a consensus idea becomes institutionalized and incentives are attached to their adoption, then it becomes much more powerful.[80]

Bandwagoning and Diffusion

Moreover, it may be that the spread of democracy and economic liberal policy is partially caused by their own diffusion—each rides a tide of success.[81] However, diffusion processes are notoriously difficult to pin down because it "is hard to distinguish true diffusion from illusions of diffusion created by global trends, correlated disturbances, or the regional clustering of domestic factors."[82] Moreover, it may be difficult to distinguish it from learning or emulation, though Ikenberry suggests that the three main varieties of diffusion are external inducement, emulation, and social learning—which combine these ideas.[83] For democracy, in particular, Huntington argues that diffusion or bandwagoning is one of the keys to understanding the spread of democracy globally. Also, other scholars find that regimes tend to match the average degree of democracy or non-democracy among their contiguous neighbors. It was found that democracy was particularly strong in the US sphere of influence.[84] One study found that . . . "[s]ince 1815, the probability that a randomly chosen country will be a democracy is about 0.75 if the majority of its neighbors are democracies, but only 0.14 if the majority of its neighbors are non-democracies."[85] Others suggest that democracy diffusion within a region has a cascading effect, and regional clustering effects, not unlike what was described above.[86]

Economic learning and diffusion also seem at play in privatization and the liberalization of economic policy worldwide. The geo-political shift in the international community came with attendant changes in international norms and world social "learning?." Most importantly, people saw that the collapse of the Soviet Union was an acknowledgment of the inherent problems of state socialism and the relative advantages of democratic capitalist countries.

The shift in power relations helped facilitate this "learning," with the change in relative power of the remaining super and great powers. These players obtained increased power within new and existing international institutions which allowed them to exercise power to shape international regimes more to their liking. Developing country autonomy was reduced when the Soviet Union collapsed, and the relative power of the US and Europe vis-à-vis developing nations was increased. The movement away from inward-oriented policies towards more "free trade" policies began during the Cold War, but with the end of the Cold War the symbolic and rhetorical acceptance of such policies has been much higher. Most countries saw the writing on the wall. This allowed a shift in norms as well as the relative aims of IGOs such as the World Bank, IMF, and GATT (later WTO). A new consensus, the Washington Consensus, began to inform leaders of countries and intergovernmental organizations agencies and IFIs about the likely developmental outcomes of market-based outcomes versus state-led outcomes.

Importantly, as implied previously, negative learning was at work as well. The parts of the developing world which pursued more statist policies were held to have performed worse economically. Although much of the developing world argued that problems of development stemmed from unequal power relations or other structural problems, this position has weakened over time.[87] Africa, in particular, was seen as having failed in its developmental pursuit, and its over-reliance upon the state in the economic domain came under increased scrutiny.[88] But these ideas were not limited to Africa. The overreliance upon statist development was seen as the problem with Eastern Europe, Latin America, Africa, and parts of Asia.[89]

Also, several countries began to move away from inward-oriented, state-led development and improved their economies dramatically: Chile, Ghana, and India are cases where the moves away from import substitution industrialization (ISI) were public, clear, and presumably successful.[90] These showcase countries were intentionally used by the Bank to spread what it believed to be the best developmental policies. Rapley argues, however, that structural adjustment was most successful through the 1990s in Latin America and least successful (in promoting growth) in Africa.[91] The trend can also be seen in Eastern Europe where nearly every country has undergone dramatic shifts in developmental approach, quite often away from state command economies toward market-driven ones.

Combined Change in Power of International Actors and Ideas

The Linking of ODA to Political Liberalization

With the end of the Cold War, the United States was the largest single bilateral donor of aid in absolute levels. In 2009, for example, the US gave about 24% of all such official development assistance (ODA) by itself.[92] The top four (US, France, Germany, and the United Kingdom) gave over half in combination. With Japan added, the number increases to over 60%. Importantly, with the end of the Cold War, the major Western powers have linked aid, at least rhetorically, to the promotion of economic and political liberalization. [93] A consensus had emerged about the need for political and economic conditions applied to development aid for real development to take place. Although the historic purpose of ODA to developing countries has been touted as promoting economic growth and alleviating poverty, aid is also known to be a foreign policy tool in which the "giving nation" promotes its own national or geopolitical interests.[94] With this in mind, American foreign aid began as a tool in the fight against communism in the developing world, with issues such as human rights, the promotion of democracy, and the opening of markets all receding to a secondary position.[95] Other countries, such as Japan and France, have been discussed as countries whose aid programs have been more mercantilist, though not exclusively so.[96]

With the fall of the Berlin Wall, however, bilateral aid became unrelated to the calculus of Cold War thinking. Three important trends emerged: overall aid levels declined until the late 1990s; donors began to pay more attention to issues of development and poverty; and several key donors tied the goals of democratization or political liberalization to aid flows in this second period.[97] Importantly for much of the developing world, and especially Africa, America, France, and the United Kingdom announced that ODA would become linked to efforts at political liberalization within a year of the fall of the Berlin Wall.[98]

In 1993, for example, and only four years after the announcements, these three countries together gave away slightly more than 50% of all ODA going to all developing countries and multilateral organizations, though between 1986 and1987, they constituted about 40% of all such.[99] Importantly, these three represented between 37% and 46% of all African bilateral aid for these same years.

These trends appear to have resulted in aid becoming more of a tool to promote democracy, development, and capitalism—though national self-interest has remained a key element of decisions concerning who gets aid and how much. In fact, beginning in the late 1990s, aid's ability to address the issues of poverty in the developing world took on new salience as orienting development aid as a Cold War tool became unimportant.

Moreover, the amount of international aid available in the Cold War period slowly increased during most of this time until it peaked in 1990. Then it fell slowly until 1997, at which time it began rising again for nearly every year through 2010. (See Figure 5.2) For example, between 1960 and 1989, the average amount of aid was $52 billion per year; while between 1990 and 2010, the average was around $91billion.[100] Although a slight decline in aid occurred from 1995 to 2001, the upward trend soon resumed. Moreover, the average level from 1995 to 2001 was still at $74 billion, nearly 1.5 times higher than the Cold War average, and it was nearly identical to aid levels during the 1980s. What this tells us is that as conditionality on aid increased, so too did the importance of aid in absolute terms.

Despite the potential for aid in promoting democratization, where there was little coordination toward political conditionality among donors, or

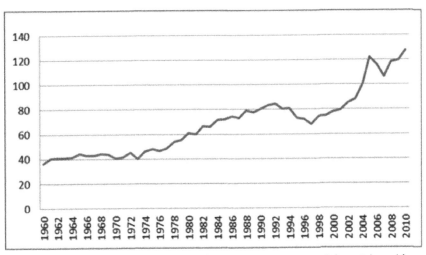

Figure 5.2   Net ODA Disbursements: Total DAC 1960–2010: 2009 Prices. Adapted from OECD, data, Net ODA disbursements, Total DAC by author

where a powerful donor protected a nation (like the US did for Zaire for many years, or more recently France for Cameroon), then such liberalization effects did not follow (at least initially).[101] Often countries with less geopolitical importance for major donors faced the most pressure to liberalize. We must remember, however, that liberalization and full democratization should not be confused.[102]

European ODA

Moreover, Europe as a whole officially linked democratization to aid early in this second period. In 1991, the European Union passed such a resolution.[103] The following year, the Maastrict Treaty listed democracy as well as respect of human rights and the rule of law as important considerations in determining the distribution of development aid from Europe.[104] Such concerns were even included in the 1995 Lomé IV accord. Moreover, in the post-Cold war period, as an organization and through its members bilateral aid Europe contributed at least 50% of all African development aid in the first half of the 1990s.[105]

Multilateral Aid: the International Financial Institutions

Structural Adjustment Policies

Most structural adjustment policies from the IMF were targeted to reduce or eliminate currency overvaluation, subsidies (e.g., food, fuel, and health), wage increases, redundant workers, and inflation. They also sought to introduce fees for service (co-pays) and raise taxes—all in order to correct budgetary and trade imbalances. World Bank structural adjustment policies were intended to increase prices to exporters (farmers), reduce imports, privatize state-owned enterprises, adopt neo-liberal economic policies (generally), and stop lending money to politicians or state-owned enterprises at below market rates. The IMF policies were called stabilization polices, and the World Bank policies, structural adjustment.

Some privatizations were the result of pressures from the World Bank and IMF, while others appear to have been the result of a change in perspective and epistemological consensus concerning public ownership of enterprise and economic growth. According to one author, the World Bank's views on privatization were ambivalent in the 1980s.[106] Although they did advocate privatization, public sector reform was still a predominant approach for reform. In fact, he cites a 1983 World Bank report, suggesting that efficiency of enterprises was more a matter of how it was managed than how it was owned.[107] In fact, from 1980 to 86 most conditions placed on loans (73%) were for public enterprise financial performance, while only 13% were for outright privatization.[108] By the late 1980s, the number of structural adjustment programs with conditions for privatization greatly increased.[109]

The IMF (as opposed to the World Bank) might have had more of an effect on privatization: it was found that countries borrowing from the IMF later privatized more assets—controlling for other variables—relative to other similar countries.[110] For each dollar a country borrowed from the IMF, it subsequently privatized assets worth approximately half that amount. In contrast, World Bank loans were not found to be significantly associated with increased privatization revenues. This could be seen as either a result of pressure from the IMF or it could be seen as a signal that better policies would be pursued once these countries were under IMF conditionality.[111]

Not all scholars agree that structural adjustment has made a significant difference for countries, especially the worst performing ones. Easterly has become a well-known critic of the Bank and has shown that between 1980 and 1999, on most major economic indices targeted by structural adjustment, having more structural adjustment loans was not correlated to better outcomes.[112] Especially in the case of Africa, the worst performing countries had "bad policy" outcomes from 1980 to 1999—despite being under IMF programs an average of almost 72% of the period.[113] In another part of his paper, however, he shows the probability that a country would experience "macroeconomic distortions" to be falling from a high of 70% of developing countries in 1980 to around 15% in 1999. So, how do we square this circle? If we accept the Cold War and post-Cold War periods as important markers, we see that the percentage of developing countries with macroeconomic distortions is between approximately 48% and 73% in the years 1980–1989.[114] The average appears to be around 54% of developing countries. By contrast, the percentage of developing countries experiencing macroeconomic distortions appears to fall from about 45% in 1990, to 40% in 1991, to a slight rise to 44% in 1992, to 35% in 1993, then missing data for 1994/95, to 21% in 1996, and continuing to fall to about 15% of countries in 1999. The average percentage of countries with macroeconomic distortion for these years is around 30%. If we predict the numbers for 1994/95 using a line, the average would be around 29% still, with a clearly declining line from 1989 onwards. Moreover, this proposition appears to hold in his analysis. Although he did not find structural adjustment loans to be linked with improved macroeconomic indicators, he did find that length of time with such loans and a measure of time both to be significant.[115] This is in keeping, but not direct evidence of, the idea that these policies were more effective in the post 1989 world, though these are slow moving, partial reforms. Moreover, according to one source, structural adjustment stabilization policies were much more rigorously followed and implemented in Africa during the post-Cold War period.[116] This is also consistent with the idea of increasing power of American interests, and the norms it backed, in this second period.

France as a Latecomer to IMF Conditionality

Additionally, many African countries found some protection against strict structural adjustment programs through the protection of the French, who were not initially four-square behind structural adjustment.[117] Having a statist approach to its economy, a Socialist as president until 1995, and majority state ownership of its own oil sector until 1996, France was poorly disposed in applying overly stringent "neo-liberal polices," especially ones involving countries in its *chase gardée* (private hunting grounds) and its allies.[118] According to Wilson, however, by the end of the 1980s, a consensus of 80–85% existed between the US and France concerning many of the specifics of structural adjustment programs.[119] One of the biggest stumbling blocks between World Bank and French views regarding structural adjustment was resolved when the CFA monetary zone was devalued in 1994. Thus, the end of the Cold War, along with the French government looking to limit their liability vis-à-vis the French franc zone, resulted in a convergence among the US, UK, France, the World Bank, and IMF about the need for conditionality, even if the particulars about sequence, timing, and scope were not all agreed upon. Moreover, one author argued that France was the most influential country within Europe when it comes to influencing European aid distribution.[120] Nonetheless, the French view came more into line with the US, UK, World Bank view soon after the end of the Cold War.

Rising Power of Multinational Corporations and Foreign Direct Investment

Unlike in the first period when multinational corporations were seen to be associated with colonialism or were the targets of economic nationalism, many developing countries began to look to multinational corporations (MNCs) [also transnational corporations (TNCs)] for sources of foreign direct investment (FDI) as a means of development—especially after the debt crisis of the 1980s when banks stopped lending to developing nations. Even before the end of the Cold War, the power of multinational or transnational firms was on the rise, and it has only been increasing since. According to Sklar, by 1999, "TNCs account[ed] for more than one-third of world output."[121]

The role of FDI has been increasing worldwide, especially from the late 1980s on. "While real world GDP grew at a 2.5% annual rate and real world exports grew by 5.6% annually from 1986 through 1999, United Nations data show that real world FDI inflows grew by 17.7% over this same period!

Additionally, MNCs mediate most world trade flows."[122] This means that corporate power might be growing faster than national power, from an economic perspective.

In another indication of corporate strength, many MNCs have more sales per year than many countries have GDPs. In 1992, right around the end of the Cold War, of the 150 largest GDPs or annual sales, General Motors had more sales (in value) than Saudi Arabia's GDP; Exxon and Ford had larger sales than Turkey's GDP; and Toyota had more sales worth more than Hong Kong's GDP. Of the top 150 countries/MNC's, almost 90 of them (60%) were corporations.[123] Moreover, their power within the US is clear.[124] By 2000, TNCs accounted for over one-third of all US formal sector employment.[125] Moreover, over 90% of US trade is conducted by trading firms (ones that both import and export).[126] Moreover, of these firms, a very few dominate within: "In 2000, for example, the top 1% of trading firms (in terms of their trade flows) account for 81% of U.S. trade."[127] These authors also find that around half of US trade flows take place between affiliates of the same MNC, that is, intra-firm trade.

In addition, the amount of FDI globally has increased dramatically following the end of the Cold War. As we can see from Figure 5.3, the amount of FDI sent to developing and developed nations has grown, but with more volume and variation for the developed world. The graph shows that there was an increase in 1989, followed by a slight dip in 1991/92, then followed by a strong increase in international FDI, even among developing nations. There were also spikes in the data for 2000 and 2007. Also we see that Africa has missed much of the increase in FDI, though this will be discussed in later chapters. Much of the FDI inflow to the developing world must be following privatization programs, which are gaining speed in parts of the developing world, and Africa in particular, especially after 2001. In fact, it is estimated that in 2010, half of all FDI went to developing nations.[128] Nonetheless, the influence of the MNCs behind these large flows offers increased power or potential power as countries seek increased investments. These opportunities for FDI certainly must follow from the increased privatization of state-owned industries or sectors with the end of the Cold War, and their strength could be partially linked the rise of BITs described above.

Transnational corporations' sales represent more and more of all sales internationally. Total world foreign direct investment (FDI) flows (inward and outward combined) were over 3.5 trillion dollars.[129] For developing areas, inflows were very important, at 620 billion dollars, representing about 37% of all FDI inflows. Of global shares of FDI, about 11% went to East Asia, 8.5% was invested in Latin America and the Caribbean, about 6% went to CIS countries (former Soviet), 5% was sent to West Asia, 3.7% for sub-Saharan Africa, 3.5% for South East Asia, about 3% for South Asia, 1.4% for North

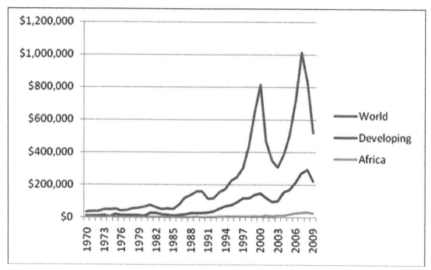

Figure 5.3 FDI Flows in Millions of Dollars. Adapted from data from UNCTAD stat by author. In US dollars, millions. Deflator for US dollar from Federal Reserve Bank, Minneapolis, Base year is chained; 1982–1984 = 100

Africa, and less than one percent for Oceana and South East Europe.[130] In terms of capital stock formation, FDI inflows for 2008 represented 12.3% for the world and 12.8% for developing countries. Moreover, the share of gross fixed capital formation was 36.7% for sub-Saharan Africa, 26.8% South East Europe, 21.8% was sent to West Asia, 21% went to CIS countries (former Soviet), 18.7% for North Africa, 15.8% for South East Asia, 15.5% was invested in Latin America and the Caribbean, 13.3% for Oceana and about 8.5% for both East Asia.[131]

Also, many large companies are more and more transnational. UNCTAD has developed the measure called the Transnationality Index (TNI), which is an average composite three ratios: foreign assets to total assets, foreign sales to total sales, and foreign employment to total employment.[132] They find that the top 100 companies worldwide have TNIs over 60% by 2008, and the top 10 developing world corporations have TNIs of over 50%.[133]

Declining Importance of Sovereignty

A growing consensus had been emerging in immediate the post-Cold War period that countries cannot have unchecked sovereignty where its account-ability is only internal, but that "responsible sovereignty" requires that a country's treatment of their citizens meets certain standards and that "sover-eignty entails obligations and duties toward other sovereign states as well as to one's own citizens."[134] Deng has argued that for states to claim sovereignty, they must meet "minimum standards of good governance or responsibility for the security and general welfare of its citizens and those under its jurisdiction."[135] Moreover, international UN peacekeeping missions in such places as East Timor, Kosovo, Rwanda, and Somalia indicate changing international norms concerning sovereignty.[136]

In fact, the then acting secretary general of the United Nations wrote in 1992 that "the time of absolute and exclusive sovereignty. . . has passed."[137] He called for states to have more of a commitment toward human rights, reflecting a rising universalist view of morality in which the international system could take notice of the internal actions of states which were in gross violation of acceptable human norms. The logic of this approach could lead to justifications toward humanitarian interventions violating the strong norm of sovereignty, especially where ethnic cleansing or genocide is apparent. Later in 1999, UN Secretary-General Kofi Annan suggested that sovereignty was being redefined in light of rising globalization and interdependence.[138] Also, in 2008, the Brookings institute convened a conference on responsible sovereignty in Berlin where international organizations and foreign policy leaders worldwide discussed the future of international security and cooperation around this idea.[139]

As such, some scholars have argued that sovereignty, as a norm, has been undermined internationally, and especially within sub-Saharan Africa.[140] Many scholars have argued that the implementation of structural adjustment and its intrusion into the domestic economic policy making is tantamount to undermining the sovereignty of African nations.[141] However, Williams holds that at the inception of the concept of sovereignty (the Treaty of Westphalia), all representatives of the nations attending accepted that states with sovereignty had obligations to their people to provide good government and provide for their basic needs and that sovereignty was always limited. Nonetheless, since the late 1980s, the international community has felt less constrained to honor sovereignty of nations which have not promoted the material well-being or economic development of their nations.

Therefore, countries which are seen to have become corrupt and unwilling to pursue the attainment of economic and material prosperity and well-being of their people may have their sovereignty called into question, even on a de jure level. In fact, with the end of the Cold War, Africa's strict adherence to state sovereignty has been somewhat lessened with the American adventure in Somalia and Nigeria's involvement in Liberia. Some scholars go so far as to suggest that countries should have to be certified by some international body (e.g., the UN) to maintain their statehood. Herbst says, "the US, and other countries, can . . . recognize that some states are simply not exercising physical control over part of their country and should no longer be considered sovereign."[142]

Nonetheless, Herbst has drawn much debate/criticism for the practicality of this suggestion.[143] Englebert and others have also argued that conflict in Africa and the lack of domestic legitimacy of so many leaders should lead to new borders or new states within Africa and undo the norm of *uti possidetus*.[144]

Moreover, beyond the IFIs and their structural adjustment policies, many other international and regional actors have attempted to engage in the creation of institutions which increase accountability or good governance through capacity building or creating information. For example, in 1995, Transparency International began collecting data on the level of corruption of most nations, including Africa. Many have suggested that the mere collection and publication of these data has placed the issue of corruption on the forefront of development workers and others.

The Extractive Industries Transparency Initiative (EITI) was also begun in 2002 to help get to the bottom of the resource curse. Begun by the UK under Tony Blair, nations which joined the initiative would publish what they paid governments for the natural resources of that country. The goal was to make known such revenues so they could be tracked and be made available for public goods. This could increase the accountability of rulers to the ruled by giving individuals data with which to work.[145] This is less seen as undermining sovereignty since it is voluntary, though some research has shown that countries that become EITI compliant obtain more aid and more FDI.[146] So far, 23 counties are listed as compliant with EITI rules and procedures, while 16 have obtained candidate status.

Finally, we discussed earlier in the chapter how ODA was linked to political reform, which necessarily impinges upon the sovereignty of nations receiving the aid. Again, aid is voluntary, but for the weakest states foregoing aid is difficult, if not impossible, under most conditions. Moreover, economic conditionality began with structural adjustment, and later HIPC and MDRI (see Chapter 7) also impinged upon sovereignty. These soft law institutions reflect the growing norms of placing countries outside of the new norms of the international community under scrutiny. This would have been less likely during the Cold War, although Amnesty International has been around since 1962. It was founded as an NGO in London, and it has always been independent of American foreign policy interests.

Counter-Trends[147]

Divided Donors

When donors encounter specific countries with a foreign policy based more on realist politics than the stated norms of democracy and development, then the pressures for democratization are greatly lessened. For example, in the case of French aid, some scholars have suggested the France did not pressure

Cameroon to democratize, at least not much past the holding of elections.[148] Moreover, the US support for the current regime in Equatorial Guinea seems to point to oil as more important than human rights or democratization. Some suggest that Equatorial Guinea has among the worst human rights and democratization records, but maintains strong ties to the US, though it does not receive much ODA from the US.[149] By contrast, where the donors work together and link aid to greater democratization, the effects can be strong in the short term, as the case of Malawi illustrates.[150]

China

More recently, China is seen as a nation that can provide some shelter from the Western liberal winds pushing African countries to institute or maintain liberal regimes or reforms begun in the wake of the end of the Cold War. Right after the end of the Cold War, though, this trend was far from clear. In 1990, Chinese per capita income was $370, while the US's level was $21, 970.[151] Also, Chinese-African trade was valued at only $3 billion in 1995. Moreover, China had only $49 million in FDI in Africa in 1990, and its great increase in FDI came 2001.[152] In addition, China had real limits to its ability to influence international institutions of liberal power such as the World Bank and IMF. It was only recently granted permanent Most Favored Nation status in the WTO in 2000.[153] Also, it had not been a significant aid donor, even as late as 2011 it gave only $2 billion in aid, compared to the US contribution of $30B and the overall OECD contribution of $128B. It would not be until after 2000–2002 that the "take-off" of Chinese trade and investment in Africa would really rise.

Importantly, around the end of the Cold War, China was not seeking to directly compete with the US; rather its economic foreign policy mostly sought out countries with which it could sell, buy, or invest and ones which would recognize it as the one China—it was not really weighing in on the emerging new norms at all.[154] Chinese recent attention in Africa has been in a search for oil and other natural resources to feed it growing economy, though its attention in Africa initially emerged in the wake of the 1989 Tiananmen massacre with China looking for more non-Western allies.[155] Even with a growing and potentially more assertive China, since it had already publicly moved away from the state socialist model of development, and it had begun allowing foreign ownership of many sectors after 1986, it seems to be on board with the liberal trading regime in broad strokes, if not the democratic liberalism.

The Attacks on September 11 and the Global War on Terror

American foreign policy again changed for a subset of countries after the terrorist attacks of September 11, 2001. Countries which could be seen as playing an instrumental role in the war on terror could receive American military and developmental aid, regardless of its levels of democracy, if it

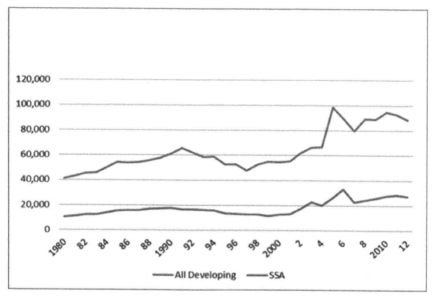

Figure 5.4   ODA from USA.

was seen as a key player. American aid had begun to wind down slowly, as
many predicted it would in a post-Cold War scenario. Following the attack
on 9–11, however, the Bush administration saw the promotion of democracy, stable societies, and development as part of American strategic interests and aid flows resumed globally and regionally, including sub-Saharan
Africa.

As we can see in Figure 5.4, US aid in constant terms rose slowly from
1980 until 1991, when it began to fall until 1997.[156] Then it slowly ticked
up until 2001, when it rose again until a peak in 2005, where it dropped and
bounced around 2008 levels.

For Africa, which received around 25–30% of American ODA, the pattern
follows the broader trend, but it does so in a less exaggerated fashion. The
largest changes in American aid for African nations have been to Sudan,
Ethiopia, and the DRC, though the numbers pale relative to the huge upticks
for countries directly involved, or more closely involved, in the wars in Iraq
and Afghanistan. These two, as well as Turkey, Pakistan, and Jordan, have
seen the most significant increases in aid allocation since 2001.[157] One set
of authors ound that change in aid patterns were not influenced by levels of
democracy globally, though they found a slight effect for Africa (at 90% significance).[158] The American preferences for stability and "winning" the war
on terror could become like the Cold War anti-communist logic, dampening
other effects when this is present. So we may expect that countries will be

expected to become more politically and economically liberal, unless doing so creates civil war, instability, or works against other short-term goals involving the war on global terror.

CONCLUSIONS

A pro-democratic, pro-capitalist, and pro-free trade America emerged from the end of the Cold War with few contenders to share center stage of the international system. America was thus better able to translate its preferences regarding the international system into actions within institutions than it was able to during the Cold War. In addition, a rising European Union had also been on the same page for many of the pro-democracy and pro-capitalist sentiments favored by Washington, at least in broad parameters. In turn, these preferences became linked to the receipt of aid both multilaterally and bilaterally: some economic conditionality began in the 1980s, but it accelerated and extended to the political spheres in the 1990s. Moreover, the ideas and norms associated with the success of liberal capitalism inherent in the lessons from the collapse of the Soviet Union, Eastern Europe, and the reform of China, all increased the power of the norms of democracy and capitalism. Plus, the reforms associated with the integration of Europe also helped bolster and accelerate tendencies towards privatization worldwide. The sweeping away of so many authoritarian regimes throughout the region created a diffusion effect for Africa as well. African authoritarian leaders had to question how they could keep demands for democracy at bay when the East Germans with the Stazi could not.

The increased interest in promoting capitalism and democracy seems to have been part of trends that had begun to emerge before the end of the Cold War, but which were later reinforced and deepened. With the end of the Cold War, we have seen an increase in the numbers of democracies, as well as countries turning away from state socialist programs, the abandoning of inward-oriented development policies as practice and as a theory, and the attendant privatization of state owned industries. Moreover, trade and investment have been on the rise since the end of the Cold War, as has bilateral investment treaties protecting much of this new investment. In addition, MNC are responsible for more and more jobs, trade, and investment worldwide, and this has accelerated post 1989. We have also seen a rise in the number of democracies as well as countries liberalizing their political systems.

Each trend has been unevenly implemented or experienced in each region. Next, we examine the regional context for these region-wide changes in economic and political institutions and practices as well as the degree to which real liberalization of political or economic institutions and practices has taken place.

NOTES

1. Michael Bratton and Nicolas van de Walle, *Democratic Experiments in Africa: Regime Transitions in Comparative Perspective* (Cambridge: Cambridge University Press, 1997), p. 8. For the importance of differences between de jure and de facto elections see Staffan I. Lindberg, *Democracy and Elections in Africa* (Baltimore, MD: The Johns Hopkins University Press, 2006).

2. For end of Cold War accelerating economic reforms that had been begun earlier, see also Nicolas van de Walle, *African Economies and the Politics of Permanent Crisis, 1979–1999* (Cambridge: Cambridge University Press, 2001).

3. See Peter J. Schraeder, *African Politics and Society: A Mosaic in Transformation 2nd Edition* (Belmont, CA: Thompson, Wadsworth, 2004), p. 132–34. Afro-Marxism was dropped by Mozambique in 1989, Cape Verde and Sao Tome and Principe in 1990, Benin, Congo, Angola, Ethiopia in 1991, and Madagascar in 1993. Somalia had abandoned it earlier in 1977, but that was not part of this trend.

4. Ibid. Tanzania dropped socialism in 1985, Ghana and Burkina Faso in 1987, and Zambia in 1991. Mali and Guinea were earlier, in 1968 and 1978, respectively

5. For an examination of the meaning of good governance in Africa, see Goran Hyden and Michael Bratton, eds., *Governance and Politics in Africa* (Boulder, CO: Lynne Rienner Publishers, 1992).

6. For this argument, see Martin Doornbos, "Good Governance": The Metamorphosis of a Policy Metaphor," *Journal of International Affairs* 57, 1 (Fall 2003): 3–17, p. 3.

7. For earlier version of this argument, with references, see John James Quinn, *The Road oft Traveled: Development Policies and Majority State Ownership of Industry in Africa* (Westport CT: Praeger, 2002), especially Chapter 9.

8. For an overview of political difficulties of implementing reforms, see Stephan Haggard and Steven B. Webb, "What Do We Know about the Political Economy of Economic Policy Reform?" *The World Bank Research Observer* 8, 2 (July 1993): 143–68; also Stephan Haggard and Robert R. Kaufman, "Economic Adjustment in New Democracies," in Joan M. Nelson et al., eds., *Fragile Coalitions: The Politics of Economic Adjustment* (New Brunswick, N.J.: Transaction Books, 1989): 57–78; Stephan Haggard and Robert R. Kaufman, *The Political Economy of Democratic Transitions* (Princeton: Princeton University Press, 1995).

9. William C. Wohlforth, "Realism and the End of the Cold War," *International Security*, Vol. 19, No. 3 (Winter, 1994–1995), pp. 91–129, p. 103, see also John Lewis Gaddis, International Relations Theory and the End of the Cold War," *International Security*, 17, 3 (Winter, 1992–1993): pp. 5–58.

10. See Robert V. Daniels, *The End of Communist Revolution* (London: Routledge, 1993).

11. For unipolar, see Charles Krauthammer, "The Unipolar Moment," *Foreign Affairs—America and the World, 1990*, Special Issue, Vol. 70, No. 1 (1990/91): 25–33. for uni-multipolar, see Samuel Huntington, "The Lonely Superpower" *Foreign Affairs* (March/April 1999); for discussion of this debate, see Stephen G. Brooks and William C. Wohlforth, "American Primacy in Perspective," *Foreign Affairs* (July/

August 2002). For other arguments on limits on American power, see Joseph S. Nye, "Limits of American Power," *Political Science Quarterly* 117, 4 (2002/2003).

12. For views on hegemony see Robert Gilpin, *U.S. Power and the Multinational Corporation: The Political Economy of Foreign Direct Investment* (New York: Basic Books, 1975); Stephen D. Krasner, "State Power and the Structure of Foreign Trade," *World Politics* 28 (April 1976): 317–47; for an overview see Robert O. Keohane, *After Hegemony: Cooperation and Discord in the World Political Economy* (Princeton, NJ: Princeton University Press, 1984), esp. Chapter 3; for a critique see Duncan Snidal, "Limits of Hegemonic Stability Theory," *International Organization* 39 (August 1985): 579–614.

13. Joseph Nye, *Is The American Century Over?(Global Futures)* (Malden, MA: Polity Press, 2015), p. 5.

14. Some data suggests that China's GDP (in PPP) has recently surpassed the US' GDP (though not using current exchange rates) in 2014, but others suggest the data is fabricated or just the wrong data for comparison of military power. See, for example, Ben Carter, "Is China's economy really the largest in the world?" BBC News (16 December 2014): Magazine. http://www.bbc.com/news/magazine-30483762

15. Adam S. Posen "Fleeting Equality: The Relative Size of the U.S. and EU Economies to 2020" *Brooking Institution, U.S.-Europe Analysis, Number 8* (September 2004), p1, p6.

16. CIA World Factbook, SV European Union, United States, SV Economy. Accessed April 15, 2014.

17. Posen "Fleeting Equality."

18. For this data, see World Bank, *World Development Report 1992* (Washington DC: World Bank, 1992): Table 3, pp. 222–23, and Table 1, pp. 218–19

19. Christopher Layne, "The Waning of U.S. Hegemony—Myth or Reality? A Review Essay," *International Security*, 34, 1 (Summer 2009): 147–72, p. 150.

20. See NATO homepage. http://www.nato.int/cps/en/natolive/nato_countries. htm Accessed January 2014.

21. Ibid., SV membership. http://en.wikipedia.org/wiki/Member_states_of_ NATO. Accessed January 2014.

22. For example, see David M. Herszenhorn, "In Crimea, Russia Moved to Throw Off the Cloak of Defeat," *New York Times* (March 24, 2014): A9. http://www.nytimes.com/2014/03/25/world/europe/ukraine.html

23. Layne, "The Waning of U.S. Hegemony," p. 149.

24. Francis Fukuyama, *The End of History and the Last Man* (New York: Free Press, 1992).

25. However, some critics are trying to get these organizations to moderate their positions. See for example, Joseph E. Stieglitz, *Globalization and its Discontents* (New York: W. W. Norton & Company, 2003).

26. Samuel P. Huntington, *The Third Wave: Democratization in the Late Twentieth Century* (Norman, OK: University of Oklahoma Press 1991).

27. The data for this section comes from Freedom House, http://www.freedomhouse.org/uploads/fiw09/CompHistData/CountryStatus&RatingsOverview1973–2009.pdf

28. All data in this section, unless specified otherwise, comes from the Freedom House website, examining regional data from 1988/89 and 1998/99. http://www.freedomhouse.org/uploads/fiw09/CompHistData/FIW_ScoresByRegion.xls. Accessed 1/12/10.

29. For transitions to democracy literature see, Dankwart Rustow, "Transitions to Democracy: Toward a Dynamic Model," *Comparative Politics* 2, 3 (April 1970): 337–63; Guillermo O'Donnell and Philippe C. Schmitter, *Transitions from Authoritarian Rule: Tentative Conclusions About Uncertain Democracies* (Baltimore: Johns Hopkins University Press 1986); Huntington, *The Third Wave*; Haggard and Kaufman, *The Political Economy*; Bratton and van de Walle, *Democratic Experiments*; Thomas Carothers, "The End of the Transition Paradigm," *Journal of Democracy* 13, 1 (January 2002): 5–21; and Lisa Anderson, ed., *Transitions to Democracy* (New York Columbia University Press, 1999).

30. Huntington, *The Third Wave*, p. 272

31. Freedom House, *Discarding Freedom: Return to the Iron Fist.* (2015) https://freedomhouse.org/sites/default/files/01152015_FIW_2015_final.pdf

32. Taken from Thomas D. Lairson and David Skidmore, *International Political Economy: The Struggle for Power and Wealth, 2nd edition* (Belmont, CA: Wadsworth, 1997), p. 66.

33. Robert Gilpin, *Global Political Economy: Understanding the International Economic Order* (Princeton: Princeton University Press, 2001), p. 219.

34. Taken from WTO/GATT homepage, SV membership. http://www.wto.org/english/theWTO_e/gattmem_e.htm.

35. The Holy Sea is an observer in the WTO and a member of the UN. The European Union is a member of the WTO. Taiwan is a member of the WTO, but not the UN.

36. Unless stated otherwise, data for Table and this section come from KOF Index of globalization, http://globalization.kof.ethz.ch/aggregation/ SV World. For Table, see category a: economic globalization. Most recently access 2012.

37. See Gilpin, *Global Political Economy*.

38. For worldwide, see Stephen D. Krasner, *Structural Conflict: The Third World Against Global Liberalism* (Berkeley & Los Angeles: University of California, 1985); for Africa, see Quinn, *The Road oft Traveled*.

39. Most of this analysis relies upon Zachary Elkins, Andrew T. Guzman, and Beth Simmons, "Competing for Capital: The Diffusion of Bilateral Investment Treaties, 1960–2000," *International Organization* 60 (Fall 2006): 811–46.

40. Ibid., p. 838.

41. Data for this section taken from Ibid., Figure 1, page 815. Data are approximations from graph.

42. Peter Young, "Privatization around the World," *Proceedings of the Academy of Political Science*, Vol. 36, No. 3, Prospects for Privatization (1987), pp. 190–206. Though, Germany had a large privatization project in the 1960s, and Chile in the early 1970s, but these sales were considered to be prior to the same wave. See, William Megginson, "Privatization," *Foreign Policy*, No. 118 (Spring, 2000), pp. 14–27

43. Nancy Brune, Geoffrey Garrett, and Bruce Kogut, "The International Monetary Fund and the Global Spread of Privatization." *IMF Staff Papers*, Vol. 51, No. 2 (2004), pp. 195–219.

44. The European project with the resulting increased competition would likely increase incentives for states to move out of competing economic sectors.

45. Brune, Garrett, and Kogut, "The IMF," p. 196; see also Ezra N. Suleiman and John Waterbury, "Introduction: Analyzing Privatization in Industrial and Developing Countries," in Ezra N, Suleiman and John Waterbury, eds., *The Political Economy of Public Sector Reform and Privatization* (Bolder, CO: Westview Press, 1990): 1–21.

46. Megginson, "Privatization," p. 14.

47. William L. Megginson and Jeffry N. Netter, "From State to Market: A Survey of Empirical Studies on Privatization," *Journal of Economic Literature* 39, 2 (June 2001): 321–89, p. 380.

48. Unless stated otherwise, data involving actual revenues raised and numbers of transactions of privatizations come from Brune, Garrett, and Kogut, "The IMF."

49. For more on Eastern European privatization, see Scott Thomas, ""The Politics and Economics of Central and Eastern Europe," in *Columbia Journal of World Business* Volume XXVIII, No. 1 (Spring 1993): 168–79.

50. Megginson, Privatization, p. 16.

51. Young, "Privatization," p. 193–94.

52. Ibid., p.200.

53. John Nellis, "Privatization in Africa: What has Happened? What is to Be Done?" in Gerard Roland, ed., *Privatization: Successes and Failures* (New York: Columbia University Press, 2008): 109–35, p. 112.

54. Calculated from "Gross domestic product (2009)." The World Bank: World Development Indicators Database. World Bank http://siteresources.worldbank.org/DATASTATISTICS/Resources/GDP.pdf. Combining Europe zone, UK, US and Japan.

55. See NATO homepage. http://www.nato.int/cps/en/natolive/nato_countries.htm

56. Although one scholar suggested that most aid from the Soviet Union to Africa ended in 1986, see Thad Dunning, "Conditioning the Effects of Aid: Cold War Politics, Donor Credibility, and Democracy in Africa" *International Organization* Vol. 58, No. 2 (Spring, 2004): 409–23.

57. See Richard Rose, "Democracy and Enlarging the European Union Eastwards," *Journal of Common Market Studies* 33, 3 (September 1995): 427–50.

58. World Bank, *Adjustment in Africa: Reforms, Results, and the Road Ahead* (Washington, D.C.: The World Bank, 1994); World Bank, *Accelerated Development in Sub-Saharan Africa* (Washington, DC: World Bank, 1981). World Bank, *Sub-Saharan Africa: From Crisis to Sustainable Growth* (Washington D.C.: The World Bank, 1989).

59. Robert Wade, *Governing the Market: Economic Theory and the Role of Government in East Asian Industrialization* (Princeton: Princeton University Press, 1990). For comparison of state-led inward oriented v state-led outward oriented v laissez-faire views, also see Quinn, *The Road oft Traveled*, pp. 17–30.

60. See for example, Michael W. Doyle, "Liberalism and World Politics," *The American Political Science Review*, Vol. 80, No. 4 (Dec., 1986), pp. 1151–69; Zeev Maoz and Bruce Russett, "Normative and Structural Causes of Democratic Peace, 1946–1986," *The American Political Science Review*, 87, 3 (Sep., 1993): 624–38.

61. For this view, see John M. Owen IV., "Iraq and the Democratic Peace," *Foreign Affairs* (Nov./Dec. 2005); also Bruce Russett, "Bushwhacking the Democratic Peace," *International Studies Perspectives* 6 (2005): 395–408.

62. Samuel Huntington, *The Third Wave*; Fukuyama, *The End of History*.

63. See Article 36 of World Bank Charter, "Prohibition of Political Activity: The International Character of the Bank."

64. World Bank, *Sub-Saharan* Africa; World Bank, *Governance and Development* (Washington, DC: World Bank, 1992).

65. See for example, David Dollar, and J. Svensson, "What Explains the Success or Failure of Structural Adjustment Programs?" *Policy Research Working Paper 1938.* (Washington, DC: World Bank, 1998); Paul Collier and David Dollar Collier, *Development Effectiveness: What Have We Learnt?* (Washington, DC: World Rank, 2001).

66. See especially Bela Balassa, "Exports, Policy Choices, and Economic Growth in Developing Countries after the 1973 Oil Shock," *Journal of Developing Economics* 18 (1985): 23–35; Anne O. Krueger, *Foreign Trade Regimes and Economic Development: Liberalization Attempts and Consequences* Vol X (Ballinger Publishing Company: Cambridge Mass., 1978); Rati Ran, "Exports and Economic Growth in Developing Countries: Evidence from Time Series and Cross Section Data," *Economic development and Cultural Change* 31 (October 1987): 51–73; and William G. Tyler, "Growth and Export Expansion in Developing Countries," *Journal of Developmental Economics* 9 (1981): 121–38. See also, World Bank, *Accelerated Development*; World Bank, *Sub-Saharan Africa*; John Ravenhill, "Africa's Continuing Crises: The Elusiveness of Development," in John Ravenhill, ed., *Africa in Economic Crisis* (New York: Columbia University Press): 1–43; Michael F. Lofchie, *The Policy Factor: Agricultural Performance in Kenya and Tanzania* (Boulder, CO.: Lynne Rienner Publishers, Inc., 1989); Jeffrey Sachs, "Introduction," in J. Sachs, ed., *Developing Country Debt and the World Economy National Bureau of Economic Research* (Chicago: University of Chicago Press, 1989), pp. 12–13. Anne O. Krueger, "Trade Policy as an Input to Development," *American Economic Association* 70, 2 (May 1980): 288–92; and Douglas Rimmer, ed., *Action in Africa: the Experience of People Involved in Government Business & Aid* (Portsmouth, N.H.: Heinemann, 1993).

67. For negative views of democracy on growth or stability see Samuel P. Huntington, *Political Order and Changing Societies* (New Haven: Yale University Press, 1968); also Guillermo A. O'Donnell, *Modernization and Bureaucratic-Authoritarianism: Studies in South American Politics* (Berkeley: Institute of International Studies/University of California, 1973, 1979). For a positive or neutral view of democracy's role on growth and stability see Atul Kholi, "Democracy and Development," in John P. Lewis and Valeriana Kallab, eds., *Development Strategies Reconsidered* (New Brunswick, N.J.: Transaction Books, 1986); also see Richard L. Sklar, "Developmental Democracy," *Comparative Studies in Society and History* 29, 4 (October 1987): 686–714. For the effects of democracy on adjustment see Haggard and Kaufman, "Economic Adjustment in New Democracies;" for majority state ownership reinforcing tendencies towards a one-party or military regime, see John J. Quinn, "The Managerial Bourgeoisie: Capital Accumulation, Development and Democracy," in David G. Becker and Richard L. Sklar, eds. *Postimperialism and World Politics* (Westport, CT: Praeger, 1999): 219–52.

68. For example see Adam Przeworski, *Democracy and the market: Political and economic reforms in Eastern Europe and Latin America* (Cambridge: Cambridge University Press, 1991), esp. pp. 113–33.

69. Alex Callinicos, "Whither Marxism?" *Economic and Political Weekly* (1996): PE9-PE17.

70. Quinn, *The Road oft Traveled.*

71. Joan M. Nelson, *Economic Crisis and Policy Choice: The Politics of Adjustment in the Third World* (Princeton: Princeton University Press, 1990); Nelson et al., eds., *Fragile Coalitions*; Jeffrey D. Sachs, "Conditionality, Debt Relief, and the Developing Country Debt Crisis," in Sachs, ed., *Developing Country Debt*, pp. 275–84; Thomas M. Callaghy and John Ravenhill, eds., *Hemmed In: Responses to Africa's Economic Decline* (New York: Columbia University Press, 1993).

72. For example, Bill Warren argued that classical Marxism was correct in viewing capitalism as the means of transforming society and bringing about economic development. Also, Richard L. Sklar and David G. Becker argued that the Third World bourgeois class was nationalistic and that development was taking place in the Third World, though unevenly so. See William Warren, *Imperialism: Pioneer of Capitalism* (London: Verso, 1980); Richard L. Sklar, "Postimperialism: A Class Analysis of Multinational Corporate Expansion," in David G. Becker et al., eds., *Postimperialism: International Capitalism and Development in the Late Twentieth Century* (Boulder, Co.: Lynne Rienner Publishers, 1987): 19–40; Becker and Sklar, "Why Postimperialism?" in Ibid., pp. 1–18.

73. Wade, *Governing the Market*

74. Ibid. For a summary of these three approaches, see Quinn, *The Road oft Traveled.*

75. Gilpin, *Global Political Economy*, p. 219.

76. Though some would say much of this ideological shift from liberal capitalism to conservative capitalism was associated with the elections of Reagan and Thatcher. See for example, Kenneth R. Hoover, "The rise of conservative capitalism: ideological tensions within the Reagan and Thatcher governments." *Comparative Studies in Society and History* 29, no. 02 (1987): 245–68.

77. John Williamson, "What Should the World Bank Think About the Washington Consensus," *The World Bank Research Observer* 15, 2 (August 2000): 251–64, 257.

78. Ibid.

79. Ibid., pp. 252–53.

80. Ibid. Also, see John Williamson, "Democracy and the 'Washington Consensus,'" *World Development* 21, 8 (1993): 1329–36.

81. See Chapter 1.

82. Daniel Brinks and Michael Coppedge, "Diffusion Is No Illusion: Neighbor Emulation in the Third Wave of Democracy," *Comparative Political Studies* 39, 4 (May 2006): 463–89, 464.

83. G. John Ikenberry "The International Spread of Privatization Policies: Inducements, Learning and 'Policy Bandwagoning,'" in Suleiman and Waterbury, *The Political Economy of Public Sector Reform*: 88–110, p. 99.

84. Ibid. See also Harvey Starr, H., C. Lindborg, C. "Democratic Dominoes Revisited: The Hazards of Governmental Transitions, 1974–1996," *Journal of Conflict*

Resolution 47, 4 (2003): 490–519; and Harvey Starr "Democratic Dominoes: Diffusion Approaches to the Spread of Democracy in the International System," *The Journal of Conflict Resolution*, Vol. 35, No. 2 (Jun., 1991), pp. 356–81

85. Kristian Skrede Gleditsch and Michael D. Ward, "Diffusion and the International Context of Democratization," *International Organization,* 60 (2006): 911–33, p. 916.

86. Ibid. See also Johan A. Elkink, "The International Diffusion of Democracy," *Comparative Political Studies* 44, 12 (2011): 1651–74, John O'Loughlin, Michael D. Ward, Corey L. Lofdahl, Jordin S. Cohen, David S. Brown, David Reilly, Kristian S. Gleditsch, and Michael Shin, "The Diffusion of Democracy, 1946–1994," *Annals of the Association of American Geographers* 88, 4 (1998): 545–74; Harvey Starr, "Democratic Dominoes: Diffusion Approaches to the Spread of Democracy in the International System," *Journal of Conflict Resolution* 35, 2 (1991): 356–81; and, of course, Huntington, *The Third Wave.*

87. See for example, Gerald M. Meier and Joseph E. Stiglitz, eds., *Frontiers of Development Economics: The Future in Perspective* (New York: Oxford University Press, 2001), and John Rapley, *Understanding Development: Theory and Practice in the Third World, 3rdEdition* (Boulder, CO: Lynne Rienner Publications, 2007).

88. World Bank, *Accelerated Development*; World Bank, *Sub-Saharan Africa*; Clapham *Africa and the International System*; Quinn, *Road oft Traveled*; van de Walle, *African Economies.*

89. World Bank, *Bureaucrats in Business.*

90. Rapley, *Understanding Development.*

91. Africa has been growing in the 2000s, however, though a debate as to whether this was because of or in spite of structural adjustment will ensue.

92. Data in this section comes from OECD announcement on ODA on April 14, 2010. http://www.oecd.org/document/11/0,3343,en_21571361_44315115_44981579_1_1_1_1,00.html

93. For overview of aid see Carol Lancaster, *Foreign aid: diplomacy, development, domestic politics* (Chicago: University of Chicago Press, 2007); for France in particular, see John James Quinn and David J. Simon, "Plus ça change, . . . : The Allocation of French ODA to Africa During and After the Cold War," *International Interactions* 32, 3 (2006): 295–318.

94. Lancaster, *Foreign aid*; see also Hans Morganthau, "A Political Theory of Foreign Aid," *American Political Science Review*, 56, 2 (1962): 301–09; R. D. McKinlay, "The Aid Relationship: A Foreign Policy Model and Interpretation of the Distributions of Official Bilateral Economic Aid of the United States, the United Kingdom, France, and Germany, 1960–1970," *Comparative Political Studies*, 11, 4 (1979): 411–63; Steven W. Hook, *National Interest and Foreign Aid* (Boulder, CO: Lynne Rienner Publishers, 1995); Alfred Maizels, and Machiko K. Nissanke, "Motivations for Aid to Developing Countries," *World Development* 12, 9 (1994): 879–900; Peter J. Schraeder, Steven W. Hook, and Bruce Taylor, "Clarifying the Foreign Aid Puzzle: A Comparison of American, Japanese, French, and Swedish Aid Flows," *World Politics*, 50, 2 (1998): 294–323; Alberto Alesina and David Dollar, "Who Gives Foreign Aid to Whom and Why?" *Journal of Economic Growth*, 5, 1 (2000): 33–63.

95. Lancaster, *Foreign Aid.*

96. Quinn and Simon, "Plus ça change;" Schraeder, Hook, and Taylor, "Clarifying the Foreign Aid Puzzle."

97. Lancaster, *Foreign Aid.*

98. Peter J. Schraeder, "Foreign-Aid Posturing in Francophone Africa," in Steven W. Hook, ed., *Foreign Aid Toward the Millennium* (Boulder, CO: Lynne Rienner Publishers, 1996): 173–90. However, many now wonder how strong this commitment really was. For example, Joseph argues that France now embraced "acceptable governance" as opposed to either "good governance" or "democracy." see Richard Joseph, "The Reconfiguration of Power in Late Twentieth-century Africa, in Richard Joseph, ed., *State Conflict and Democracy in Africa* (Boulder, CO: Lynne Rienner Publishers), ftn. 27. Nonetheless, Mitterand's original quote only stressed political liberalization and not democracy per se. See also Quinn and Simon, "Plus ça change."

99. OECD, *Development Co-operation: Effort and Policies of the Members of the Development Assistance Committee* (OECD, 1998), calculated from Table 3, p. a5–6.

100. Calculated from OECD table marking its 50th anniversary. http://webnet.oecd.org/dcdgraphs/ODAhistory/ Figure 5–2 also from this source.

101. Nikolas Emmanuel, "Undermining Cooperation: Donor-Patrons and the Failure of Political Conditionality" *Democratization* 17, 5 (2010): 856–77.

102. Nicolas van de Walle, "Elections without Democracy: Africa's Range of Regimes," *Journal of Democracy* 13, 2 (April 2002): 66–80; Michael Bratton and Eric C. C. Chang, "State Building and Democratization in Sub-Saharan Africa: Forwards, Backwards, or Together?" *Comparative Political Studies* 39, 9 (November 2006): 1059–83.

103. See Gorm Rye Olsen, "Europe and the Promotion of Democracy in Post Cold War Africa: How Serious is Europe and For What Reason," *African Affairs* 97 (1998): 343–67, 344.

104. Ibid.

105. Ibid., p. 344–45

106. Cook, "Privatization."

107. World Bank, *World Development Report 1983* (Washington, D.C.: World Bank, 1983). Cited in Ibid.

108. Paul Mosley, "Privatization, Policy-Based Lending and World Bank Behavior," in Paul Cook and Colin H. Kirkpatrick, eds., *Privatisation in Less Developed Countries* (London: Harvester Wheatsheaf, 1988).

109. Paul Cook and Colin H. Kirkpatrick, "Privatisation in Less Developed Countries An Overview', in Paul Cook and Colin H. Kirkpatrick, eds., *Privatisation in Less Developed Countries* (London: Harvester Wheatsheaf, 1988).

110. See Brune, Garrett, and Kogut, "The IMF." They controlled for the effects of the initial size of the state-owned sector, fiscal imbalances, per capita income, the depth of capital markets, and the quality of government. These same results could not be extended to World Bank loans. However, past 1986, the World Bank required countries to meet IMF conditionality before they would be considered for loans.

111. Ibid. The authors argue that it was more from credibility, but they pool countries of all levels of development together.

112. William Easterly, "What did structural adjustment adjust? The association of policies and growth with repeated IMF and World Bank adjustment loans," *Journal of Development Economics* 76 (2005): 1–22. See also Paul Mosely, Turan Subasat, and John Weeks, "Assessing Adjustment in Africa," *World Politics* 23 (1995): 1459–73.

113. Calculated from Ibid (Easterly), Table 1, p. 5

114. Ibid. Data in this section are taken from a graph (Figure 3), on page 14. Numbers are approximations from graph.

115. The variable "time trend" was significant for budget deficit/GDP current account def/gdp (in one model), black market premium, and real interest rates (in one model). Also, cumulative time spent in IMF was significantly linked with budget deficit (except when time trend was included), inflation, black market premium, overvaluation (except when time trend is included), and real interest rates.

116. van de Walle, *African Economies*, p. 69.

117. Ernest J. Wilson, III, "French Support for Structural Adjustment Programs in Africa," *World Development*, Vol. 21, No. 3 (1993): 331–47.

118. Schraeder, Hook, and Taylor, "Clarifying the Foreign Aid Puzzle;" Robert Aldrich and John Connell, eds., *France in World Politics* (New York: Routledge 1989); Jacques Adda and Marie-Claude Smoots, *La France face au Sud: le miroir brisé* (Paris: Karthala 1989).

119. Wilson, French Support for Structural Adjustment," p. 334.

120. Olsen, "Europe and the Promotion of Democracy."

121. Richard L. Sklar, Postimperialism: Concepts and Implications," in David G. Becker and Richard L. Sklar, eds., *Postimperialism and World Politics* (Westport, CT: Praeger, 1999): 11–36, p. 13.

122. Bruce A. Blonigen, "Foreign Direct Investment Behavior of Multinational Corporations," *NBER Reporter: Research Summary* (Winter 2006).

123. See Lairson and Skidmore, *International Political Economy*, p. 112–14.

124. And with the recent Supreme Court decision of Citizens United, MNCs cannot be limited in political expenditures.

125. A. B. Bernard, J. B. Jensen, and P. K. Schott, "Importers, Exporters and Multinationals: A Portrait of the Firms in the U.S. that Trade Goods," *NBER Working Paper No. 11404,* (June 2005), p. 2.

126. Ibid.

127. Ibid., p. 3.

128. See Lairson and Skidmore, *International Political Economy*, p. 116.

129. UNCTAD, *World Investment Report: Transnational Corporations, Agricultural Development, and Agriculture* (Geneva: United Nations, 2009): Annex Table, B1.

130. Calculated from Ibid.

131. Ibid., Annex Table B3.

132. Ibid., p. 39n22.

133. Ibid. p. 19.

134. Francis Deng, Sadikiel Kimaro, Terrence Lyons, Donald Rothchild, and I. William Zartman, *Sovereignty as Responsibility* (The Brookings Institution, Washington D.C., 1996). See also, *A Plan for Action: A New Era of International*

Cooperation for a Changed World: 2009, 2010, and Beyond (Washington, DC: Managing Global Insecurity, Brookings Institute, 2008), p. 11.

135. Francis M. Deng, "Reconciling Sovereignty with Responsibility: A Basis for International Humanitarian Action," in John W. Harbeson and Donald Rothchild, eds., *Africa in World Politics: The African State System in Flux* (Boulder: Westview, 2000): 353–78, 357.

136. Helen Stacy, "Relational Sovereignty," *Stanford Law Review*, 55, 5 (May, 2003): 2029–2059; see also Christopher Clapham, "Sovereignty and the Third World State," *Political Studies* 47, 3, Special Issue (1999): 522–37.

137. Boutros Boutros-Ghali, *An Agenda for Peace: Preventive Diplomacy, Peacemaking and Peacekeeping* (New York: United Nations, 1992), cited in Francis Mading Deng, "State Collapse: The Humanitarian Challeng4 to the United Nations," in I. William Zartman, ed., *Collapsed States: The Disintegration and Restoration of Legitimate Authority* (Boulder, CO: Lynne Rienner Publishers, 1995): 207–19, p. 212.

138. For an overview, and cite for Annan's comments, see Stanley Hoffmann, "The Debate about Intervention," in Phil Williams, Donald, M. Goldstein, and Jay M. Sharfitz, eds., *Classic Readings and Contemporary Debates in International Relations* (Belmont, CA: Thomas Wadsworth, 2006): 667–74.

139. http://www.brookings.edu/events/2008/0715_mgi.aspx

140. David Williams, "Aid and Sovereignty: Quasi-States and the International Financial Institutions," *Review of International Studies* 26 (2000): 557–73.

141. Ibid. See Also Clapham *Op. cit.*

142. Jeffrey Herbst, *States and Power in Africa: Comparative Lessons in Authority and Control* (Princeton: Princeton University Press, 2000); 264.

143. John James Quinn, "W(h)ither the African State (System)?" *International Politics* 38, 3 (September 2001): 437–446; Edmond J. Keller, "Reexamining Sovereign States in Africa," *International Studies Review* 4, 1 (Spring, 2002), pp. 197–200.

144. See Pierre Englebert, *State Legitimacy and Development in Africa* (Boulder, CO: Lynne Rienner, 2000); also Francis M. Deng," Reconciling Sovereignty with Responsibility," For descriptions of reduced sovereignty, see Williams, "Aid and sovereignty."

145. See for example, Paul Ocheje, "The Extractive Industries Transparency Initiative (EITI): Voluntary codes of conduct, poverty and accountability in Africa," *Journal of Sustainable Development in Africa* 8, 3 (2006): 222–39. http://www.jsd-africa.com/Jsda/Fall2006/PDF/Arc_the%20Extractive%20Industries%20Transparency%20Initiative.pdf

146. For EITI section, see Liz David-Barrett and Ken Okamura, "The Transparency Paradox: Why do Corrupt Countries Join EITI?" *European Research Centre for Anti-Corruption and State –Building Working* Paper No. 38 (November 2013). http://eiti.org/files/The-Transparency-Paradox.-Why-do-Corrupt-Countries-Join-EITI1.pdf

147. That is counter trends apparent at the time. The conclusion will deal with more current ones.

148. For example, see Emmanuel, "Undermining cooperation."

149. Adam Nossiter, "U.S. Engages With an Iron Leader in Equatorial Guinea," *New York Times,* May 30, 2011. Also, Equatorial Guinea only received 0.25 million dollars from the US in any year from 2003–2009, out of a total of around $4,000 million for all of SSA. See OECD, http://stats.oecd.org/Index.aspx?DatasetCode=TABLE2A accessed 10/24/2011.

150. Emmanuel, "Undermining cooperation."

151. Word Bank, *World Development Report 1992: Development and the Environment* (Washington, DC: World Bank, 1992), Appendix, Table 1.

152. For 1990, Barry Sautman and Yan Hairong, "Trade, Investment, Power and the China-in-Africa Discourse," *The Asia-Pacific Journal* http://japanfocus.org/-Yan-Hairong/3278/article.pdf; for 2001, see BBVA Research, Economic Watch: China, (October 12, 2011): http://www.bbvaresearch.com/KETD/fbin/mult/111014_ChinaWatch_ofdi_tcm348–273161.pdf?ts=7112011

153. Adam Davidson, "Come On, China, Buy Our Stuff!" *New York Times* (January 25, 2012). http://www.nytimes.com/2012/01/29/magazine/come-on-china-buy-our-stuff.html?pagewanted=all&_r=0

154. See, Richard J. Payne and Cassandra R. Veney, "China's Post-Cold War African Policy," *Asian Survey*, 38, 9 (September 1998): 867–79; Denis M. Tull, China's engagement in Africa: scope, significance and consequences," *Journal of Modern African Studies*, 44, 3 (2006), pp. 459–79; Ian Taylor, "China's foreign policy towards Africa in the 1990s", *Journal of Modern African Studies* 36, 3 (1998): 443–60.

155. See Tull, China's engagement in Africa; also Taylor, "China's foreign policy."

156. Data from OECD.statextracts. Aid (ODA) disbursements to countries and regions [DAC2a]. http://stats.oecd.org/Index.aspx?DatasetCode=TABLE2A# accessed April 16th, 2013. Aid from US in constant 2012 dollars.

157. Todd Moss, David Roodman, and Scott Standley, "The Global War on Terror and U.S. Development Assistance: USAID allocation by country, 1998–2005," *Center for Global Development* Working Paper 62 (July 2005), see Table 1. However, the used only USAID data and not ODA data.

158. Ibid., see Table 5.

Chapter 6

The Partial Decentralization of Political Power in Africa

Limited Multiparty Competition and Rising Civil Society

Within a decade of the end of the Cold War, a nearly complete makeover of the political institutions of sub-Saharan Africa had occurred, at least in outward form. In fact, nearly every country in the region had adopted new constitutions leading to multiparty electoral regimes. This represented a clear break from the Cold War period, when one party (de facto or de jure) or military rule was the norm.[1] Moreover, many African countries even established term limits for presidential tenure: something nearly unthinkable for most African polities during the Cold War.

Despite the significant changes in political institutions in the region, most countries in sub-Saharan Africa have not become Western-style democracies: many countries are still governed by many of the same political elites who held control prior to the transitions, significant levels of political power remain in the hands of political leaders, and most of these countries have had only marginal increases in measures of political and civil rights. Therefore, the region experienced a *partial* liberalization of the prevailing political institutions and some practices of sub-Saharan Africa following the end of the Cold War. It is important to study institutional arrangements as they shape the ability of groups to gain and maintain access to office—including their strategies to do so.[2] We now explore the regional context to see the reforms and political institutions that have emerged as well as some explanations as to why.

THE RELATIVE RAPID ADOPTION OF MULTIPARTY REGIMES

Again, the move to adopt multiparty regimes, at least in name, quickly spread throughout the region. Before 1989, only three or four countries had been multiparty electoral regimes for any length of time.[3] A few others have attempted to implement multiparty regimes during the Cold War period, but most were interrupted with periods of military rule (e.g., Nigeria, Ghana) and did not become established. The dominant political institutions of the region during the Cold War were one- or no-party states; however, within five years after the Cold War, no de jure one-party regimes remained.[4]

The third wave, or the "second liberation of Africa," is often said to have commenced in the region with the call for a National Assembly in Benin in 1989, which convened in February of 1990 and was followed by multiparty elections in 1991.[5] Region-wide, between 1989 and 1994, 29 counties held what would be called "founding elections:" ones that moved the country away from one-party to multiparty regimes. Over a third of these occurred in just 1993.[6] An additional 11 countries held such elections from 1995 to 1997.[7] By 1997, only a handful of African countries had failed to hold multiparty elections.[8] This "third wave" swept through Africa in less than a decade after the end of the Cold War, and a majority of these elections were conducted within the first half of that decade. The international, regional, and domestic pressure to hold elections was strong enough that even the staunchest holdout countries soon held elections: Nigeria in 1999, Uganda, in 2005, and the Democratic Republic of the Congo (DRC, formerly Zaire) in 2006. Sudan held multiparty elections in 2010, and it even allowed a referendum whereby Southern Sudan became independent on 9 July 2011.[9] By early 2011, aside from Eritrea, Somalia, and Swaziland, nearly every African country had changed its constitution and held multiparty elections.[10]

Figure 6.1 illustrates the frequency of nations holding founding multiparty competitions since 1989.[11] In pre-1989, four countries had been holding multiparty elections. In 1989, this number rose to five. Two more countries

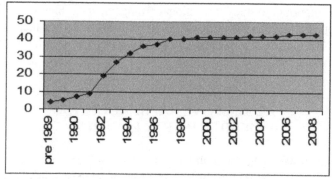

Figure 6.1   Cumulative Founding Multiparty Elections.

were added to the list in 1990 and 1991 each, but the greatest rise began in 1992 and continued through 1997. As we can see, by 1997 and 1998, the rate at which countries were holding founding elections was leveling off. From Figure 6.1, we can see that this was clearly a clustering event, giving evidence of a common regional or international shock, which led to a new regional, institutional equilibrium—not unlike in the first period.

Freedoms Associated with New Electoral Regimes

Not only did nearly all African countries hold multiparty elections, but the aggregate levels of political and civil rights in the region also rose, though only slightly. Looking at Figure 6.2, we see that Sub-Saharan Africa went from an average level of political and civil rights between 2 and 2.5 from the 1970s to 1980s, to between 3.5 and 4 from 1999 onwards (the numbers were inverted, so higher meant more rights).[12] The average level of freedoms in the region went from "not free" to "partly free."[13]

In addition, we see that many more countries were coded as free and partly free than were so coded prior to 1989. For example, in 1975, only three countries were ranked "free," 12 were considered "partly free," and 26 countries were considered "not free."[14] In 2014, ten countries were coded as free, 19 were coded as partly free, and 20 were coded as not free.[15] So, sub-Saharan Africa went from having just over 60% of its ranked countries listed as not free, down to around 41%, while the percent coded as free rose from about 7% to about 20%.[16] The percent of countries ranked as partly free rose from 30% to 39%. These numbers reinforce the idea that a region-wide, but partial, political liberalization occurred.

This increase in the number of countries between authoritarianism and democracy (partly free) is consistent with a new literature examining countries existing in a "grey zone," though they are held to be unlikely to transition into a consolidated democracy.[17] These regimes are often called "hybrid regimes" or "competitive authoritarian."[18] Within the African context, the executive branch has faced limited legislative and judicial constraints on its power.[19]

Levels of Freedoms of Elections

Second, significant variation existed in exactly how free and fair the founding and post-founding elections were. Between 1989 and 2001, van de Walle coded such elections with a two when it was considered to be "free and fair," with a one for "somewhat free and fair," and with a zero for "not free and fair." The average of 87 legislative elections from between 1989 and 1994 was 1.15, with free and fair elections representing 55.5% of the total. Importantly, Bratton has argued that none of the "late elections," held

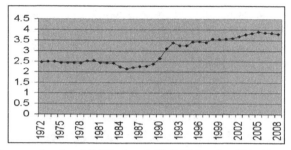

Figure 6.2   Average Levels of Political and Civil Rights for SSA. *Note*: Numbers are inverted: Higher Numbers Mean more Rights

between 1995 and 1997, were considered free and fair (reducing free and fair elections in the region to 43.5% for 1989 to 1997).[20] As Lindberg has argued, however, the holding of less than completely free and fair elections could have a positive aspect in the longer run: after three of four such elections, the more free and fair such elections themselves become.[21]

The region has witnessed a radical change in institutions with the widespread adoption of new electoral regimes and the recognizing of opposition parties. The levels of freedom in many countries have not changed very much, however, and this may suggest that these are hybrid electoral authoritarian regimes adopting the window dressing of democracy to obtain increased domestic and international support for the leaders and their governments. So are these changes breaks with the past or continuations?

EXAMINATION OF THE NEW NORMAL AND THE PARTIAL FRAGMENTATION OF POLITICAL POWER

Types of Executive Branch

The basic outlines of the new African political institutions are described below. Looking at the type of executive systems in the region, 19 countries can be listed as presidential, 24 as hybrid, five as parliamentary, one as a monarchy, and one as a "true" collapsed state.[22] (See Table 6.1). The transitional nations have not yet held multiparty elections, but they are coded among the others as to what they are slated to become. The collapsed state is not double-counted.

Presidential systems are defined as those in which the president is elected for a fixed term, the president has a vice president instead of a prime minister, and the president does not serve in jeopardy of dismissal by the legislative branch prior to the end of the fixed term (not counting impeachment).[23]

Table 6.1 Emerging Executive Forms in SSA*

	Pure Presidential System [19]	Modified or Hybrid Presidential system [24]	Parliamentary [5]	Monarchy [1]	Transitional+/ Failed* States[1] [transitional double counted]
Free	Benin, Ghana	Cape Verde, Namibia, Sao Tome and Principe, Senegal	Botswana, Lesotho, Mauritius, South Africa	Ø	Ø
Partly Free	Burundi, Comoros, Kenya, Liberia, Malawi, Nigeria, the Seychelles, Sierra Leone, Zambia	Burkina Faso, Central African Republic, Djibouti, Guinea Bissau, Madagascar, Mozambique, Niger, Tanzania, Togo, Uganda	Ø	Ø	Ø
Not Free	Angola, Eritrea+, the Gambia, Republic of the Congo, South Sudan+, Sudan, Zimbabwe	Cameroon, Chad, Cote d'Ivoire, Democratic Republic of the Congo, Equatorial Guinea, Gabon, Guinea, Mali, Mauritania, Rwanda	Ethiopia	Swaziland	Eritrea+, South Sudan+, and Somalia*

*Both Zimbabwe and Kenya had had a prime minister's position until 2013. Benin has had periods with and without a prime minister, though as of January 2014, it does not have one. Also, Congo had had a prime prior to 2009. South Sudan is also presidential.

These tend to concentrate power in the hands of an executive, though term limits can reduce this power. A country is coded as presidential if the president was listed as both head of state and head of government and could not be voted out with a simple vote of no confidence.

Many more African nations can be described as a hybrid Presidential system where the president is independently elected, but a prime minister is listed as head of government. However, since nearly all of these Presidents in the region also enjoy majority party support in their systems, few countries have experienced a true equivalent of cohabitation, such as that found twice with the French Fifth Republic.[24] Therefore, the prime ministers in these countries are usually weak. This makes these hybrid systems quite similar to a presidential one in practice, outside of periods of cohabitation.[25] Nonetheless, a more competitive party structure could lead to bigger swings in relative power vis-à-vis the president and the prime minister (and the legislature) should the election return less than a majority for the president's party. Therefore, the potential for more fragmentation of power exists in this version of the system.

Next, five African countries can be listed as parliamentary systems, despite some having the title of head of government officially listed as president. If the country had a head of government who was elected from the parliament and could be removed in a vote of confidence, then it was considered a parliamentary system. For example, in Botswana and South Africa, the president is elected by the national assembly, can be removed by a vote of no-confidence, and usually serves in office for the same length as the national assembly. One key difference here is that he or she is both head of state and government.[26] In Mauritius, the prime minister is the real head of government and is responsible to the legislative assembly, though he or she is appointed by the president.[27] The president is elected for a five-year term—also by the national assembly. This would seem to give the assembly relatively stronger powers, appointing both president and prime minister. In Lesotho, the leader of the majority party is automatically the prime minister. Ethiopia also has a parliamentary system, with a prime minister responsible for daily government, and an elected president by both houses.

One country can be considered a monarchy: Swaziland. Lesotho has a hereditary monarch, but this person has no executive power. Therefore, it is coded as a parliamentary system. Finally, a few countries have transitional governments: Eritrea, South Sudan, and Somalia. Somalia is considered to be a failed state. Above, Eritrea and South Sudan were listed presidential, though they were considered to be going through a transitional period.

Electoral Systems

The most common types of electoral system in Africa tended toward single member district plurality (SMDP), proportional representation (PR) within

Table 6.2   **Electoral System Types Emerging in the Region**

Plurality Systems (With bloc voting*)	Plurality with Run-Off or Second Round	Proportional Representation (PR)	Mixed Plurality and PR
Botswana, Eritrea, Ethiopia, the Gambia, Ghana, Kenya, Liberia, Malawi, Mauritius* Nigeria, Sierra Leone, Swaziland, Tanzania, Uganda, Zambia, Zimbabwe	CAR, Congo-Brazzaville, Gabon, Madagascar, Mali, and Mauritania	Angola, Benin, Burkina Faso, Burundi, Cape Verde, Equatorial Guinea, Guinea Bissau, Mozambique, Namibia, Niger, Rwanda, Sao Tome and Principe, South Africa, and Togo.	Cameroon, Chad, Comoros, Congo-DRC, Cote d'Ivoire, Djibouti, Guinea, Lesotho, Senegal, Seychelles, and Sudan.

multi-member districts, or a mixed system using some combination of these two.[28] However, some countries had a French-type system version of SMDP, where one candidate needed a majority in the first round or they entered into a runoff (RO) comprised of the top two candidates (SMD-RO) or a plurality of the remaining candidates. In 2014, twenty-one countries had single member district elections based upon some type of plurality election. Of these, fifteen countries had SMDP or a close variation upon it.[29] (See Table 6.2) An additional six countries of these countries had single member elections with a two-round system.[30] One country, Mauritius, has the party block vote system[31] in multimember districts, which can increase disproportionality greatly.[32]

Fourteen countries had proportional representation systems to fill most of their seats, with some slight variations. For example, Burundi's elections featured some gender and ethnic balancing, while Namibia had six appointed seats, but 72 of 78 were distributed through PR.[33] Eleven of the remaining countries featured a mix of electoral systems, either mixed member plurality or parallel systems. For example, Comoros elected 24 members with SMD (RO), and 9 from regions; and Senegal elected 90 with SMDP and 60 with PR. Eritrea had yet to hold legislative elections, but it is listed as SMDP. Most former British colonies tended to have SMDP; while most former French colonies appear to have had mixed systems or PR. Two of the three Belgium colonies had PR, and Congo-DRC had a mixed system. All the former Portuguese colonies have adopted some form of PR.

POLITICAL PARTIES AND PARTY SYSTEMS

Dominance of One Political Party

It appears to be the case that elections in most countries in sub-Saharan Africa have resulted in one large majority party, often a second, but quite junior, minority party, and then many fragmented and very small or transitional parties.[34] This is a strong parallel with the first period and decolonization. Van de Walle suggests similarly that there is a large dominant party surrounded by several small and fragmented parties.[35] Empirically, Lindberg shows that from 1989 to 2003, the average share of seats for the largest party in the region was 63%.[36] As in the first period, the winning party in the first set of de jure competitive elections usually kept its majority for several election cycles, if not longer.

Therefore, we can describe many African countries as having a one-party dominant system, so far.[37] Here I define a one-party dominant system as one where a single political party maintains a legislative majority as well as the presidency (where elected independently) for several elections cycles. Should this dominant party be later defeated in elections, this is not considered here to be a nullification of the term, but a transition change away from a one-party dominant system—unless the party which came to power maintains a clear majorities for several cycles—then the dominant party just switched or realigned. The term is used here descriptively and in a more limited manner than others have used it. Also, the term here can include either democracies or non-democracies.

Therefore, some 22 countries in the region can be seen as one-party dominant since the founding elections, or since the last introduction of multiparty regime constitutional regimes.[38] In fact, many of these majorities come close to supermajorities. The similarities with the first period are strong on this level. Angola, Botswana, Burkina Faso, Cameroon,[39] Chad, Cote d'Ivoire,[40] Djibouti,[41] Equatorial Guinea, Ethiopia, Gabon, the Gambia, Guinea,[42] Lesotho,[43] Mozambique, Namibia, Rwanda,[44] the Seychelles, South Africa, Sudan, Tanzania, Togo,[45] Uganda,[46] and Zimbabwe can be counted as one-party dominant (so far). Several others could be so counted with coalitions (as opposed to a single party), such as Comoros, Congo-Brazzaville, and Mauritania.

The astute reader of African politics may have noticed a few "free countries" were in this list. The Botswana Democratic Party (BDP) has held a significant majority in that country since independence. In fact, the BDP has averaged a 79.6% of seats in the legislature over the last four election cycles. In Namibia, the ruling South West Africa People's Organization (SWAPO) initially obtained a 57% share of seats in the lower house. Since 1994, this party has obtained at least 73% of the seats. Even in in South Africa, during the post-apartheid period, the African National Congress (ANC) has won between 62% and 69% of the seats since the first election in 1994.[47]

Even in those countries which have elections that led to a change in which majority party ruled the country, the winning party is almost always associated with the winning president's party, and it usually wins by a large majority. So they are majority party systems, though not in an unbroken chain as in the one-party dominant systems. For example, although parties have changed majorities in Nigeria, the house always had a majority of one party. Updating the data to though mid-2010, the winning party held an average of 64.5% of the seats.[48] For only the most recent elections, the largest party received 63.9% of the seats.[49]

A few countries did not feature majority parties for at least two election cycles. These include the Central African Republic (CAR), the Democratic Republic of the Congo (DRC), Kenya, Lesotho,[50] Liberia,[51] Malawi, Niger, Sao Tome and Principe, and Senegal. Mauritius and Senegal had coalitions which functioned like majority parties and could therefore have had majorities the whole time if we count the coalition. A few others did not have a majority party after only a single election: Guinea-Bissau (in 2004), Madagascar (2007), Mali (2002), Mauritania (2006), and Sierra Leone (1996), Zambia (2006), and Zimbabwe (2008). For those countries where this loss of majority was for the most recent election, this could signal a realignment or an outlier depending of later developments.

Since many independents join ruling party coalitions, the true strength of the ruling party could be vastly understated by a simple measure of seats held, and the leaders could actually rule with a de facto legislative coalitional majority (or even presidential coalition). In fact, smaller parties and independents often bandwagon with the majority, but only after the elections: by being outside the party, the leaders of these parties may have greater leverage in obtaining resources than they would from within the party.[52] In fact, in many countries, the number of independents easily outnumbered the number of many other minority parties: in Uganda, there were 43 independents in the last election, 32 in Mali, 31 in the Cote d'Ivoire, 13 in the DRC, 12 in Congo-Brazzaville, and nine in Liberia.[53]

Among the most fragmented party structures can be seen in the DRC where the largest party obtained only 14% of the seats, and it took the largest nine parties together to comprise 51%.[54] In addition, over 105 parties had at least one seat (and 54 parties had exactly one seat), and 13 seats were held by independents. Despite the clear fragmentation of parties in the DRC, Kabila's legislative coalition was counted at 260 of the 500 seats in 2013.[55] Therefore, a coalition that would sustain a majority emerged, and no vote of confidence would likely unseat him.

Importantly, and this represents a break from the past, some countries which have instituted multiparty elections have seen changes in the parties and leadership that have ruled the countries through elections: Benin, CAR,[56] Cape Verde, Comoros, Ghana, Kenya, Liberia, Madagascar, Malawi, Mauritania, Mauritius, Niger, Nigeria, Sao Tome and Principe, Senegal, Sierra Leone, and Zambia. These countries in which parties have changed hands may provide later incentives for institutional deepening in the region, especially if the turnover of power becomes institutionalized. According to Geddes, at least in the Latin American context, political elites are most likely to engage in meritocratic reform of their bureaucracies under conditions of two or more parties of equal strength that are sometimes in power and sometimes out of power. This could lead to the institutionalization of stronger bureaucracies in the region with a predictable alternation in ruling political party.[57]

Weakness of Rival Political Parties

Beyond the large majority party, one smaller main opposition party has often existed. Even the largest second parties, however, have tended not to be very strong (measured by size). Looking at available data prior to mid-2014, the second party held an average of nearly 18% of the seats in the lower house. This ranged from a high of nearly 47% of the seats (Ghana) to a low of just under 1% (in Gabon, one party had one seat of 120). Of the 44 countries in the sample, only nine countries had second parties holding at least a third of the seats.[58] The average spread in percentage between the winning and second place party (for seats) is 46.6%. Those countries with much closer margins (within 20%) include these: Benin, Cape Verde, the DRC, Ghana, Guinea Bissau, Ivory Coast, Kenya, Lesotho, Madagascar, Niger, Sao Tome, and Zambia. Some of these (aside from DRC) could become two-party systems, but that remains to be seen.

Third or fourth parties tended to be too small and weak to be in a position to gain enough votes to contest for real power in the near term. In fact, the largest two parties together usually held around over three-fourths, or 76%, of all legislative seats from 1989 to 2003. As of 2014, the largest party held an average of 63.9% of the seats, while the largest two had an average of 80% of all seats.[59] The average size of the third winning party (in the last elections available) was 6.3% of the seats,[60] though nearly half (48.8%) of them had 5% or fewer of the seats. Ten percent of these countries had zero seats for third parties. Interestingly, the average number of parties holding seats in the legislature between 1989 and 2003 was higher than one might expect, at 6.6.[61] By mid-2010, the average number of parties in the lower house increased slightly to 7.3%.[62]

Role of Ethnic Parties

One very important difference associated with political parties in this second period is that few political parties are overtly or explicitly linked with ethnic identity. Some of this may be a choice where leaders or would-be leaders of ethnic groups decide to bandwagon with a larger party to obtain access to resources, rather than to be in the opposition. Moreover, and very importantly, at least twenty-two countries have bans on "particularistic" parties, and six others have laws which could be used to exclude ethnic or religious parties.[63] Four of the nine "free" countries had such bans, twelve of twenty-three "party free" countries did, and six of sixteen of the "not-free" countries did. For the laws with language which could be so used, two were found in partly free countries, while four were from not free countries. Therefore, slightly more than half African countries had bans serving as effective barriers to ethnic parties. Examining the latest available data on parties in African legislatures, no dominant parties (in either first or second place) have any apparent ethnic or religious names attached.[64]

One problem with this approach by names is that parties could have this purpose without having the name in place. For example, we know that in Kenya several parties were more closely aligned with some ethnic groups than others, though none of them were clearly identified as such by the name of the party. Basedau et al. identify a couple of countries which have banned parties for being overly religious or ethnic: the Movement démocratique républican (MDR) was banned as a Hutu party; and the Islamic Party of Kenya (IPK) was also banned.[65]

Party Institutional Strength

Despite the apparent dominance of one large majority party in most states in Africa, the literature describes African parties as "plagued by weak organisations, low levels of institutionalisation, and weak links to the society they are supposed to represent," as well as having high levels of volatility.[66] As such, African parties continue to be characterized as personalist, clientelist, and weakly institutionalized.[67] Kuenzi and Lambright argue, however, that with repeated elections and more time, these parties are becoming more institutionalized.[68] They ranked thirty sub-Saharan African countries that had at least two sequential multiparty elections by level of the institutionalization of their parties from three to nine, where three is the least institutionalized and nine the most. Countries with an aggregate score of eight or above were considered to have institutionalized political parties. Botswana, the Gambia, Namibia, Senegal, and South Africa were so classified. Those between six and eight were closer to being institutionalized, and these were Zimbabwe, Cape Verde, Malawi, Cote d'Ivoire, Mauritius, CAR, Seychelles, and Sao Tome (although they labelled Zimbabwe and Cote d'Ivoire as "hegemonic in transition.")[69] Those below six were classified as inchoate. These were (in reverse rank order [from six to three]) Burkina Faso, Congo, Kenya, Madagascar, Benin, Eq. Guinea, Gabon, Ghana, Mauritania, Zambia, Djibouti, Togo, Cameroon, Lesotho, Mali, Niger, and Comoros.

FACTORS MILITATING TOWARD THE CONTINUED CONCENTRATION OF POLITICAL POWER IN SUB-SAHARAN AFRICA

Although a partial liberalization has emerged, the political elite continue to control significantly high levels of political and economic power. Although more liberal political institutions are in place in Africa, much of the foundational aspects required to sustain a democracy remain weak in the region. Below we examine some of the more important of these.

Per Capita Incomes Still Low/Poverty Still High

Many scholars feel that democracy has prerequisites of development for it to endure in certain societies, and we see that most sub-Saharan African nations are still in an area of concern in this regard.[70] And some scholars in political science feel that countries below 2,000 per capita are especially susceptible to democratic reversals.[71] In 2010, two decades after the end of the Cold War, the average income in the region (in 2005 dollars) between 2006 and 20012 was right about $1,785.[72] This includes highs of $13,732 in Equatorial Guinea and $12, 980 for the Seychelles. If we exclude these two, then the next wealthiest country is Gabon, at $6,331. Many African countries had per capita incomes under $300, such as Burundi, the DRC, Eritrea, Ethiopia, and Liberia. Some wealthier countries had per capita incomes above $4,000, such as Botswana, Equatorial Guinea, Mauritius, Namibia, the Seychelles, and South Africa. So, average levels of wealth are still quite low. Only three countries are above the $6,000; mark which some think is required for stable democracy, and most are below the $2,000 level usually considered to be very fragile.

Not only are per capita income averages low in many countries, but also significant numbers of their citizens live on less than $2 a day. In fact, within the region, only South Africa, Gabon, and Kenya have fewer than 40% of its citizens living on the two dollar a day level.[73] This does not auger well for a vibrant democratic citizenry, nor does it auger well for an emerging entrepreneurial environment, given weak domestic markets.

Increased, but Still Low, Literacy Rates

Again, literacy is part of the underpinning of more liberal societies, and it remains quite low in Africa, despite some improvement since independence. For example, the percentage was 61% for the region (based upon available data), but with a high of 91.3% (Equatorial Guinea) and a low of 19% (Niger).[74] Several countries had sub-Saharan literacy rates of less than 50%: Burkina Faso, Chad, Cote d'Ivoire, Ethiopia, Guinea, Mali, Mozambique,

Niger, Senegal, and Sierra Leone. Data was missing for South Sudan and Somalia, which are probably among the lowest.

Continued Weakness of "Civil Society"

At the time of the "founding" elections following the end of the Cold War, few organizations existed which could mount an effective national political campaign. Civil society did often (and temporarily) form a united protest movement dislodging former authoritarian leaders or forcing elections upon the political elite. But this unity usually fragmented after the unifying object was successfully removed (i.e., the former authoritarian rule).

Part of the reason for the weakness of civil society in this second period is similar to the first.[75] Most post-independence, authoritarian African regimes continued colonial policies regarding civil society: few permitted strong interest groups to compete for policy preferences. Fewer still allowed strikes by labor, especially in state-owned sectors. In fact, Tordoff wrote that labor unions were actually more constrained in the post-independence period than during the colonial period![76] States wanted unions weak or tamed for several reasons: first states were usually the largest employer, and unions would direct their demands for wages at the government itself; inflation could follow from higher wages; the government feared strikes; powerful unions could widen urban-rural divides; and unions could become a potential threat as a rival form of power.[77] He suggested this was a pattern for nearly all interest groups for most of the post-independence period: that they were often weaker post-independence through the Cold War.

Also, rare were the African countries that allowed a free press to blossom during the Cold War period.[78] Only a few countries had a print press listed as free from 1980 to 1989: Botswana, the Gambia, and Mauritius. Interestingly, Nigeria had a press that was ranked as either free or partly free for these years.[79] Nine other countries had a print press ranked as partly free for several years (i.e., Burkina Faso, Cote d'Ivoire, Ghana, Lesotho, Liberia, Senegal, South Africa, Zambia, and Zimbabwe). In 1989, combining print press and broadcast, only Mauritius and Nigeria were ranked as free. Botswana, the Gambia, Senegal, and Sudan were listed as partly free (although Sudan had been not free for most of the prior period). Thirty-seven other countries were ranked as not free. Nonetheless, the most visible organizations which could form an incipient civil society to compose additional political parties (e.g., traditional or ethnic leaders, church groups, labor unions, youth groups, and business groups) still face similar problems as they did during the early decolonization and independence period.[80]

Civil society in Africa remains quite weak, even with new elections, since the level of wealth is so low and since so few major economic activities have been outside of the state realm for very long.[81] One scholar says civil society is weak due to the "miserable economic conditions of contemporary African states . . . [as well as] the weakness of the domestic private sector."[82] Also, given majority state ownership of most capital-intensive industries, banks, or mineral or oil exporting sectors during the Cold War era, a private indigenous business class had few opportunities to accumulate wealth outside of the state.[83] Bratton suggested that the strongest civil societies were located in countries where more economic resources existed outside of direct state control, especially where significant domestic industrialization has taken place, such as in Kenya, Zimbabwe, or South Africa.[84] However, Zimbabwean civil society has clearly been weakened since the failed transition to democracy.

Even those who feel that civil society was central to the regional move away from authoritarianism may feel that it is too weak to lead to consolidation of democracy. Thus, it helped promote liberalization and not democracy per se. Gyimah-Boadi argued:

> Civil society remains too weak to be democracy's mainstay, not only in Nigeria and Zaire (where transitions have become stalemated), and in Burkina Faso, Cameroon, Ghana, Kenya, and Togo (where transition outcomes are still ambiguous), but also in Benin, Malawi, South Africa, and Zambia (where outcomes have been more clearly successful). In nearly all cases, the ability of civil society to help deepen democratic governance and put it beyond reversal remains in serious doubt.[85]

More recent events have not contradicted these insights, and despite elections that were later held in most of these countries, the ones in doubt are not coded as free. Fortunately, not too many countries have reverted, but so many appear to exist in the grey zone between authoritarianism and more democratic systems.[86]

Continued Neopatrimonial Practices

Beyond the relative weakness of alternate organizations, perhaps the most important trend illustrating the continued consolidation of power by the political elite in the region is the emergence, in most countries, of one-party dominant or majority party systems in a context of neopatrimonial rule. In these cases, the peculiar advantages enjoyed by incumbents are strong: they control most of the media, the army, the courts, the bureaucracies, and most of the funding within the nation. Reflecting this, recall the finding that whoever won the presidency usually also won a majority of seats in the legislature. This appears to be true in both the immediate post-colonial elections and the "founding" elections of post-1989.

Within sub-Saharan Africa, the amount of professional wage positions distributed through state apparatus remains high. The average percentage of wage employment through the state in the region was 35.9% in the late 1980s.[87] Where countries had majority state ownership of industries of mining or oil, the average share of state wage employment was as high as 71%.[88] In Tanzania, for example, state employment represented more than three quarters of public sector workers in the 1980s. According to another source, and from a sample of six major countries, parastatal workers averaged about 58% of all public employees within the civil service.[89] So "normal" state workers, such as teachers, postal workers, bureaucrats, and so forth, only made up about 42% of state workers.[90] Therefore, in states with significant role in the economy, they could control up to 75% of formal employment, and if hiring and firing decisions have a political element, then opposition party members would probably forfeit state sponsored formal sector employment while in the minority. In fact, states routinely used such patronage to cement their power into a single party in the first period.[91] In Kenya, after founding elections were held, Moi made clear to state employees that civil servants found supporting the opposition would be sacked.[92]

Moreover, once a party won power, the political elite of the party used the "traditional" political and economic levers of the state to further reinforce their rule: they had control over most high paying jobs, they controlled the state media, and they had use of the coercive power of the state. Also, where their majorities were large enough, they could simply change the rules of the game to maintain their power. These things were at work in both periods. For example, in Kenya, the ruling party KANU used its power to establish the rules of the elections which favored a KANU victory, including needing 25% of the vote in five of eight provinces, control of voting registration, control of the media, use of fraudulent state resources to buy votes, the use of police and courts to restrict the right of assembly, pre-election violence to divide the pro-farming groups and other potential opposition groups, and, finally, voter fraud.[93] The parallels with the first period are strong, short of the complete elimination of the opposition from the polls. Other events also resulted in a fragmented opposition, but Moi and KANU had an active hand in maintaining a plurality of votes with the new elections, and the international community condoned this behavior by accepting quick elections in lieu of widespread institutional reform. In fact, donors pressured minority parties to participate in elections and the national assembly instead of boycotting them.[94]

Also, the people usually in charge of setting up the transitional elections have been the incumbent political elite that used the power of office to help steer the results in its preferred direction. So incumbents had significant input in the shaping of the new procedures of competition and could form them in ways that would favor incumbents, or they hoped would favor them, and the later in the reforms that these transitions took place, the more learning they had and perhaps the better able they were to shape the results.

As discussed before, in the early elections (1989–1994), over a third of these founding elections resulted in a change in the chief executive (37.9%), while for the latter elections (1995–1997) only around 7% did so.[95] Thus, incumbents were likely to keep power in over 60% of the cases, and even in loss, the former leaders were likely to form a main opposition party, often later recapturing power.[96] As in the first period, the former ruling party (competing in the new elections) often had disproportionate access to people with leadership skills and experience in campaigning and governing.

Perhaps the best evidence of incumbency advantage, in general, comes from the results of these new elections. From 1990 to 2012, of 169 elections held in the region, 114 (or 67.5%) resulted in the election of the incumbent leader.[97] If we include succession within party, this becomes an incumbent victory for 130 of 169 elections (nearly 77%). However, 39 elections did result in the victory of the opposition leader at the polls (23%). Even though this number is small, we must remember that only around 20% of the continent is ranked as free, and not all free countries had changed the party in power.

Continued Role of Authoritarian Leaders

The spread of elections was also only a partial liberalization of politics as so many former ruling parties and elites continued to hold power following founding elections. Several scholars suggest that a true measure of a democracy is the alteration of the parties and leaders in power.[98] As mentioned elsewhere, in much of sub-Saharan Africa, the political party which had been in charge prior to the adoption of multiparty regimes tended to become the new ruling party afterwards—and where it was not, it was usually the main opposition party.[99] Examining founding elections, Bratton and van de Walle show that in 15 of 29 elections (52%), the incumbents (heads of the former ruling party) remained in control. In a few cases, the outcome was mixed, but in only 11 of 29 (38%) elections between 1989 and 1994 were the incumbents clearly ousted. In another study, and for elections held between 1995 and 1997, only a third of African elections led to an alteration in power.[100]

Similarly, Ishiyama and Quinn showed that the former dominant party (FDP) was quite likely to either win a majority under the new electoral rules or become the most powerful opposition party.[101] Examining several elections between the years of 1989 and 2000, it was found that the leaders of the former dominant party remained in power in 15 of 21 countries studied (about 70%).[102] Another scholar showed that between 1990 and 1999, half of the old guard of autocratic leaders still held effective power after the new elections.[103] Therefore, leaders of the formerly dominant parties were later able to become president or prime minister, as the cases of Kenya and Ghana illustrate. Nonetheless, the opposition is faring better in the new period compared to the old: according to Goldsmith, by 2001, in 78 elections, 21 resulted in an opposition victory (about 27%), this compared with the earlier period of one opposition victory out of 126 (about 0.8%).[104]

Even should elections remove the incumbent leader or even if a candidate from an opposition party wins, this does not necessarily mean that the new leadership is radically different form the old guard. As Lindberg illustrates, even when leaders are replaced, it is usually by someone who had been in the upper echelons of the former ruling party. Even with "free and fair elections," members of the old autocratic guard were voted out of power in only 12% to 17% of elections from 1990 to 2003.[105] Where incumbent leaders step down due to term limits, they are as likely as not replaced by someone who had been powerful in the incumbent's party. Moreover, even where candidates from opposition parties win elections, as in Ghana and Kenya, the replacements were usually linked to the old guard: Kufour had been a member of Rawling's cabinet, and Kibaki had been vice president under Moi.[106] Nonetheless, Lindberg does show that with more and more elections, more and more members of the old guard do drop out, with a high of 50% gone by the fourth election cycle.[107]

Importantly, a new trend is emerging in the post-Cold War period: the peaceful and electoral removal and/or replacement of the chief executive. Well-known cases of the alteration of power for the chief executive through elections include these: Benin, Botswana, Ghana, Kenya, Namibia, Nigeria, Senegal, South Africa, Tanzania, and Zambia. This turnover of power does not always translate into an alteration of party in power, however. For example, in Namibia, South Africa, and Tanzania, the political party that won the first founding election has remained in power since, even if particular leaders have left office. This has also been true in Botswana since independence. Nonetheless, and returning to the idea of turnover, some scholars have shown that most African presidents are now leaving office because of term limits, voluntary retirements, or electoral losses—compared to two-thirds that were removed through violence or coups as in the prior period.[108]

Continued Elite Control of the Economy

Beyond controlling large number of jobs channeled through "traditional" state bureaucracies, African states continue to have significant control over many parts of the formal economy, which in turn impacts multiparty democracy. As we will see in the next chapter, a partial privatization of state-controlled industry has begun, but as a percentage of formal sector employment, the number remains high. And when political elites control significant elements of the economy, this can be used to increase both their economic and political power. This was seen during the Cold War period, and the logic should be no different in the second period.

With the change in the international system after the end of the Cold War, and the economic crises that so many countries with majority state ownership experienced, many of these neopatrimonial regimes were under significant stress. It was this stress that led to the openings for reform, along with the international pressure. In Chapter 8, I argue that those countries most in need of international sources of revenue to sustain neopatrimonial systems allowed for reforms which led to a greater increase in political and civil rights compared to other similar African countries (see Chapter 8). This is because their access to resources to continue to run patronage machines was in decline from a combination of failed domestic economies, lack of comparative advantage in exporting, and international linkages of aid or ODA to economic and political liberalization. Countries which had featured majority state ownership of most capital-intensive industries and therefore followed more inward-oriented development policies, and this went against their natural comparative advantages. One major exemption would be countries with significant mining or oil export sectors; although they may have followed policies that went against their comparative advantage, continued access to resources from these normally lucrative sectors would have continued. Also, countries which were more outward-oriented (or less inward) were more likely to have kept a viable agricultural export sector which could have helped continue to fund the patronage machine. So, in the short term, state ownership weakened civil society and strengthened the political elite. Moreover, majority state ownership of most or all industry (as well as mines and banking sectors (see Chapters 4 and 7)) virtually ensured that no important business class could rise to compete for power with the political elites, as the commanding heights of the economy were already occupied.[109] Nonetheless, all countries in Africa were vulnerable enough to international and domestic pressure to adopt at least the outward appearance of political reforms by allowing multiparty elections to take place, however, free and fair they may or may not have been.

Even with more party competition, African systems tend to be dominated by large parties, and these parties and their leaders tend to undergird their power through access to, and distribution of, patronage. Therefore, the patrimonial core of the prior systems seems to be intact. As discussed previously, state ownership and/or control of many parts of the economy allowed the political elite to capture revenue streams as well as direct jobs and resources to their followers. Majority state ownership has also been linked with corruption.[110] And even though many countries are privatizing many former majority state-owned industries (see next chapter), the state remains a significant economic player as well as the source of so much employment for so many states. In fact, the control of significant amounts of bureaucratic and economic resources by ruling political elites is still the case, and they use these resources to remain in power—through the ideological support for these practices as well as the number of companies they control are in decline.

Nonetheless, as in the period immediately following independence, states in the region in the second period continued to have weak business classes, though not as weak as in the prior period.[111] for those countries in which the state had owned most of the capital-intensive industries during the Cold War, this trend should have been worse, but it is generally true for most countries of the region. Therefore, in most countries, no strong commercial class existed that was independent of state support and could easily and quickly become organized into an opposition party—if this class even had desired to do so—as Przeworski suggests is required for democracy to move forward.[112] Moreover, after years of high levels of taxation and policies that harmed agricultural exporting sectors, few groups existed that could translate their economic power into political power. The most notable exceptions were Cote d'Ivoire, Kenya, and Zimbabwe—though Mugabe has neutered this potential class of agricultural opponents once they backed the opposition: he allowed the forcible taking of farms held by the white minority and had these lands pass to political loyalists (under the banner of giving to the veterans of the war of liberation).

Not only was the domestic bourgeoisie weak relative to the state, but most people in the region employed in the formal sector continue to be employed by the state. The state employed anywhere from a third to nearly three quarters of all formal sector employees near the end of the 1980s. Those where the state featured MSO had an average employment level of 70%, while non-MSO was still high at 37%.[113] According a World Bank source, the average level of total employment by state-owned enterprises was 21.5% between 1986 and 1991, right before or at the transition. This number excluded "normal" employment for the state, such as teachers, police, bureaucrats, and so forth.[114] This meant that significant numbers of jobs were at stake in the outcomes of elections in the region, especially where the legacies of the government were more dirigist. However, even many years after the end of the Cold War, state employment in sub-Saharan Africa remains high by international standards.[115]

Unchanged Self-Interest of Incumbents in Holding Power

Ruling elites are assumed to be power maximizers in this analysis, and when faced with growing pressure for democratization from below in addition to those from international forces, they are assumed to attempt to design new institutions that would have the appearances of democracy while still maintaining as much power as possible.[116] This assumption appears to reflect African realities and is shared by many African scholars. Therefore, the international and domestic pressure for political and economic reforms was felt most strongly by countries that were not self-sufficient in providing funding for their patronage systems. However, most political elites facing the need to adopt reforms attempted to implement only the minimal amount necessary to satisfy international and domestic constituencies. Minimal reforms would also maximize their likelihood of maintaining power. This was the goal, but as with Gorbachev and his designs to create a more open Soviet system, reform efforts can sometimes overtake the original plans of their designers (we could also add the French revolution to this point).

However, countries with fewer domestic resources to mobilize in the service of their patronage system were more likely to adopt more significant reforms; they could not risk being penalized and having their access to resources for patronage lost. However, many regimes would agree to partial reforms and then retreat from them after obtaining the resource flows, as Zaire was known to have done many times. However, with the end of the Cold War, and Mobutu's diminished importance to the international community, and his refusal to implement significant reforms, he was indeed cut off from international resource flows. Also, some scholars have shown that countries where leaders adopted reforms later in this process than others were better able to rig the system and win later elections.[117] Often, however, these countries were in less desperate economic straits. Mugabe is one of the few former leaders of an independence movement left in the 1990s who could draw on anti-colonial nationalism to remain in power and fight the forces of democracy: incumbents at the end of the Cold War were rarely the ones who led the march to independence in the second period, nor had many a track record of bringing about prosperity, and many had lost the patronage needed to maintain their regimes.

FACTORS MILITATING IN FAVOR OF THE FRAGMENT POLITICAL POWER

Despite so many aspects of the continued consolidation of power, some countries adopted polities which helped fragment power, though these were unevenly adopted throughout the region. Even though many rulers look at elections as a way of maintaining power, they could also become a means of limiting power, especially over time. Here the fragmentation could be away from mere personal rule or away from ruling parties or other institutions of power.

The Holding of de jure Elections

As already discussed, nearly every African country has moved from some form of one-party rule or military rule to a version of rule where election outcomes have to be respected as an extension of the rule of law (at least de jure). Therefore, although many countries have single, large dominant parties that approximate the same power of one-party states, most hold elections that might matter, and many have elections which have mattered. Moreover, specifically in a study of African elections, Lindberg has shown that the holding of de jure free and fair elections, even when they are clearly not de facto free and fair initially, will—over time—lead to the holding of elections which improve in their level of fairness.[118] He does not argue that the countries became more democratic, per se, but that the elections became freer over time. Thus, when political stakes in elections are high, more and more demands over the propriety of elections emerge from society. Therefore, the holding of multiparty elections is clearly one of the most important fragments of political accountability.[119]

Term Limits

Since so many of these systems centralized power in the hands of one person, term limits could become an indispensable potential check on personal power (if only temporally). In fact, many Presidential systems have term limits, which help nullify some of the advantages of incumbency and the consolidation of power into the hands of just one person. Parties associated with past presidents are strong, but not as strong as ones with a president running as an incumbent: Rawlings' party lost only after did not run, but his heir apparent did. Heir apparents are not as strong as former leaders. They do not have the same name recognition. Also, he or she might be weakened in a power struggle over who will win the nomination.

With the end of the Cold War, and the adoption of new constitutions, many presidential systems have prohibitions against the chief executive serving more than two terms. For example, examining 38 presidential systems from 1990 to 2005, Posner and Young show that 32 of them had imposed term limits.[120] However, of these thirty-two, the leaders of 18 countries came face to face with the realities of terms limits, and half of them tried to change the constitution to extend their ability to remain in power. Of these, three failed (Malawi, Nigeria, and Zambia) and six succeeded (Chad, Gabon, Guinea, Namibia, Togo, and Uganda).[121] Since then, Burkina Faso, Cameroon, and Niger have also had term limits removed or extended as the incumbent encountered these limits.[122] In every such case, the incumbent won the subsequent election.

In the nine countries where the chief executive stepped down due to term limits, the former President's party sometimes lost the next contested set of elections. For example, in Benin, Cape Verde, Ghana, Kenya, Mali, and São Tomé and Príncipe, the candidate from the former president's party has lost. In Mozambique, the Seychelles, South Africa, and Tanzania, by contrast, the candidates which ran as the candidate for their parties retained the office of president.[123] Botswana has recently introduced term limits, despite being a parliamentary system. These examples have the possibility of becoming norms and what maybe the new African "normal" politics, though this is far from assured.

Rising Power of Opposition Parties and Some Alternation in Power

Some fragmentation of political power can be seen clearly in the few countries where the parties that lost the founding elections would later capture a majority in the legislature or the executive branch. In Cape Verde, Ghana, Guinea Bissau, Kenya, Lesotho, Liberia, Madagascar, Mali, Nigeria, Senegal and Sierra Leone, parties which did not win the founding elections have later come to hold a majority of seats in the lower house.[124]

However, given the tendency for a one-party dominant system to emerge under these conditions, chances for the opposition to take power do not seem strong, even if one party was successful in doing so one time. One place where opposition parties seem to be more vibrant, ironically, is where the former dominant party (FDP) lost the founding election, and they became the major opposition party. Looking at the data from Ishiyama and Quinn, when the FDP had less than a majority (but more than 0), their average percent seats was 28%, which is more than double the average for Lindberg's data for second parties.[125] Of the 30 data points where the FDP had more than zero, but less than 50%, in only six cases did they hold 13% or fewer of the seats. Therefore, opposition parties comprised of formerly dominant parties appear to have more seats than newer parties arising out of the ashes of the one-party systems. However, other opposition parties may be gaining, if only slightly, as elections continue. In a study looking at party strength over elections, Rakner and van de Walle show that the average percentage of seats for second parties rises to 21.4% for third elections and over 27% for third and fourth round election cycles.[126]

Ghana is probably the best example where an opposition party is strong, and an alternating two-party system is emerging. In Ghana, the seats won by the non-ruling party rose from 4% in 1993, to 30% in 1996, and stayed around 40% thereafter (46% in 2000, 40% in 2004, and 46% in 2008).[127] Moreover, Ghana has met the "two turnover" rule, with Rawlings' party winning the founding elections, losing the elections when the successor in his party, Atta Mills, lost to Kufor for two cycles. After Kufor was ineligible to run for elections due to term limits, the parliament swung back to Rawlings' party again. Nonetheless, despite the potential ability to wrest control away from the rule party, most opposition parties remain fragmented and weak.

Federalism

Most African countries have had unitary forms of government. During the Cold War period, only Nigeria had any real long-term experience with federalism,[128] though in the DRC (Zaire), regional governments had significant de facto power during the First Republic.[129] Also, several other countries have experimented with federal systems: Cameroon, Zaire/DRC, Kenya, Senegal/Soudan, Sudan, and Uganda. Most of the others emerged out of the colonial period with unitary forms of government, which meant that sovereignty was not divided or shared, and that winning at the national level meant gaining ultimate authority for all state revenues and polices. This greatly increased the political control of those winning national elections as they had no competing, autonomous governing institutions with which to share power.

In the second period, one scholar suggests that Ethiopia, Nigeria, South Africa, and Tanzania were among the few with federal systems (as of 1997).[130] According to another source, we can count Comoros, Ethiopia, Nigeria, and South Africa, with Sudan in transition to federalism.[131] The Democratic Republic of the Congo (DRC) may also be considered a federal system as members of the senate are elected by provincial assemblies.[132] Interestingly, the constitution of the DRC is silent on the issue, though some suggest that it may be leaning toward a federal system.[133] In addition, Sudan was considered a transitioning federal system, though the South has recently left the federation. Federal systems within authoritarian countries would not pose a real limit on power, though as countries democratize, the impact of federalism as a means of fragmenting power should grow. Nonetheless, most countries remain non-federal.

Bicameralism

Eighteen of forty-eight countries (around 38%) are listed as having two houses: Botswana, Burundi, Congo-Brazzaville, the DRC, Ethiopia, Gabon, Lesotho, Liberia, Madagascar, Mauritania, Namibia, Nigeria, Rwanda, Senegal, South Africa, Sudan, Swaziland, and Zimbabwe. Of these, the DRC, Ethiopia, Nigeria, South Africa, and Sudan are federal where one should expect a second house, though neither Comoros nor Tanzania have a second house and are held to be federal by some. Going by levels of freedoms, it seems that both free and partly free nations are nearly two-to-one unicameral to bicameral, whereas in not free countries it is nearly evenly divided.

Of these with two houses, only a few—Gabon, Liberia, Nigeria, and Zimbabwe—had direct elections of most or all of its members to the second house. The rest were the result of appointments by the executive branch, or indirect elections from lower level governments, or some combination of these two. In Swaziland, most are appointed by the King, though some are appointed by the house. Also, most recently, Lesotho's 33 senators were comprised of 22 traditional chiefs and those who are appointed by the king.[134]

Limited Domestic Resources Available to Political Elites

Africa was nearly universally singled out as the worst economic performing region, especially since the publication of the so-called Berg Report.[135] It mostly remained so through the late 1990s. Although the attributed causes of economic problems were debated, this framed the debate about African growth for years to come. In fact, most countries in sub-Saharan Africa had low per capita incomes, low levels of investment from abroad, high and growing debt levels, declining shares of international trade, and low or negative growing economies. From 1970 onwards, nominal GDP in sub-Saharan Africa grew more slowly than any other region, while real GDP growth rates declined.[136] For most of the Cold War period, after independence, regional growth of per capita GDP was 0.05%.[137] However, from 1980 to 1987, African GDP per capita growth was negative 2.8.[138] The average GDP per capita in 1987 was $330.[139] These countries were not rich, nor were they growing. Moreover, these conditions were generally worse in countries which had featured majority state ownership of industries (especially if they did not have oil).[140]

Moreover, increased pressures from rising oil prices and declining exports led most African countries into very high levels of debt and debt servicing, which increased these countries' vulnerability to external pressures for economic and political reform. In fact, around the end of the Cold War, the region had debts as a percentage of GDP of 80%, and debt service as a percentage of exports at 14.7%.[141]

Externally Imposed Conditionality

The economic performance of the region was so bad, that most African countries began to be under structural adjustment requirements by the World Bank and IMF, beginning in the mid-1980s. In fact, by 1989, over thirty African countries were "actively engaged in wide-ranging programs of economic reform or structural adjustment."[142] And within a few years (1993), nearly every African country was under, or had been under, some structural adjustment program.[143] Although the programs for each country varied, "four basic elements are always present: currency devaluation, the removal/reduction of the state from the workings of the economy, the elimination of subsidies in an attempt to reduce expenditures, and trade liberalisation."[144] Clapham and others suggest that this undermined the very sovereignty of such nations. However, as described in the next chapter, implementation of most programs was at best incomplete, though more implementation followed with the end of the Cold War.

The requirements of structural adjustment were mostly to return to the market the most basic economic decisions and to implement free(r) trade. The prior distortions away from free trade were meant to create industrialization, but they also afforded valuable political rents to politicians, which they parted with only reluctantly. (See next chapter for more on Structural Adjustment.)

Rising Power of Civil Society/Protests

Despite the absolute weakness of African civil society discussed previously, it may be rising relatively in the post-Cold War period, and many argue that it was pivotal to mobilize against tyranny. In fact, civil society seems to have played this role in many of the transitions away from authoritarianism in the region in the 1990s as well as in the first period against colonial rule.[145] Protests from civil society were clearly evident during the widespread movement toward political liberalization in the region.[146] In fact, Bratton and van de Walle argued that protests were the key elements in the liberalization of the region.[147] However, the link between protests and democratization does not seem to be so clear cut.[148] According to their own data, in five out of 14 cases (35.7%), no widespread protests occurred, even though these countries would later liberalize. Moreover, where widespread protests did take place, eleven out of twenty-eight did hold democratic elections (39.3%). Importantly, of the 42 countries under study, 40 had significant political reforms (95%), despite variance of protests. However, political elites were certainly aware of protests in neighboring nations and may have made choices to avoid them preemptively.

Nonetheless, civil society was strengthened and deepened as a result of the massive protests as well as the transition to more liberal regimes. In fact, Bratton and van de Walle illustrate nicely the degree to which certain groups within civil were involved in protests (e.g., students, civil service, unions, churches, and defectors from the political elite).[149] Clearly, how the state responded to these protests mattered, and this response impacted the nature and timing of reforms. According to Bratton:

> In response to popular protest and donor pressure, African political leaders created political openings—for example, by releasing political prisoners and abandoning one-party constitutions—that improved the legal environment for free expression and association. There is considerable evidence that previously closed political space was occupied by genuine manifestations of civil society, namely by structures of associations, networks of communication, and norms of civic engagement.[150]

Bratton also argues that Africa's civil society was engaged and strengthened through the national conferences held mostly in Francophone West Africa.[151] These intentionally brought together elites from various aspects of social, civil, political, and economic spheres to draft a new social order. When they demand sovereignty, a critical point in transitions occurs. These conferences were loosely based upon France's early assemble of les trois états. [152]

Also, the rising economic and political power forming outside of the state may help strengthen civil society in the long term. As discussed previously, some argue that a powerful private sector is necessary for democracy to survive; for example, Przeworski argues that democracy requires a bourgeoisie with divided interests for democracy to take place.[153] Otherwise, as Moore suggests, a dependent bourgeois class is likely to be a junior partner in an authoritarian state.[154] Quinn showed that the few African countries which did have longer runs of multiparty politics did not feature majority state ownership of oil, mining, or most capital-intensive industry.[155] However, as discussed elsewhere in this chapter (and the next), a significant amount of the market and its regulation remain in political elites' hands, though this is diminishing slowly.

A similar view can be taken of civil society generally: it is weaker the more space the state takes up. However, the direction of action between civil society and the state is not unidirectional. A complicating aspect of analyzing civil society is that civil society may actually need an institutionalized and predictable state for it to arise: the state has to promote and allow civil society to become more powerful before civil society can be strong enough to challenge or restrain the state. Should a weakly entrenched civil society come to oppose the state in a semi-authoritarian environment, state support would probably be withdrawn, or leaders of civil society could face active repression—either of which necessarily weakens civil society.[156] Nonetheless, civil society remains a latent force for democracy as more human capital which could be used one day for leadership is spread throughout the body politic.

Rising Power Non-governmental Organizations (NGOs)

The one area where civil society may be much stronger relative to the decolonization period is for non-governmental organizations (NGOs). Not all NGOs are domestic, though international NGOs make an effort to work with domestic civil society and channel money into areas of mobilization outside of the state. As states become less able to provide traditional public sector goods, NGOs are the likely substitutes.[157] In fact, the rise of neo-liberalism and NGO provision of social services was a coincidence with mutual reinforcing tendencies.[158] However, NGOs funded from abroad, represent sources of organization and funding outside of traditional ruling elite power.

NGOs have increased significantly in numbers, and they have more access to resources. According to one source, NGOs numbered in the 100s during the early independence period, but they numbered around 25,000 in 2005.[159] The

United Nations also coordinates much of its work with NGOs: they worked with around 41 in 1948, and they recently work closely with around 1,350.[160] In Kenya for example, the number of NGOs increased nearly threefold from 1978 to 1988.[161] Importantly, USAID began to work specifically with NGOs to increase the latter's capacity and strength in the region as a way of improving civil society.

The movement toward stronger indigenous NGOs in Africa really began in the late 1980s.[162] Aside from Kenya and South Africa, NGOs in most African countries had been "characterized by small and institutionally weak nongovernmental sectors. In recent years, this situation has been changing rapidly in a number of countries as more pluralistic modes of governance have been accepted and pursued."[163] NGOs are gaining strength within the region.

Not only are NGOs increasing in number and importance, they are also distributing more and more aid on behalf of nations or intergovernmental organizations. This was done in part to combat perceived corruption by not having these resources flow (directly) through the hands of the ruling political party and its leaders. How much aid NGOs distribute is somewhat in dispute, though the numbers appear to be high: they distributed between \$2.2bn to \$2.5bn in 1992/3, depending on the source.[164] Moreover, the Overseas Development Institute suggests that these numbers underrepresent the real flows. NGOs distribute an average of 5% of donor (OECD) bilateral aid, ranging from a low of 1% for Japan to a high of 30% for Sweden.[165] Official donors (including nations) are channeling more of their aid through NGOs. In the 1970s, only about 1.5% of NGO revenues came from official donors, while this has risen to over 30% in the mid-1990s.[166] In the post-Cold War period, "[n]on-governmental organizations have been increasingly recognized [by the USAID] as indispensable to creating and sustaining the civil society framework fundamental to long-term sustainable development in the newly independent nations of the former Soviet Union as well as in traditional developing countries."[167] Although USAID (the American Aid agency) does not publish how much it channels through NGOs, in 1995 Al Gore announced that the administration would have about 40% of development assistance (one type of aid) distributed through NGOs.[168] Within Africa, NGOs managed over \$1 billion by 1990, and this amount has more than tripled to \$3.5 billion.[169]

The World Bank, as well, is channeling more money through NGOs with the end of the Cold War. From 1973 to 1988, NGOs were involved with only around 6% of projects funded by the Bank, whereas by 1990 NGOs were directly involved in some way with over 22% of Bank-funded projects.[170] This number rose to 50% by 1994. Importantly, the Bank began to prefer indigenous NGOs to international ones over time. From 1973 to 1991, 40% of NGOs on Bank projects were international, but by 1994, indigenous NGOs represented over 70% of such organizations on bank projects.[171] Given donors' wishes to avoid corrupt and poorly governed states, more of their development aid has been steered toward NGOs in the past two decades.

However, with the rise of sources of power outside their control, many African states have responded by passing legislation limiting NGO power or access to resources. For example, "since 1991, governments in Botswana, Ghana, Kenya, and Zimbabwe have proposed or enacted legislation designed to strengthen official authority over NGOs—usually under the guise of developing a national regulatory framework for associations."[172]

In Kenya, a board supervising NGOs is stacked with government representatives, and its decisions cannot be appealed. Some NGOs have to renew registration every five years, and the bureaucracy is under the direct control of the president. Ghana is also thinking of passing regulation to rein in the autonomy of their NGOs.[173]

Nonetheless, NGOs are stronger than they were in the immediate post-independence period, and they stand as a potential source of finances and expertise outside of official state channels. However, NGOs are still potentially weak, and many are parochial. NGOs have to abide by local laws, norms, and protocols or risk being banned or kicked out of the country.

Privatization

Although this will be discussed in much more depth in the following chapter, the partial privatization of so many former state-owned enterprises necessarily partially weakens the political strength of the political elite *in the long term*. Also, in the short-term, the political elite could be politically weakened due to the layoffs that are associated with privatization that may be blamed upon the state, though it is almost always the new owners who do the actual firing. In the Zambian case, privatization resulted in decreases of between 20% and 28% of workers for such firms.[174] Therefore, privatization will result in fewer resources under the direct control of the political elite to dispense as patronage. Should citizens outside of the ruling elite be the ones who come into ownership of such property or stock, they may be able to form a class or group of individuals that is able to fund opposition political parties or candidates.

Nonetheless, privatization in the short term can bolster the power of the political elites, as the money raised from the privatization of assets in Africa can lead to great short-term windfalls, often on the order of one percent of total GDP.[175] This can give temporary possible relief to a patronage based society as well as likely to result in corruption as the political elites steer undervalued properties to their supporters or members of their rank. In fact, domestically, those most likely to have funds to purchase privatized resources are the current political elite. This leads to a contradiction in motives as foreigners are more likely to infuse money into the system, but loyalist will benefit from a transfer to them.

Most African nations, nonetheless, have begun to privatize. In fact, only ten African countries did not have recorded privatization activity by 2001.[176] However, those sectors that have been privatized have tended to be small- and medium-level enterprises, at least initially (see next section). Such acts of privatization are not likely to form the basis of an autonomous bourgeoisie in the short-term. In fact, most of the large-scale firms are usually privatized to foreign investors, although the smaller and medium size firms are being privatized to indigenous owners. It is too soon to tell how many are really political insiders unlikely to form a political or economic check on the ruling party. In fact, some accounts suggest that privatization has exactly enriched the ruling class and their friends in places such as Uganda, Zambia, Burkina Faso, and Cote d'Ivoire.[177] In addition, one report suggests that Mugabe and ZANU-PF leaders came to own 40% of the land "liberated" from the white Zimbabwean framers (although this is not privatization, the distributional element is similar).[178]

Nonetheless, some have suggested that privatization has promoted the creation of a tiny wealthy class, as opposed to a broad indigenization leading to a middle class.[179] Tanzania appears to have the most privatizations going to nationals: one study found that two-thirds of small-scale privatizations in Tanzania went to citizens. By contrast, even in Tanzania, the larger firms went to foreign firms, many from South Africa.[180] Nevertheless, the seeds of a class are planted which may one day have interests at odds, or partially at odds, with the ruling political elite. Regardless, much of the privatization is going to foreign companies that may be seen as less of a threat to the political power of the ruling elite.

Weakened Legitimacy for Coups

In the first period, coups were seen as a way of consolidating power. Often, and especially in the francophone countries, coups would be consolidated with a change in constitution and a plebiscitary election, resulting in a one-party regime. Coups were, in fact, the most common means of transferring power, which would usually bring more power into the military. However, with the end of the Cold War, successful coups have been less frequent than during the Cold War period, though attempted coups have been on the rise.[181] Comparing eleven years before the end of the Cold War (1979–1989) and eleven years after (1990–2001), we see that during the first period twenty-six successful coups took place in fourteen countries.[182] By contrast, after 1990, only 13 successful coups were carried out in eleven countries, and a few of these were to install democratic regimes. The initial differences post-1990 and pre-1990 is stark. According to one source, between 1960 and 1980, coups, violent overthrows, or assassinations were responsible for the vast the majority of cases of African leaders leaving power. In the 1990s, this fell to around 50%, and between 2000 and 2005, it was under 20%.[183] According to another source, coups represented between 40 and 50% of all leadership changes between 1960 and 1990; this fell to 24.6% in the 1990s and to 13.3% in the 2000s.[184]

Norms

Most of the international norms discussed in the last chapter were being diffused throughout the region as well as internationally, and citizens were growing weary of supporting regimes which were not democratic, did not produce economic growth, were seen as overly corrupt, did not provide public goods, and/or could not support the levels of patronage to key constituencies. The basis of their rule was undermined under these conditions. Also, with the collapse of one-party ideology linked with the socialist development model, it became less supported in Africa as well. In fact, a one-party state with majority state ownership came to be seen as a failed path to development both internationally and regionally. The only "legitimate" potential claims for one-party rule was to fight against ethnic division, but so many one-party states seen are ruling for a narrow ethnic elite anyways; and this form of potential legitimacy was not widely available by the time of the end of the Cold War.[185]

REGIONAL OR INTERNATIONAL ORGANIZATIONS THAT HELP FRAGMENT POWER

The African Union, Democracy, and Coups

In 1997, the Organization of African Unity (OAU) undermined the regional norm of complete state sovereignty, at least rhetorically, when it passed a resolution condemning coups d'etat in the region. In its inception, the OAU had a policy of non-interference in the affairs of member states. With this change, the unconstitutional overthrow of a country's government was no longer seen as strictly a domestic concern for that country, but it became seen as a concern for the region and regional governance. Moreover, the Assembly of Heads of States barred member countries whose leaders were overthrown, but not replaced in "credible" elections from attending the 2000 meeting.[186] The AU would go on to describe possible sanctions to be invoked against countries which interrupted constitutional rule, including such measures as "denial of visas to coup-plotters, commercial restrictions, and restrictions on government contacts."[187] The country in question would, however, have six months to reestablish a constitutional order before the AU could apply sanctions. Nonetheless, this rhetoric was turned to action, when President Ahmed Kabbah was overthrown in May 1997. The coup was condemned internationally, and the OAU held that other African states had a duty not to cooperate with the new military regime.[188] The OAU/AU also condemned similar unconstitutional actions in Cote d'Ivoire, Comoros, Madagascar, Mauritania, and Togo.[189] More recently, the AU condemned the coup in Niger in 2010 and urged them to restore constitutional order.[190] The sanctions have included official condemnations as well as the suspension of participation in Union activities. These actions are far from the sending of troops, though they show a rising regional norm.[191]

Not only did the regional organization condemn unconstitutional overthrows of regimes, it explicitly endorsed democracy and good governance. In the African Union charter, it is called to "promote democratic principles and institutions, popular participation and good governance."[192]

AU—NEPAD

In 1999, several prominent African leaders came together to propose an African initiative to help end some of the enduring economic, political, and social problems of Africa. Presidents Mbeki of South Africa, Obasanjo of Nigeria, Bouteflika of Algeria, and, later, Wade of Senegal suggested a system whereby African governments submit to peer review to improve their collective challenges. This would result in the New Partnership for Africa's Development (NEPAD). According to one scholar,

> NEPAD is an African programme for African development that came into being as the result of the joining together of the Millennium Partnership for the African Recovery Programme (MAP) and the OMEGA Plan at the request of the Organization of African Unity. The New African Initiative, which is now officially referred to as NEPAD, was approved by the Lusaka summit on 11 July 2001. The Partnership is a commitment by African leaders to get rid of poverty and to place the African continent on a path of lasting growth and development. It is founded on African states practising good governance, democracy and human rights, while working to prevent and resolve situations of conflict and instability on the continent.[193]

Symbolically, NEPAD is similar to the Lagos Plan of Africa in that its mission flows from general Pan African ideals, such as African unity and self-reliance. However, unlike the Lagos Plan of Action, it did not stand in complete contrast to the policies proposed by the World Bank and other IFIs; rather, it called on African leaders to adopt economic and political systems that were more democratic, accountable, and efficient. The protocol calls for improvement in governance, African leadership to solve African problems, anchoring African solutions to African resources, facilitating and accelerating economic interdependence, and NEPAD goals should be linked with Millennium Development goals. It is an attempt for Africans solving African problems, but with some help from the outside. The implicit contract of NEPAD with the West is that countries which comply with, or conform to, NEPAD audits would obtain more international aid and investment than those which did not.[194]

Thus far, thirty African countries have signed on as members of the African Peer Review Mechanism (APRM), and between 2006 and 2011, 14 countries were peer reviewed.[195] These fourteen are these: Ghana, Rwanda, Kenya, South Africa, Algeria, Benin, Uganda, Nigeria, Burkina Faso, Mali, Mozambique, Lesotho, Mauritius, and Ethiopia. Although many can question the effectiveness of NEPAD, the fact that such a high profile organization has embraced many of the goals of democracy and good political, economic and corporate governance, as well as regional cooperation and integration necessarily helps reinforce regional norms away from complete sovereignty of leaders and creates expectations of economic and political accountability, which in turn helps with tendencies for the fragmentation of economic and political power.

The End of Apartheid in South Africa

The end of apartheid in South Africa has resulted in many important regional effects. First, opposition to white rule was THE unifying foreign policy goal of African nations after decolonization, once it was accomplished, this common plank for the region was removed.[196] The end of apartheid resulted, therefore, in more scrutiny placed upon the authoritarian nature of countries in the region: once the hated common enemy was gone, the problems of corruption and authoritarianism were no longer in the shadow of institutionalized racism. They were out in the open and could be seen as the next regional problem. This was especially so when the new regime put into place in South Africa was seen as a democratic model.

The end of apartheid also allowed South Africa to emerge as a major regional player, with significant legitimacy, especially with the personage of Nelson Mandela at its helm. It was the most developed economically, it had the largest economy, and it was a source of economic investment. In fact, South Africa's economy was worth almost half of the rest of the continent's economy combined in 2006, at 56%.[197] In fact, Nelson Mandela engaged South Africa in several regional tasks. NEPAD as well could only have begun with South African support by a post-apartheid regime.

INTERNATIONAL PRESSURES TO LIBERALIZE

Several scholars have made the argument that the liberalization in the region (within particular countries) was clearly tied to international pressures to introduce *multiparty* elections, and not democracy per se.[198] Moreover, the linking of aid to political liberalization was shown to be more successful in the post-Cold War than during it.[199] African leaders understood, or should have, that they were no longer in the same geo-political environment and had different bargaining power in the second period. Moreover their high levels of dependence upon foreign aid mandated careful attention to the desires of donors. The credibility of the donor to cut aid in the absence of reform was much greater with the end of the Cold War, and African leaders should have understood this as such.[200] This can be seen in that most countries introduced some political reforms to avoid being cut off by Western backers.

A few countries tested this commitment and ran afoul of the international mood and lost funding: Mobutu had bilateral aid discontinued in 1990 by France, the United States, and Belgium.[201] Moreover, France, a longtime supporter of this large francophone country, informed Mobutu that he was not invited to the next francophone summit.[202] In 1991, the European Union followed suit and refused to provide all but humanitarian aid to Mobutu. So clearly, Zaire had fallen far from the embrace of its erstwhile Western allies. Also aid was suspended to Burundi following a coup in 1993, and aid was suspended to Nigeria after elections were annulled for the same year.[203] Togo too, followed in the footsteps of Mobutu and had aid suspended in 1991, by the US, France, and Germany. Military aid was suspended by the US and France the following year.[204] Founding elections were held in 1993, though they were not free and fair, and aid levels continued to be minimal.

By contrast, Rwanda (pre-genocide) chose not test the international will vis-à-vis democratization. President Habyarimana was advised at the Franco-African summit at la Baule in June 1990 to promote multiparty politics and the advice was taken.[205] Within a month, and despite no apparent domestic push for democratization, he announced that a transition to multiparty elections would be held, though he fully intended to ensure that the ruling party, which was renamed the MRNDD (Mouvement républicain national pour la démocratie et le développement) would control the system, while only tolerating small opposition parties.[206] Rwanda was trying to get ahead of the liberalization game.

Again, the international pressure was for reform and not full democracy per se, and African leaders would try to implement the least amount of reform possible to please the international community in order to avoid losing international financial backing. According to Brown, the political conditionality attached to aid in the post-Cold War period often encouraged a transition to an electoral democracy that was merely "electoral" in form, and which often had negative outcomes such as fomenting rivalries and interethnic violence.[207] Moreover, many attempts at reform proved disappointing to advocates of democracy, with backsliding, civil war, and military coups occurring in places such as Malawi, Central African Republic, and Madagascar—rather than a full democracy.[208] Bratton and van de Walle make a similar point arguing that parts of the international community could be appeased by an extremely weak standard of democracy.[209]

Dunning argues that threats to cut off aid by Western powers were more credible in the post-Cold War environment, and his idea is quite consistent with this analysis. Additionally, many African countries found some protection against strict structural adjustment programs through the protection of the French, who were not four-square, initially, behind structural adjustment.[210] As discussed before, having a statist approach to their economy, as well as majority state ownership of their own oil sector until 1996, France was initially a weak supporter of "neo-liberal polices," especially ones involving countries in their African sphere of influence.[211] As Wilson argued, by the end of the 1980s, a consensus existed between the US and France concerning many aspects of structural adjustment programs.[212] By 1994, World Bank and French views concerning structural adjustment was reconciled when the CFA was devalued. Thus, with the end of the Cold War, in a concensus emerged among the US, UK, France, the World Bank, and IMF about the need for conditionality, even if the particulars about sequence, timing, and scope were not all agreed upon.

CONCLUSION

So it seems that in Africa, with the end of the Cold War, African political institutions and practices became more liberal, though the greater majority cannot be considered to be democracies as such. Even this change is important, as many more fragments of political accountability came into force which can help perpetuate and strengthen these more liberal institutions and practices. De jure elections have been held in nearly every country; the freedoms enjoyed by most African citizens have increased; the press has enjoyed more freedom than ever before; elections have resulted in the removal of politicians in several countries; term limits have forced some incumbents to step down from running for election; even when term limits were extended, they were sometimes later respected; more and larger majority state-owned enterprises have been, and are being privatized (see next section) which removed economic power from the state elite; and more aid has been funneled outside of official state channels.

However, many aspects of African politics demonstrate the continued concentration of power in the hands of the elites in many countries. Most countries are either not free or only partly free; when elections do take place, most winning parties have a clear or super majority; many former authoritarian leaders, or their heirs, retained leadership; civil society remains weak; and businesspeople control less of the economy than in other regions of the world. Also, with most countries adopting either presidential or hybrid presidential systems, in conjunction with significant majorities for a single party, the fragmentation of power has been only partial. However, should more relatively free and fair elections occur, especially with term limits, these partial fragments of political accountability may deepen. Civil society may become stronger, legislatures may do more than rubber stamp, and the norms of rising political and civil rights may become more and more entrenched in the region.

NOTES

1. See Chapter 3.

2. For the importance of institutions see Douglass C. North, *Institutions, Institutional Change and Economic Performance* (Cambridge: Cambridge University Press, 1990); Douglass C. North, *Structure and Change in Economic History* (New York: W. W. Norton & Co., 1981); Oliver E. Williamson, *The Economic Institutions of Capitalism: Firms, Markets, Relational Contracting* (New York: The Free Press, 1985); James E. Alt and Kenneth A. Shepsle, *Perspectives on Positive Political Economy* (Cambridge: Cambridge University Press, 1990); Peter Gourevitch, *Politics in Hard Times: Comparative Responses to International Economic Crises* (Ithaca, NY: Cornell University Press, 1986); and Ruth Berins Collier, *Regimes in Tropical Africa: Changing Forms of Supremacy, 1945–1975* (Berkeley: University of California Press, 1982).

3. These were Botswana, Mauritius, and the Gambia, though the Gambia underwent a coup in 1994 which ended this record. This view also excludes the limited franchise nations of Rhodesia and South Africa as only whites could participate, and the majority was excluded from effective participation in elections.

4. Michael Bratton and Nicolas van de Walle, *Democratic Experiments in Africa: Regime Transitions in Comparative Perspective* (Cambridge: Cambridge University Press, 1997), p. 8. For the importance of differences between de jure and de facto elections see Staffan I. Lindberg, *Democracy and Elections in Africa* (Baltimore, MD: The Johns Hopkins University Press, 2006).

5. Although Namibia held elections in 1989, many Africanist scholars treat Namibia and South Africa and their independence or more tied to the end of apartheid than other more dominant regional forces. Also, other countries held elections before Benin, but the National Assembly of 1989 was seen by many as a symbolic watershed.

6. Bratton and van de Walle, *Democratic Experiments*, p. 197, Table 7. This list includes Namibia and South Africa. Ten of 29 were in 1993.

7. Michael Bratton "Second Elections in Africa," *Journal of Democracy* 9, 3 (1998): 51–66, p. 44

8. These were Nigeria, Somalia, Swaziland, Uganda, Zaire (later DRC), and recently established Eritrea. Also, South Sudan has yet to hold a national election since the referendum for autonomy in 2011. Data taken from various sources, including Nicholas van de Walle, "Presidentialism and Clientism in Africa's Emerging Party Systems" *The Journal of Modern African Studies* 41, no. 2 (June 2003): 297–322 and other internet resources, especially African Election Database. The Gambia had elections before the coup in the late 1994. IPU Parline, African Elections Database.

9. Jeffrey Gettleman, "After Years of Struggle, South Sudan Becomes a New Nation," *New York Times* (July 9, 2011): http://www.nytimes.com/2011/07/10/world/africa/10sudan.html?pagewanted=all

10. Though Somaliland held elections in 2005. See African Elections Database. Sudan held elections in 2010. http://africanelections.tripod.com/about.html. Also, this analysis does not include the newly established South Sudan.

11. Data taken from various sources, including Lindberg, *Democracy and Elections*; and van de Walle, "Presidentialism and Clientism." Also, the Gambia is counted twice, once as having elections prior to the transition, and once as having an election following a coup in the early 1990s.

12. Numbers taken from Freedom House. Some adjustment was made for the years, 1989–1990 when numbers were not exactly corresponding to calendar years. Each number is subtracted from 8 so higher numbers mean more rights.

13. It would have to rise to 5.5 to become free (the region not shown on scale).

14. Freedom House, SV African countries, 1975. http://www.freedomhouse.org/template.cfm?page=439

15. Freedom House, S.V. African Countries, 2014. http://www.freedomhouse.org/report-types/freedom-world#.U0au_qK9Ymo This list included South Sudan. For analysis of sub-scores, see John W. Harbeson. "Promising Democratization Trajectories in Africa's Weak States," in John W. Harbeson and Donald Rothchild, eds., *Africa in World Politics: Reforming Political Order* (Boulder, CO: Westview, 2009).

16. The denominators were different for the two different time periods. In 1975, only 41 countries were ranked, while in 2014, 49 were.

17. For example, see Thomas Carothers, "The End of the Transition Paradigm," *Journal of Democracy* 13, 1 (January 2002): 5–21; Jeffrey Herbst, "Political Liberalization in Africa after Ten Years," *Comparative Politics* 33 (April 2001): 357–75. However, one author suggests that repeated de jure elections, even if flawed, lead to de facto free and fair in Africa over time. See Lindberg, *Democracy and Elections*. For quality of democracy in Africa, see Larry Diamond, "Is the Third Wave Over?" *Journal of Democracy* 7, 3 (1996): 20–37; Bratton and van de Walle, *Democratic Experiments*; Christopher Clapham, *Africa and the International System: The Politics of State Survival* (Cambridge: Cambridge University Press, 1997); Richard Joseph, "The Reconfiguration of Power in Late Twentieth-Century Africa," in Richard Joseph, ed., *State, Conflict, and Democracy in Africa* (Boulder, CO: Lynne Rienner

Publishers, 1999): 57–82; Richard Joseph, "Africa, 1990—1997: From Abertura to Closure," *Journal of Democracy* 9, 2 (1998): 3–7; Crawford Young, "The Third Wave of Democratization in Africa: Ambiguities and Contradictions," in Joseph, ed., *State, Conflict, and Democracy*: 15–38; Nicolas van de Walle, "Elections without Democracy: Africa's Range of Regimes," *Journal of Democracy* 13, 2 (April 2002): 66–80.

18. Although this is a large literature, examples include these: Larry Diamond, "Thinking About Hybrid Regimes," *Journal of Democracy* 13 2 (2002): 21–36; and Steven Levitsky and Lucan A. Way, "The Rise of Competitive Authoritarianism," *Journal of Democracy* 13.2 (2002): 51–65. See their sources, as well as above footnote, for more citations.

19. Carothers, "The End of the Transition Paradigm."

20. Bratton "Second Elections in Africa," Table 1, p. 54.

21. Lindberg, *Democracy and Elections.*

22. Data in these sections come from several sources: Freedom House, *CIA World Factbook*, *African Elections Database*, and *Africa South of the Sahara.* All are available on line, though I used *African South of the Sahara* reference material. When Eritrea and South Sudan are included, there are 19 presidential systems although they are transitional. This is as of 2014.

23. For similar views see Arend Lijphart, *Patterns of Democracy: Government Forms and Performance in Thirty-Six Countries* (New Haven: Yale University Press, 1999), p. 118; see also Adam Przeworski, Michael Alvarez, José Antonio Cheibub and Fernando Limongi, "What Makes Democracies Endure," *Journal of Democracy* 7, 1 (1996): 39–55.

24. Although Senegal's President Wade had to cohabit from his election in April 2000 until the legislative elections gave him a majority in 2001. A new constitution also changed the presidential term from 7 to 5 years, though the next elections will be one year apart. However, a president could dissolve the parliament should he or she be without a majority. See http://www.cia.gov/cia/publications/factbook/geos/sg.html#Govt

25. Cohabitation occurs when the president is of one party and the prime minister is of another party. Since there is a dual executive in hybrid systems, this would weaken the lead administrator necessarily.

26. John D. Holm, "Botswana: A Paternalistic Democracy," in Larry Diamond, Juan J. Linz, and Seymour M. Lipset. *Democracy in Developing Countries: Africa, Volume II* (Boulder, CO: Lynne Rienner Publishers, 1988), p. 186. The same is true for South Africa.

27. *CIA World Factbook*, SV Mauritius. https://www.cia.gov/library/publications/the-world-factbook/geos/mp.html

28. Unless specified elsewhere, data rechecked by International Institute for Democracy and Electoral Assistance (International IDEA): Table of Electoral Systems Worldwide http://www.idea.int/esd/world.cfm Last accessed February 3, 2014.

29. Not all seats are SMDP in Zimbabwe, but 120 or 150 are. In Swaziland, 55 of 60 are SMDP. Mali had 147 of 160 seats distributed by SMDP; Mauritius had 62 of 66 elected by SMDP and had 4 appointed by the supreme court. See www.electionworld.org SV countries. Togo as of 2003.

30. Comoros had a minority of seats elected indirectly by local legislatures. See African Elections Database, S.V. Comoros.

31. "Party Block Vote is a plurality/majority system using multi-member districts in which voters cast a single party-centered vote for a party of choice, and do not choose between candidates. The party with most votes will win every seat in the electoral district." Taken from African elections database: http://africanelections.tripod.com/terms.html#Electoral_Systems. Djibouti was in this category until 2012.

32. For vote disproportionality, see Lijphart, *Patterns of Democracy*.

33. Namibia had 72 of 78 distributed through PR, and 6 appointed. http://www.electionworld.org/index.html

34. In the analysis of party systems, we only look at post-transition results, if there was a transition, or after 1989, which ever was later. And if there were changes in the constitution, we only include the post-constitutional trends, unless data of Lindberg, *Democracy and Elections* or van de Walle, "Presidentialism and Clientism."

35. van de Walle, "Presidentialism and Clientism were used."

36. Lindberg, *Democracy and Elections*, Table 18.

37. For an in-depth discussion of pros and cons for various terms for one party dominance, see Matthijs Bogaards, "Counting Parties and Identifying Dominant Party Systems in Africa," *European Journal of Political Research* 43 (2004): 173–97. See also, Renske Doorenspleet and Lia Nijzink, eds., *One Party Dominance in African Democracies* (Boulder, CO: Lynne Rienner Publishers, 2013).

38. As of 2014.

39. The ruling party in Cameroon (Cameroon People's Democratic Movement (RDPC)) had a 48.8% plurality in the founding elections, but soon became a one-party dominant system. The next elections saw their majorities grow from 61% to 83% and to 85% in 2007. Calculated from http://africanelections.tripod.com/cm.html. Unless states otherwise, data and information comes from African Elections Database or Wikipedia SV elections in the country.

40. Until coup in 1999. Then after long war, no clear dominant party.

41. For most elections, the largest party of the coalition had 100% of the seats. 2008 saw a boycott of elections by the opposition.

42. Until the coup in 2008, then new party plus allies got a slim majority in 2013. http://en.wikipedia.org/wiki/Guinean_legislative_election,_2002

43. Although the Lesotho Congress for Democracy (LCP) replaced the Basutoland Congress Party (BCP) in elections, it was a segment of the BCP led by the former leader of the party so the leadership is mostly continuation rather than change.

44. Post genocide. The FRP has had a majority in each election, though the last with only 51%. However, of the elected seats, they won 77% of the contested seats.

45. In 1994, the ruling party lost a majority, and two parties formed a coalition, but the president would not seat the nominated prime minister, and the parties pulled out, and the a new coalition formed with the ruling party, who would go on to have majorities from then on.

46. For years, Uganda had a nonpartisan (but which was views by many as really a one party system), system.

47. See also, Roger Southall, "The Centralization and Fragmentation of South Africa's Dominant Party System," *African Affairs* 97 (1998): 443–69.

48. Author's updating of Lindberg's *Democracy and Elections* data through 2010. Rakner and van de Walle show that in fourth round elections, the average for top parties falls to 41.9%, though they only have three countries in this list. See Lise Rakner and Nicolas van de Walle, "Opposition Weakness in Africa," *Journal of Democracy* 20, 3 (July 2009): 108–21, p. 110.

49. Taken from African elections database. Coalitions listed as such were combined. Vacant seats reduced the denominator. If only elected offices were listed, but not parties, only those were included. Accessed October 2014.

50. Starting in 2007, prior to that one party or its fragment had majorities.

51. After the war.

52. Implication form analysis of van de Walle, "Presidentialism and Clientism."

53. African Election Databases, SV countries and most recent elections.

54. African Election Databases, SV DRC 2011 elections.

55. Freedom House, SV DRC, http://www.freedomhouse.org/report/freedom-world/2013/congo-democratic-republic-kinshasa#.VD1Wm1ex1bI

56. Although the elected government was overthrown in 2013.

57. Barbara Geddes, "A Game Theoretic Model of Reform in Latin American Democracies," *The American Political Science Review* 85, 2 (1991): 371–92.

58. This excludes Eritrea, Somalis, South Sudan and Swaziland.

59. Data takes from African Elections Database, accessed Jan 31, 2011. http://africanelections.tripod.com Accessed October 2014. Parline and Wikipedia was used for some more recent elections.

60. Ibid.

61. With the number for Senegal in 2001 changed from 49 to 10. See http://africanelections.tripod.com/sn.html

62. Author's updates of Lindberg's data, *Democracy and Elections*.

63. Matthias Basedau, Matthijs Bogaards, Christof Hartmann and Peter Niesen, "Ethnic Party Bans In Africa: A Research Agenda," *German Law Journal* 8, 6 (2007): 617–34, p. 630. However, Moroff argues that Kenya had no such ban until 2008, see Anika Moroff "Ethnic Party Bans in East Africa from a Comparative Perspective," *GIGA Research Programme: Violence and Security* No 129 (April 2010). Uganda had bans on all parties until 2002, when it introduced such bans. The Inkatha Freedom Party is identified with Zulu ethnicity, but it is in third place in South Africa, though it could claim to be a regional party. Nonetheless, South Africa has no such ban.

64. African Elections Database, accessed Jan 25, 2011. http://africanelections.tripod.com

65. Basedau et al. "Ethnic Party Bans," p. 631.

66. In the analysis of party strength, we only look at post transition results, if there was a transition. And if there were changes in the constitution, the most recent trends, unless we use the data of Lindberg or van de Walle. For quote see Van de Walle and. K.S. Butler, "Political parties and party systems in Africa's illiberal democracies." *Cambridge Review of International Studies* 13, 1 (1999): 14–28: p. 15

67. O. Van Cranenburgh, "Tanzania's 1995 multi-party elections: The emerging party system," *Party Politics* 2, 4 (1996): 535–547; Bratton and van de Walle,

Democratic Experiments; Michelle Kuenzi and Gina Lambright, "Party System Institutionalization in 30 African Countries," *Party Politics* 7, 4 (July 2001): 437–68.

68. Kuenzi and Lambright, "Party System Institutionalization."

69. Ibid. p. 461.

70. See, especially, Seymour Martin Lipset, "Some Social Requisites of Democracy: Economic Development and Political Legitimacy," *American Political Science Review* 53 (March, 1959): 69–105. For overview of this literature, see Chapter 8.

71. See the work of Przeworski and Limongi who argue that democracies are quite fragile at below $2000 percapita; they only tend to last 9 years of fewer. Adam Przeworski and Fernando Limongi, "Modernization: Theories and Facts," *World Politics* 49, 2 (Jan., 1997): 155–83. Between $2000 and $6000, they could last longer. Above $6000, they have never failed.

72. World Bank, *World Development Indicators*, S.V. Economic Policy & Debt: National accounts: US$ at constant 2005 prices: Aggregate indicators. http://databank.worldbank.org/data/views/variableSelection/selectvariables. aspx?source=world-development-indicators#

73. Based upon the 2009 *UN Human Development Report*, http://hdr.undp.org/sites/default/files/reports/269/hdr_2009_en_complete.pdf Table 1, less than $2 a day, 2000–2007.

74. These numbers come from the World Bank, *World Development Indicators*, S.V. Literacy rate, adult total (% of people ages 15 and above), http://data.worldbank.org/indicator/SE.ADT.LITR.ZS?page=3. Averages were made for 1990-latest available.

75. For some recent classic works on civil society in Africa see Robert Fatton, "Predatory Rule: state and civil society in Africa (Boulder, CO: Lynne Rienner Publishers, 1992); Jean-Francois Bayart, *The State in Africa: the politics of the belly* (New York, Longman, 1993); John W. Harbeson, Donald Rothchild, and Naomi Chazan, eds., *Civil Society and the State in Africa* (Boulder, CO: Lynne Rienner Publishers, 1994);

76. William Tordoff, *Government and Politics in Africa, 3rd Edition* (Bloomington and Indianapolis: Indiana University Press, 1997), p. 117.

77. Ibid.

78. Unless states elsewhere data for this section is taken from Freedom House, SV freedom of the press.

79. Many countries had a broadcast press that was less free (unless both were not free) than print press aside from the Gambia and Mauritius.

80. For an overview of these groups in the immediate post-colonial times, see Immanuel Wallerstein, "Voluntary Associations," in James S. Coleman and Carl G. Rosberg, Jr., eds., *Political Parties and National Integration* (Berkeley & Los Angeles: University of California Press, 1964): 318–39; also Elliot J. Berg and Jeffrey Butler, "Trade Unions," in Coleman and Rosberg, eds., *Political Parties*, pp. 340–81; and William John Hanna, "Students," in Coleman and Rosberg, eds., *Political Parties*, pp. 413–43.

81. Henry Bienen and Jeffrey Herbst, "The Relationship between Political and Economic Reform in Africa," *Comparative Politics* 29, 1 (Oct. 1996): 23–42; E.

Gyimah-Boadi, "Civil Society and Democratic Development," in E. Gyimah-Boadi, ed., *Democratic Reform in Africa: The Quality of Progress* (Boulder, CO: Lynne Rienner Publishers, 2004): 99–119.

82. Gyimah-Boadi, "Civil Society," p. 108.

83. For majority state ownership and impacts on business classes, see John J. Quinn, "The Managerial Bourgeoisie: Capital Accumulation, Development and Democracy," in *Postimperialism and World Politics.* David G. Becker and Richard L. Sklar, eds (Westport, CT: Praeger, 1999): 219–52. For its impact on economic policy, also John James Quinn, *The Road oft Traveled: Development Policies and Majority State Ownership of Industry in Africa* (Westport, CN: Praeger, 2002); also World Bank, *Bureaucrats in Business: The Economics and Politics of Government Ownership* (Washington, DC: World Bank, 1995); for other links between state ownership and patronage see Roger Tangri, *The Politics of Patronage in Africa: Parastatals, Privatization, & Private Enterprise* (Trenton, NJ: Africa World Press,1999), Richard Sandbrook, *The Politics of Africa's Economic Recovery* (Cambridge: Cambridge University Press, 1993), and Barabara Grosh and Rwekaza S. Mukandala, eds., *State-Owned Enterprises in Africa* (Boulder, CO: Lynne Rienner Publishers, 1994).

84. Michael Bratton, "Beyond the State: Civil Society and Associational Life in Africa," *World Politics* 40, (April 1990): 407–30, p. 427.

85. E. Gyimah-Boadi, "Civil Society In Africa," *Journal of Democracy* 7, 2 (1996): 118–32, p. 119.

86. Carothers, "The End of Transition Paradigm."

87. Data from Peter S. Heller and Alan A. Tait, "Government Employment and Pay: Some International Comparisons." Occasional Paper 24. (Washington, D.C.: International Monetary Fund, October 1983); secondary sources are listed for each country in Chapter 4 under **Jobs**. However, here we have 18 countries instead of just eight, but their numbers were the primary source of information for many countries.

88. Ibid.

89. Peter R. Fallon and Luiz A. Pereira da Silva, "Recognizing labor market constraints in Mozambique," in David L. Lindauer, Barbara Nunberg, eds., *Rehabilitating government: pay and employment reform in Africa* (Washington, DC: World Bank, 1994): 82–102, p. 86–7. Only six of the ten countries had data for this column.

90. Calculated from Ibid.

91. See for example, Quinn, "Managerial Bourgeoisie."

92. M. Githu, 'Kenya's opposition and the crisis of governance," *Issue: A Journal of Opinion* 21, 1–2 (1993), p 30, cited in Stephen Brown, "Authoritarian Leaders and Multiparty Elections in Africa: How Foreign Donors Help to Keep Kenya's Daniel Arap Moi in Power Author," *Third World Quarterly* 22, 5 (Oct., 2001): 725–39, p. 726.

93. Ibid.

94. Ibid.

95. Ibid., Table 1. However, this does compare a six year period to a three year one.

96. See John Ishiyama and John James Quinn, "Phoenix from the Ashes: The Formerly Dominant Parties in Africa," *Party Politics.* Vol. 12, No. 3 (May 2006): 317–40.

97. Data from this section comes from Giovanni Carbone, "Elections and leadership changes: How do political leaders take (and leave) power in Africa?" CAI (26 February 2014): http://www.consultancyafrica.com/index.php?option=com_content &view=article&id=1651:elections-and-leadership-changes-how-do-political-leaders-take-and-leave-power-in-africa-&catid=42:election-reflection&Itemid=270

98. Samuel P. Huntington, *The Third Wave: Democratization in the Late Twentieth Century* (Norman: University of Oklahoma Press, 1991), 266–67. Though Huntington discusses a two turn-over rule, here we are discussing only one.

99. Ishiyama and Quinn, "Phoenix from the Ashes;" van de Walle, "Elections without Democracy." Unless they boycotted the elections, then they often lost all access to power.

100. Bratton "Second Elections in Africa," p. 56

101. Ishiyama and Quinn, "Phoenix from the Ashes." These countries had been coded as either one party competitive or plebiscitary. See Bratton and van de Walle, *Democratic Experiments.*

102. van de Walle, "Presidentialism and Clientism," p. 300; see also above note.

103. Bruce Baker, "The Class of 1990: How Have the Autocratic Leaders of Sub-Saharan Africa fared? *Third World Quarterly,* 19, 1 (1998): 115–27.

104. Arthur A. Goldsmith, "Donors, dictators and democrats in Africa," *Journal of Modern African Studies,* 39, 3 (20001): 41–36, taken from Table 2, pp. 420–21.

105. Lindberg, *Democracy and Elections,* p. 65.

106. Ibid.

107. Ibid., p. 77. He argues that it begins with second elections. It is also hard to tell of this is merely a maturation effect given life spans, independent of political life spans.

108. Posner and Young, "Institutionalization of Political Power."

109. Quinn, "Managerial Bourgeoisie."

110. For a discussion of majority state ownership on corruption, see John James Quinn, "The Effects of Majority State Ownership of Significant Economic Sectors on Corruption: A Cross-Regional Comparison," *International Interactions* 34, 1 (2008): 81–128.

111. John James Quinn, "Democracy and Development," in Emmanuel Nnadozie, ed., *African EconomicDevelopment* (New York: Academic Press, 2003): 231–258. Gyimah-Boadi, "Civil Society in Africa."

112. See Adam Przeworski, *Democracy and the market: Political and economic reforms in Eastern Europe and Latin America* (Cambridge: Cambridge University Press, 1991).

113. Quinn, *The Road oft Traveled,* p. 39.

114. World Bank, *Bureaucrats in Business,* Table A5, Share of State-Owned Enterprieses in Emplyoment, 1978–1991, pp. 288–89. This report is for unweighted average. Using weighted averages, it would be 16.4.

115. Ibid. Though this data source ends at 1991.

116. Unless they realistically thought they might lose power, then they might want more power outside of the state as a backup.

117. Bratton, "Second Elections in Africa."

118. Lindberg, *Democracy and Elections.*

119. Richard L. Sklar, "Developmental Democracy," *Comparative Studies in Society and History.* 29, 4 (October 1987): 686–714.

120. Posner and Young, "Institutionalization of Political Power." They leave out the five parliamentary systems as well as Somalia, Swaziland, Eritrea, Sudan, and the Comoros.

121. One source suggests that Moi tried to change the constitution of Kenya behinds the scenes, but given the negative feedback, he did not launch a full out effort. See Napoleon Bamfo, "Term Limit and Political Incumbency in Africa: Implications of Staying in Power Too Long with References to the Cases of Kenya, Malawi, and Zambia" *African & Asian Studies,* 4, 3 (2005): 327–355.

122. Reuters, "FACTBOX-Africa's presidents prolong their rule." Fri Aug 7, 2009 8:09am. http://www.reuters.com/article/idUSL7120283; Kathryn Sturman, "Niger: Who Needs Presidential Term Limits?" 17 August 2009. All Africa.com; Will Ross, "Cameroon makes way for a king," BBC News, Friday, 11 April 2008. Also, the term limits were removed Burkina Faso, but reinstituted following popular protests. However, the incumbent ran for a third term in 2005, arguing that the term limits did not apply retroactively. See Freedom House, Countries at the Cross Roads 2002, Burkina Faso, country report. See also CIA factbook SV specific countries. See also, Economic Commission for Africa, *Rapport sur la gourvcenance en Africa II* (Addis Ababa: Economic Commission for Africa, 2009): p. 26.

123. African Election Database, SV particular countries, http://africanelections. tripod.com/index.html Accessed Feb 12, 2010.

124. Ibid.

125. And for the same time period. However, this analysis only included former competitive and plebiscitary one-party states. Calculated form Ishiyama and Quinn, "African Phoenix."

126. Rakner and van de Walle, "Opposition Weakness in Africa," p. 110.

127. Calculated from African Electoral Database, S.V Ghana.

128. See for example, Sklar, "Developmental Democracy."

129. Crawford Young and Thomas Turner, *The Rise and Decline of the Zairian State* (Madison, WI: University of Wisconsin Press, 1985), p. 31–42.

130. Dean E. McHenry, Jr., "Federalism in Africa: Is it a Solution to, or a Cause of, Ethnic Problems?" Presented at the Annual Meeting of the African Studies Association in Columbus, Ohio, November 1997.

131. Forum on Federalism, http://www.forumfed.org/en/federalism/by_country/ index.php Also, Sudan has now been partitioned, North and South.

132. CIA World Fact book, SV. DRC, SV government.

133. Thomas Turner, "Congo-Kinshasa leans toward federalism." Federations Magazine (October/November 2007): 4–5. http://www.forumfed.org/en/products/ magazine/vol7_num1/congo.php

134. The French Senate Webpage: http://www.senat.fr/senatsdumonde/english/ lesotho.html

135. World Bank, *Accelerated Development in Sub-Saharan Africa* (Washington, DC: World Bank, 1981).

136. Thomas M. Callaghy, "Africa and the World Political Economy: More Caught between a Rock and a Hard Place," Harbeson and Rothchild, eds., *Africa in World Politics*: 43–82, p. 44; See also, Ravenhill, *Africa in Crisis*; Callaghy and Ravenhill *Hemmed In*;

137. See Pierre Englebert, *State Legitimacy and Development in Africa* (Boulder, CO: Lynne Rienner Publishers, 2000), p. 2.

138. World Bank, *Sub-Saharan Africa: From Crisis to Sustainable Growth* (Washington, DC: World Bank, 1989), Table 1, 221.

139. World Bank, *World Development Report 1989* (Washington DC: World Bank, 1989), Tables 1 and 2, pp. 164–67.

140. See Chapter 8.

141. World Bank, *World Development Report 1989*, Table 24, p. 211.

142. Edward V.K. Jaycox, "Structural Adjustment in sub-Saharan Africa: The World Bank's Perspective," *Issue: A Journal of Opinion*, Vol. 18, No. 1 (Winter 1989), pp. 36–40, p. 36.

143. Clapham, *Africa*, p. 171. He lists the exceptions of Angola and SACU countries.

144. J. Barry Riddell, Things Fall Apart Again: Structural Adjustment Programmes in Sub-Saharan Africa, *The Journal of Modern African Studies*, Vol. 30, No. 1 (Mar., 1992), pp. 53–68, p. 53.

145. See Gyimah-Boadi, "Civil Society in Africa;" also Harbeson, Rothchild, and Chazan, *Civil Society*; and John W. Harbeson, "Externally Assisted Democratization: Theoretical Issues and African Realities," in John W. Harbeson and Donald Rothchild, eds., *Africa in World Politics: The African State System in Flux* (Boulder, CO: Westview Press, 2000): 235–262.

146. Michael Bratton and Nicolas van de Walle, "Toward Governance in Africa: Popular Demands and State Responses," in Goran Hyden and Michael Bratton, *Governance and Politics in Africa* (Boulder, CO: Lynne Rienner Publishers, 1992): 27–56.

147. Bratton and van de Walle, *Democratic Experiments in Africa*, p. 117.

148. For empirical critique of Bratton and van de Walle, see Joel D. Barkan, "Regime Change in Africa," *Journal of Democracy* 10.2 (1999) 165–70.

149. Bratton and van de Walle, "Toward Governance in Africa." p. 32.

150. Michael Bratton, "Civil Society and Political Transition in Africa," *Institute for Development Research Reports* 11, 6 (1994), p. 6.

151. Ibid.

152. For links of these conference to French national assembly, see Pearl T. Robinson, "The National Conference Phenomenon in Francophone Africa," *Comparative Studies in Society and History*, 36, 3 (July 1994): 575–610; for conference in Togo and Benin, with an emphasis on associational groups, see John R. Heilbrunn, "Social Origins of National Conferences in Benin and Togo," *The Journal of Modern African Studies*, 31, 2 (June 1993): 277–99.

153. Przeworski, *Democracy and the Market*.

154. Barrington Moore Jr., *Social Origins of Dictatorship and Democracy: Lord and Peasant in the Making of the Modern World* (Boston: Beacon Press, 1966).

155. Quinn, "The Managerial Bourgeoisie;" John J. Quinn, "The Impact of State Ownership of Resources on Economic and Political Development in Sub-Saharan Africa." *Ufahamu* Vol. XXI, No 1and 2 (Winter/Spring): 60–79.

156. Bratton suggests that civil society needs strong states to be strong, "Beyond the State." I remember Richard Sklar asking the question, "What happens to the strength of civil society in Nigeria (or any other country) the day after a coup?" Therefore, and by implication, civil society's absolute strength and organizational ability clearly matters, but so too does the level of freedom in society to organize and petition government. See decision model by Quinn in *Road oft Traveled*. Assumptions are perceptions of victory or likelihood of repression are weighed by actors in whether to push for protests or reforms.

157. Firoze Manji and Carl O'Coill, "The Missionary Position: NGOs and development in Africa." *International Affairs* 78, 3 (2002): 567–83.

158. Ibid.

159. Michael Holman, "Welcome to the Aid Business," *Open democracy* (June 2005). http://www.globalpolicy.org/component/content/article/176/31419.html

160. Sam Chege, "Donors shift more aid to NGOs: But cooperation between governments and NGOs is critical for greater effectiveness," *African Recovery* http://www.un.org/ecosocdev/geninfo/afrec/vol13no1/aid2ngo.htm

161. Manji and O'Coill, "The Missionary Position," p. 579.

162. Overseas Development Institute (ODI), "NGOs and Official Donors," Briefing paper 4 (August 1995), see sections "Official donors and southern NGOs." http://www.odi.org/sites/odi.org.uk/files/odi-assets/publications-opinion-files/2644.pdf

163. *USAID Support for NGO Capacity-Building: Approaches, Examples, Mechanisms* (Washington, DC: Office of Private and Voluntary Cooperation, USAID, July 1998), p. 21.

164. Overseas Development Institute, "NGOs and Official Donors."

165. Ibid., Table 1.

166. Ibid.

167. *USAID Support for NGO Capacity-Building: Approaches, Examples, Mechanisms* (Washington, DC: Office of Private and Voluntary Cooperation, USAID, July 1998), p. 1.

168. Cited in Carol Lancaster, *Foreign Aid: Diplomacy, Development, Domestic Politics* (Chicago: University of Chicago Press, 2007), p. 250, endnote #70.

169. Chege, "Donors shift more aid to NGOs."

170. Data in this section from ODI, "NGOs and Official Donors."

171. Ibid, ODI, box "NGOs and the World Bank."

172. Gyimah-Boadi, "Civil Society In Africa," p. 125.

173. Ibid.

174. John Nellis, "Privatization in Africa: What Has happened? What is to Be Done?" *Fondzione Eni Enrico Matte* (October 2005): 18. http://ageconsearch.umn.edu/bitstream/12200/1/wp050127.pdf

175. Nancy Birdsall and John Nellis, "Winners and Losers: Assessing the Distributional Impact of Privatization," Center for Global Development, Working Paper No 6., (May 2002).

176. John Craig, "Privatisation and indigenous ownership: evidence from Africa." *Annals of Public and Cooperative Economics*, 73, 4 (2002): 559–76.

177. See Ibid for overview on literature on effects of privatization on indigenization in Africa.

178. David Smith, "Mugabe and allies own 40% of land seized from white farmers—inquiry" *The Guardian* (Tuesday 30 November 2010 13.59 EST), summary/subtitle: "Zimbabwean president is said to have used the land reforms to reward his supporters rather than ordinary black Zimbabweans."

179. Roger Tangri and Andrew Mwenda, "Corruption and Cronyism in Uganda's privatization in the 1990s," *African Affairs* 100 (2001): 117–133.

180. Taken from Nellis, *Privatization in Africa*.

181. For a discussion of coups in post-Cold War period, see John F. Clark, "The Decline of the African Military Coup," *The Journal of Democracy* 18, 3 (2007): 141–55.

182. The data on coups in this section is taken from Patrick J. McGowan, "African Military Coups D'etat, 1956–2001: Frequency, Trends and Distribution," *Journal of Modern African Studies*, 41, 3 (2003), pp. 339–70; some also comes from Data for this section on coups comes from Coups d'état events, 1946–2009. Monty G. Marshall and Donna Ramsey Marshall, Center for Systemic Peace, July 30, 2010. http://www.systemicpeace.org/inscr/inscr.htm

183. Posner and Young, "Institutionalization of Political Power," taken from Figure 1.

184. Giovanni Carbone, "Elections and Leadership Changes."

185. In Kenya, Zaire, Cameroon, and many other countries, regional difference or ethnic divides were seen in what could have been the all-inclusive one party state. Even Cote d'Ivoire after Boigney became seen as such.

186. See Theodore J. Piccone, *International Mechanisms for Protecting Democracy*, (Washington, D.C.: Democracy Coalition Project, 2004). See Also, Williams, "From non-intervention to non-indifference."

187. Piccone, *International Mechanisms*

188. Williams, "From Non-Intervention to Non-Indifference."

189. Ibid, also Piccone, *International Mechanism*.

190. Nossiter, "Niger Capital"

191. Williams, "From Non-Intervention to Non-Indifference

192. Cited in Ibid.

193. Patrick Chabal, "The Quest for Good Government and Development in Africa: Is NEPAD the Answer? *International Affairs (Royal Institute of International Affairs 1944-)*, Vol. 78, No. 3 (Jul., 2002), pp. 447–462, ftn #1.

194. See Taylor, *NEPAD*, p. 45.

195. Taken from NEPAD webpage http://www.nepad.org/economicandcorporategovernance/african-peer-review-mechanism/about Accessed February 3, 2012. Webpage last updates, 2011. Last accessed, August 4, 2015.

196. For overviews of African foreign policies, see Stephen Wright, ed., *African Foreign Policies* (Boulder: Westview, 1999); Wright, Gilbert M. Khadiagala and Terrence Lyons, eds., *African foreign policies: power and process* (Lynne Rienner Publishers, 2001); and John James Quinn, "African Foreign Policies," in Robert Denemark et al., eds., *The International Studies Compendium Project* (Oxford: Wiley-Blackwell, 2010): 24–46.

197. Taken from World Bank, 2006, http://siteresources.worldbank.org/DATA-STATISTICS/Resources/GDP.pdf

198. Stephen Brown, "Foreign Aid and Democracy Promotion: Lessons from Africa," *The European Journal of Development Research* 17, 2 (June 2005): 179–98; see also Richard Joseph, "Africa, 1990–1997: From *Abertura* to Closure," *Journal of Democracy* 9, (1998): 3–17. If fact Joseph calls them virtual democracies. Joseph, Richard, "Democratization in Africa after 1989: Comparative and Theoretical Perspectives, *Comparative Politics* 29, 3 (Apr., 1997): 363–82.

199. Thad Dunning, "Conditioning the Effects of Aid: Cold War Politics, Donor Credibility, and Democracy in Africa," *International Organization* 58, 2 (Spring 2004): 409–23.

200. Ibid.

201. Unless states otherwise, the data from this section come from *Africa South of the Sahara 1999* or *2001* (London: Europa Publications Limited, 1999, 2001): SV Democratic Republic of the Congo.

202. John James Quinn, "Diffusion and escalation in the Great Lakes Region: the Rwandan genocide, the rebellion in Zaire, and Mobutu's Overthrow," in Steven E. Lobell and Philip Mauceri, eds., *Ethnic conflict and international politics: explaining diffusion and escalation* (New York: Palgrave Macmillan, 2004): 111–32.

203. Bratton and van de Walle, *Democratic Experiments*, pp. 241–42.

204. Africa South of the Sahara, SV. Togo, 2004.

205. Gérard Prunier, *The Rwanda crisis: History of a genocide* (Columbia University Press, 1995), pp. 76–77.

206. Ibid., 127.

207. Brown, "Foreign Aid and Democracy Promotion," p. 182.

208. Ibid.

209. Bratton and van de Walle, *Democratic Experiments*, pp. 241–42.

210. Ernest J. Wilson, III, "French Support for Structural Adjustment Programs in Africa," *World Development*, 21, 3 (1993): 331–47.

211. Peter J. Schraeder, Steven W. Hook, and Bruce Taylor, "Clarifying the Foreign Aid Puzzle: A Comparison of American, Japanese, French, and Swedish Aid Flows," *World Politics* 50, 2 (1998): 294–323; Robert Aldrich and John Connell, eds., *France in World Politics.* (New York: Routledge 1989); Jacques Adda and Marie-Claude Smoots, *La France face au Sud: le miroir brisé* (Paris: Karthala 1989).

212. Wilson, "French Support for Structural Adjustment," p. 334.

Chapter 7

The Partial Fragmentation of Economic Power in Africa

The Liberalization of Economic Policies and Partial Privatization

Not only did the political institutions of the region undergo a massive reordering in the wake of the second geopolitical shift, but the economic institutions and practices of the region did as well. Like the political reforms, we can see a significant region-wide outward appearance manifestation of economic reforms, but, in reality, these changes only represent a partial, but important, fragmentation of economic power throughout the region. The extent of the economic liberalization also varied within the region. The adoption of many of these reforms began in the mid- to late-1980s, but their pace accelerated following the new geopolitical alignment.[1]

The most noticeable evidence of the partial liberalization of economic power and greater exposure to markets for the region are these: (1) a move away from inward-oriented economic policies; (2) greater flows in international trade; (3) a region-wide increase in the number, and importance, of acts of privatization of majority state-owned industries; and (4) a rise in levels of foreign direct investment (FDI). Moreover, the region has also seen (5) increased African membership in intergovernmental organizations established to lower trade barriers, increase trade flows, and/or increase economic regional integration, and (6) an attendant rise in bilateral investment treaties. Several of these actions can be seen as both causes and consequences of liberalization.

Despite the emergence of region-wide and significant reforms in economic institutions and practices, the legacy of so much prior state control over these economies means that the state remains a significant player. The continued strength of the governing political elites in most countries can be seen through continued control over, and ownership of, much of their economies. Evidence for the continuing consolidation of economic power can be seen in the following: (1) large and significant components of the economy continuing to be in state hands, especially oil or mining sectors, (2) the state remains the largest employer of formal wage (non-agricultural) employment, and (3) one party which exercises power with only a small likelihood of losing elections. This last point is more relevant in conjunction with the fact that so much of the economy and so many jobs remain controlled and distributed by political elites. The apparent causes of many of these trends on regional, domestic, and international levels, are addressed in this chapter, though the influence of the international level was mostly addressed in Chapter 5.

EVIDENCE FOR THE PARTIAL FRAGMENTATION OF ECONOMIC POWER

Dramatic Decline in Inward-Oriented Economic Policies

As discussed in prior chapters, the political elite in most countries in the region consolidated its control over the economic domain partially through the use of inward-oriented development policies. This helped channel economic power through the political process rather than the market, though this tendency was stronger in some countries than in others.[2] Countries with majority state ownership were more inward-oriented, though Afro-Marxist and socialist countries followed such policies from an ideological basis.[3] Inward-oriented policies (moderate or strong) are those which result in incentive structures which are biased toward, or distinctly favor, production for the domestic market. The average rate of effective protection is medium to high and is fairly widespread; direct import controls and licenses are present and may be pervasive; and the exchange rate favors imports over exports.[4] The most common inward-orientated policies which added greatly to government power, aside from direct government ownership of industry, were tariffs, non-tariff barriers, currency overvaluation, and export taxation although inflation and budget deficits were ostensibly domestic in nature, they also came under pressure for liberalization. These, however, often resulted in negative current account balances and low growth, thereby necessarily impacting economic foreign relations and policies.

Tariffs/NTBs

Sub-Saharan Africa had strongly protected markets prior to the second geopolitical shift, the trade-weighted average of tariffs for eighteen sub-Saharan countries in 1987 was 27.78%.[5] In the same year, Burkina Faso had a weighted tariff level of 52.8% in 1987. Also, Kenya's average tariff level was 35%. Finally, Benin, Burundi, Ghana, and Senegal had average tariff levels near 30%. By another index, with 10 being no tariffs and 0 being total, Africa had an average tariff rate of 4.16 in 1985.[6] Perhaps more importantly, African countries often used non-tariff barriers (NTB) to reduce economic competition.

Using an index for the level of NTBs, which runs from 0% to 100%, eighteen countries in the region had an average of 69%—though the region as a whole had a range of tariffs from 14.9% to 100%.[7] Countries such as Benin, Congo, Sierra Leone, Tanzania, Zambia, and Zimbabwe featured NTBs of 100%—usually as a result of the country's control over foreign currency. It must be kept in mind that, although tariff numbers reflect overall real levels of protection, effective protection for non-agricultural goods was usually much higher.

With the end of the Cold War, however the economic liberalization of tariffs became more common in the region. For example, the average tariff level on all products (weighted and from 2000 to 2004) was 11.46%.[8] (Compare to 27.78 above). Some of the countries with the lowest tariffs in the post-Cold War period were these: Botswana (1%), Madagascar (3.6%), Namibia (0.5%), and Swaziland (0.6). Some of the countries with higher tariffs were these: Djibouti (26.8%), Nigeria (18.5%), Seychelles (23.4%), Sudan (19.6%), and Zimbabwe (18.7%). Importantly, the highest numbers in the second period are still lower than the average for the first. According to another source, but using an inversed index of average tariffs, the number went from 4.16 to 7.4 and from 1985 to 2009 (where an increase indicates fewer tariffs and ten was the upper limit for free trade).[9]

Looking at another measure of restrictions on trade (Figure 7.1), which includes tariffs as well measures for as non-tariff barriers (NTBs), Africa seemed to be at a status quo or have a very slight rise in liberalization (from around 25 to almost 30) until 1996, when the levels began to rise dramatically, from 32.18 to 44.76. (See Figure 7.1) Thus, it seems from the graph for Africa suggests that some log jam in protectionist policies broke in 1996, which is coincident with the transition from the GATT to the WTO after the end of the Cold War, as well as being within seven years of the end of the Cold War.[10]

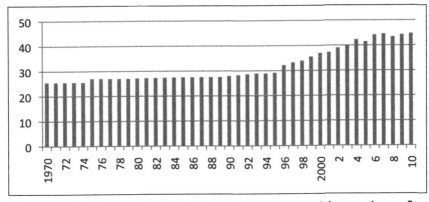

Figure 7.1   Restrictions on Trade SSA Average 1970–2010. [Higher numbers reflect fewer restrictions.]

Examining these data by country, one can see that nearly every country showed a decrease in restrictions (represented by a rise in graph). Only Angola, Botswana, Burkina Faso, Ethiopia, Lesotho, Malawi, and Zimbabwe showed a slight increase in levels of protectionism.[11] Countries with over a 50% improvement in this index were these: Benin, Burundi, Congo-Brazzaville, Ghana, Kenya, Madagascar, Mali, Mauritius, Nigeria, Rwanda, Senegal, Sierra Leone, Tanzania, Uganda, Zambia, and Zaire (the DRC).

Agricultural Taxation Levels

African countries were renowned for higher levels of taxation on agricultural exports compared to countries in other regions during the Cold War, though regional variation was high.[12] According to one source, from 1970 to 1989 Africa had an average of 51% direct and indirect taxes on agricultural exports, compared to between 25% and 28% levels for Asian, Latin American, and Mediterranean countries.[13] Moreover, for the 24 African countries in this sample, the mean tax rate for important export crops was 42%. From another source, the average taxes on the most important export crops from 1966 to 1986 for 25 countries was 66.7%.[14] Government controlled or created monopsonies were part of the reason for such high taxes, though one scholar sees more of the cause in the sunk costs for farmers and low discount factors.[15]

Since the end of the Cold War, African taxation rates on exports have declined, albeit slowly and unevenly. Using the nominal rate of assistance as a tax measure, we see that the average level of taxation on agricultural exports from 1966 to 1989 was 39%, while from 1990 to 2005 it was 27.7%.[16] This represents an average decline of about 11.3%.[17] In fact, African governments have long been pressured by the World Bank to raise producer prices by directly lowering taxes or devaluing the currency (since currency overvaluation is a tax on exporting and a subsidy for importing). According to the World Bank, in a study of 28 countries, 17 countries lessened agricultural taxation rates from 1981–1983 to 1989–1991.[18] Of these 17, three countries saw decreases of over 100% in the real protection coefficient, one saw a change between 50 and 100%, while the remaining 13 had very low decreases in taxation rates. By contrast, 11 moved in the opposite direction, with two having more than a 50% increase in the real protection coefficient (Guinea-Bissau and Zambia).

Even looking at non-exported agriculture, we see the prices coming closer to reflect market values, thereby reducing government's role in this sector. For such crops, African farmers were subsidized, on average, during the first period at a rate of about 20.4%. For example, Liberia, Nigeria, Cameroon, CAR, Congo, Gabon, Niger, and Senegal all subsidized cassava. However, corn (maize) was sometimes taxed (Malawi, Mali, Zimbabwe, Zambia, and

Tanzania) and sometimes subsidized (Burkina Faso, Namibia, South Africa, Kenya, Somalis, and Ethiopia). By 1990, the nominal rate of assistance to farmers fell to 5.6%, reflecting a decrease of 14.7%. Finally, looking at non-tradable agricultural goods (as opposed to imported or exported crops), we see that during the first period (1966–1989), there was a small tax, at 0.6%, which increased to 2.3% during the second period. This is an increase in taxes of about 1.7%.

Looking at the most comparable measures between the two periods, and using the nominal rate of assistance, it appears that both subsidies and taxes on tradables decreased significantly, as did taxes on non-tradables, though the levels were lowest for non-tradables. It seems that the government footprint has decreased in the second period, though export taxes still remain around 25%, subsidies on imports are at about 6%, and taxes on domestic only crops are about 2%. The other measures show a higher taxation on export crops, and they also appear to be lower for the second period.

Currency Overvaluation Levels

As van de Walle indicated in 2001, countries made the most progress on the stabilization measures of the International Monetary Fund (IMF) which include several of the inward-oriented policies of concern.[19] By far, the most important of these was currency overvaluation. Looking at pre- and post-Cold War data, we see that during the Cold War, sub-Saharan African countries had an average ratio of the parallel market rate of 5.70 (where a one means no distortion), while after 1990, these countries had an average of 1.45 (excluding Zaire and Angola).[20] In another calculation which excluded CFA currency countries (as well as DRC and Angola), we see that average for this ratio was 17.97 during the Cold War, and 2.54 after.[21] So a significant decrease in currency overvaluation occurred for most countries. For CFA countries, the rate (as measured here) was 1.094 for both periods.[22] As the reader should remember, currency overvaluation acts as a tax (or transfer) on exports and subsidies on imports, and its decline is clearly a movement away from one of the most impactful inward-oriented policies.[23]

Inflation

Another interesting turn around financial indictor is inflation, which seems to have been (mostly) wrung out of many African economies. According to African governance indicators for inflation, in 2007, the average for countries with data (not including Somalia) was 97.8 (where 100 is the best). Nearly every country had a score of 99.8 or higher, save for Zimbabwe which scored a zero.[24]

Using the rate of inflation itself (and excluding Zimbabwe), we find that the average level of inflation for 2007 was about 7%.[25] This average is quite low by historic, Third World standards. By way of contrast, in sub-Saharan Africa from 1980 to 1987, the average level of inflation was 15.2%. This included such highs as 95.2% for Uganda and 53.5% for Zaire.[26] The countries with lower levels of inflation for these years included Liberia at 1.5% and Gabon at 2.6%.

Budget Deficits

Despite the curbing of budget deficits being a key World Bank and IMF target, not all African countries have fared as well here (nor has the US and many European countries for that matter), though clearly this picture looks better for the region. In 2000, the African average budget deficit was −4%, including a high of 11.7% for Gabon, and a low of −41% for Eritrea (where a negative number is a deficit and a positive one a surplus).[27] Thirty-seven countries had negative averages and ten had positive averages.[28] By 2007, the average for the region was positive 2.3%, with a low of −24.6% for Zimbabwe and a high of 124.9% for Sao Tome and Principe. Also, in 2007, twenty-seven countries had budget deficits, while twenty had surpluses. This compares to only ten with surpluses from before.

In the late 1980s, the average government deficit/surplus for the region from 1985 to 1989 was *negative* 5%.[29] This included lows of −22% for Burkina Faso and −14% for Niger, to highs of 14.5% for Botswana and 11.5% for Benin. Overall, of the countries included, 37 had budget deficits and five had budget surpluses. This appears to be a significant regional turnaround, especially in the number of countries with budget surpluses.

Current Account Balances

According to World Bank data, from 1980 to 1989, African countries ran an average current account balance of −9.97% as a percentage of gross national income (GNI). Even with changes in policy environments, current account balances from 1990 to 2000 were slightly worse with an average of −11.15%.[30] In comparison, from 2004 to 2008, sub-Saharan countries had a small surplus in current account balances.[31] These were negative from 2008 to 2009, but returned to black for 2010–2011.

Greater Trade Flows

Beginning in the 1970s, but only rising slowly, African countries have been increasing their involvement in global economic participation.[32] In 1970, the aggregate index of levels of economic globalization for sub-Saharan Africa was 30.15 (See Figure 7.2).[33] This compares to a world average of 39.4. This index rose slowly until 1987, when numbers stayed around the same until

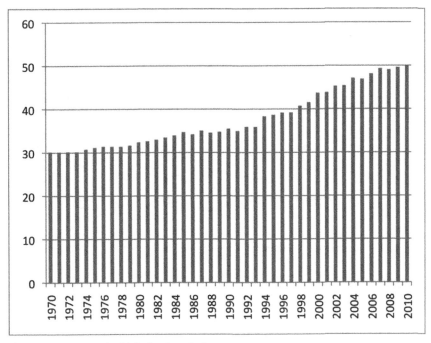

Figure 7.2   Economic Globalization, Index.

1994, when they rose steadily until 2006, when they stayed right around 49 for the next few years (compared to a world average of around 62 in 2010).

The data for African economic flows tell a similar story. It began at a relatively low level in 1970 and slowly rose or maintained its levels until 1987. Then from 1987 to 1993, the levels were about the same, until a big uptick takes place in 1994. Then we see some volatility until 2000, when it picks up until 2008, and then it has remained at this level. This a clear indication that trends in Africa were reflecting world trends (see Chapter 5, Figure 5.1), though African levels began at much lower levels of economic integration and the absolute levels are still lower. If we examine only trade flows, Africa does indeed appear to have much higher levels of integration than in the first period. In the Cold War period, levels of flows in this index were 39.9, while for the second period the average was 50.4. This represents an average increase of 26%. From start to end, the percentage change increase was just over 50%.

Most countries saw a 10% or greater increase in such flows. The countries with the greatest increases in economic flows (over 40%) were these: Angola, Cape Verde, Ethiopia, Ghana, Lesotho, Madagascar, Mozambique, Nigeria, Rwanda, Sudan, Uganda, and Zimbabwe. Those with lower than 10% were these: Botswana, Burkina Faso, Djibouti, Swaziland, the Seychelles, and

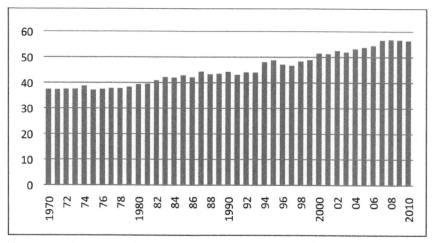

Figure 7.3 Congruence between Voters and Members 1990–2010. Accept greater income differences. *Notes*: Q: To exhort people to greater effort, we should be willing to accept bigger differences in wage levels. The difference in mean has been multiplied with 100 and subtracted from 100. Hence, a score of 100 indicates perfect congruence, no difference in the mean.

Togo, South Africa, Zambia. Four saw small declines in flow: Gabon, Kenya, Mauritania, and Malawi.[34] At first glance, it seems to be the case that most of the countries with the largest increases in these flows were ones that had begun with some of the lowest levels. These were also usually countries that either (1) had featured majority state ownership (MSO) of industries (and the attendant strongly inward-oriented policies) during the first period or (2) which had undergone significant domestic turmoil or violence affecting their economies.

As discussed elsewhere, countries that had featured majority state owner-ship of industry or mining or oil exporting sectors had more inward-oriented trade policies during the Cold War period.[35] So the countries which had less than 10% increases were ones that had not featured MSO or did not have domestic turmoil and therefore started from a higher level. For example, Botswana only had a 2% increase, but its level was at 70; and Gabon had a negative 5% in flows, but its level was 69.2. By contrast, countries with significant inward-oriented policies or great civil disruptions often had the largest increases. Rwanda had a 60% increase, but its average score on the KOF index was 17, compared to the regional average of 50.[36] Uganda also had a 60% increase, but it only reached the level of 28.9 in the post-Cold War period. Ethiopia was at 23, and so forth. These examples suggest that much of this movement is actually regression toward the mean, among countries with disruptions or which ended poor policies.[37]

Partial Privatization of State-Owned Enterprises, Banks and Marketing Boards

As discussed in Chapter 5, Africa (along with the Middle East) represented about 3% of all revenue raised from privatizations between 1988 and 1998, internationally.[38] In terms of the sheer number of privatization transactions, and from the longer time period of 1980–2004, the region witnessed the second highest frequency of transactions internationally, though it ranked at the bottom for the value of the assets sold.[39] Most of the earliest divestitures were of smaller firms of lesser value, where few jobs were to be lost.[40] Although some privatizations occurred in sub-Saharan Africa before the end of the Cold War, most occurred after 1990.

Prior to 1990, only fifteen sub-Saharan African countries had begun to privatize any of their state-owned assets, though Guinea, Mozambique, and Malawi had the largest number of acts of privatization. They also were among the earliest to begin.[41] Cote d'Ivoire, Togo, and Uganda had between 22 and 34 acts each.[42] Benin, Central African Republic, Zaire (DRC), Madagascar, Mauritania, Niger, Nigeria, Senegal, and Togo each had between 10 and 20 acts of privatization. Burundi, the Gambia, Ghana, Guinea Bissau, and Mali each had fewer than ten. Recalling from Chapter 4, Africa was estimated to have nearly 3000 public enterprises (PEs) in the 1980s, with Guinea having over 180, Malawi over 100, and Cote d'Ivoire with nearly 150.[43] Moreover, these numbers are probably also underestimates and quite conservative. According to one source, Africa underwent 334 privatizations prior to 1990.[44] These are estimated to have been worth 2.6 billion dollars.[45]

With the end of the Cold War, the number of privatizations and their value increased drastically. For example, between 1991 and 2002, roughly 2,300 acts of privatization were recorded in Africa, with total sales estimated at $9 billion.[46] Moreover, from 2000 to 2008, the amount of money raised climbed to $12.5 billion.[47] In fact, most African countries only seriously undertook real attempts later in the 1990s. For example, Burkina Faso began in 1994, Burundi in 1992, Cameroon in 1996, Cote d'Ivoire in 1991, and Mali in 1996.[48] In fact, the number of transactions between 1990 and 1996 for the region was 2054, compared to the 334 prior to 1990.[49]

Most privatization programs followed a pattern of some initial ones occurring by the mid-1990s, though the more highly valued firms occurred much deeper in the process.[50] For example, the largest sale in Benin (from 1988–2007) was in 2007, representing 55% of all revenue to that point.[51] In Burkina Faso, the largest sale in 2006 represented 92% of revenue raised since 1994. Gabon, too, sold assets in 2007 comprising 94% of all revenue raised. Kenya, which had over 100 transactions between 1988 and 2008, had sales in the last four years (up to 2008) worth 83% all revenue raised. Typically, the largest

10 or 12 SOEs could account for over 70 to 80 of the assets of all SOE for the country during the first period.[52] These largest of them tended to be among the last to be privatized, if at all.

Importantly, the difference in the government's average share of sectors before and after the Cold War fell significantly, from 89.1% to 10.3%. For example, in the manufacturing and industry sector, such ownership fell from 79.7% to 7.9%. For agriculture, agroindustry, and fisheries, state average ownership fell from 79.5% to 1.6%; for services, tourism and real estate, the percentage fell from 70.2% to 14.3%; for trade it fell from 95.3% to 3.3%; for transport from 97.6% to 4.9%; for financial institutions, government average ownership fell from 86.7% to 8.2%; and the decline for water was 100% to 12.5%.[53] The decline was less steep for other sectors of the economy, reflecting some continued state influence. For example, the average state ownership for the energy sector was 88.3% before and 46.5% after.[54] Also for telecoms, the average share of government ownership fell from 95.8% to 42.8%. Nonetheless, it appears that the state still owned less than a majority of these sectors, while they had majority ownership of most of the sector before privatizations.

In major mining and petroleum exporting sectors, most countries maintain significant or even majority shares, though with some exceptions.[55] For example, Ethiopia, Tanzania, and Ghana sold important chunks of these sectors. The Ashanti gold mines in Ghana were privatized successfully in 1993/4, representing 47% all of divestiture revenue from 1989 to 1998.[56] Some countries which had privatizations in petroleum include South Africa, Cote d'Ivoire, Togo, Uganda, and Zambia.

Despite some movement on privatization in mining, most countries which had had majority state ownership of mining or oil kept majority ownership of most of this sector during the second period, though some countries had some limited sales and partial privatization. Benin maintains its state-owned petroleum extraction and processing industry, and Togo still owns 100% of its phosphate sector. In fact, the government of Togo declared its phosphate mines and public utilities to be "strategic," which placed them outside consideration for privatization.[57] By contrast, several mining and oil nations have engaged in limited and partial privatization. In 1989, Nigeria privatized parts of two petroleum companies, raising $8.5 million as well as selling part of Unipetrol for $9.7 million in 1991. The largest privatization was in 1993 when the NNPC oil field nationalized from the British was sold to other private companies.[58] Nonetheless, Nigeria still owns between 60 and 80% of its petroleum parastatals.

Angola experienced a partial privatization of this sector, though its control of the oil sector remains quite strong. In 1992, the state petroleum sold enough of its share to result in a decline of ownership to 41% for approximately two-thirds of its total output. Nonetheless, the petroleum law of 2004 invests all ownership rights for petroleum in the parastatal, though in practice exploitation is done through production sharing agreements. Although this law opened up bidding and reduced the prior monopoly, the SOE remains an important player.[59] The DRC now also appears to have begun with partial privatization, but not by privatizing the copper parastatal, per se; rather parastatal began engaging in joint ventures. In fact, over 80% of Gecamines' mines are associated with joint ventures.[60]

Zambia may be the country which has had the most significant privatization program of a major mining export sector. Copper was Zambia's life blood of exporting and for government revenue from independence onwards. In 1997, Zambia sold two mines Nkana and Nchanga which were part of Zambia Consolidated Copper mines (ZCCM) and raised $220 million. In 1998, other aspects of ZCCM were sold raising an additional $385 million. Even this was done reluctantly, and only as a last resort. Zambia agreed to sell its holdings in Consolidated Copper Mines (ZCCM) only after losing millions of dollars for years.[61] In fact, prior to the sale, the government rejected an offer from a South African/Canadian/American/British consortium known as Kafue to purchase these mines and assume its past debt.[62] The deal would have been for $130 million, with $75 million in debt assumption, and $500 in rehabilitation and expansion. Finally, with the IMF threatening not to release another tranche of $350 million, and the price of copper plummeting, Zambia finally agreed to sell in November 1999 for $90 million.[63]

Even with many acts of privatization, state control through ownership in Africa remains fairly high. The share of state-owned enterprises in sub-Saharan Africa (as a percentage of GDP) was 18.7% from 1978 to 1985, declining only to 17.9% from 1986 to 1991.[64] Ironically, Ghana, which was a poster child for the World Bank and IMF for policy transitions, showed an increase of SOE share of GDP from 5.8% to 8.4% between these two periods using this measure.[65] Only Guinea appeared to have a significant decline of SOE activity between these two periods, (i.e., from 25% to 9%), though a footnote indicates that this more likely reflected a measurement error rather than a real decrease in state economic activity.[66] There was, however, a slight decrease of SOE investment as a percentage of GDP for Africa between these two periods: from 28.9% to 26.4%.[67] Nevertheless, the share of SOE in employment increased between these two periods, from 15.85% to 17.1%.[68] Also, the government share of GDP has not changed much, with an average of 16.14% from 1979 to 1989, compared to 15.96% from 1990 to 1999.[69] The average for 2000 to 2010 is similar at 15.63%. So there has been a slight decrease, but government shares remain high.

Even so, some regional momentum for the withdrawal of the state from the economy has been afoot in the region, even if only rhetorically. The Organization for African Unity, for example, announced in 1985 that an increased role for private sector enterprise would be beneficial for development.[70] Despite some support for this reform, the obstacles for the African region were greater than elsewhere: there were more countries with significant majority state ownership, the capital markets were not deep, and few stock exchanges existed.

Partial Privatization of Banking

According to one source, during the 1970s, over a third of African countries enjoyed a monopoly within the banking system.[71] By 2001, no African country had such a monopoly. In West Africa, the bank restructuring began between 1989 and 1990.[72] In 1990, state ownership of banks was close to or had declined below 30% in Benin, Cote d'Ivoire, Mali, Niger, Senegal, and Togo. Only Burkina Faso had above 40%.[73] According to another study, Botswana, the Gambia, Mauritius, the Seychelles, and South Africa held less than 10% ownership of banking assets; Cote d'Ivoire, Kenya, Nigeria, and Zambia held between 10 and 24%; Ghana, Lesotho, Malawi, Rwanda, and Tanzania held between 25 and 59%; and Ethiopia held more than 60% ownership of banks in 2000–2002.[74] Many of these were still further privatized: By 2003, Ghana held less than 12.1%; Kenyan MSO banks had less than 1.1% of all assets, Nigerian MSO banks were down to 4.7%; and Rwandan state-owned banks held less than 6.6% of assets.[75]

Privatization/Liberalization of Marketing Boards

As discussed elsewhere, most African countries had marketing boards which had been monopsonies (single buyers) during the Cold War, though the genesis of such boards was nearly always during the colonial period. In fact, during the 1980s, the "processing and exporting of commodities was almost entirely in the hands of marketing boards" for sub-Saharan African countries.[76] Within a decade of the end of the Cold War, however, many of these monopsonistic marketing boards had been eliminated. In fact, by 1999, monopoly boards had become the exception rather than the rule.[77] Nigeria eliminated its agricultural marketing board in 1986, while Madagascar and Niger had eliminated marketing boards for some crops by 1994.[78] In other cases, the major marketing board has allowed other private companies to compete with them, such as in Burundi with coffee and Tanzania with cashew nuts.[79] The World Bank listed four countries that were eliminating marketing boards for export crops: Nigeria, Mozambique, Guinea, and Guinea Bissau. Countries with mixed reforms are (still government in control, but prices linked to world prices) were these: Kenya, Burundi, the Gambia, Malawi, Niger, Uganda, Zimbabwe, Benin, Burkina Faso, Cameroon, Cote d'Ivoire, Mali, Rwanda, Sierra Leone, Zambia, and Chad.

In many other countries, marketing boards were reformed rather than privatized: producer prices were more strongly linked with world prices in an attempt to reduce administrative inefficiencies. In fact, the countries that eliminated significant government intrusion into the domestic market for at least one major food were these: Benin, Burkina Faso, Cameroon, CAR, Congo, the Gambia, Guinea, Guinea-Bissau, Kenya, Madagascar, Malawi, Mali, Mauritania, Mozambique, Nigeria, Senegal, Tanzania, Togo, and Zambia.[80] The abdication of control over a domestic crop should have been easier politically as more bureaucratic reach would be required to regulate commodities which did not move through a major port or airport, and the state's ability to tax these markets in most states was probably nil.[81] Countries that the World Bank categorized as having made few or no real reforms for export marketing boards as of 1994 were these: Ghana, Madagascar, CAR, Congo, Gabon, Senegal, and Tanzania.[82] Since 1994, other countries have eliminated their marketing boards. Cameroon liberalized its export market for both coffee and cocoa in 1994; Cote d'Ivoire liberalized its marketing for coffee after 1999; and Uganda liberalized, though the former marketing board does regulation.[83]

Rise of Foreign Direct Investment

Another potential indicator of economic resources flowing outside of states' hands (and more in the market) can be seen in the level of foreign direct investment (FDI).[84] The levels of FDI have been higher in the region recently, especially with more privatization of resources, though it began from a very low base. And as we saw in a prior chapter, around 1.8% of all long-term private investment to Third World went to Africa, with a significant portion of this small amount only going to Angola, Nigeria, and South Africa.[85] In 1989, the percent of FDI which came from privatizations in Africa was 0.6; this rose slowly from 1990 to 1995, to an average of 6%, with a high of 16% in 1994.[86]

As discussed before, the most valuable privatizations have occurred more recently, and most of these involved significant foreign ownership, especially in mining and telecommunications, which is FDI by definition. For example, the sale of Ashanti Gold Mines and the partial privatization of oil in Angola were bought primarily by multinational corporations. In a survey of privatization in eight African countries, five of them had foreign sales representing over 60% of all sales, and six had over 50% of sales being foreign. Only two had less than majority foreign purchasers as a percentage of sales, though much of this would change later.[87]

In terms of revenues coming into the region, we can see from Figure 7.4 that FDI really started to flow slowly with the end Cold War, though its rate of increase really took off after a decade. The line seemed to bump along until 1990, when it began to increase rapidly.[88] Figure 7.4 also included a line representing FDI going to non-Southern African nations to exclude the possibility that this is all going to South Africa (with the end of apartheid), though South Africa received a disproportionate share. This graph is consistent with the data on privatization: first, that it only really took off during the decade following the end of the Cold War, and, second, the later one goes from that point, the higher the value of the assets sold. Eventually this line will become curvelinear if most of the FDI is from privatization (as at some point the state will run out of things to privatize), but clearly some of it is. It could well be that 2008 was the inflection point: it is too early to tell.

Also the amount of FDI as a percentage of gross fixed capital investment has grown recently, as one would expect. In 1995, it only represented about 6% of all fixed capital investments. This grew to 12% in 1997 and to around 15% between 2000 and 2004 and rose again to around 27% from 2006 to 2008.[89] As privatizations have increased in the region, this number has increased, necessarily (as most sales of large firms have been to foreign companies).

It should be noted, again, that most of these new inflows of FDI have been to countries with mining and oil operations, along with South Africa, so it is not evenly distributed throughout the region. Figure 7.5 shows a chart of countries in sub-Saharan Africa which received at least $4 billion in FDI in 2008.

Although South Africa is the most industrialized country in Africa, it should be remembered that it has significant mining operations; however, this sector does not comprise as much as a percentage of exports as in other countries. In 2007, for example, in crude materials (inedible) and minerals and fuels, it exported $13,898 million worth.[90] In contrast, Gabon, clearly an oil/mineral export, sold exporter $5.8 million worth of petroleum abroad. But for Gabon, this represented around 80% of exports, while for South Africa, it was less than 22% of exports.[91]

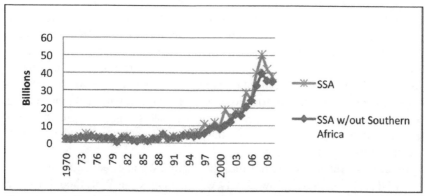

Figure 7.4   Inflow of FDI to Sub-Saharan Africa: 2010 Current US Dollars.

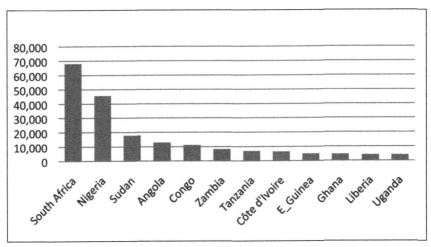

Figure 7.5   Countries with $4 billion or more in FDI 2008. Adapted from UNCTAD, *World Investment Report*, Table Annex Table B2 by author

Membership in Binding Trade or Monetary Regimes

Belonging to a binding trade or monetary regime necessarily limits a country's ability to control its economic foreign policy in the same manner as not belonging to this regime. Although countries may leave organizations, doing so come at some reputational costs. This could be in the form of an external fragment of economic accountability or an agency of restraint, which can limit a future government's ability to reverse a policy decision.[92] International treaty obligations can be ignored, but it is done at one's peril or reputation.

African Nations Joining WTO

One of the clear differences between the two periods for the region is the level of participation in the GATT/WTO. Moreover, those that did belong during the Cold War had the ability to avoid reciprocity with developed nations, while gaining access to their markets for many goods.[93] In terms of African involvement in the WTO, we see that currently most African countries are full members of the WTO, and even 37 had been members of GATT. Of these 37, eight joined GATT after the end of the Cold War but before it became the WTO. Additional two countries joined the WTO as such. All but one of these members of the WTO from Africa joined in 1995 or 1996 (the WTO began on January 1,1995): Cape Verde joined in 2008. An additional six countries are observer nations, so 45 countries may well be members within five years.

The WTO is also a stronger institution than the GATT ever was. As mentioned in Chapter 5, WTO rules are more binding than GATT rules were.

Gilpin suggested that the WTO was much more institutionalized.[94] Also, developing countries were routinely allowed exceptions to both tariff and non-tariff barriers, especially with the use of quantitative restrictions on imports.[95] These are less stringent in the WTO, though some de facto division remains.

Regional Trade Organizations

African countries have embarked on a series of South-South regional trade agreements, which were originally intended to be part of a non-Western, African-centered approach to development.[96] The Organization of African Union began the African Economic Community (AEC) in 1991 with the goal of the final integration of the continent into one market. As African countries were not anywhere near such a goal, the leaders decided to create a series of regional economic communities (RECs) to facilitate a partial move toward the complete economic integration of Africa. Once each region was closer to full integration, the whole of Africa could be merged together. Established under the guidance of the AU, the RECs were to be intermediate steps toward integration, with a hope for even a common currency.

Some of the more important regional trade organizations/treaties in the region included the Economic and Monetary Community of Central African (CEMAC/EMCCA), the Preferential Trade Area (PTA) which became the Common Market of Eastern and Southern Africa (COMESA), the Economic Community of West African States (ECOWAS), theWest African Economic Community (CEAO) [later the West African Economic and Monetary Union (UEMOA)], and the Southern African Development Community (SADDC, later SADC). With the end of the Cold War, some more integration appears to be occurring in some of the regions, though it could be debated whether or not increased intra-regional trade is an unqualified good, as much of this increase could be reduced overall trade or trade diversion behavior.

Some other important regional trading blocs, RECs, or custom unions that should be mentioned were the East African Community (EAC), which included Kenya, Tanzania, and Uganda and which has expanded to include Rwanda and Burundi. The Mano River Union (MRU) is comprised of Guinea, Liberia, and Sierra Leone. In Central Africa, the Economic Community of Great Lakes Countries (ECGLC) includes all the former colonies of Belgium: Burundi, Rwanda, and Zaire.[97] In Southern Africa, one of the most integrated regional trade organizations was the South African Customs Union (SACU). In this organization, none of the countries (i.e., Botswana, Lesotho, Swaziland, or South Africa) had tariffs or non-tariff barriers (NTBs) against each other.[98]

As we can see in Figure 7.6, trade within several of these groups, as a percentage of all trade, seems to have dropped from around 8.1% in 1970, to 5.15% in 1980; it then rose to around 7.6% in 1990, and it increased further

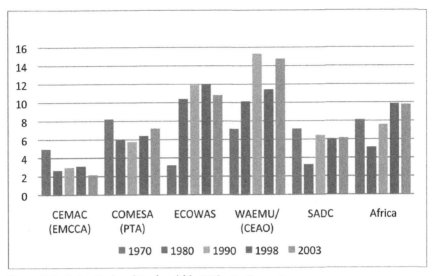

Figure 7.6 Intra-Regional Trade within RECs: By Percentage.

to around 9.85% in 1998. In 2003, it remained around 9.75%. These numbers reflect an average of all intra-African trade as a percentage of all African trade (imports and exports). [99] Thus, some intra-regional increase in trade has increased to new levels, but only around a 20% increase from 1970, though this represents around a 32% increase from 1980.[100] There is some debate as to whether these increases are trade creating or distorting. Nevertheless, it appears to be higher in the post-Cold War period compared to the Cold War period.

Bilateral Free Trade Agreements

Beyond membership in regional or worldwide trade organizations, bilateral trade treaties can also be a form of economic accountability and move countries closer to neo-liberal policies. As mentioned in Chapter 5, a veritable explosion in bilateral trade treaties has emerged, which could be both cause and effect for rising international investment. Many African countries have signed significant numbers of these agreements since the end of the Cold War. Some of these BITS were with other African nations, but many more were with developed countries. Africa had early experience with BITs, signing the most of any region in the 1960s.[101] By the end of the Cold War, Africa had signed 149 BITs, though this number increased to 428 by 1999. Nearly half of these were with developed countries (172), while 168 were with other developing nations, of which 44 of them were with other African nations. Thus, 41 African nations had BITs, compared to only 21 during the 1980s.

Over 31 African nations signed 50% or more of their BITs after the end of the Cold War (through January 1, 2000). South Africa signed the most in this period, with 22 followed by Zimbabwe (18), Ghana (15), Mauritius (10), and Cape Verde (9). Not all of these BITs were in force as of January 2000, but they express intent and aspiration.[102]

Those countries where most of the BITs were signed prior to the end of the Cold War are fewer in number. Of these, the Francophone countries had the most, such as Cameroon (7), Democratic Republic of the Congo/Zaire (6), Cote d'Ivoire (5), Gabon (6), and Senegal (10). With more time, these may shift to having more BITs, but they were not part of the quick trend in the 1989 though the end of 1999 movement.[103] Also, these numbers do not reflect the role membership in multilateral trade agreements would have.

FACTORS FACILITATING FRAGMENTATION OF ECONOMIC POWER/LIBERALIZATION OF POLICIES

To explore why a political elite presumably engaged in economic liberalization that may have jeopardized its hold on power, one must understand the elite's relative position and bargaining power. The relative strategic importance of African nations became less with this second geopolitical change. Africa also was of low economic importance to the West and its allies, especially with the end of the Cold War. In addition, many African nations had experienced near total failure to achieve economic development, resulting in fewer domestic resources to draw upon as well as higher debts and lower levels of investment from abroad. This necessarily increased most of Africa's dependence upon official development assistance (ODA) as well as the IMF and the World Bank Funding. Then with the IMF and World Bank linking economic reforms to more debt forgiveness, the aid-dependent nations had less ability to refuse, especially where their domestic economies were in tatters. Also, with rising American power, many international and regional organizations were more actively enforcing norms consistent with free trade. Finally, the international community pressed for less government control, more accountability, less corruption, and more economic efficiency.

Moreover, domestic pressures reinforced these trends for the decentralization of economic power, and the partial political fragmentation of power has allowed for more of a possibility for competition for domestic economic policy. Therefore, the new environment permitted domestic constituents to pressure their government for economic policies that would benefit them, though not all pressures domestically were for liberalization: this cut both ways.

Low Trading Levels/ Strategic Importance and High Dependence of Africa to Rest of World

With the end of the Cold War, African nations could no longer play the East against the West to obtain increased aid or strategic assistance from either the United States or the Soviet Union.[104] As most African states are relatively weak militarily as well as economically underdeveloped, they became less important once their threat to balance against one side or the other disappeared. The Russian presence in Africa all but disappeared, but with some modest replacement by China. In fact, US aid internationally fell right after the end of the Cold War, and it only began to increase again after the 9/11 attacks in 2001.

Beyond its decline in geo-political importance, sub-Saharan Africa was also becoming less important to international markets, as a source of either exports or imports. The regional share of exports of food and other primary products declined from 17% to 8% from 1970 to 1990.[105] (See Figure 7.7) In terms of total world trade shares, Africa declined from around 5% at independence to less than 2% in 2000.[106] Looking at only exports, the levels were even lower; sub-Saharan Africa's share of world exports fell nearly every year from 1970 to around 2000.[107] In 1970, its percentage of merchandize exports was 3.4% and in 2000, it was 1.5%. This rose slowly to 2.4% by 2011.

Also, despite many years following independence, the region remained heavily dependent on one or two crops or minerals for exports in the 1990s: over two-thirds of the countries in the region had one commodity or crop account for 50% or more of total exports.[108] This, in combination with the decrease of Africa as a player in the post-Cold War context, reduced their strategic importance to other great powers.

Moreover, Africa was becoming less relevant as a purchaser of world products. As Figure 7.8 indicates, in 1970, Africa imported only around 3.3% of the goods internationally. This trend see-sawed back and forth until 1981/82, but it took a clear direction falling from 3.6% to a low of 1.3% in 2002. Since then, Africa has become a better market, and their share of imports has slowly increased to around 2% of world trade since 2009. Nonetheless, per capita incomes in Africa remain low for most of the continent.

In the decades since the end of the Cold War, as we can see in both graphs, there has been a bit of a turn around, often attributed to the associated rising demand from developing China and India. America, as well, has decided to diversify away from reliance upon Middle Eastern oil, making African oil and mineral exports somewhat more important in the late 1990s. These exports, along with their rising value, are often credited with the recent higher average economic growth levels in Africa. In fact, the terms of trade for African nations have been quite positive since 2000.

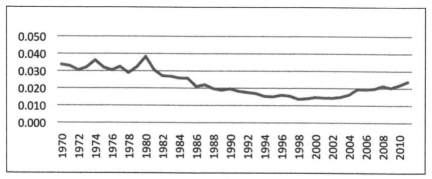

Figure 7.7   Merchandize Exports as Percentage of World: Sub-Saharan Africa.

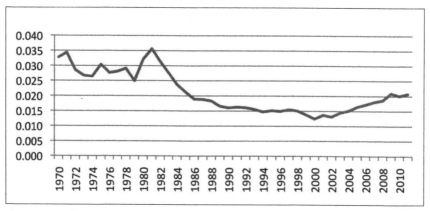

Figure 7.8   African Imports as Percentage World. Adapted from UNCTAD stats by author

So, some of the increase in exports could be a result of terms of trade as much as a turnaround in policy, though there must be some effect from lower levels of currency overvaluation. (See Figure 7.9)

African Poor Economic Situation Prior to 1989 and Rising Debt

The poor performance of most sub-Saharan African economies during the Cold War period is well known, and it adds to the subcontinent's international marginalization and status as the home of so many weak states. In fact, Africa was nearly universally singled out as the worst economic performing region, especially since the publication of the so-called Berg Report.[109] Although the attributed causes of economic problems were debated, this framed the debate about African growth for years to come. From 1970 onwards, nominal GDP in sub-Saharan Africa grew more slowly than any other region, while real

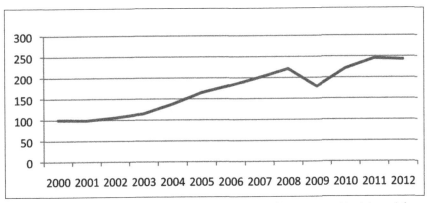

Figure 7.9 Terms of Trade for Exports Sub-Saharan Africa 2000=100. Adapted from UNCTAD stats by author

GDP growth rates declined.[110] For most of the Cold War period, after independence, regional growth of per capita GDP was less than 0.5%.[111] In fact, from 1980 to 1987, African GDP per capita growth was −2.8 and the average GDP per capita for that last year was $330.[112]

There has been a contentious debate concerning the causes of slow growth in the region. The view that most of Africa's problems are externally driven was a strong sentiment in the decolonial period and can even be seen in many documents, such as the Lagos Plan of Action; however, this view is not well accepted internationally, or especially in the West in the post-Cold War period. Even regionally, this has become seen more and more as mere camouflage for poor African leadership. The emergence of NEPAD as an institution to increase accountability reflects this fact (see below). In fact, the intellectual conclusions drawn vis-à-vis African poor economic performance help give World Bank and IMF programs of economic conditionality greater legitimacy internationally.

Debts

Debt became the thin edge of the wedge that has led to the externalization of economic foreign policy witnessed throughout much of sub-Saharan Africa.[113] As most students of African politics know, higher and higher debts for the region were linked with more and more of export revenues being tied to debt servicing. In fact, international actors, especially a group called Jubilee, argued that the debts of the Third World were a worldwide moral issue and an important constraint on their development. Significant debt forgiveness would follow, but only after economic conditionality was followed (see below). Moreover, with the debt crisis triggered by Mexico's announcements that they were no longer servicing debts, private banks abruptly stopped lending to nations—which up to that point had been considered to be in very low risk of non-repayment. The sources of most new loans to African nations were developed nations or international financial institutions (IFIs). The IFIs would later require economic policy changes for continued support.

In fact, debt loads in Africa grew significantly in the wake of the OPEC oil shocks, especially in terms of debt servicing: rising oil prices, in conjunction with declining traditional exports led most countries in the region to high levels of debt servicing.[114] As Figure 7.10 shows, debt as a percentage of exports rose from 77% in 1980 to nearly 250% in 1993/1994.[115] This number began to decline slowly from this point, but the trend downward moved more quickly from 2002 onwards, until around 2007, when it seems to have stabilized just above 50%. So the HIPC and MDRI programs (see discussed later) did significantly impact levels of debt, especially as a percentage of exports. Since the total debt as percentage of GDP appears to have a different slope in places, it also appears that exports from Africa were on the rise as well as debts being in decline.

Externally Imposed Structural Adjustment

As a result of these mounting debts and continued struggles of the economies of the region, in conjunction with changing views among experts in the IMF and World Bank as to what led to sustainable development, some African countries began to be under structural adjustment requirements by the World Bank and IMF. Beginning in the 1980s, they would grow in number and

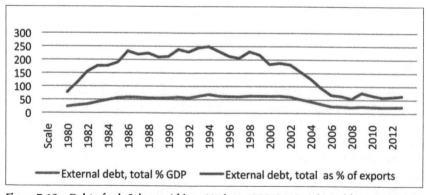

Figure 7.10   Debt of sub-Saharan African Nations 1980–2012. Adapted from IMF World Economic Outlook Database by author

importance from 1986 onward. According to several sources, by the mid-1980s, the need for structural adjustment was apparent even to the French, who had been hold outs against these "Anglo-Saxon" driven institutions. In fact, France had opposed overly strict structural adjustment policies prior to the mid-1980s. By the late 1980s, she was soon more on board with the need for conditionality in lending—in part due to the cost associated with the backing of the CFA zone.[116] By 1993, France announced that it would have no more balance of payment support for countries not fulfilling terms with the IMF and World Bank.[117] Therefore, by the late 1980s onwards, the perspective of the World Bank and IMF began to shape the framework within which all Western aid policy was set.[118]

It should be remembered that structural adjustment was clearly an emerging and evolving policy well before the end of the Cold War. Edward Jaycox, former regional vice president for Africa at the World Bank, suggested that only a relatively few African countries had adopted structural adjustment programs between 1980 and 1985 (e.g., Malawi, Togo, Ghana, and Kenya). According to another scholar, the earliest such programs to begin in Africa were in 1980/81 for Kenya, Malawi, Mauritius, and Senegal.[119] Jaycox suggests that 1986 was the turning point year, and by 1989, over thirty African countries were "actively engaged in wide-ranging programs of economic reform or structural adjustment."[120] And within a few years (1993), nearly every African country was under, or had been under, some structural adjustment program.[121]

Although the programs for each country varied, "four basic elements are always present: currency devaluation, the removal/reduction of the state from the workings of the economy, the elimination of subsidies in an attempt to reduce expenditures, and trade liberalisation."[122] Many scholars suggest that structural adjustment, per se, undermined the very sovereignty of such nations. Nonetheless, implementation of most of these programs was at best incomplete, though more implementation followed with the end of the Cold War.

Although structural adjustment helped balance some economic policies, Africa, and other developing regions, continued to struggle with debt burdens associated with past policies, price shock, and other elements of international trade. In 1996, the Heavily Indebted Poor Countries (HIPC) initiative was launched to ensure that developing nations could get out from under onerous debt. The price for this was the acceptance of compliance with structural adjustment terms for three years, after which some debts would be relieved. In 2005, a more robust version of this program was expressed through the Multilateral Debt Relief Initiative (MDRI), which would result in 100% debt forgiveness from the IMF, World Bank, and African development fund (AfDF) for nations fulfilling the terms of

HIPC. Countries which met the following four goals could qualify for debt relief. Countries had to:

1. be eligible to borrow from the World Bank's International Development Agency, which provides interest-free loans and grants to the world's poorest countries, and from the IMF's Extended Credit Facility, which provides loans to low-income countries at subsidized rates.
2. face an unsustainable debt burden that cannot be addressed through traditional debt relief mechanisms.
3. have established a track record of reform and sound policies through IMF- and World Bank supported programs
4. have developed a Poverty Reduction Strategy Paper (PRSP) through a broad-based participatory process in the country.

They were required to complete HIPC, which then could lead to complete debt forgiveness. Countries had to:

1. establish a further track record of good performance under programs supported by loans from the IMF and the World Bank.
2. implement satisfactorily key reforms agreed at the decision point
3. adopt and implement its PRSP for at least one year.[123]

Of the 48 sub-Saharan African countries, 30 arrived at the "post-completion-point" which meant they had qualified under strict IMF and World Bank conditions necessary to obtain debt forgiveness. Four more are at an interim point, and three remain at a pre-decision point. The implication is that the majority of countries within the region were required to meet a relatively high bar of compliance with the economic policies of the IMF financial policy requirements at the end of the Cold War, and this helps explain the compliance of this aspect more than privatization. These programs were clearly a strong fragment of economic accountability as it reduced the discretion of domestic decision makers. Should these countries not have brought their economic policies into line with neo-liberal thinking, future loans would not have been obtained, and debt forgiveness would not have been possible. They also instituted the very reforms which would make African economies more exposed to market forces.

In terms of direct impact, and in keeping with this analysis, structural adjustment, HIPC, and MDRI appear to have most impacted fiscal policies. It also appears that the World Bank and IMF cared the most about getting fiscal policies right, as significant violations of these were likely to lead to suspension of countries in the post-Cold War period. Moreover, by making all World Bank loans contingent on IMF policy approval, this doubled down on the international pressure on these sets of policies. In fact, oftentimes reforms were centered upon the reform of state ownership enterprises rather than privatization. Privatization was often contemplated after the failures, or perceived failures, of such reforms.

As mentioned in Chapter 5, the signals to countries concerning privatization coming from the World Bank were mixed in the 1980s: they advocated privatization, but public sector reform was actually more of a priority.[124] In fact, a 1983 World Bank report suggests that it was more interested in efficiency than ownership.[125] Between 1980 and 1986, only 13% of conditions were placed forcing privatization.[126] By the late 1980s, in contrast, the number of structural adjustment programs with conditions for privatization greatly increased.[127]

But when one examines structural adjustment requirements, one must remember that both the IMF and World Bank have areas in which they will not negotiate, those in which they are somewhat open to negotiation, and those in which they are quite open. The same could be said for African elites: they too have domestic constituents and pressures which complicates their negotiations with these IFIs. It might be useful to think of a Putnam two-level game where both the negotiators at the IFIs and the African elites have space in which to negotiate that is partially limited by domestic or organizational considerations.[128] Also, both have incentives to exaggerate the limits of the domestic or internal side to achieve a better outcome (with the least conditionality on the part of African elites, and the most on behalf of the IFI officials). And like in other negotiations, both have an interest in arriving at a mutually agreed upon solution: where would the IFIs be if no one took their aid? And where would African elites be without debt renegotiation or forgiveness? In fact, van de Walle suggests that African elites adopted the aspects of structural adjustment that were the easiest to implement, and the easiest to reverse, all while keeping the taps open. Moreover, Tangri suggests that privatizations were mostly driven by international financial institutions, and even if leaders were willing (and most were not very willing), domestic constraints limited actions in these areas.[129] And this matches the empirical record where few privatizations emerged early, and the more important ones followed later, if at all.

Dependence upon Aid

Another historic source of international weakness for sub-Saharan Africa flows directly from the combination of the evolution of aid regimes and prior poor economic performance in the region.[130] Given the poor economic performance of so many countries in sub-Saharan Africa prior to the end of the Cold War, and the high levels of debt accumulated by so many, many such countries were quite vulnerable to international pressure.

As we can see from Figure 7.11, net ODA (per capita) increased to Africa in the mid-1970 and seems to have peaked in most categories by the early 1990s.[131] It declined until 2001 and began moving upwards since. As a percentage of gross capital formation, it peaked at nearly 40% in the early 1990s and declined to around 20% in the late 2000s. As a per capita number, however, it had an early peak at nearly the same time as the other indicators, dropped until 2000, when it increased until the last two years, though these are current dollars. The overall impression is one of increased African dependence upon aid from the mid-1970s to the 1990s.

Importantly, aid represents significant sources of funding for African regimes. Also, aid as a percentage of government revenue is another indication of African dependence upon the international community, which continues in the post-Cold War period. From 1990 to the present, African countries (for which there were data) had and average level of 67.7%. This included countries with averages of above 80%, such as Burkina Faso, Burundi, CAR, DRC, Ethiopia, the Gambia, Liberia, Madagascar, Mali, Niger, Rwanda, Sao Tome and Principe, and Sierra Leone. Some of these were near or above 100% (i.e., Burkina Faso, DRC, Liberia (over 400%), Madagascar, Niger, Rwanda, Sao Tome and Principe, and Sierra Leone). Some were below 10%, but these were few: Botswana, Equatorial Guinea, Seychelles, and South Africa. Although FDI is increasing, it is not as a fungible source as revenue for governments, though it could have substitution effects. Moreover, as identified in the prior discussion of FDI, it was negligible during the 1980s and

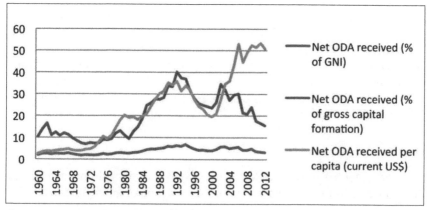

Figure 7.11   Net ODA to SSA 1960–2012.

early 1990s. Only recently have FDI flows increased significantly, but they still lag behind other regions.

Political Liberalization

One of the first elements that could help explain greater economic fragmentation may come from the increased levels of domestic political and civil rights in the region since 1989. Although several chapters in this work suggest that international pressures helped with the partial democratization of the region, the partial democratization of the region also allows for more fragmentation of economic power and the possibility of economic reforms down the road. The expansion of the political sphere to include more voices means that parties or interest groups interested in voicing economic policy proposals have more freedom to do so. Although democratic systems could pursue inward-oriented policies, but they might not. The political elites even those overseeing significant aspects of the economy of the nation, now have to compete (at least formally) in an expanded political environment for economic policy. Also, new private owners of large farms, factories, businesses, and other profitable sectors are likely to be able to overcome their collective action costs to pressure the government to change or soften policy that would otherwise adversely affect them in more free countries. These may be merely latent groups in some countries where domestic owners of productive factors are few and far between. Nonetheless, the political party in power necessarily has already overcome its collective action costs and will be a force to reckon with should they oppose these emerging domestic economic forces. Many times, compromise is possible. Also, the opposition can sweep into power and find ready backers in those on the previous other side of the policy debate with the now out-of-power incumbents.

Private owners, however, may not all want neoliberal policies and, depending on if they own scarce of abundant factors of production, may actually favor of inward-oriented policies.[132] Thus, privatization may not reduce pressures for protectionism; they could actually increase societal pressures for such policies from the owners of these sectors if the new owners want protection. Nonetheless, *ceteris paribus*, a more open political system should allow those who favor more outward-oriented policies a better chance to change or soften policy, at least compared to the first period where protectionist forces seemed to have a lock on African economic foreign policy. Also, more private ownership of industry should lead to a diversification of interests and hence increase the potential for those who would want more open policies. Also, while these current trends of more liberal policies are in place entrepreneurs are creating businesses based upon the calculus of making money under more liberal policy regimes, which could make them likely powerful supporters of those policies, especially should they become exporters.

The legitimacy of the political elites to continue in the political and economic status quo was clearly undermined as their economies performed so poorly in the 1980s, and as they became more aid and loan dependent. Nonetheless, I argue, as do many others, that the neopatrimonial tendencies of political elites remain and these elites try to maintain as much control over their economies (like over their political systems) as they can facing particular constraints of international, regional, and domestic power. Also they are partially limited in their choice of economic policy and institutions given prevailing ideas about efficiency and fairness, beyond particular material constraints, coming from IFIs, though these constraints clearly matter to them.

With political liberalization, would-be political elites could take up the baton of economic reforms either as a means of obtaining political power by advocating popular reforms or as a means of improving their economic outcomes should they represent private economic interests, or as a matter of beliefs about what is good for the nation. Any of these, or some combination of them, in conjunction with political openness can deepen economic reforms. There is the possibility, however, that populist economic policies which would move away from market openness could also mobilize voters.

Role of UN in Promoting Economic Liberalization

Even the United Nations has changed its stance vis-à-vis the positive role that private enterprise can play in economic development. In 2002, the United Nations International Conference on Financing for Development convened in Monterrey, Mexico and formulated what would be called the Monterrey consensus. It called for a partnership between private sector actors and government to work together for development.

The United Nations Development Programme (UNDP) has on their website the recognition for the need of *private enterprise* to help meet development goals:

> UNDP recognizes that achieving the Millennium Development Goals (MDGs) depends on vibrant economic growth driven by markets and private enterprises that create jobs, provide goods and services for the poor and generate tax revenues to finance essential social and economic infrastructure.

The private sector—from large multi-national companies to small enterprises and cooperatives servicing local markets—also has an essential role to play in achieving broader UNDP goals in areas such as energy and environmental service delivery, crisis prevention, gender equality and democratic governance.[133]

Regional or International Forces Facilitating Liberalization/Less Corruption

With the end of the Cold War, many international actors have attempted to create institutions or information that can help limit "poor governance," which can include reducing corruption as well as increasing political and civil rights by the way of making government more accountable to its citizens.[134] As discussed in Chapter 5, organizations such as Transparency International (TI) engage in comparative exposure of corruption internationally, including sub-Saharan Africa. By researching and listing levels of corruption by country, it can facilitate the ability of citizens of a country to pressure their governments by providing them information they may not otherwise have. We cannot compare pre- and post-Cold War numbers since TI began in 1995 (when it only rated South Africa). By 2000, it had 17 African countries, and by 2006, it had 45 African nations listed. In 2005, only two African countries scored above a 5, which TI suggests is the commonly seen threshold for serious corruption. Moreover, in 2006, Chad, the Democratic Republic of the Congo, Sudan, and Guinea were at the bottom of the global ranking that year.[135] By 2014, several more African countries scored above average, Botswana, Cape Verde, Seychelles, Mauritius, Lesotho, Namibia, Rwanda, Ghana, and South Africa, but the rest were just at average or well below. Only 4 of the lowest ten are African: Eritrea, South Sudan, Sudan, and Somalia.[136]

The Extractive Industries Transparency Initiative (EITI) was also begun in 2002 to help get to the bottom of the resource curse.[137] As discussed in Chapter 5, it required publication of what companies paid governments for the natural resources of that country. Of the 23 countries that are listed as compliant with EITI rules and procedures, fourteen are from sub-Saharan Africa.[138] Of the 16 candidate countries, seven are from sub-Saharan Africa. Both of these organization are trying to reduce levels of corruption in African (and other) countries in order to promote development. In fact, many IGOs and particular governments have divisions charged for reducing corruption.[139] Even the OECD, the UN, and the USAID have elements created to reduce corruption in developing nations.

LIMITS TO ECONOMIC LIBERALIZATION AND THE
FRAGMENTATION OF ECONOMIC POWER

Continued Government Ownership, Control
of Employment, and Spending

Despite the gains in momentum for privatization, the balancing of budgets, and the other associated liberal reforms of economic policies in sub-Saharan Africa, African governments still control significant aspects of their economies, especially though spending and jobs. First, as discussed above, much privatization has occurred, but large-scale mining and oil sectors have tended to remain in state hands, and this can reinforce tendencies toward corruption.[140] As already mentioned, Nigeria, Benin, and Togo have kept majority state ownership in their mineral or oil sectors. Also, the types of privatizations made initially were where fewer jobs were at stake or where the value of the sectors was low.

Gwartney, Lawson, and Block measured the size of government enterprises as a share of the economy for 1975, 1980, 1985, 1990, and 1995. They created an index from 0 to 10, where 10 is the least amount of government involvement in the economy and 0 the most. Most countries, even in 1995, were at four or lower (where the number of government owned industries is "substantial" and "private enterprises are generally small.") More importantly, of countries within sub-Saharan Africa, only a few countries had their indexes indicated a movement away from government involvement, such as Ghana (from 0 to 2), Niger (4 to 6), and Senegal (from 4 to 6). All the others had the same numbers from 1975 to 1995, or they had more government involvement (e.g., Botswana (8 to 6), and Tanzania (2 to 0)).[141]

Beyond ownership, the government share of GDP does not appear to have decreased very much. In fact, African countries saw a slow and steady increase of government spending as a percentage of GDP, aside from 1982 to 1986.[142] From 1980 to 2002, governments grew in size almost 3% per year. Moreover, post-1990, government growth increased to around 4.4% per year. [143] As a result, we see, by time increments, slow rises in government spending: African government spent 28.43% of their GDP in 1980, 26.72% in 1990, 31.42% in 2000, and 33.82% in 2002.[144] This number, however, could reflect a shrinking economy as much as an increase in government size.

Continued Government Importance to Wage employment

Also, the state remained the largest employer of all non-agricultural formal sector work. During the early 1980s, the percentage of workers in the formal sector who worked for the state was quite high in Africa, at 59.7%.[145] For those countries with majority state ownership, that number rose to around 76%, and those with less than majority state ownership still had around 40% of all formal sector employment through the state.[146] In a sample of seven major countries, parastatal workers averaged about 58% of all public employees within the civil service. Therefore, "normal" state workers, such as teachers, postal workers, bureaucrats, and so forth, made up about 42% of state workers.[147] Overall, the average percentage wage employment through the state in Africa was 52.9% by the late 1980s.[148]

The end of the Cold War does not yet seem to have marked a significant decrease in public wage employees. In fact, as an average, people working for state-owned enterprises (beyond teachers, bureaucrats, and so forth) increased from 17.1% in 1989 to 18.3% in 1991, according to the World Bank.[149] A mixed picture can be seen across countries concerning these levels. In an IMF study of just civil service jobs in a sample of 38 countries, it was found that about one-third of the countries for which there was comparable data saw a decline in civil service employment.[150] By implication, however, two-thirds had either no changes or increases. It must be remembered, however, as a percentage, in the context of rising populations, just providing the same level of services could mean the number of civil service jobs would have to grow just to stay even in the 1989–1996 period. Also, since many privatized firms in Africa shed many jobs, were liquidated or, the number of jobs distributed through the state may be quite high only because (now) private sector employment shrank so much. Nonetheless, these numbers should be lower relative to Africa's recent history.

Increased Political Freedoms, but Still One-Party Dominance

As we saw in the last chapter, the region has seen a nearly region-wide adoption of multiparty elections in the post-Cold War period, though a wide variation of levels of political and civil rights remains. In 2014, for example, only nine countries in the region were ranked as "free." Twenty countries were rated "partly free;" and eighteen countries were ranked "not free."[151] And in most of these countries, even the free ones, a single party tends to dominate the office of president as well as the legislature. Therefore, the level of real accountability is higher, but the region as a whole is better described as partly free, by way of average. (See prior chapter for more details)

Continued Weakness of Domestic Business Class

Nonetheless, despite recent acts of privatization, to date the potential for a vibrant business class is still weak in many countries. The markets in Africa are thin, per capita incomes are very low, market size is small, and high levels of corruption reduce business opportunities. Beyond direct impacts of corruption, the weak state syndrome affects business and government both. According to a recent survey of African businesspeople in 27 countries, companies complained about weak infrastructure, including access to electricity and poor roads (and missing rail) as key constraints on business.[152] In fact, most large firms surveyed in the study operated their own electrical generators (over 70% in such countries as Mauritius, Burundi, Malawi, Burkina Faso, Benin, Angola, Congo DR, Guinea-Bissau, Senegal, Mali, Cameroon, Kenya, Rwanda, Tanzania, Uganda, Nigeria, Cape Verde, the Gambia, Mauritania and Niger).[153] Moreover, finding finance was also a problem for entrepreneurs: most answered that financing for business came mostly from internal finance (as opposed to from a bank or credit supplier).[154] In addition, potential businesspeople face routinely significant red tape as well as the pitfalls of bribery.[155]

The weakness of the indigenous business class is even clearer if one distinguishes by the citizenship and minority status of owners. The same survey examined black-owned versus minority- or foreign-owned businesses and found that although "indigenous" (black host nationals) owners controlled most manufacturing firms in 13 of 14 countries examined, the minority-owned or foreign-owned firms were the ones that hired the most workers.[156] This would be a proxy for size and potential political power. Moreover, in 11 of 14 countries, minority firms had more than 50% value added for their sector.[157] This is important as minority (non-black African) owners can be marginalized politically, and they are unlikely to prove to be a strong constraint on political power aside for economic issues affecting their particular firms. Non-nationals and ethnic minorities might face more uncertainty vis-à-vis property rights as well as potential nationalist backlashes, as the Chinese in Indonesia, the Indians in Uganda, the Belgians and Greeks in Zaire, the white famers in Zimbabwe, and the Jews in pre-WWII Europe experienced. All of them had their land or property appropriated or had populist protests or riots rise up against them, for reason of their minority ethnic or racial or religious status.

Most Agriculture Small Holders with Usufruct
Land Rights or in State Hands

Since over 85% of farms in sub-Saharan Africa are less than 2 hectares in size, and since 35% of Africa GNP is produced by agriculture, and since over 70% of Africa's food supply comes from small holders, most people engaged in this sector of the economy would likely have problems overcoming their collective action costs and becoming politically powerful.[158]

Part of the reason for the structure of agriculture being so is that many countries in Africa did not allow for the formation of privately owned large farms during the Cold War. In fact, many countries nationalized land ownership in the early independence period. For example, in Nigeria all land is owned by the state, but leases of up to 99 years can be obtained. Other states that nationalized large land holdings were Angola, Mozambique, and Zambia (where there had been white settlers) as well as Benin, Burkina Faso, and Uganda.

Another factor potentially limiting the power of farmers as a political group is that in most of Africa, land is owned communally and is therefore governed by customary law. This necessarily means that the land in question cannot (under these conditions) become a means of capital accumulation for the farmers using it, because it cannot be sold. Moreover, most people doing the actual farming (up to 70%) are women, who are often locked out of land ownership through customary law or traditional practices.[159] In sum, farmers face obstacles to political power through the lack of a solid economic foundation—even if they could overcome their collective action costs and try to act politically, they could lose their access to land if the customary leaders opposed their political agendas.

Finally, even where laws exist allowing private ownership of land, they are often confusing, therefore improved land governance could make a difference in output and prosperity.[160] Byamugisha argued that Africa "has 202 million hectares or half the world's total holdings of useable uncultivated fertile land."[161] In fact, only 10% of rural occupied land in Africa is registered, adding to the confusion.[162] Even where registration is occurring, often it is communal lands still governed by usufruct land rights as opposed to land ownership per se. Byamugisha suggests that efficiency returns through better governance could take place short of privatization of land. This is a weaker form of economic accountability, but it is a start.

CONCLUSION

From the analysis, it is clear that a region-wide shift in economic institutions and practices following the end of the Cold War occurred. These trends began in the late 1980s, but they increased greatly in speed and scale with the rise of American power at the end of the Cold War. The most significant and widespread changes were evident in fiscal reforms, removal of impediments to trade, and some privatization of previously state-owned companies. The evidence for the economic liberalization can be seen in the greater flows of trade and investment, the greater number of neoliberal reforms adopted, and the movement towards privatization of industries as well as mining and petroleum sectors.

Much of the pressure for economic reforms had come from the international community. The adoption of such reforms was clearly linked with the preferences of America and its allies, as were the changes in policies vis-à-vis bilateral and economic lending under their control. In fact, IMF and World Bank conditionality was a key element in African elites adopting these reforms. Moreover, the failure of inward-oriented policies, in conjunction with rising costs of importing fuel in the 1970s and 1980s, increased the vulnerability of African leaders on these external sources of funding. Moreover, the debt crisis virtually eliminated private bank loans as a source of accessing resources. FDI began to avoid Africa as well, especially with the opening up of Eastern Europe and China in the early 1990s.

This partial fragmentation of economic power has resulted in more economic power existing beyond the reach of the political elites, as political elites per se (though they may have used their office to obtain private property). The partial political reforms should also help bolster civil society and create or strengthen fragments of economic accountability. In turn, these fragments of economic accountability could become sources of support for fragments of political accountability. These fragments of accountability can be external as well as internal as economic policy has more sources of international and domestic checks: from exposure to market competition internationally, regional, and domestically; to policy having to be approved by the World Bank and IMF; for economic policies being inviting for FDI to find its way there; to competitive elections which allow economic interest groups to lobby for their most preferred policies; to the rising power of legislatures which could be a check on bad policies; and to external international and regional organizations looking at levels of corruption within countries which could have an impact on economic efficiency.

Should these economic reforms be maintained and stability in economic policies give rise to a stronger business class, we should see continued domestic pressure for the continuation of these policies. Whoever is "winning" as a result of these more liberal reforms may become politically active and defend their new positions. And, as larger and larger sections of African economies are privatized, or as state monopolies simply quit the field, the space for a rising bourgeoisie increases. Moreover, "learning" both at home and abroad, has discredited many of the statist policies. Also the legitimacy of capitalism vis-à-vis development seems to be a strong international norm. It remains to be seen how powerful, or effective, these fragments of economic and political accountability will be in creating environments for "good" economic policy and "good" economic foreign policy. Also, some autonomy is often recognized as required for "good" policy; this dilemma is hard to work out, though compared to Africa's economic condition in the 1980s, it is likely to be an improvement.[163]

Nonetheless, the political elite in Africa still controls the lion's share of formal sector employment, agriculture is still dominated by small farmers with weak claims on land, and the domestic business classes and civil society are still emerging and weak. Also, many states continue to hold majority state ownership of mining or petroleum companies as well as many of the largest companies. All of these things are made even more powerful with the continuation of one-party control of most polities in the region and where the party is unlikely to lose an election.

Moreover, the self-interest of so many politicians in neopatrimonial societies has not been in implementing these economic and political reforms, and some may seek to reverse them once their vulnerability decreases. This would allow them to increase their control over economic resources, which can then be distributed politically. This tension remains, and the next few decades will tell us which way Africa will proceed. But so far, some economic power is fragmenting, but state elites have enormous assets and strong political majorities. Opposition parties, civil society, and external constituencies interested in African political and economic liberalization need to help create or maintain sources of economic and political power outside of the state in order to keep the delicate balance of democracy and capitalism alive and well—lest the overconcentration of economic and political power return to the hands of the political elites in the region.

NOTES

1. For the end of the Cold War accelerating economic reforms that had been begun earlier, see also Nicolas van de Walle, *African Economies and the Politics of Permanent Crisis, 1979–1999* (Cambridge: Cambridge University Press, 2001).

2. John James Quinn, *The Road oft Traveled: Development Policies and Majority State Ownership of Industry in Africa* (Westport, CT: Praeger, 2002); see also Robert H. Bates, *Markets and States in Tropical Africa: the Political Basis of Agricultural Policies* (Los Angeles and Berkeley, CA: University of California Press, 1981); Roger Tangri, *The Politics of Patronage in Africa: Parastatals, Privatization, & Private Enterprise* (Trenton, NJ: Africa World Press, 1999).

3. For state ownership leading to more inward-oriented politics, see Quinn, *The Road oft Traveled*; John J. Quinn, "The Managerial Bourgeoisie: Capital Accumulation, Development and Democracy," in David G. Becker and Richard L. Sklar, eds., *Postimperialism and World Politics* (Westport, CT: Praeger, 1999): 219–52. For ideology, see Crawford Young, *Ideology and Development in Africa* (New Haven: Yale University Press, 1982); also Ibid.

4. The Berg Report, as it was called, made the case that African economic problems were primarily about policies, see World Bank, *World Bank Development Report 1987* (Washington, D.C., 1987), p. 82.

5. The tariff and non-tariff numbers in this section were compiled from the *Handbook of Trade Control Measures of Developing Countries: A Statistical Analysis of Trade Control Measures of Developing Countries 1987* (Geneva: United Nations Conference on Trade and Development, 1987).

6. Economic Freedom of the World 2011, for years 2009 and 1985; http://www.freetheworld.com/release.html

7. UNCTAD, *Handbook of Trade Control Measures.*

8. World Bank, *African Development Indicators 2006*, Table 6.1, p. 40.

9. Calculated from Economic Freedom of the World, 4Aii (Mean tariff rate) 2009, 1985.

10. These included (hidden import barriers, mean tariff rate, taxes on International trade, and capita account restrictions (see Ibid. SV measures). It is also the year of the opening of the World Trade Organization (WTO). See http://www.wto.org/english/thewto_e/thewto_e.htm

11. Remember these are relative, so slight increases in protectionist countries which had been mostly open nations may mean that the former countries still have fewer/ lower barriers than countries with large decreases in trade barriers, but which started at high levels of protectionism. Not all countries had data for this category.

12. For example, Tanzanian taxes were much higher than Kenyan ones, see Michael Lofchie, *The Policy Factor: Agricultural Performance in Kenya and Tanzania* (Boulder, CO: Lynne Rienner Publishers, 1989); more generally, see Michael F. Lofchie, "The New Political Economy in Africa," in David E. Apter and Carl G. Rosberg, eds., *Political Development and the New Realism in Sub-Saharan Africa* (Charlottesville: University of Virginia Press, 1994): 160–165.

13. Margaret McMillan, "Why Kill the Golden Goose? A Political-Economy Model of Export Taxation," *The Review of Economics and Statistics,* February 2001, 83(1): 170–84.

14. Quinn *Road oft Traveled*, calculated from Table 2.1, p. 39.

15. McMillan, "Why Kill the Golden Goose?"

16. For data (and sample) for this section, see Kym Anderson and Ernesto Valenzuela, "Estimates of Distortions to Agricultural Incentives, 1955 to 2007," Aggregates, spreadsheet at www.worldbank.org/agdistortions, (Washington DC: World Bank, October 2008). The nominal rate of assistance to farmers (NRA) is used for all (primary) Agriculture, Value of production-weighted average, Exportables, Importables, and non-Tradables. The countries included are Benin, Burkina Faso, Cameroon, Chad, Cote d'Ivoire, Ethiopia, Ghana, Kenya, Madagascar, Mali, Mozambique, Nigeria, South Africa, Sudan, Tanzania, Togo, Uganda, Zambia, and Zimbabwe.

17. The difference is statistically significant (with a t-test at $p = 0.00$).

18. The data from this section come from World Bank, *Adjustment in Africa: Reforms, Results, and The Road Ahead* (Washington, D.C: World Bank, 1992), Figure 3.4, p. 79.

19. van de Walle, *African Economies.*

20. World Bank, *World Bank Indicators, 2000*. Disk. Both Angola and Zaire (DRC) had extraordinarily high currency overvaluations, with ratios of 51,000,000,000 and 514,000,000,000 during the Cold War, and for 5,360,000,000 and 128,000,000,000

after 1990, each respectively. Since means are sensitive to outliers, they are not included in the average, as they do not represent the new normal for other countries in the region.

21. CFA countries are excluded to examine only those countries in which elites had control over the currency overvaluation levels.

22. Although the World Bank argued that the CFA zone was overvalued by 50% or more. But given the measure (comparing official rates to black market rates), and the backing of liquidity by the French, we would not see much overvaluation here as the black market rates should not differ from official rates with complete convertibility.

23. See Bates, *Markets and States.*

24. Robert I. Rotberg and Rachel M. Gisselquist, *"2009 Index of African Governance Data Set,"* downloaded from http://www.nber.org/data/iag.html [downloaded 2/17/2010]. The latest year in the 2009 index was 2007.

25. Ibid. Taken from pdf report, p. 193. http://www.nber.org/iag/2009/iag2009.pdf

26. World Bank, *Sub-Saharan Africa: From Crisis to Sustainable Growth* (Washington, DC: World Bank, 1989), Table 1, p. 221. The overall average is weighted.

27. Ibid., p. 195.

28. Somalia is excluded from all these calculations.

29. World Bank, *African Development Indicators,* Table 7.1.

30. Calculated from World Bank Win*Stars, Vol. 4.2 World Bank African Database 2002.

31. International Monetary Fund, *World Economic and Financial Surveys: Regional Economic Outlook: Sub-Saharan Africa* (Washington, DC: International Monetary Fund, 2012), Table 1.1, p. 3.

32. Although African globalization is rising, it is doing more slowly than world levels. Also, the term "Africa" herein refers to sub-Saharan Africa, unless states otherwise.

33. These data on globalization come from the KOF Index of Globalization. Available on line http://globalization.kof.ethz.ch/ accessed most recently February 2014. Taken from Africa, but North African countries (and Yemen) removed.

34. Only including the countries for which data were available.

35. Quinn, *The Road oft Traveled.*

36. Rwanda did not have MSO, but it had a horrific period of violence that disrupted export markets. Uganda had both effecting it.

37. Regression to the mean occurs when above average performance or underperformance returns to "normal". For example, a player performing at their best is more likely to return to long term performance than keep getting better and better. Or a batter in a slump, more appropriately, can quickly climb in statistics until the return to the prior "normal." If this were not true, a bell curve (or some normal distribution) could not describe the event.

38. William Megginson, "Privatization," *Foreign Policy,* No. 118 (Spring, 2000), p. 16.

39. Nancy Brune, Geoffrey Garrett, and Bruce Kogut, "The International Monetary Fund and the Global Spread of Privatization," *IMF Staff Papers* Vol. 51, No. 2 (2004), pp. 195–219.

40. Tangri, *The Politics of Patronage*, p. 42.

41. With 76, 65, and 35, respectively. See, Oliver Campbell White and Anita Bhatia, *Privatization in Africa* (Washinton, DC: The World Bank, 1998), Appendix 1, pp. 138–39. See also Paul Bennell, "Privatizing in Sub-Saharan Africa: Progress and Prospects during the 1990," *World Development* 25, 11 (1997): 1785–1803. Bennell's numbers are different for these three countries at 49, 2, and 46. However, for Mozambique, he only includes larger-scale privatization, see p. 1789.

42. Bennell, "Privatizing," p. 1789. This was from 1980 to 1989.

43. John R. Nellis, "Public Enterprises in Sub-Saharan Africa," in Barbara Grosh and Rwekaza S. Mukandala, eds., *State-Owned Enterprises in Africa* (Boulder, CO: Lynne Rienner Publishers, 1994), p. 5.

44. White and Bhatia, *Privatization in Africa* Appendix 1, 138–39. This analysis excludes the 301 cases where dates were not known, though they were probably post 1990 (and the lion's share are from Angola).

45. Deduced from World Bank Privatization data, up to 1989.

46. Thierry D. Buchs, "Privatization in Sub-Saharan Africa: Some Lessons from Experiences to Date", *International Finance Corporation*, mimeo (2003). http://www.nioclibrary.com/privatization/e025.pdf

47. Calculated from World Bank Privatization data, 2000–2007. And there might be some double counting, but the numbers are suggestive.

48. Deduced from World Bank Privatization data, 1989–2007.

49. White and Bhatia, *Privatization in Africa,* Appendix 1, pp. 138–139. This analysis excludes the 301 cases where dates were not known, though they were probably post 1990 (and the lion's share are from Angola).

50. Tangri, *The Politics of Patronage*, p. 42.

51. Unless otherwise noted, data come from, or is compiled from, World Bank privatization database. 1988–2007. http://data.worldbank.org/data-catalog/privatization-database

52. Ravi Ramamurtri, "The Search for Remedies," in Ravi Ramamurtri and Raymond Vernon, eds., *Privatization and Control of State-Owned Enterprises* (Washington, D.C: The World Bank, 1991): 7–28, 15.

53. Ibid. Table 4, p. 10.

54. The data in this section come from Ibid.

55. These data come from World Bank privatization database.

56. Kojo Appiah-Kubi, "State-Owned Enterprises and Privatisation in Ghana," *The Journal of Modern African Studies*, Vol. 39, No. 2 (Jun., 2001), pp. 197–229, p. 209. See Ted Projects, http://www1.american.edu/TED/ghangold.htm.

57. Tobert Barad, "Privatization of State-Owned Enterprises: The Togolese Experience," in Grosh and Mukandala, *State-Owned Enterprises in Africa*, p. 177.

58. *Africa South of the Saharan* 2008, (London; Europa Publications Limited, 2007), p. 890.

59. Taken from http://www.slideshare.net/EPetrilli/angola-bidding-process Accessed 2/4/10.

60. Michael J. Kavanagh, "Gecamines of Congo Will Seek Profit From Takeovers, Audits," *Bloomberg* (October 6, 2011). http://www.bloomberg.com/

news/2011–10–06/gecamines-of-congo-will-seek-profit-from-takeovers-audits-1-.
html

61. Quinn, *The Road oft Traveled.*

62. "Overpricing Zambia's Family Silver," *The Economist* 347, 8067 (May 9, 1998), p. 46.

63. "Selling the Family Copper," *The Economist* 353, 814 (November 6, 1999): 49.

64. World Bank, *Bureaucrats in Business: The Economic and Politics of Government Ownership* (Washington, DC: World Bank, 1999), table A1, p. 269 (weighted averages).

65. Ibid.

66. Ibid., p. 319.

67. Ibid. Table A.3, p. 277.

68. Ibid., Table A.5, p. 289.

69. Calculated from World Bank Indicators, General government final consumption expenditure (% of GDP). http://data.worldbank.org/indicator/NE.CON.GOVT. ZS?page=3

70. Peter Young, "Privatization around the World," *Proceedings of the Academy of Political Science*, Vol. 36, No. 3, Prospects for Privatization (1987): 190–206, 201.

71. Van de Walle, *African Economies*, p. 75.

72. Jean Paul Azam, Bruno Biais, Magueye Dia, *Privatization versus Regulation in Developing Economies: The Case of West African Banks*, Working Paper Number 315 (February 2000), p. 7. http://wdi.umich.edu/files/publications/workingpapers/ wp315.pdf

73. Ibid.

74. Taken from James A. Hanson, "The Transformation of State-Owned Bank," in Gerard Caprio, Jonathan L. Fiechter, Robert E. Litan, and Michael Pomerleano, eds., *The Future of State-Owned Financial Institutions* (Washington, DC: Brookings Institution Press, 2004), p. 14.

75. See George R, G. Clarke, Robert Cull, and Mary Shirley, "Empirical Studies," in G. Caprio, J. Fiechter, R. Litan, and M. Pomerleano, eds., *The Future of State-Owned Financial Institutions* (Washington, DC: Brookings Institution Press, 2004): 280–81.

76. Andrew W. Shepherd and Stefano Farolfi, *Export crop Liberalization in Africa: A review* (Rome: Food and Agriculture Organization of the United Nations, 1999), p. iii.

77. Ibid.

78. World Bank, *Adjustment in Africa*, p. 81.

79. Ibid., p. 82.

80. Ibid, Table 3.3, p. 85.

81. During my tour in the Peace Corps in Zaire (now DRC), the state tried to impose price controls on domestic produce and signs appeared in the markets displaying the state regulated price (between 1984 and 1985). No market woman would sell to us at those prices. They just silently shook their head no when the sign was pointed to, and they restated their negotiating price. The signs disappeared within a few weeks and were never mentioned again.

82. World Bank, *Adjustment in Africa*, Table 3.2, p. 84. However, while in Ghana in 2001, it was clear that other companies were collecting cocoa and farmers sold to them instead of COCOBOD, but technically they were collecting on behalf of COCOBOD. Personal observations on the road from Legon to Suyani and back. Ghana 2001. At one truck stop, the COCOBOD buyer's hut was in ruin and unstaffed, while a private one across the road was open and full of coffee.

83. Mylène Kherallah, Christopher Delgado, Eleni Gabre-Madhin, Nicholas Minot, and Michael Johnson, *The Road Half Traveled: Agricultural Market Reform in Sub-Saharan Africa* (Washington, D.C.: International Food Policy Research Institute, 2000): p. 10.

84. It is where investment in a company is at least 10%, when it is less, it is considered to be portfolio investment.

85. Original source, van de Walle, *African Economies*, p. 268.

86. White and Bhatia, *Privatization in Africa*, Appendix E, pp. 148–149. 1989–1995, for ten African countries.

87. Kayizzi-Mugerwa, "Privatization in sub-Saharan Africa." Table 5, p. 17. Samples from 1990–1997, before many of the largest sales emerged. For example, in Kenya which had the prior smallest percent foreign sales, in 2007 it had its the largest sale ever ($390 million) and it was to a French company. See World Bank Privatization Database. Also, "French company takes over state-owned Kenyan telecommunications firm," *BBC Worldwide Monitoring* (December 25, 2007 Tuesday) (source Daily Nation, Nairobi, in English 25 Dec 07).

88. Taken from UNCTAD webpage, UNCTADstat, http://unctadstat.unctad.org/TableViewer/dimView.aspx the number are deflated to 2010 levels using OECD deflator for US, "Deflators for Resource Flows from DAC Countries"(2010=100) (updated April 2012) http://www.oecd.org/document/11/0,3746,en_2649_34447_1894347_1_1_1_1,00.html

89. UNCTAD, *World Investment Report: Transnational Corporations, Agricultural Development, and Agriculture* (Geneva: United Nations, 2009): See figure II.2, p. 42. (This includes North Africa).

90. Taken from *Africa South of the Sahara 2011*, SV. South Africa, p. 1152. This number excludes mineral components listed under basic manufactures, like cut diamonds, iron, steel, and worked gold—which are worth another 26,000 or so million dollars.

91. Calculated from Ibid., SV South Africa and Gabon.

92. For economic accountability, see John J. Quinn, "Economic Accountability: Are Constraints on Economic Decision Making a Blessing or a Curse?" *Scandinavian Journal of Development Alternatives and Area Studies* 19, 4 (December 2000): 131–169. For agency of restraint, see Paul Collier in "Learning from Failure: The International Financial Institutions as Agencies of Restraint in Africa," in Andreas Schedler et al., *The Self-Restraining State: Power and Accountability in New Democracies* (Boulder, CO: Lynne Rienner Publishers, 1999): 313–330.

93. Joanne Gowa and Raymond Hicks, "The most-favored nation rule in principle and practice: Discrimination in the GATT," *Review of International Organization* 7 (2012): 247–266.

94. Robert Gilpin, *Global Political Economy: Understanding the International Economic Order* (Princeton: Princeton University Press, 2001), p. 219.

95. Arvind Subramanian, and Shang-Jin Wei, "The WTO promotes trade, strongly but unevenly," *Journal of International Economics*, 72, 1 (2007): 151–75, p.156; see also, Gowa and Hicks, "The most-favored nation rule."

96. For an introduction and overview of economic integration and economic integration in Africa, see Femi Babarinde, "Regionalism and Economic Development," in Emmanuel Nnadozie, ed., *African Economic Development.* (New York: Academic Press, 2003): 473–498; for more recent views, see Yongzheng Yang and Sanjeev Gupta, "Regional Trade Arrangements in Africa: Past Performance and the Way Forward," *IMF Working Paper* (Washington, DC: International Monetary Fund, 2005).

97. *Handbook of Trade Control Measures of Developing Countries: A Statistical Analysis of Trade Control Measures of Developing Countries 1987* (Geneva: United Nations Conference on Trade and Development, 1987), S.V. Zaire.

98. *Africa South of the Sahara 2011* S.V. South Africa.

99. Calculated from Yang and Gupta, "Regional Trade Arrangements in Africa," Table 3, p. 17.

100. See Ibid for debate. These authors suggest that high regional trade could reflect international marginalization.

101. The data for this part comes from UNCTAD, *Bilateral Investment Treaties 1959–1999* (New York: United Nations, 2000): p. 5. http://www.unctad.org/en/docs/poiteiiad2.en.pdf

102. Of course Eritrea and Namibia (and South Africa) would have all of their BITs signed in the post-Cold War period.

103. See UNCTAD data base on BITS http://www.unctad.org/Templates/Page.asp?intItemID=2344&lang=1

104. Christopher Clapham, *Africa and the International System* (Cambridge: Cambridge University Press, 1996); William Reno, *Warlord Politics and African states* (Lynne Rienner Publishers, 1999); Stephen Wright, ed., *African Foreign Policies* (Boulder: Westview, 1999); Gilbert M. Khadiagala and Terrence Lyons, eds., *African Foreign Policies: Power and Process* (Lynne Rienner Publishers, 2001); for summary of comparative African foreign polices over time see, John James Quinn, "African Foreign Policies," in Robert Denemark et al., eds., *The International Studies Compendium Project* (Oxford: Wiley-Blackwell, 2010): 24–46.

105. Thomas M. Callaghy, Africa and the World Political Economy: Still Caught between a Rock and a Hard Place," in John W. Harbeson and Donald Rothchild, eds., *Africa in World Politics: The African State System in Flux* (Boulder, CO: Westview Press, 2009): 39–71, p. 44.

106. van de Walle, *African Economies*, p. 265.

107. Taken from UNCTADstat, merchandize exports. All of Africa, without Northern Africa.

108. van de Walle, *African Economies*, p. 265.

109. World Bank, *Accelerated Development in Sub-Saharan Africa* (Washington, DC: World Bank, 1981).

110. Thomas M. Callaghy, "Africa and the World Political Economy: More Caught between a Rock and a Hard Place," in Harbeson and Rothchild, *Africa in World Politics*: 43–82, p. 44; see also, Thomas F. Callaghy and John Ravenhill, eds., *Hemmed In: Responses to Africa's Economic Decline* (New York: Columbia University Press, 1993).

111. Pierre, Englebert, *State Legitimacy and Development in Africa* (Boulder, CO: Lynne Rienner Publishers, 2000), p. 2.

112. See World Bank, *Sub-Saharan Africa*, Table 1, p. 221; per capita numbers come from World Bank, *World Development Report 1989* (Washington DC: World Bank, 1989), Tables 1 & 2, pp. 164–67.

113. Clapham, *Africa*.

114. For a nice linking of OPEC and debt, see David F. Gordon, "Debt, Conditionality, and Reform: The International Relations of Economic Restructuring in Sub-Saharan Africa," in Callaghy and Ravenhill, *Hemmed In*: 90–129.

115. Data from IMF World Economic Outlook Database. Debt as % of GEP and debt as % or Exports. http://www.imf.org/external/pubs/ft/weo/2012/01/weodata/weorept.aspx?sy=1980&ey=2013&scsm=1&ssd=1&sort=country&ds=.&br=1&c=6 03&s=D_NGDPD%2CD_BX&grp=1&a=1&pr1.x=54&pr1.y=9#notes

116. See, for example, Ernie Wilson, "French Support for Structural Adjustment Programs in Africa." *World Politics* 21, 3 (1993): 331–47.

117. Gordon Cumming, "French Development Assistance to Africa," *African Affairs*, 94, 376 (July 1995): 383–98, p. 390. Jean-Paul Fuchs, *Pour une politique de développement efficace, maîtrisée, et transparente: Rapport au Premier minister.* Paris: La documentation Française (1995), p. 48. This was the Balladur approach.

118. Cumming, "French Development Assistance to Africa," p. 387.

119. Clapham, *Africa*, p. 170.

120. Edward V.K. Jaycox, "Structural Adjustment in sub-Saharan Africa: The World Bank's Perspective." *Issue: A Journal of Opinion* 18, 1 (Winter, 1989): 36–40, p. 36.

121. Clapham, *Africa*, p. 171. He lists the exceptions of Angola and SACU countries.

122. J. Barry Riddell, "Things Fall Apart Again: Structural Adjustment Programmes in Sub-Saharan Africa," *The Journal of Modern African Studies* 30, 1 (Mar., 1992), pp. 53–68, p. 53.

123. Unless otherwise stated, data and information in this section is taken from the IMF factsheet, "Debt Relief Under the Heavily Indebted Poor Countries (HIPC)." December 2011. http://www.imf.org/external/np/exr/facts/hipc.htm

124. Paul Cook and Colin H. Kirkpatrick, eds., *Privatisation in less developed countries* (Brighton: Wheatsheaf Books, 1988).

125. World Bank, *World Development Report 1983* (Washington, DC: World Bank, 1983).

126. Cook and Kirkpatrick, "Privatization, Employment and Social Protection in Developing Countries," in Cook and Kirkpatrick, *Privatisation*, p. 888.

127. Ibid.

128. Robert D. Putnam, "Diplomacy and domestic politics: the logic of two-level games," *International Organization* 42, 3 (June 1988): 427–60.

129. Tangri, *The Politics of Patronage*, p. 129.

130. Carol Lancaster, *Aid to Africa So Much To Do, So Little Done* (Chicago: University of Chicago Press, 1999).

131. Unless states otherwise, data for ODA and ODA graphs taken from World Bank Indicators, http://data.worldbank.org/data-catalog/world-development-indicators—accessed June 2014. Some were in aggregate, some were aggregated by author, but from the same source, such as ODA as percent of government revenue.

132. See Quinn, *Road oft Traveled*.

133. UNDP and private sector: http://www.undp.org/content/undp/en/home/ourwork/povertyreduction/focus_areas/focus_private_sector/_jcr_content/contentPar/

134. See, for example, Goran Hyden and Michael Bratton, eds., *Governance and Politics in Africa* (Boulder, CO: Lynne Rienner Publishers, 1992); Martin Doornbos, "Good Governance": The Metamorphosis of a Policy Metaphor," *Journal of International Affairs* 57, 1 (Fall 2003): 3–17.

135. See Transparency International, SV regional factsheet. http://archive.transparency.org/policy_research/surveys_indices/cpi/2006/regional_highlights_factsheet, May 8, 2014.

136. Taken from IT website, http://www.transparency.org/cpi2014/results

137. For seminal works on resource curse, see Jeffrey D. Sachs and Andrew M. Warner, "Fundamental Sources of Long-Run Growth," *American Economic Review.* 87, 2 (1997); Jeffrey D. Sachs and Andrew M. Warner, "Natural Resource Abundance and Economic Growth," (December 1995). NBER; and R.M. Auty, "The Political Economy of Resource-Driven Growth" *European Economic Review* 45 (2001): 839–46, and R.M Auty, ed., *Resource Abundance and Economic Development* (Oxford, UK: Oxford University Press, 2001).

138. For EITI section, see Liz David-Barrett and Ken Okamura, "The Transparency Paradox: Why do Corrupt Countries Join EITI?" *European Research Centre for Anti-Corruption and State –Building Working* Paper No. 38 (November 2013). http://eiti.org/files/The-Transparency-Paradox.-Why-do-Corrupt-Countries-Join-EITI1.pdf

139. See, for example, the World Bank anti-corruption page and its list of links: http://web.worldbank.org/WBSITE/EXTERNAL/WBI/EXTWBIGOVANTCOR/0,,contentMDK:20710269~menuPK:1746889~pagePK:64168445~piPK:64168309~theSitePK:1740530,00.html

140. John James Quinn, "The Effects of Majority State Ownership of Significant Economic Sectors on Corruption: A Cross-Regional Comparison," *International Interactions* 34, 1 (2008): 81–128.

141. James Gwartney, Robert Lawson, and Walter Block, *Economic Freedoms of the World 1975—1995* (Canada: Fraser Institute, 1996), Table II-B, p. 264. Not all African countries were included, although 31 were.

142. Shenggen Fan and Anuja Saurkar, "Public Spending in Developing Countries: Trends, Determination, and Impact," EPTD Discussion Paper 99 (Washington, DC: International Food Policy Research Institute, 2003).

143. Ibid., p. 3.

144. Ibid., Table 2.3, p. 35.

145. Taken from Peter S. Heller and Alan A. Tait, "Government Employment and Pay: Some International Comparisons," Occasional Paper 24 (Washington, D.C.: International Monetary Fund, October 1983).

146. John J. Quinn, "The Impact of State Ownership of Resources on Economic and Political Development in Sub-Saharan Africa," *Ufahamu* Vol. XXI, No 1and 2 (Winter/Spring): 60–79, Table 1, p. 67.

147. Calculated from Ibid.

148. Calculated from Quinn, *Road oft Traveled*, Table 2.1, p. 39.

149. World Bank, *Bureaucrats in Business*, Table A.5.

150. Ian Lienert and Jitendra Modi, "A Decade of Civil Service Reform in Sub-Saharan Africa," *IMF Working Paper* A Decade of Civil Service Reform in Sub-Saharan Africa—WP/97/179 (December 1997): 1–47

151. Freedom House, S.V. African Countries, 2014. www.freedomhouse.org. This list included Somaliland.

152. Vijaya Ramachandran, Alan Gelb, Manju Kedia Shah, *Africa's Private Sector: What's Wrong with the Business Environment and What to Do About It* (Washington, DC: Center for Global Development, 2009).

153. Ibid., Figure 2.5, p. 27

154. Ibid. Figure 2.12, p. 41.

155. Ibid. pp. 34–37.

156. Ibid. See Figures 3–1 and 3–3.

157. Ibid., Figure 3.2, p. 56.

158. For argument, see Bates, *Markets and States*. Data cited in Joseph Shields and Jonathan Elist, "The key to unlocking Africa's multi-billion dollar agriculture opportunity: great managers," *Africa Policy Journal* (Feb. 2013). http://apj.fas.harvard.edu/the-key-to-unlocking-africas-multi-billion-dollar-agriculture-opportunity-great-managers/

159. "World Bank: Africa held back by land ownership confusion," BBC News (23 July 2013). http://www.bbc.com/news/business-23421548

160. For more details, see Frank F. K. Byamugisha, *Securing Africa's land for shared prosperity: a program to scale up reforms and investments* (Washington D.C.: World Bank and Agence Française de Développement, 2013). http://www-wds.worldbank.org/external/default/WDSContentServer/WDSP/IB/2013/05/31/000445729_20130531122716/Rendered/PDF/780850PUB0EPI00LIC00pubdate05024013.pdf

161. Ibid., p. xv.

162. Ibid., p. 55.

163. For a discussion of the positive or negative effects of democracy on economic policy or outcomes, see Giovanni Sartori, "Rethinking Democracy: Bad Polity and Bad Politics" *International Social Science Journal* 129 (August 1991): 437–51. For which countries having the fewest number of fragments of economic accountability leading to worse economic outcomes, see Quinn, "Economic Accountability."

Chapter 8

Prior Majority State Ownership, Geopolitical Shifts, and Later Political Liberalization in Africa

A Statistical Analysis

As discussed elsewhere in this book, the arrival of region-wide elections, and the attendant increases in political and civil rights in sub-Saharan Africa, has been seen as a "second liberation" or the arrival of the "third wave" to the region.[1] Despite a nearly region-wide adoption of multiparty elections in the post-Cold War period,[2] a wide variation in the of levels in the political and civil rights remains. In 2014, ten countries were coded as free, 19 were coded as partly free, and 20 were coded as not free.[3] In 1975, for example, only three were ranked "free," sixteen were considered "partly free," and twenty-five countries were considered "not free."[4] Therefore, clearly a wave of political liberalization has swept through the region.

In this chapter, I argue that one of the best predictors of a significant increase in levels of political and civil rights in the post-Cold War period in the region was *majority state ownership* (MSO) of most of a country's capital-intensive manufacturing during the Cold War period.[5] The causal nexus is complex, but a clear argument can illustrate how ownership structures led to worse economic outcomes in some sub-Saharan African countries, which then impacted later levels of freedoms. Those countries with MSO of most of their capital-intensive industries followed more inward-oriented policy regimes during the Cold War period, which led to a loss of exports, which led later to less access to hard currency as well as fewer economic resources to distribute as political patronage. In turn, these countries were more vulnerable vis-à-vis the rising international and domestic pressures for political and economic liberalization manifest in the post-Cold War period. By contrast, countries with lucrative mineral or oil exporting sectors (whether owned by the state or not) were less likely to have lost their ability to export and then had more hard currency and economic resources available to maintain the political system. Also, countries which had maintained a strong agricultural exporting base were less vulnerable to external pressure. Therefore, non-MSO, mineral exporting, and oil exporting countries retained more economic resources available for patronage through exporting—thereby, they were less vulnerable to later domestic and international pressures for democratization. I argue that all sub-Saharan African countries were somewhat vulnerable to international and domestic pressures for political reforms, and that all adopted significant changes in their political institutions. The ones that were the most vulnerable to international pressure, however, experienced the largest increases in political and civil rights.

DEMOCRACY AND ITS SOURCES

Any understanding of the partial political liberalization (or the partial democratization) in Africa needs to be understood in the context of overlapping perspectives of democratization, each with a different emphasis. The "endogenous" democratization literature may represent the longest tradition in the literature on modernization and democratization in political science,[6] with clear empirical support.[7] The strong correlation between economic development and political rights and freedoms has led to the conclusion that development and wealth create demands for greater political inclusion of powerful interests—which leads to more democracy.[8] Empirically, and theoretically, the key variables for predicting later democratization are higher levels of literacy, higher per capita incomes, a rising middle class, higher levels of urbanization, and other variables accompanying modernization.[9] O'Neil refers to these as structural variables.[10] Importantly few of the structural variables normally associated with democracy were strong in Africa, even after some forty to fifty years of independence.[11]

    The endogenous democracy literature has been criticized on several fronts. On the one hand, Rustow, O'Donnell, Schmitter, and others have argued that structural variables have not mattered for explaining regional democratic transitions.[12] In fact, much of this "transitions" literature uses a path-dependent, contingent approach within regions, making specific predictions problematic.[13] O'Neil refers to this approach as "process."[14] The transitions literature usually examines notable crises and other events, and their sequences, leading to a decision to hold elections. For Rustow, however, transitions to democracy are a piecemeal, ad hoc extension of power, following no precise formula. Between the crisis and the decision, the transition is conditioned by mixtures of alliances, luck, personal actions, pact creation, negotiations, and other elements of political agency. Looking at Africa from this perspective with the notable exception of South Africa,[15] few countries followed the course of Latin America through "elite pacts" or "fissures among the elites" as a means to initiate transitions.

In one of the seminal works on transitions in sub-Saharan Africa, Bratton and van de Walle discover several variables that predicted democratization or political liberalization.[16] They found that national conferences, the number of post-independence elections, military intervention (of the right kind), frequency of political protests, overseas development aid, opposition cohesion, and percentage of legislative seats held by the majority just before the transition were all statistically linked with the probability of a transition. Most of their significant variables were measured during the transition—consistent with the transitions literature and the use of process variables. Some legacy or structural variables were included, though they were considered to be less important than the process variables, especially their key variable of protests. Importantly, most of their significant findings were domestic variables, and not regional or international.[17]

One well-known critic of the "transitions to democracy" approach characterizes it as sharing five common themes.[18] The first one addresses the underlying *telos* of transitions: that one is moving away from dictatorial rule and towards democracy, in an inevitable or "normal" fashion. Second, the democratization process unfolds in a set sequence of events.[19] Third, the elections are of crucial importance to transitions.[20] Fourth, that "underlying conditions in transitional countries—their economic level, political history, institutional legacies, ethnic makeup, sociocultural traditions, or other 'structural' features—will not be major factors in either the onset or the outcomes of the transition process."[21] Fifth, that the states in which these transitions are taking place are "coherent, functioning states."[22] Assumption number four above necessarily pits this second tradition against the more traditional endogenous democratization literature.

A second major critique to the endogenous democracy theory comes from Przeworski and Limongi, who argued that democratization occurs after authoritarian collapse and not from modernization.[23] After a collapse, they argue, countries are equally likely to introduce either democratic or authoritarian forms of government. They attribute strong association between incomes and democracy to democracy's fragility at lower income levels, but endurance at higher ones.[24] Later researchers would suggest that "exogenous democratization" was at play, but they also argued that this argument went too far in the complete repudiation of endogenous influence on democratization, especially in the pre-WWII period.[25] Others have suggested that by only coding authoritarian collapses that resulted in democratic regimes, as opposed to including collapses establishing all new authoritarian regimes, that their results were misleading.[26]

Similar to Przeworski and Limongi, many Africanists see a democratic opening most likely to emerge from the collapse of prior patronage systems. Economic collapse can lead to the de-legitimization of the regimes, resulting in widespread protests against them.[27] For some, the protests and riots arise from long-term economic decline, or austerity-induced liberalization programs, or in light of a decrease of domestic legitimacy for the incumbent regimes themselves.[28] By contrast, these protests then help create a democratic opening.[29] The more traditional explanation for the onset and durability of African democratic regimes during the Cold War (the Gambia, Botswana, and Mauritius) attributed causation to British legacy or small size.[30]

Finally, many scholars look to changes in external forces or international norms and ideologies to explain the political changes in Africa, though domestic forces are also clearly part of the explanation. Harbeson discusses "externally assisted democratization" where pre-existing (but some latent) domestic forces for democratization were assisted by international forces in the post-Cold War period.[31] Levitsky and Way argue that external pressure is greatest (or most effective) where "leverage" and "linkage" are both strong.[32] To explain, leverage is the amount of pressure that the international community can place on governments, while linkage is exposure of international pressure or linkage into the society itself. For example, aid (ODA) would be a source of leverage, while trade and private investment are sources of linkage. They show that, in Africa, international leverage tends to be strong, but international linkages tend to be weak, which places most of the continent in their third weakest category for democratization. Finally, they argue that where international leverage and linkage are both weak, these countries are the least likely to democratize.[33]

Other external influences that have been used to help explain the African liberalization are these: (1) the extension of the "third wave" to Africa through a democratic demonstration effect; (2) the increased legitimacy of democracy (and capitalism) and its diffusion associated with the end of the Cold War; (3) the lack of a socialist champion after the fall of the Soviet Union; (4) the linkage in the 1990s of ODA to political liberalization and the attendant uncertainty of how committed the international players were in this decision; (5) previous economic conditionality imposed upon faltering African economies; (6) learning associated with failures of state-led development in Eastern Europe and Africa; and (7) the demonstration effect showing the fragility of authoritarianism in the wake of its collapse in Eastern Europe.[34] To bolster the point about ODA, even relatively, mercantilist France required that African recipients of French bilateral aid have economic agreements with the International Monetary Fund (IMF) in 1993, in what would be called the Balladur Doctrine.[35]

New Hybrid Hypothesis

As is clear from earlier parts of the book, I hold that the partial African liberalization in the second period resulted from a combination of external pressures, shifts in international norms, the linking of these norms to aid and debt relief, the collapse of the Soviet Union, the undermining of the legitimacy of state-socialism, international learning, and an important, internal "legacy" variable that helped lead to the ultimate domestic, economic undermining of many patronage regimes.[36] This chapter hopes to show that the variable of *majority state ownership* of *most capital-intensive industries* in an African nation for most of the Cold War is a robust predictor of later political liberalization. The causal linage is complicated and indirect; and it requires both international and domestic explanations. Nonetheless, the logic should be easily comprehensible to political economists. It requires one to imagine the position of African political leaders from 1989 to 1994 as they weighed their prospects for maintaining power as well as their likely ability to obtain the resources necessary to maintain a patronage regime, even as they saw Eastern European systems collapse and liberalization beginning to sweep through that region, and as they heard announcements from their primary donors and many multilateral agencies that future lending or aid would become dependent upon political and economic liberalization.

To make this argument, I first argue that most African polities exhibited strong elements of neo-patrimonial rule.[37] This type of rule occurs where "the chief executive maintains authority through personal patronage, rather than through ideology or rule of law."[38] Whether the terms neopatrimonial, patrimonial, patronage systems, weakly institutionalized systems, or rent seeking are used, many scholars of Africa have held that patronage was the primary glue of the political systems following independence.[39] In these regimes, access to, and the political distribution of, economic resources is the primary political currencies of the realm. Therefore, countries based primarily upon patronage which lose access to significant flows of patronage are quite likely to collapse from within, as no ideological or institutional legacies would endure in the absence of the lost patronage ties and opportunities.[40]

Next, we need to understand that many (but not all) countries in sub-Saharan Africa, within a decade or two after independence, chose to nationalize major sectors of their economies or to have a state-led and state-owned development plans.[41] As a result of many overlapping ideological, nationalistic, and political motives, countries from Ghana, to Tanzania, to Nigeria, to Congo, to Zambia, to Zaire (now DRC), to Guinea came to have majority state ownership of their most important economic sectors.[42] Even such "capitalist" countries as Botswana, Kenya, Cote d'Ivoire, and Senegal had significant government involvement in their economies, though they did not have majority state ownership of either most capital-intensive industries or their largest mineral or oil export sector.

I hold that countries in which the government came to own over 50% of most capital-intensive industries (but excluding countries with lucrative mining or oil exporting sectors) would later lose their ability to export internationally for several reasons: (1) the industries that were state-owned became less competitive, in general, as they were run primarily for reasons of political patronage and not economic efficiency; (2) majority state ownership of industries in Africa resulted in, or deepened, inward-oriented policies that would destroy or greatly weaken their traditional agricultural exporting sector; and (3) Africa had no comparative advantage in capital-intensive industries and could not—as a stylized fact—be competitive exporting the products from this sector.[43] Therefore, these policies undermined exports from their (potential) comparative advantage in agriculture, but were not replaced by industrial exports, given the very nature of import substitution industrialization (ISI) as well as having no particular comparative advantage for exports from such a sector in capital-scarce Africa, and this made these countries uniquely dependent upon international sources of hard currency (such as aid or loans). And aside from oil or mining states, Africa tended not to draw much foreign direct investment (FDI) (outside of South Africa). In fact, according to Callaghy, the amount of bond money going to Africa in 1991 was 0, compared to $2.4B for East Asia and $1.9B for South Asia.[44]

Inefficiency of State owned Sectors

Why are majority state-owned sectors more likely to be economically inefficient? The World Bank has long been critical of the growth impact of state-owned sectors on these economies, though their level of analysis vis-à-vis ownership tends to be sector-by-sector and not country-by-country.[45] Theoretically, where the state owns more than 50% of the stock in a company, it has passed a tipping point because it can win any contested votes on the board.[46] This should represent an uncontested level of control through voting, though other sources of power exist, clearly.[47] Therefore, with majority state ownership, the representatives of the political elites can control the key elements of the corporation with their majority voting power: they can control the treasury, the accounting procedures, the hiring policies, and many other key decisions in a company. Also, it often argued that politicians who manage enterprises or bureaucracies seek to maximize political support, and not economic efficiencies. Therefore, it should follow that such industries should not be internationally competitive—even if they could be potentially.[48] Although groups with less than majority shares of ownership can come to run companies, they cannot do so against the wishes of a majority of owners or a majority owner. Where the state is a minority owner, by contrast, the balance of other stockholders could potentially overcome their collective action costs and vote in a different leadership. And this managerial team would likely maximize economic returns, and not political ones, as per the likely preferences of most stockholders.[49]

The empirics support the logic of neo-patrimonialism and state ownership. State-owned enterprises in Africa are notoriously inefficient, and these sectors have long been criticized for being run for short-term political gains over long-term economic considerations. They are also overstaffed and routinely subsidized! Clarke found that majority state-owned firms were much less likely to export than were other similar firms.[50] This variable was negatively and significantly associated with manufactured exports in eight African countries. Moreover, he found that custom and trade regulations that were viewed as reducing exports were also significantly linked to lower exports from the manufacturing sector. And since his surveys were from 2002 to 2004, this was well after some significant economic liberalization reforms had already taken place. These data would likely have been even worse during the Cold War.

MSO and Inward-Oriented Policies and Exporting

African countries with majority state ownership of either their mineral export sectors or most of their capital-intensive industries featured had more inward-oriented policies than other similar countries during the Cold War period.[51] These inward-oriented policies favor the importation of goods over the exportation of goods and undermined both traditional and modern exporting sectors, aside from minerals or oil. The World Bank defines them as:

> [o]nes which result in incentive structures that are biased toward, or distinctly favor, production for the domestic market: The average rate of effective protection is medium to high and is fairly widespread, direct import controls and licenses are present and may be pervasive, and the exchange rate favors imports over exports.[52]

In the short-term, these economic policies, including restrictions on import licenses and access to hard currency, as well as tariff protections, all could be distributed politically and could further ensconce a political elite in power in a patronage system. For the longer term, however, inward-oriented polices proved not to be sustainable economically, and therefore, the political structures built upon these foundations could not endure.[53]

One major assumption of this argument is that political elites who take ownership of sectors take on the interests of that sector vis-à-vis trade policy. Since the industries the political elites came to own were capital-intensive, and since capital is scarce in Africa,[54] and since owners of scarce factors are harmed under conditions of free trade (Stolper-Samuelson theorem), then the owners of these scarce factors (i.e., political elite) would prefer protectionist policies.[55] These capital-intensive sectors would have withered if they had faced international competition, and their ability to provide patronage would have been lost. Therefore, the political elites which own scarce factors take on the interests of protectionism (or inward-oriented policies). When the political elites who own scarce factors discover their strong preference for protectionism, they adopt the preferred protectionist policies nearly without fail: they have more instruments at hand (e.g., state media, jobs in other sectors, access to currency, access to import licenses, police, military, prison). This analysis rejects the implicit assumptions of pluralism: that the political elites are neutral bystanders or referees in a match of societal forces.[56] When they own scarce factors, they become both players and referees. Political elites become the most powerful interest group in the nation, and they has already overcome their collective action costs vis-à-vis endogenous tariff battles.

Other countries followed an import substitution policy associated with inward-oriented policies. In fact, private owners of capital-intensive industries in capital-scarce countries should also seek protectionist policies, though they may or may not "win" in the society-wide competition for trade policies; they would have to compete with export-oriented interest groups. In these cases, where the political elites do not own factors of production, these societies more resemble a pluralist competition, though usually in Africa under authoritarian constraints. However, I argue that the policy distortion is greater, and more certain, under conditions of majority state ownership of scarce sectors: this relationship between majority state ownership and more inward-oriented policies in the region during the Cold War has been shown empirically.[57] For example, the average level of currency overvaluation for African countries with MSO from 1966 to 1986 was over six times higher than it was for non-MSO countries: 210% and 33%, respectively.[58] As a result of this and other policies, farmers came to exit such export markets through smuggling, shifting to crops for the domestic market, or leaving agriculture altogether. It is well known that the traditional agricultural export sector declined dramatically in countries with high currency overvaluation,[59] though it is less well known that MSO was so highly linked with currency overvaluation.

Capital-Intensive Industries and Exporting

Countries with majority state ownership of most capital-intensive manufacturing industries should not have been able to export much by way of industrial goods internationally out of this new sector. First, no African country enjoyed a clear comparative advantage in capital-intensive manufacturing industries, and, following with ideas of Heckscher-Ohlin, therefore, they would not be able to export very much out this sector (aside from a few niches sectors here and there). According to this theory, exports from countries use abundant factors as the major inputs—and rarely scarce factors.[60] With minerals or oil, by contrast, much of the comparative advantage comes from the mere existence of the abundant resource of the oil or mineral itself—and not the associated capital-intensive nature of extraction. In fact, most African countries export crude, not refined petroleum, consistent with having no comparative advantage in capital. For example, refined petroleum exports are less than 2% of Angola's crude exports, and neither Congo nor Nigeria lists refined petroleum among its exports.[61]

Adding to its inability to be very competitive internationally, African capital-intensive sectors have no particular compensating advantage in management skills, access to market, or other sources of entrepreneurial talents to overcome this basic lack of comparative advantage.[62] Additionally, outside of Mauritius and the Great Lakes region, few African countries have had a comparative advantage in labor, which can be an abundant factor important for an exporting manufacturing industry. In fact, most of Africa is much less densely populated than the rest of the world. Given the lack of comparative advantage in either capital for the whole region, or labor for most of the region—as well as the relative inefficient nature of state-owned industries[63]—African, countries had little significant merchandized exporting from majority state-owned (or any capital-intensive) manufacturing (not including mineral sectors, of course).[64]

Bringing these three parts of the argument together, I argue that capital-intensive industries should not be internationally competitive for exports and these problems were made worse by the inherent inefficiencies of state-owned enterprises, especially in the Third World. Finally, since African MSO countries followed more inward-oriented policies, and had especially high levels of currency overvaluation, they tended to undermine their traditional agricultural export base. In sum, these countries should have lost their ability to export, unless they enjoyed or found a significant mineral or oil exporting sector. Over time, these inward-oriented policies linked to majority state ownership of industry led to economic and export stagnation or failure.

New International Context

Not only did African elites in majority state owned, but without oil or mining, (MSO-WOM) countries face declining sources of revenue from their exporting base for patronage needs, but they also faced dwindling prospects for access to international sources of loans, investment, and aid with the end of the Cold War. As discussed elsewhere, beginning in the 1980s, but culminating in the post-Cold War period, several events converged to limit the African political elites' ability to obtain international funding and hard currency without programs of economic and/ or political liberalization. The Third World debt crisis led to fewer loans from private banks; the switch to systematic economic conditionality by the International Monetary Fund (IMF) and World Bank in the mid- to late-1980s reduced lending for countries with inward-oriented policies;[65] with investment opportunities in Asia and the newly liberated Eastern European countries, less private investment was flowing to the region;[66] the even more rigid enforcement of structural adjustment in the post-Cold War period reduced such funding even further; and the linking of ODA to political liberalization in the 1990s reduced aid to non-liberalizing countries.[67] African elites had to decide whether to test the commitment of donors to reducing aid in the future if they did not adopt some measures of liberalization. Thus, as Brown held, "the threat of political conditionality (whether explicit or not) can be sufficient to exact political liberalisation without altering aid delivery."[68] This would suggest, in the terms of Levitsky and Way, that the international community would have more influence over countries with failed domestic economies, as the latter should have been more aid dependent.[69]

Therefore, African countries that lost the most access to domestic and international sources of funding for their patronage systems should have become (or should have perceived themselves to have become) the most vulnerable to both domestic opposition and international pressures for democratization.[70] I argue that countries with MSO of industry, but without viable mining or petroleum sectors (MSO-WOM), were the most likely to face a full-blown political crisis due to a clear lack of domestic and international economic resources at the end of the Cold War, and they should not have seen any easy way out of their circumstances in the near term. External sources of funding were set against the inward-oriented development path as well as authoritarian politics from 1989 onwards, and these countries had lost most of their domestic ability to produce exports.

Other Countries

By contrast, as a matter of logic and empirics, countries that had relatively more outward politics should have been able to maintain more of their traditional agricultural export sectors and therefore should have been less vulnerable to international pressures in the post-Cold War period. Despite widely held views that Africa suffered uniformly from agricultural malaise during the Cold War, some countries had growing agricultural export sectors. In fact, the 1981 Berg Report which outlined a story of general agricultural failure in the region during the 1960s and 1970s found six countries with higher than 3% annual growth in agricultural output in its study (Cameroon, Ivory Coast, Kenya, Malawi, Rwanda, and Swaziland).[71] None of these countries had majority state ownership of most industries. The Berg report also showcased seven countries with stagnant or negative agricultural output during the same period (Angola, Congo, Ghana, Mauritania, Mozambique, Togo, and

Uganda).[72] All had majority state ownership of most industries, or its largest mineral or oil exporting sector. In addition, the two countries the report used to highlight especially poor agricultural performance were Ghana and Tanzania, both of which had majority state ownership.[73] Similarly, Robert Bates' well-known book outlining the problems of African agriculture and markets features three countries with especially poor agricultural policies (Nigeria, Zambia, and Ghana), and one (Kenya) with strong agricultural policies.[74] The three with poor performance also had MSO of their economies, while the latter did not.

Also, countries with lucrative mineral or oil exporting sectors (either state-owned or privately-owned) should have been less constrained by the international community at the end of the Cold War. Not only did oil and mining countries have domestic sources for streams of patronage, they were also more likely to lure in foreign direct investment (FDI).[75] Following from the above logic of patronage politics, they were less likely to feel pressure to democratize as they had a guaranteed source of revenue from which to continue to support a patronage system, even if at reduced levels.[76] Although these countries might face what some call the "mineral resource curse"[77] (with or without majority state ownership), and they too would lose their agricultural export sector, they would not lose all their access to hard currency and funding for patronage—unless the mineral or oil sector went bust.[78] Should oil or mineral sectors lose their ability to export, they would more resemble the countries which had featured majority state ownership of industry.

By extension, and to be consistent with the logic of this argument, states that found oil or lucrative mining strikes in the immediate post-Cold War period are expected to have been less vulnerable, or should have perceived themselves to be less vulnerable, to pressures from the international community to democratize. They would have had a source of revenue and investment not linked to economic or political conditionality—which would allow a patronage system to be constructed or maintained without more than token steps taken toward political liberalization.[79]

Finally, leaders of countries with many natural resources could choose a strategy other than democratization—warlord politics.[80] In countries where diamonds, petroleum, or other natural resources were available, leaders could retreat from providing a large-patronage network through public goods to maintaining power by providing such assets to a smaller coalition backed by military force. Then, private good provision replaces public good provision in these societies, and the pretense of ruling in the public interest is reduced or eliminated. The availability of such resources of importance to multinational corporations creates a revenue stream that some very self-interested rules could use as a basis of rule, this could result in a collapsed state. Reno suggests that war lord politics were at work in was the cases of Liberia, Sierra Leone, and Zaire (now the DRC).[81]

Other Africanists have made similar arguments about the loss of patron-age and collapse, though their ideas tended to be generalized to the region as a whole, or they do not distinguish according to the structural variable of majority state ownership. In fact, several African scholars have argued that democracy could emerge out of the ashes of a collapsed patronage system.[82] Grosh suggested a similar argument to this one, though not couched in these terms. She holds that there are two types of countries: "those that used repressed economy policies long enough to cause their economies to collapse and those that used the policies less severely and whose economies grew slowly but positively."[83] She did not show, however, which countries would be in which group in an *a priori* fashion. Similarly, Quinn, using a decision model, showed that one of the variables most likely to lead to political change in African countries was an economic collapse.[84]

Hypothesis

This chapter argues that countries in sub-Saharan Africa with majority state ownership of most capital-intensive manufacturing industries (but without major mining or oil exporting sectors) [MSO-WOM] during the Cold War period are the ones most likely to have had the greatest increases in political and civil rights in the post-transition period. I argue that the legacy effects of majority state ownership (MSO) of industries from the 1960s through the 1980s affected the economic trajectory of sub-Saharan African countries, which later made them more vulnerable to international pressure. I test this hypothesis using a cross-sectional OLS regression analysis where the independent variable of majority state ownership (a dummy variable) during the Cold War period is regressed on post-transition levels of political and civil rights (1995–2005), using other control variables from the literature on democracy and neopatrimo-nialism. The complex, path-dependent and often ad hoc nature of the transition is not measured or tested directly.[85] Therefore, this analysis is testing these variables' effects upon later liberalization, rather than democratization process per se. This is a better test in light of the purpose of the book: to see how Africa liberalized, politically and economically following from a geopolitical shift. Also, Geddes tests transitions away from authoritarianism in a similar fashion.[86] Nonetheless, first I examine some initial evidence to support this hypothesis.

Initial Evidence

Examining the average differences in levels of political and civil rights (from Freedom House) between the two periods (1979–1989 and 1995–2005), a regional increase in rights of 1.2 is evident out of a scale of seven.[87] And as we saw before, only nine countries were considered to be free in 2009. By contrast, examining only countries with prior MSO of industry, but without significant mining or oil exporting sectors (MSO-WOM), the average increase in rights for this category was 2.95, and this number is well over twice the overall mean. Additionally, all countries with a two-point (or more) increase in political or civil rights were MSO-WOM, except for Malawi. Additionally, if the average change for all of Africa is examined excluding MSO-WOM countries, the average increase in political and civil rights for the whole region was only 0.45.[88] Therefore, *there was only slightly more than a half a point average increase in political and civil rights for the region of sub-Saharan Africa when MSO-WOM countries are excluded.* It seems that the greatest gains in political liberalization in Africa can be attributed primarily to these countries.

Next, it should be noted that the average level of currency overvaluation for African countries with MSO from 1966 to 1986 was over six times higher than it was for non-MSO countries: 210% and 33%, respectively.[89] It is clear that traditional agricultural export sectors declined dramatically in countries with high currency overvaluation,[90] though it is less well known that the high levels of currency overvaluation were tried to MSO.

Moreover, we can see that MSO-WOM countries had worse agricultural exporting experiences, on average. From 1980 to 1985, during the heart of economic decline in the region,[91] countries with MSO-WOM experienced an average annual percent growth of food exports of *negative* 4.12%.[92] Using only volume (since price could interfere with inferences), these same countries showed a similar average annual decline from 1980 to 1985, *negative* 4.2.[93] By contrast, countries without MSO of most industries (excluding oil or mineral exporting countries) had an average annual food export rate of *positive* 0.07% per year.[94] The volume of agricultural exports for these countries was an average annual growth rate of *positive* 2.76%.[95] Although volatility is notorious for agricultural output, given problems with drought, floods, and so forth, here the predicted patterns vis-à-vis this theory are supported. Although these are far from stunningly positive numbers, they represent absolute differences of 4.18% and 6.96% for value and volume, respectively, between these two categories of countries (again excluding all major mining or oil exporting countries).

Also, we can see that MSO-WOM countries had an average of 4.57% of total exports from manufacturing from 1975 to 1985.[96] By contrast, countries without majority state ownership of most industries, or significant oil or mineral exporting sectors, had an average of 13.56% of manufacturing exports during our period, which was nearly three times as high.[97] Moreover, three of these latter countries had averages above 20%.[98] Nonetheless, given the lack of comparative advantage in capital-intensive industries, and few countries with abundant labor, manufacturing in Africa may have some natural limits to it, regardless of ownership. Nonetheless, clearly one category has done better than the other.

Also, the levels of growth were lower for MSO-WOM countries, at −0.654—compared to 0.82 for other countries.[99] If we remove all countries with significant oil or mineral exporting sectors which could suffer from the mineral/oil resource curse, the numbers are −0.65 and 1.14, respectively.[100] In terms of capital accounts, as a percentage of gross national income, MSO countries averaged −14.18%, while non-MSO or oil or mining countries had an average of −8.35.[101] Both did poorly, one did much worse. Finally, examining the inflows of foreign direct investment from 1980 to 1989, MSO-WOM countries had an average of $4.46 million a year, and non-MSO-WOM countries had an average of $40.26 million a year.[102] Dividing this number between mineral/oil producers and those without, we see that most of this FDI went to mining or oil countries, with an average of $80.69 million per year, the remaining countries received an average of $11.06 million. This latter amount is still nearly two and a half times the expected amount of FDI than for MSO-WOM countries.

These negative exporting outcomes, lower growth levels, and lower levels of FDI should make such countries more dependent upon other external sources of funding. The facts bear this out. In fact, MSO-WOM countries received much more aid: the average in 1989 was 21.66% of GDP, while that for non-MSO-WOM was 10.54%—or nearly half.[103] The levels of debt for this category were also much higher, at 137.87% compared to 87.9% for the other countries, or over one and a half times higher. Therefore, they had been more dependent upon loans and aid than other such countries.

So, it appears that MSO-WOM countries had lower growth, had a declining agricultural export base, had a lower manufacturing export base, had higher debts, obtained less FDI, and had more reliance upon international aid at the end of the Cold War than did other African countries.[104] I feel that leaders in countries without expected potential revenues from oil or mining, or likely FDI, and who had declining or dilapidated agricultural sectors, few expectations for exporting from the industrial sectors, who had high loan liabilities, and who relied on a fifth of their GDP from ODA (like leaders from former MSO countries), should have seen themselves as more vulnerable to the international community than those that had viable agricultural export sectors, viable manufacturing sectors, lower debts, or mineral or oil sectors in existence (or soon coming on line).

Design and Methodology

In this design, I test the effects of legacy variables near the end of the Cold War period on levels of political and civil rights after the main transition period. As such, I test the average levels of our independent variables for 44 countries from the period of 1979 to 1989, or levels right at 1989, to see if these legacy variables were linked to the levels of political and civil rights from 1995 to 2005.[105] This approach tries to capture the effect of the legacy variables (which is often ignored) on later levels of freedoms, without examining the contingent, path-dependent effects which are clearly harder to model or predict. Therefore, I do not trace out the links between the structural variables and the process ones, however, a statistically significant finding would mean that the structural variable mattered, on average, through the potentially divergent processes that occurred. I do not claim that these latter variables did not matter, just that legacy effects did, and their effects are isolated through this method. Also, I do not draw out exactly how legacy effects play out in the transition period other than on their *a priori* likely influences.[106] Moreover, I do not test democratization, per se, but rather changes in political and civil rights.[107]

LIST OF VARIABLES, OPERATIONALIZATION, AND CHOICE OF COUNTRIES

Data for each variable come from a variety of sources. Most of legacy variables are averages of eleven years before the "second wave" or are representative of levels for about a decade before 1989.[108] The dependent variable, level of political and civil rights, is measured by the average level of political and civil rights averaged from 1995 to 2005.[109] This captures the average of freedoms for about a decade after the transition process.

The first independent variable is a dummy variable for the existence of majority state ownership of capital-intensive industry—but excluding countries which also had a significant mineral or petroleum exporting sector. It is coded as one when the state owned more than 50% of most of its capital-intensive industries (regardless of the size of this sector), unless the country was a major oil or mineral exporter for a significant part of the first period.[110] Otherwise, it was coded as a zero. The coding for these data comes from various sources.[111] (See Appendix I for categories of countries).

By a matter of logic, one other legacy, or structural, variable should be a very good predictor of the present level of political and civil rights: past levels of political and civil rights. This variable comes from Freedom House and is the political and civil rights per country from 1979 to 1989, averaged. If the levels of rights did not change much, or if all changed by a similar amount, then this variable should be significant and positively linked with later levels. I also include the legacy of type of colonization, as many scholars have argued that it matters a great deal to later political outcomes.[112] Therefore,

I included a dummy variable pertaining to colonial heritage, whether British, Belgian, or Portuguese.[113] French, Spanish (one country), and not colonized (two countries) are lumped together into the default category against which the other dummy variables are contrasted.[114]

The second set of legacy variables comes from the work of Bratton and van de Walle. These scholars distinguish between different kinds of authoritarian regimes based upon the extent of participation and competition. They distinguish four types of neopatrimonial regimes in Africa. They find that former competitive one-party systems have the best chance of making a successful transition to democracy. I test this by including a dummy to show whether a country was a competitive one party system, plebiscitary, or a military.[115] I exclude their variable of "white settler polity" as both Namibia and South Africa are excluded from this analysis, given their very different relationships with the international community prior to the end of the Cold War.[116] I also included size of population.[117]

Another set of variables included flows from the modernization literature. Many societal wide development variables have been linked with levels of democracy in the past: literacy, per capita incomes, a rising middle class, levels of urbanization, a rising class of business owners, and other variables associated with endogenous democratic theory. From this list, I include wealth, growth, and levels of urbanization.[118] Wealth is measured by the level of 1989 GDP per capita and logged.[119] This is the level of wealth just at the cusp of the transition. Also included is a longer average of growth before the transition, 1979–1989.[120] The level of urbanization is in percentage form.[121]

Another important legacy variable comes from Easterly and Levine who argue that ethnic or linguistic fractionalization was among the primary causes of poor economic policy, poor educational outcomes, "political instability, inadequate infrastructure, and weak institutions."[122] I use the 1986 measure.[123] Also a variable from Englebert's work on legitimacy is included, as he demonstrated empirically that non-legitimate countries had worse policy outcomes and should also lead to more failed polities.[124]

Since many thinkers have shown that the existence of a significant mineral or petroleum exporting sector can be detrimental to democracy, a dummy variable for this is included.[125] New oil or mining is a dummy variable for countries that became oil or mining exporters in the transition period, as such a find should make regimes less vulnerable to international or domestic pressure by increasing resource flows domestically, as well as leading to more FDI.[126] Also included is a variable measuring the percentage of Muslims, as recent scholarship has suggested that Islam may be inimical to democratic practices.[127] Also, the existence of civil wars should have a negative impact on the democratization process and a measure of it is therefore included.[128]

Finally, some movement could be due to the perceived failure of Communism and socialism at the end of Cold War. Also countries that lost access to resources from the USSR would be more vulnerable as well.[129] Therefore, a dummy variable for countries that were either Afro-Marxist or socialist for a majority of the years from 1979 to 1989 is also in the model.[130]

Therefore, the primary independent variable is this: majority state ownership of capital-intensive industries during the Cold War, though it excludes countries with a significant mineral or oil exporting sector (MSOWOM). The control variables are these: the political and civil rights from 1979 to 1989 (polciv79), legitimate regimes (legit), competitive one party regimes (comp), military regimes (military), per capita GDP from 1989 (logged (pdppc89ln)), GDP growth 1979–1989 (growth 79–89), percent of years in civil war, percent Muslim, urbanization, ethnolinguistic fractionalization, population, mining or oil exporting, new mining or oil in the second period, socialism, Afro-Marxism, and former colonial status: British, Portuguese, and Belgian.[131] The variables of number of elections and plebiscitary elections were excluded as they proved to be collinear with other variables.[132] Also, the measure of multiparty was better captured in the freedom house numbers than with a dummy.[133]

The Models

In order to test the effects of legacy variables during the Cold War period upon levels of political and civil rights following the transition period, they are tested from the pre-transition period (1979–1989) on the averages of political and civil rights for 44 countries after the transition period (1995 to 2005).[134] I do not test the process variables which occurred from 1990 to 1994 (the dates for this transitional period), except for the variable of new oil/mining. It is included because the discovery of new oil or mining during the transition would clearly impact the perception of how much patronage would exist to maintain a patronage-based political system. Excluding this variable does not change the outcomes of our models much, nor does it affect the main variable at all.[135] I include all of the countries from Bratton and van de Walle's sample of variables of 47 countries, though I exclude South Africa and Namibia as unique experiences during the first period.[136] I also exclude Somalia as it broke into several parts, and the main rump is a collapsed state. This results in a sample size of forty-four.

Model 1 is the complete model with all of our variables. Model 2 is included as some may suggest that other legacy variables accounted for the levels of political and civil rights, such as colonial heritage, so a second model is estimated without it. Model 3 leaves out all variables possibly caused by MSOWOM.[137] Then Model 4 uses instrumental variables to control for possible

Table 8.1   Models and Findings

Dependent Variables	(1) Polciv9505 OLS	(2) Polciv9505 OLS	(3) Polciv9505 OLS	(4) Polciv9505 2SLS
Independent Variables				
Intercept	**4.49+**	3.96	**3.55+++**	**1.622++**
	(2.64)	(3.0)	(0.789)	(0.735)
Majority State	**1.426++**	**1.23++**	**1.20++**	**1.167++**
Ownership	(0.516)	(0.519)	(0.564)	(0.545)
Freedom House	**0.425++**			**0.646++**
1979–1989	(0.24)			(0.15)
Legit	0.699	0.944	0.905	
	(0.593)	(0.719)	(0.719)	
Competitive one party	0.133	−0.138		
	(0.465)	(0.427)		
Military regime	0.005	−0.053		
	(0.425)	(0.369)		
Average GDP/Pop	−0.348	−0.158		
1989ln	(0.346)	(0.417)		
Growth 79–89	0.119	0.114		
	(0.094)	(0.09)		
Urbanization	0.009	0.006		
	(0.12)	(0.011)		
Civil War	**−1.28++**	**−1.567++**		**−2.19+++**
	(0.553)	(0.59)		(0.626)
Percent Muslim	−0.008	−0.004	−0.005	
	(0.007)	(0.007)	(0.005)	
Population	0.002	0.001	−0.007	
	(0.006)	(0.006)	(0.009)	
Ethnolinguistic	−0.61	0.435	0.008	
fractionalization	(0.595)	(0.736)	(0.85)	
Mining/oil Dummy	0.083	−0.09	−0.142	
	(0.41)	(0.457)	(0.445)	
New mining/oil	**−1.239++**	**−1.54+++**	**−1.98+++**	**−1.09+**
Dummy	(0.457)	(0.385)	(0.37)	(0.638)
Portuguese Dummy	0.65	0.615	−0.123	0.395
	(0.579)	(0.658)	(0.704)	0.634
British Dummy	−0.314	0.222	0.162	0.0090
	(0.519)	(0.429)	(0.377)	(0.504)
Belgian Dummy	**−1.95++**	**−1.90++**	**−2.08+++**	−0.722
	(0.856)	(0.866)	(0.622)	(0.63)
Afro-Marx Dummy	−0.79	0.22	0.144	**2.06++**
	(0.677)	(0.94)	(0.741)	(0.88)
Socialist Dummy	−0.114	−0.138	−0.71	
	(0.494)	(0.615)	(0.558)	
N	44	44	44	42
R-squared	0.742	0.694	0.608	0.573
Corrected	(robust)	(robust)	(robust)	0.656
R-squared				

+++ significance $p < 0.01$; ++ significance $p < 0.05$; + significance $p < 0.10$; Significant findings in bold.

endogeneity as some could argue that several of the independent variables are not independent of one another.[138] This is the more traditional alternative to the approach used in models 2 and 3, though dropping endogenous variables could be a robustness check. I use the robust variables found from models 1–3, and then all the variables from Model 1 are used as instrumental variables to shape the possibly endogenous variables in the main equation. The data are estimated in STATA13, and each model is tested for heteroskedasticity and multicollinearity.[139]

The estimations were also run with an alternative measure (an interval level, but technically ordinal) of government ownership as some might object to a dummy variable for state ownership (and as a robustness check). Variable IIB was taken from Gwartney, Lawson, and Block.[140] It was the average of state ownership and intrusion, rated from 0 to 10. After running the model, however, I found that this variable was not significant (or ever close to significant) in any model—either with or without the majority state ownership dummy in the model, though MSO was always significant where included. Due to less data, inclusion of it dropped the N from 44 to 26.[141] It was therefore not included in the models.

FINDINGS

As can be seen from Table 8.1, strong support for the hypothesis is found: countries that had featured majority state ownership of their capital-intensive industries in the first period, but which did not have major oil or mining export sectors (MSO-WOM), were positively and significantly correlated with higher levels of political liberalization in the second period when compared with other similar countries. This meets the expectations of the logic set forth in this chapter and other elements of the book as a whole. For every model, countries with prior MSO of industries, but without significant mining or oil exporting sectors, had an average increase in political and civil rights between 1.67 and 1.426 in a scale out of 7.

Several other variables were also robust across the models in which they were included. These were the prior levels of political and civil rights, the percentage of time the state had civil war in the first period, and new oil rents found in the transition period. The variable for Belgian colonization, however, was significant in models 1–3, but not in model 4. The variable for Afro-Marxist was significant in Model 4 only. The variables for civil war, finding new oil or mining in the transition period, and being a former Belgian colony all militated against higher, later levels of political and civil rights. By contrast, MSO-WOM, prior level of political and civil rights, and Afro-Marxism predicted for higher later levels of rights in the post transition period (though the sign for Afro-Marxism was negative in Model 1).[142]

Several of the other variables were never significant: the historic legitimacy of the country, competitive one party states, military regimes, per capita GDP in 1989, growth from 1979–1989, urbanization, percent Muslim, population, ethnolinguistic fractionalization, mining or oil exporting counties, former Portuguese colonization, former British colonization, or having been socialist (as opposed to Afro-Marxist).

INTERPRETATIONS AND CONCLUSIONS

Therefore, it seems that most of the traditional structural variables from the endogenous democratization literature from the first period could not account for the changes in levels of political and civil rights for the region in the second period: growth, levels of GDP, and urbanization were insignificantly linked in each model. Perhaps using the truncated sample of only African cases meant there was not enough variation on these variables to confirm these findings. Nonetheless, this means, as per the regional transition to democracy literature, some of these variables did not matter much here. I did find that some legacy or structural variables did matter, but they are of another ilk. Having had majority state ownership of industry during the Cold War period, the prior levels of political rights, having been colonized by the Belgians, or having a legacy of internal conflict are powerful predictors of post-transition levels of freedoms—although the Belgian variable was insignificant in one model, and Afro-Marxist was significant in only one.

The robust finding for prior levels of political and civil rights in the models means that, on average, most countries' levels of political and civil rights prior to the transition were good predictors for after the transition, *ceteris paribus*. Countries with more freedoms were likely to have more freedoms afterwards, on average; and more authoritarian countries were more likely to remain more authoritarian, on average. Two of the three most democratic countries, Botswana and Mauritius, remained so. Similarly, countries like Angola, Burundi, Cameroon, Chad, Cote d'Ivoire, Equatorial Guinea, Guinea, Mauritania, Rwanda, Sudan, Swaziland, Congo-Kinshasa, and Zimbabwe all remained or became not free in the post-transition period.

As for some of Bratton and van de Walle's variables, I found no support for the idea that the type of neopatrimonial system mattered, though I did not test transitions to democracy directly as they did. By contrast, the analysis sought to explain post-transition changes in levels of freedoms.[143] Nor were some other legacies, such as levels of legitimacy, or ethnolinguistic fractionalization, or type of colonization, found to be significant, save for Belgian colonization in Models 1, 2, and 3.

Unexpectedly, being a mining or oil exporter did not seem to matter. Since they were not likely to democratize in either period, this non-finding is quite consistent with the logic set out herein. They had continued access to autonomous sources of patronage, the ruling elite wanted to maximum power, and these countries were less vulnerable to the international pressure to democratize following the end of the Cold War. However, the resource curse theory which links oil to lower levels of political and civil rights is supported indirectly with the variable of new mining or oil. Here countries that may have been vulnerable to international pressure to liberalize politically suddenly became less vulnerable to this pressure as newly discovered economic resources were going to be coming on line. This could give leadership a strong promise of new resources and could resist some of the international, regional, and domestic demands for political liberalization. This is quite consistent with the overall of logic of this paper: that leaders are presumed to preserve patronage based regimes when possible. Next, the negative association and significance of civil war should be mostly self-evident. Long civil wars do not bode well for later higher levels of political and civil freedoms.

Finally, the weaker results for Belgian and Afro-Marxism are suggestive that they probably matter, but they are not robust findings. We have to remember a few things about Belgian colonies, however: they represent only three of the 44 cases, two of them are bicommunal (Rwanda and Burundi), and the third is the Democratic Republic of the Congo. Therefore, some of this could be due to a small sample size, though many people have argued that Belgian colonization was especially poor.[144] Also, I included the variable of Afro-Marxism and socialism partially to make sure that the effects attributed to MSO were not reducible to them. In fact, excluding Afro-Marxism and/or socialism from the estimation models, I find that the MSO coefficient changes only by a tiny amount, but it remains strongly significant, with the same sign. Moreover, the exclusion of MSO-WOM does not result in Afro-Marxism becoming significant in the first three models. With some logic, we can see that neopatrimonial regimes might be likely to break down where the regime was both former MSO and former Afro-Marx, thereby losing the support of the USSR in the immediate post-Cold War period while having lost significant levels of exports during the Cold War. Most of their breakdown, however, should be attributed to their choice of nationalizing scarce factors and taking on the sector's trading preferences, leading to inward-oriented development policies, and the ensuing negative effects.

Therefore, the literature suggesting that the African countries most likely to reform were those which experienced a collapse of their patronage systems has been supported here. Although other Africanists have argued that collapsed patronage regimes may be the most likely to transition or democratize, the arguments I have read did not have a story, *a priori*, about which would likely collapse and why. My argument illustrates which countries are mostly to follow this path *a priori*, in the wake of the second geopolitical shift. The theoretical story and empirics are quite consistent with each other.

Tying this analysis to the work of Przeworski and Limongi's theory, however, they would predict that only half of the countries which had patronage systems fall apart would have had increases in rights, while the other half should have remained authoritarian or become more authoritarian within this set of countries. I hold that post-Cold War pressures led to a systematic adoption of more freedoms for the most vulnerable countries as access to resources was tied to economic and political liberalizations and not the flip of a coin (or a 50/50 chance), which they argued.

Looking at Figure 8.1 below, we can map which countries had the greatest gains in liberties looking at prior levels of political freedoms and MSO-WOM. The left-hand access is the net change in freedoms (the higher the greater the increase of rights in the two periods), and the bottom axis is the prior average levels of freedoms from 1979 to 1989 (with the number inverted so the lower, the more authoritarian). The key shows that squares represent

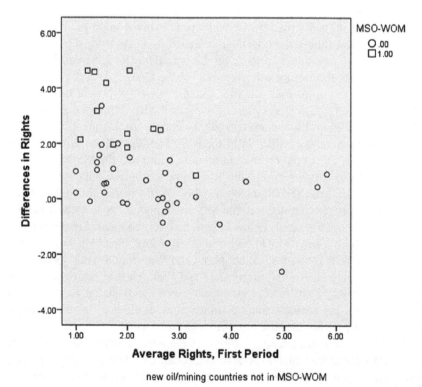

new oil/mining countries not in MSO-WOM

Figure 8.1   Differences in Levels of Freedom, Prior Levels of Freedoms, and MSO-WOM

MSO-WOM, and circles represent the rest. As the reader can see, nearly all the countries with large positive changes in freedoms are from our category of interest (and had been more authoritarian in the first period). In fact, nearly all of the countries which had two point increases or more were former MSO countries. Only one country with greater than a two point increase is not from this category. The former MSO-WOM countries experienced an average increase in rights of 2.95.

Przeworski and Limongi's predictions should look more like the circles (the universe of non-MSO countries or those with mining or oil (old or new)). Here the average increase in rights between the two periods was 0.45 points. This can be seen where half of the data points are close to or above 0.45, while the other and half were at or below (sometime well below) 0.45—despite the nearly region-wide adoption of more liberal electoral systems. So the average regional effects outside of our variables account for less than half a point increase in the region.

Moreover, as mentioned above, only one country in this latter category increased by more than 2 points, though a couple of them decreased by about two points. Perhaps during the Cold War, when international demands for political liberation were more muted, these two categories of countries might have more resembled the blue circles (i.e., where a few increased, a few decreased, and most changed very little.). Nonetheless, with international diplomatic pressure linking aid to democratization, with the ideological collapse of state-led development, with the fall of the Soviet Union as an African patron, and with IFIs pushing for more accountability, good governance, and more open markets, the most vulnerable countries were less able to resists such pressures in the post-Cold War environment. At the end of the Cold War, MSO-WOM countries suffered from the combined problems of high debts, low growth, limited export options, limited FDI, and aid dependency. They also did not have significant domestic natural resources under their control to substitute for an external revenue stream, unless they were in the category of new oil or mining. The leaders of such countries were, therefore, the most likely to see themselves in a situation without sufficient sources of patronage from domestic sources, or old international sources, to maintain their patronage systems. They would have to turn to the international community and to embrace the latter's priorities as a way to turn the spigot for international resource flows back on, to reduce debt burdens, and to readjust their own economies to the creation of more domestic economic wealth.

In sum, the hypothesis that African countries with majority state ownership of industries, but without oil or mining, would be the countries likely to liberalize the most at the end of the Cold War has been supported. The empirical evidence supports the logic set out before. Like the transitions literature, I found that many structural variables such as urbanization, growth, and levels of income, did not seem to matter in this sample, though I found that some other, less-well studied, ones did. With the wave of democratization sweeping sub-Saharan Africa, the countries which appear to have had greater increases in their levels of freedoms in the second period were those which were former MSO countries without mining or oil. The other variables found to be significant for predicting changes in later levels were these: prior levels of freedoms, new oil or mining, civil wars, Belgian colonization, and Afro-Marxism, though Belgian colonization was insignificant in one model and Afro-Marxism in three. These structural variables were significant some, most, or all of the time. I leave to future studies how these may or may not have followed particular transition archetypes. I also leave to future studies how durable these changes shall prove to be, though as discussed elsewhere, there is some reason for optimism.

NOTES

1. For research on this, see Larry Diamond, "Is the Third Wave Over?" *Journal of Democracy* 7, 3 (1996): 20–37; Michael Bratton and Nicolas van de Walle, *Democratic Experiments in Africa: Regime Transitions in Comparative Perspective* (Cambridge: Cambridge University Press, 1997); Christopher Clapham, *African and the International System: The Politics of State Survival* (Cambridge: Cambridge University Press, 1996); Richard Joseph, "The Reconfiguration of Power in Late Twentieth-Century Africa," in Richard Joseph, ed., *State, Conflict, and Democracy in Africa* (Boulder, CO: Lynne Rienner Publishers, 1999): 57–82; Richard Joseph, "Africa, 1990–1997: From Abertura to Closure," *Journal of Democracy* 9, 2 (1998): 3–7; Crawford Young, "The Third Wave of Democratization in Africa: Ambiguities and Contradictions," in Richard Joseph, ed., *State, Conflict, and Democracy in Africa* (Boulder, CO: Lynne Rienner Publishers, 1999): 15–38; Nicolas van de Walle, "Elections without Democracy: Africa's Range of Regimes," *Journal of Democracy* 13, 2 (April 2002): 66–80; E. Gyimah-Boadi, ed., *Democratic Reform in Africa: The Quality of Progress* (Boulder, CO: Lynne Rienner Publishers 2004); Michael Bratton and Eric C. C. Chang, "State Building and Democratization in Sub-Saharan Africa Forwards, Backwards, or Together?" *Comparative Political Studies* 39, 9 (November 2006): 1059–1083; Staffan I. Lindberg, *Democracy and Elections in Africa* (Baltimore, MD: The Johns Hopkins University Press, 2006). For third wave, see Samuel P. Huntington, *The Third Wave: Democratization in the Late Twentieth Century* (Norman, OK: University of Oklahoma Press 1991).

2. For example, see van de Walle, "Elections without Democracy;" Bratton and Chang, "State Building and Democratization;" and Lindberg, *Democracy and Elections*.

3. Freedom House, S.V. African Countries, 2014. http://www.freedomhouse. org/report-types/freedom-world#.U0au_qK9Ymo. This list included South Sudan.

For analysis of sub-scores, see John W. Harbeson, "Promising Democratization Trajectories in Africa's Weak States," in John W. Harbeson and Donald Rothchild, eds., *Africa in World Politics: Reforming Political Order* (Boulder, CO: Westview, 2009).

4. Freedom House, SV African countries, 1975.

5. For prior arguments linking MSO to negative economic or political outcomes in the region, see John James Quinn, *The Road oft Traveled: Development Policies and Majority State Ownership of Industry in Africa* (Westport, CN: Praeger, 2002); John J. Quinn, "The Managerial Bourgeoisie: Capital Accumulation, Development and Democracy," in David G. Becker and Richard L. Sklar, eds., *Postimperialism and World Politics* (Westport, CT: Praeger, 1999): 219–52; and John James Quinn, "The Effects of Majority State Ownership of Significant Economic Sectors on Corruption: A Cross-Regional Comparison," *International Interactions* 34, 1 (2008): 81–128.

6. For basic paradigm, see W.W. Rostow, *The Stages of Economic Growth: A Non-Communist Manifesto* (New York: Cambridge University Press, 1960); Seymour Martin Lipset, "Some Social Requisites of Democracy: Economic Development and Political Legitimacy," *American Political Science Review* 53 (March, 1959): 69–105.

7. See, for example, Ibid.; Robert W. Jackman, "On the Relationship of Economic Development to Political Performance," *American Journal of Political Science* 17 (1973): 611–21; Kenneth Bollen and Robert W. Jackman, "Political Democracy and the Size Distribution of Income," *American Sociological Review* 50, 4 (August 1985):438–57; Adam Przeworski and Fernando Limongi, "Modernization: Theories and Facts," *World Politics* 49 (January 1997): 155–83.

8. Ross E. Burkhart and Michael S. Lewis-Beck, "Comparative Democracy: The Economic Development Thesis," *The American Political Science Review*, Vol. 88, No. 4 (Dec., 1994): 903–910.

9. Lipset, "Social Requisites;" Robert H. Bates, *Market and States in Tropical Africa: The Political Basis of Agricultural Policies* (Los Angeles: University of California Press, 1981); Bratton and van de Walle, *Democratic Experiments*; Robert J. Barro, "The Determinants of Democracy," *Journal of Political Economy* 107, 6 (1999): s158-s183.

10. Patrick H. O'Neil, "Revolution from Within: Analysis, Transitions from Authoritarianism, and the Case of Hungary," *World Politics* 48, 4 (1996): 579–603, p. 580.

11. Gyimah-Boadi, *Democratic Reform in Africa*; John James Quinn, "Democracy and Development," in Emmanuel Nnadozie, ed., *African Economic Development* (New York: Academic Press, 2003): 231–58.

12. Dankwart Rustow, "Transitions to Democracy: Toward a Dynamic Model," *Comparative Politics* 2, 3 (April 1970): 337–63; Guillermo O'Donnell, and Philippe C. Schmitter, *Transitions from Authoritarian Rule: Tentative Conclusions About Uncertain Democracies* (Baltimore: Johns Hopkins University Press, 1986); Huntington, *The Third Wave*; Stephan Haggard and Robert R. Kaufman, *The Political Economy of Democratic Transitions* (Princeton: Princeton University Press, 1995); Bratton and van de Walle, *Democratic Experiments*; Thomas Carothers, "The End of the Transition Paradigm," *Journal of Democracy* 13, 1 (January 2002): 5–21; and

Lisa Anderson, ed., *Transitions to Democracy* (New York: Columbia University Press, 1999).

13. For example, see Ibid; and Valarie Bunce, "Rethinking Recent Democratization: Lessons from the Postcommunist Experience," *World Politics* 55, 2 (2003): 167–92. Rustow did not write only about regional transitions, see Rustow, "Transitions to Democracy." Bratton and van de Walle, *Democratic Experiments* is an exception as they do run regression analyses to test which path dependent processes predict in the African cases. Finally, O'Neil wrote about structural preconditions that affected the transition as they played out in Hungary, see O'Neil, "Revolution from Within."

14. O'Neil, "Revolution from Within," p. 580.

15. See Bratton and van de Walle, *Democratic Experiments*. Also, South African has been routinely considered to have a distinct developmental trajectory due to its apartheid past, it lack of ODA from international sources, and its much higher level of economic development.

16. Ibid.

17. They found ODA and structural adjustment to be insignificant in explaining the variation in the transition to democracy.

18. Carothers, "The End of the Transition Paradigm."

19. See Bratton and van de Walle, *Democratic Experiments*. They share this, and the next, assumption.

20. For how elections are key to later liberalizations, see Lindberg, *Democracy and Elections*.

21. Carothers, "The End of the Transition Paradigm," p. 8.

22. Ibid. See also Bunce, "Rethinking Recent Democratization," pp. 170–71.

23. Przeworski and Limongi, "Modernization;" See also Barbara Geddes, "What Do We Know about Democratization after 20 Years? *Annual Review of Political Science* 2 (1999): 115–44.

24. Later research would argue that Przeworski and Limongi ("Modernization") went too far in their complete repudiation of endogenous influence on democratization. Charles Boix and Susan C. Stokes, "Endogenous Democratization," *World Politics* 55, 4 (2003): 517–49.

25. Boix and Stokes, "Endogenous Democratization."

26. Ryan Kennedy, "The Contradiction of Modernization: A Conditional Model of Endogenous Democratization," *The Journal of Politics* 72, 3 (July 2010): 785–98.

27. Robert H. Bates, "The Impulse to Reform in Africa," in Jennifer A. Widner, ed., *Economic Change and Political Liberalization in sub-Saharan Africa* (Baltimore: The Johns Hopkins University Press, 1994): 13–28; Nicolas van de Walle, "Neopatrimonialism and Democracy in Africa, with an Illustration from Cameroon," in Widner, *Economic Change*: 129–57; Peter M. Lewis, "Economic Reform and Political Transition in Africa: The Quest for a Politics of Development," *World Politics* 49, 1 (1996): 92–129; and Bratton and van de Walle, *Democratic Experiments*. Haggard and Kaufman make an argument about crisis transitions for Latin American and Asia, though they hold that the conditions under which the reforms occur that change their trajectory, see Haggard and Kaufman, *The Political Economy*.

28. For an argument about mass mobilization and transitions in Eastern Europe, see Bunce, "Rethinking Recent Democratization."

29. Bratton and van de Walle, *Democratic Experiments*; Lewis, "Economic Reform."

30. See Diamond, "Third Wave Over?" Also, the Gambian government was overthrown in 1994.

31. John W. Harbeson, "Externally Assisted Democratization: Theoretical Issues and African Realities," in John W. Harbeson and Donald Rothchild, eds., *Africa in World Politics: The African State System in Flux* (Boulder, CO: Westview Press, 2000): 235–62.

32. Steven Levitsky and Lucan A. Way, "Rethinking the International Dimension of Regime Change." *Comparative Politics* 38, 4 (July 2006): 379–400.

33. Ibid., p. 388.

34. For examples, see Huntington, *The Third Wave*; Harbeson, "Externally Assisted Democratization;" Marina Ottaway, "African Democratisation and the Leninist Option," *Journal of Modern African Studies* 35, 1 (March 1997): 1–15; Clapham, *African and the International System*; Carol Lancaster, "Africa in World Affairs," in Harbeson and Rothchild, *Africa in World Politics*, pp. 208–34; Joseph, "The Reconfiguration of Power;" Joseph, "Africa, 1990–1997;" and Thomas M. Callaghy and John Ravenhill, eds., *Hemmed In: Responses to Africa's Economic Decline* (New York: Columbia University Press, 1993).

35. See Gordon Cumming, *Aid to Africa: French and British Policies from the Cold War to the New Millennium* (Aldershot: Ashgate, 2001), p. 101; Jean-Paul Fuchs, *Pour une politique de développement efficace, maîtrisée, et transparente: Rapport au Premier minister* (Paris: La documentation Française, 1995), p. 48; John James Quinn and David J. Simon, "Plus ça change, . . . : The Allocation of French ODA to Africa During and After the Cold War," *International Interactions* 32 (2006): 295–318.

36. Here the term legacy variable refers to any long-standing structural variables in place prior to the end of the Cold War (pre-1989, and it is measured as an average from 1979 to 1989). The importance of personal action or path dependent contingencies during a transition is not denied: these events are black-boxed in this analysis. However, if these variables that arose during the path dependent contingencies matter more than the systematic variables, then no significant co-variation with the structural variables would be found as all that would matter is the variation following the path dependent random walk, not the probabilities of following the structural predisposition. To the degree that the path dependent somewhat randomize variables (dependent on deals, personalities, and quirks of the case) matter, they might strengthen or weaken the effects of these variables, depending on accidental covariation. Therefore, the expectation is that some structural variables travel well and are generalizable.

37. Others tend to apply it to all of sub-Saharan Africa equally. I argue that some are more neo-patrimonial than others, i.e., those with MSO. Recently some scholars argued that neo-patrimonialism was quite varied in Africa, or they have more resources to distribute than others. See Anne Pitcher, Mary H. Moran, and Michael Johnston, "Rethinking Patrimonialism and Neopatrimonialism in Africa." *African Studies Review* Volume 52, Number 1 (April 2009): 125–56.

38. Bratton and van de Walle, *Democratic Experiments*, p. 458.

39. Bates, "The Impulse to Reform;" Thomas M. Callaghy, *The State-Society Struggle: Zaire in Comparative Perspective* (New York: Columbia University Press Callaghy 1984); Clapham, *African and the International System*; Pierre Englebert, *State Legitimacy and Development in Africa* (Boulder, CO: Lynne Rienner Publishers, 2000); Goran Hyden, *African Politics in Comparative Perspective* (Cambridge: Cambridge University Press 2006); Richard Sandbrook, *The Politics of Africa's Economic Recovery* (Cambridge: Cambridge University Press, 1993); Quinn, *The Road oft Traveled*; Roger Tangri, *The Politics of Patronage in Africa: Parastatals, Privatization, and Private Enterprise* (Trenton, NJ: Africa World Press, Inc., 1999); van de Walle "Neopatrimonialism and Democracy;" Crawford Young, "The Third Wave of Democratization in Africa: Ambiguities and Contradictions," in Joseph, *State, Conflict, and Democracy*, pp. 15–38.

40. I hold that post-Cold War shifts in norms matter, but they are not measured directly in the model. But to the degree they matter, they should matter equally across the two categories of countries in the analysis and result in differences in the second period.

41. Paul Kennedy, *African Capitalism: The Struggle for Ascendancy* (Cambridge: Cambridge University Press, 1988); Tony Killick, *Development Economics in Action: A Study of Economic Policies in Ghana* (London: Heinemann, 1979); Stephen D. Krasner, *Structural Conflict: The Third World Against Global Liberalism* (Berkeley & Los Angeles: University of California, 1985); and Quinn, *Road oft Traveled*.

42. For state ownership and control of assets, see Barbara Grosh and Rwekaza S. Mukandala, eds., *State-Owned Enterprises in Africa* (Boulder, CO: Lynne Rienner Publishers, 1994); Quinn, *The Road oft Traveled*; D. Michael Shafer, "Capturing the Mineral Multinationals: Advantage or Disadvantage," *International Organization* 37, 1 (Winter 1983): 93–119; Tangri, *The Politics of Patronage*; Sandbrook, *The Politics of Economic Recovery*; World Bank. *Sub-Saharan Africa: From Crisis to Sustainable Growth* (Washington, D.C.: World Bank, 1989); World Bank, *Accelerated Development in Sub-Saharan Africa: an Agenda for Action* (Washington, D.C.: World Bank1981); Crawford Young, *Ideology and Development in Africa* (New Haven: Yale University Press, 1982). No clear predictors of which countries nationalized and which ones have been established to the best of my knowledge. In fact, some of the richest countries at independence chose this course, such as Ghana and Zambia.

43. For an earlier iteration of this argument, see Quinn, *Road oft Traveled*.

44. Thomas M. Callaghy, "Africa and the World Political Economy: More Caught between a Rock and a Hard Place," in Harbeson and Rothchild, *Africa in World Politics*, p. 46. Moreover, he also show that capital flight for these years amounted to 80% of GDP for Africa for the same year (compared to less than 20% for the two Asia areas. Ibid.

45. World Bank, *Sub-Saharan Africa*; World Bank, *Accelerated Development*.

46. See Malcolm Gladwell, *The Tipping Point: How Little Things Can Make a Big Difference* (London: Little Brown and Co., 2000).

47. See Albert O. Hirschman, *Exit, Voice, and Loyalty: Responses to Decline in Firms, Organizations, and States* (Cambridge, MA: Harvard University Press, 1970). Also, minority ownership confers power, but owners of a miniority of shares would

be more accountable to the wishes of the other stockholders, who would not accept financial losses or high levels of corruption which eliminated profits; see Quinn, "The Effects of Majority State Ownership."

48. Bates, *Markets and States*; Quinn, *The Road oft Traveled*; Sandbrook *The Politics of Africa's Economic Recovery*; Tangri, *The Politics of Patronage*; World Bank, *Accelerated Development*; van de Walle *African Economies*; World Bank *Sub-Saharan* Africa.

49. Mancur Olson, *The Logic of Collective Action: Public Goods and the Theory of Groups* (Cambridge, MA: Harvard University Press, 1965).

50. George R. G. Clarke, "Why Don't African Manufacturing Enterprises Export More? The Role of Trade Policy, Infrastructure Quality and Enterprise Characteristics (October 2004). Available at SSRN: http://ssrn.com/abstract=602661-- though he used firm-level data from a later period.

51. See Quinn, "The Managerial Bourgeoisie;" and Quinn, *Road oft Traveled*.

52. World Bank, *World Bank Development Report*, p. 82.

53. To use Marxist terms, the economic substructure that supported the political superstructure was not sustainable, therefore, neither was the political superstructure upon which it rested.

54. Ronald Rogowski, *Commerce and Coalitions: How Trade Affects Domestic Political Alignments* (Princeton: Princeton University Press, 1989).

55. Quinn, *The Road oft Traveled*.

56. See Theda Skocpol, "Brining the State Back In: Strategies of Analysis in Current Research," in Peter B. Evans, Dietrich Rueschemeyer, and Theda Skocpol, eds., Brining the State Back In (Cambridge: Cambridge University Press, 1985): 3–43.

57. Quinn, "The Managerial Bourgeoisie;" and Quinn, *The Road oft Traveled*; John J. Quinn, "The Impact of State Ownership of Resources on Economic and Political Development in Sub-Saharan Africa," *Ufahamu* Vol. XXI, No 1and 2 (Winter/Spring 1993): 60–79.

58. Quinn, *The Road oft Traveled*, p. 39. this number includes 25 countries, but no CFA countries as France controlled the exchange policy.

59. Ibid; Mike F. Lofchie, "The New Political Economy in Africa," in David E. Apter and Carl G. Rosberg, eds., *Political Development and the New Realism in Sub-Saharan Africa* (Charlottesville: University of Virginia Press, 1994): 160–65; Bates, *Market and States*; World Bank, *Accelerated Development*.

60. For overview of Heckscher-Ohlin, see Richard E. Caves, Ronald W. Jones, *World Trade and Payments: an Introduction* (Boston : Little, Brown, 1985).

61. See *Africa South of the Sahara 2007*, (London; Europa Publications Limited, 2006), S.V. countries.

62. For African lack of capita or abundant labor, see Rogowski, *Commerce and Coalitions*.

63. World Bank, *Accelerated Development*. Sandbrook, *The Politics of Africa's Economic Recovery*; Tangri, *The Politics of Patronage*.

64. For an overview of Stolper-Samuelson, see Caves and Jones, *World Trade and Payments*; for application to politics, see Rogowski *Commerce and Coalitions*; for application to Africa; see Quinn, *Road oft Traveled*.

65. Jeffrey Sachs, "Conditionality, Debt Relief, and the Developing Country Debt Crisis," in Jeffrey Sachs, ed., *Developing Country Debt and the World Economy National Bureau of Economic Research* (Chicago: University of Chicago Press, 1989): 275–84; Carol Lancaster, "Economic Restructuring in Sub-Saharan Africa", *Current History: Africa* 1989 (May 1989).

66. Callaghy, "Africa and the World Political Economy."

67. van de Walle, *African Economies*; Cumming, *Aid to Africa*; Lancaster, "Africa in World Affairs."

68. Stephen Brown, "Foreign Aid and Democracy Promotion: Lessons from Africa," *The European Journal of Development Research*, 17, 2 (June 2005): 179–198.

69. Levitsky and Way, "Linkage versus Leverage."

70. Lewis, "Economic Reform;" Bratton and van de Walle, *Democratic Experiments*.

71. World Bank, *Accelerated Development*, p. 1.

72. Ibid., p. 2.

73. Ibid. p. 26.

74. Bates, *Markets and States*.

75. William Reno, "Africa's Weak States, Non-state Actors, and the Privatization of Interstate Relations," in Harbeson and Rothchild, *Africa in World Politics*: 286–307.

76. Bates argues that natural resources that can be taxed make countries less likely to democratize. See Bates, "The Impulse to Reform."

77. For mineral resource curse, see P. Stevens, "Resource Impact: Curse or Blessing? A Literature Survey." *Journal of Energy Literature* 9, 1 (2003): 1–42; R. M. Auty, ed., *Resource Abundance and Economic Development* (Oxford, UK: Oxford University Press, 2001); Jeffrey D. Sachs and Andrew M. Warner, "Fundamental Sources of Long-Run Growth." *American Economic Review*. 87, 2 (1997); Michael Ross, "The Political Economy of the Resource Curse," *World Politics* Vol. 51 (1999): 297–322; and Terry Lynn Karl, *The Paradox of Plenty: Oil Booms and Petro-States* (Berkeley and Los Angeles: University of California, 1997). For tie to majority state ownership, see John James Quinn and Ryan Conway, "The Mineral Resource Curse in Africa: What Role Does Majority State Ownership Play?" Centre for the Study of African Economies (CSAE). African Economic Development. St. Catherine's College, Oxford. March 16–18. http://www.csae.ox.ac.uk/conferences/2008-edia/papers/285-quinn.pdf

78. Zambian copper, for example, lost money in the 1990s. "Overpricing Zambia's Family Silver," *The Economist* 347, 8067 (May 9, 1998); and "Selling the Family Copper," *The Economist* 353, 814 (November 6, 1999). The theory was tested including and excluding Zambia, but the results did not differ significantly.

79. Equatorial Guinea, Chad, and Sudan are listed as new oil countries.

80. William Reno, *Warlord Politics* (Boulder, CO: Lynne Rienner Publishers, 1998).

81. Ibid. He also suggested that Nigeria was a good candidate for this outcome as well.

82. Bates, "The Impulse to Reform;" Barbara Grosh, "Though the Structural Adjustment Minefield: Politics in an Era of Economic Liberalization," in Widner, ed., *Economic Change*: 29–46; and Lewis, "Economic Reform."

83. Grosh, "Though the Structural Adjustment Minefield," p. 43.

84. Quinn, *The Road oft Traveled*, pp. 176–77.

85. Such as military pro-democratic intrusion and role of protests. See Joel D. Barkan, "Regime Change in Africa," *Journal of Democracy* 10, 2 (1999) 165–70.

86. Geddes, "What do we know about democratization?"

87. Political or civil rights run from 1 (the most democratic) to 7 (the most authoritarian). Political and civil rights were averaged. And as described below, Namibia, Somalia, and South Africa are dropped for consistency. I also rounded throughout.

88. Again, excluding South Africa, its former colony Southwest Africa (now Namibia), and Somalia, as well as the countries which found new mineral or oil in the transition period. They were not included in MSO-WOM.

89. Quinn, *The Road oft Traveled*, p. 39. This includes 25 countries, but no CFA countries as France controlled the exchange rate policy. Here MSO oil and mining are clumped with MSO-WOM.

90. Ibid; Lofchie, "The New Political Economy in Africa;" World Bank, *Accelerated Development*.

91. For example, see John Ravenhill, "Africa's Continuing Crises: The Elusiveness of Development," in John Ravenhill, ed., *Africa in Economic Crisis* (New York: Columbia University Press, 1986): 1–43. And this is before most countries were exposed to systematic structural adjustment requirements on the part of the World Bank, see Lancaster, "Economic Restructuring."

92. Calculated from World Bank, *African Development Indicators*, 1992, (Washington D.C: World Bank), Table 5–36, p. 98.

93. Calculated from Ibid., Table 8–8, p. 231.

94. Calculated from Ibid., Table 5–36, p. 98. This does not mean that other Africa countries did wonderfully, just that they did better within a regional comparison. Countries with oil or mineral export sectors were excluded, as they are notorious for declines in their competing exporting sectors, especially agricultural exports. This is referred to as the mineral resource curse, see endnote 77.

95. Calculated from World Bank, *African Development Indicators*, Table 8–8, p. 231.

96. Taken from World Bank, Win*Stars 4.2, Manufactured Exports ad % or total exports. However, many missing data are evident. (Given the declines in agricultural exports, this 4.57% represents a percentage of a diminishing denominator).

97. And they did not have the declining agricultural sector!

98. Ibid. Just for clarification, I am not arguing that without MSO African countries would be NICs, rather that MSO made economic developmental problems worse in the region. No panacea is offered; Africa would still have had other challenges, but these countries would have experienced overall higher levels of growth, though lower than the most rapid developers.

99. And it was statistically significant at 10%, but this is the population, not a sample.

100. This is to remove any doubts about resource curse effects affecting this subcategory.

101. This data came from World Bank *African Development Indicators*, 2000. SV current account %GNI. This is an average from 1980–1989.

102. Taken from UNCTAD. *World Investment Directory* http://www.unctad.org/en/docs/iteiit20075_en.pdf Table 1, p. 3. Accessed 6/8/10.

103. All the data in this section, unless otherwise stated, come from Bratton and van de Walle's data in *Democratic Experiments*. Aid flows and debt are from 1989, while growth is averaged from 1965 to 1989.

104. However, the frequency of protests, the key variable for Bratton and van de Walle in *Democratic Experiments*, is lower for MSO countries at 6.23, compared to non-MSO or mineral or oil exporting countries, at 10.54.

105. This gives us an average of eleven years before and after Africa's transition period for most data. Since Bratton and van de Walle's date the transition to democracy begin with Namibia's change in 1989, and since this country is excluded, the two periods are before and after their transition period. Also, the use of two periods is a better test of the theory than panel data would provide. Panel data would require the assumption that year 1 in period one would predict year 1 in period 2 well, and that it would predict year 1 in period 2 better than it could predict year 2 in period 2 or year 4 in period 2. The claims are that—on average—legacies from the first period affect trends the second period.

106. This could be something to be test in the future, after the initial ground is set. However, if this test produces no fruit, there is not point.

107. Thus, this view of democracy that key components of democracy are really fragments of accountability. Richard L. Sklar, "Developmental Democracy," *Comparative Studies in Society and History* 29, 4 (October 1987): 686–714. Joseph also raises this debate. See, Joseph, "The Reconfiguration of Power."

108. The exception is Zimbabwe where I run data from 1980–1989, because it was still under white minority rule (and not considered to be independent by many) until 1979/1980.

109. See data at: http://www.freedomhouse.org/template.cfm?page=1. The numbers are subtracted from 8 to be inverted. Therefore, the political and civil rights scores were added together and divided by 2. Then the 11-year period was added up and divided by 11. Data from Polity IV did not code as many countries and too many countries were in transition or anarchy, leading to missing data or having anarchic countries coded a 0. Under this coding scheme Somalia or DRC under war was more democratic (and less bad) then mildly autocratic countries. This is clearly a Lockean view, as opposed to a Hobbesian one. The death toll for the region after the collapse of Mobutu suggests the latter perspective.

110. This is defined this as five years or more. Logically, long enough to have private sectors to wither on the vine and have legacy effects set in.

111. MSO is when the government owns more than 50% or of most capital intensive industries. The most important sources for coding were these: "The Library of Congress Country Studies Website: http://lcweb2.loc.gov/frd/cs/cshome.html; Quinn, *Road oft Traveled*; Quinn, "Managerial Bourgeoisie;" and Quinn, "The Effects of Majority State Ownership; 'Leslie L. Rood, "Nationalisation and Indigenisation in Africa," *Journal of Modern African Studies* 14, 2 (1976):427–47; *Africa South of the Sahara*, S.V. (various years and countries); and Kennedy, *African Capitalism*; and Investment Promotion Network at Pananet at www.ipanet.com., and

"The Library of Congress Country Studies Website," at http://lcweb2.loc.gov/frd/cs/cshome.html. One check comes from J. Gwartney, R. Lawson, and W. Block. *Economic Freedom of the World*, 1975–1995 (Vancouver: The Fraser Institute, 1996). Where their (IIB) index registers a two or less, I code as a 1; where it was an 8 or higher, I code as a zero.

112. For example, Jennifer Widner, "Political Reform in Anglophone and Francophone African Countries," in Widner, *Economic Change*: 49–79, p. 51.

113. Data from Bratton and van de Walle data set obtained their data set from The South African Data Archive (ICPSR). International- University Consortium for Political and Social Research (ICPSR). Political Regimes and Regime Transitions in Africa, 1910 [sic (1989)]—1994. Michigan, Ann Arbor: ICPSR –producer, 1997. South African Data Archive- distributor, 2000. Given the disorder of Somalia, it is excluded.

114. Including France as an independent dummy variable would lead to multicollinearity. When it was included, the VIF [Variance inflation factor] was greater than four. Including categories with two of fewer would capture country effects more likely than colonial ones.

115. I leave out dictator, as all of the variables included would lead to the dummy variable trap. Also, with its inclusion, the VIF was >4. Plebiscitary was also dropped with a VIF>10 hence creating multicolinearity.

116. Namibia has no data from the first period as it was still under colonial rule. South African is often treated as distinct from the region. It had an apartheid past, leading to international isolation. In fact, South Africa did not receive ODA until 1993. See World Bank, *World Development Report 1997* (Washington, DC: World Bank, 1997), Table 12.1, p. 305.

117. The source was Bratton and van de Walle, *Democratic Experiments*. I also had included the legacy variable of the number of past elections, but it introduced multicollinearity.

118. Adding more would create multicollinearity.

119. Source, Bratton and van de Walle, *Democratic Experiments*.

120. This variable is the average of real GDP per capital chain series from Penn World tables, 1979–1989.

121. Source: Bratton and van de Walle, *Democratic Experiments*.

122. William Easterly and Ross Levine, "Africa's Growth Tragedy: Policies and Ethnic Divisions," *Quarterly Journal of Economics*, 112, 4 (November 1997): 1203–50.

123. The original source was Charles Lewis Taylor and Michael C. Hudson. *World Handbook of Political and Social Indicators* 2nd Edition (New Haven: Yale University Press, 1982). I obtained them from http//:weber.ucsd.edu\~proeder\elf.htm. Checked in March 2006. This variable is mostly considered to be time invariant.

124. Englebert, *State Legitimacy and Development*. Data available at http://www.politics.pomona.edu/penglebert/

125. Michael Ross, "Does Oil Hinder Democracy?" *World Politics* 53, 3 (2001): 325–61; Nathan Jensen and Leonard Wantchekon, "Resource Wealth and Political Regimes in Africa," *Comparative Political Studies* 37 (September 2004): 816, 26p.

126. Equatorial Guinea, Chad, and Sudan are listed as new oil/ mineral countries.

127. Huntington, *The Third Wave*; Samuel P. Huntington, *The Clash of Civilizations and the Remaking of the World Order* (New York: Simon and Shuster, 1996); for overview of the debate as well as empirical findings, see Manu I. Midlarsky, "Democracy and Islam: Implications for Civilizational Conflict and the Democratic Peace," *International Studies Quarterly* 42 (1998): 485–511.

128. I would like to thank a prior anonymous reviewer for this suggestion. The data represent the percent of the years in which a civil war occured from 1979–89. Taken from Correlates of War database, intra-war. http://www.correlatesofwar.org/cow2%20data/WarData/IntraState/Intra-State%20War%20Format%20(V%203-0).htm

129. Marina Ottaway, "From Political Opening to Democracy," in Marina Ottaway, ed., *Democracy in Africa: The Hard Road Ahead* (London and Boulder: Lynne Rienner Publishers 1997): 1–15; Jeffrey Herbst, "The Fall of Afro-Marxism," *Journal of Democracy* 1, 3 (Summer 1990): 92–101.

130. I used the coding from Peter J. Schraeder, *African Politics and Society: A Mosaic in Transformation* 2nd Edition. Belmont, CA: 2004, p. 132. However, I coded Zimbabwe as Afro-Marxist as this was their officially espoused ideology. I also checked these against, Herbst, "The Fall of Afro-Marxism;" Edmond J. Keller and Donald Rothchild, eds., *Afro-Marxist Regimes: Ideology and Public Policy* (Boulder, CO: Lynne Rienner Publishers, 1987); and Young, *Ideology and Development*.

131. France is excluded as to reduce multicollinearity. So the other colonial dummies are understood as French colonization and the few independents. The Variance Inflation factor needs to be less than 4.

132. The VIF was quite high at >11 for number of elections. It was probably most collinear with previous levels of political and civil rights, though colonial legacy would also correlate with the number of past-elections. When both plebiscitary with comp were in the same model, the VIF was above 10.

133. However, no necessary correlation existed between the other variables for types of rule and the freedom house numbers.

134. I used averages from two periods and OLS because this is a better test of our theory than panel data would provide. Also, some of our data are from only 1989, from Bratton and van de Walle *Democratic Experiments*. The use of panel data requires the assumption that year 1 in period one would predict year 1 in period 2 well, and that it would predict year 1 in period 2 better than it could predict year 2 in period 2 or year 4 in period 2. I do not claim so strong a causal link. The claims are that—on average—legacies from the first period affect trends the second period—but not the variance within the second period per se. As such, movement around the mean in each period is not predicted by movement around the mean in the first—which is the implication of panel data: that there is a one-to one correspondence data point to data point. As a result, this methodological procedure is too exact to use in this instance. I understand that panel data would allow country intercepts, but it does not answer the question being posed. Also, the correlation between 1995–2005 with 2014 levels of freedoms were 0.82 (Pearson's R), and it was significant at $p => 0.01$, and the average change was an increase in rights of 0.08 (FH).

135. Although civil and AfroMarxism, were slightly impacted.

136. See above endnote concerning these countries.

137. Test for heteroskedasticity was near $p < .05$, so I ran it with robust corrections. All models without the adjusted R square fit this same criterion. Since MSO has been shown to be linked to more inward-oriented policies, corruption, and lower levels of political, this could impact (directly or indirectly) levels of wealth, growth, and even civil wars. See Quinn Op. cit. So these are left out of #3.

138. The independent variables included in this estimation were majority state ownership without mining or oil, political and civil rights from 79–89, new oil or mining, civil war, Afro-Marxism and the colonial dummies of British, Belgian, and Portuguese. The variables considered to be (potentially) endogenous were these: majority state ownership without mining or oil, political and civil rights from 79–89, Afro-Marxism, and civil war. All the independent variable from model one were used as instruments. I included all the colonial dummies in the estimation as independent variables and as IVs in the 2SLS as some prior reviews have suggested that colonization should be the real cause and not this variable.

139. The score test for heteroskedasticity was calculated on each model where feasible. None was found in models 1 and 2. Also, the variance inflation factor was used as is mentioned elsewhere in the paper. Model 3 used robust correction after finding evidence of heteroskedasticity.

140. See Gwartney, Lawson, and Block. *Economic Freedom of the World.*

141. When included, MSO remained significant.

142. Running the regression with and without Zambia resulted in the same outcomes vis-à-vis sign and significance for this variable. In an earlier version of this chapter, Zambia was included in this group as the mining revenues dried up during the second period. However, the model works either way. For simplicity, Zambia was excluded in this version.

143. Though I did run their equation from page 224, Model F, which uses a similar dependent variable and included our variable of interest. The result was that MSO was positively and significantly linked with later levels of freedoms. Their variable for military intervention remained significant, though their other variables, including protests, became insignificant. This does demonstrate a robust rejection of their finding, but it shows that MSO-WOM is robust.

144. For example, see Catharine Newbury, *The Cohesion of Oppression: Clientship and Ethnicity in Rwanda, 1860–1960* (New York: Columbia University Press, 1988); see also Mahmood Mamdani, *When Victims become Killers: Colonialism, Nativism, and the Genocide in Rwanda* (Princeton: Princeton University Press, 2001).

Chapter 9

Conclusions

When Elephants Fight

In the wake of two global geopolitical shifts, WWII and the end of the Cold War, African nations experienced significant, if not revolutionary, changes in their political and economic institutions and practices. As outlined in the first chapter, these changes in Africa's institutions and practices can be linked to the several aspects of the new geopolitical environments that emerged: the new system leaders, or would-be leaders, tried to establish positive and negative incentives to secure allies (or ward off potential adversaries) seeking to establish their leadership in the international system. They created both bilateral and multilateral incentives to achieve foreign policy goals, including access to markets, assess to aid, and even coercion or military force. Each geopolitical shift created a window of opportunity for a new equilibrium to be created, allowing the rising powers to institutionalize the newly arising norms or their preferred norms. The analysis has shown that system leaders tried to shape the environment to be as beneficial, or non-hostile for themselves as possible, while maintaining leadership within the international system.

Moreover, in the wake these significant geopolitical realignments, "learning" and lessons about what caused the shifts takes place: approaches, ideas, and ideologies associated with the "losing" camp weakened in their legitimacy, especially vis-a-vis results, while those of the "winning" camp were enhanced. Ideas mattered as independent sources of power, but they also gained strength as reflections of the material resources placed behind them. Changes in the power of ideas also resulted in changes in their moral legitimacy, which shifted after each geopolitical realignment.

Within this context of newly shaped incentives, along with the new lessons drawn from the recent change, the set of constraints and opportunities facing other leaders, especially those of weaker nations, were transformed. Leaders and would-be leaders of sub-Saharan African states, who were the most dependent on external resources to hold power, have to respond to these significant geopolitical shifts in power, ideas, norms, and sets of incentives in order to maximize their chances of obtaining or maintaining their domestic power. These responses became reflected in the choices regarding the nature of their domestic political and economic institutions as well as in their economic and political foreign policies.

In this work, I have illustrated how two widely recognized and significant geopolitical changes in the international system have led to changes in international constraints and opportunities facing the political leaders (potential and actual) of African political movements. I explored how these two geopolitical changes occurred in a relatively quick fashion, which meant that both region-wide changes in African institutions occurred within particular intellectual and ideological contexts. I then discussed how these changes in the material and intellectual environments impacted the options of African leaders, or would-be leaders, in regard to obtaining or maintaining power or guiding their nations toward the goal of development. In their collective responses to new international material, intellectual, and ideational forces, African societies have undertaken two region-wide overhauls or changes in domestic political and economic institutions, as well as in their economic foreign policies.

In the first geopolitical shift, we saw the decline of European colonial powers and the rise of American and Soviet power in the wake of WWII. In this context, colonialism became untenable for several reasons. First, both of the rising powers opposed colonialism, though their opposition stemmed from differing mixes of self-interest and principle. On the one hand, America had long opposed colonialism: it shut markets to American traders and firms, it was at odds with the US free trade agenda, and its continuation was seen as a potential source of radicalization of newly emerging leaders in the developing world. The ethos justifying European colonial empires was also at odds with America's emphasis on self-determination and democracy. On the other hand, the USSR opposed colonization as a means of gaining allies among the developing world, as well as being part and parcel of its anti-imperialism ideology, which saw capitalism at the heart of imperialism (and hence colonialism).[1] It was also partially a missionary zeal of conversion of those who could be converted, and the recently colonized countries were likely candidates. The Soviet leaders who found themselves at the helm of the socialist/ communist movement necessarily had to oppose colonialism, though it created opportunities for them to gain allies in the larger Cold War struggle.

Second, the rising diplomatic, military, and economic power of the US and USSR was clearly greater than the diplomatic, military, and economic power of the declining colonial powers, UK and France. In fact, these latter nations were junior partners to the US in NATO (until France (partially) withdrew), and both were under the US umbrella protecting Western Europe (although both did have nuclear weapons). This disproportionate power gave both the US and USSR more ability to back the new norms of national self-determination and anti-colonialism. Importantly, especially among the Western allies, American preferences for free trade became enshrined into treaties, institutions, and new international norms governing access to military, diplomatic, and economic resources. For example, the US held a reluctant UK to the Atlantic charter following the war. Also, the free trade preferences of the US and UK (outside of their colonies) were enshrined into the Bretton Woods institutions of the International Monetary Fund, the World Bank, and the General Agreement on Tariffs and Trade. Moreover, Marshal Fund money was (partially) tied to behavior which would lead to rising free trade and the quick decolonization of the former colonies. The Dutch had such funds suspended as a result of their military efforts to retake Indonesia.

Fifth, colonialism as an idea had become indefensible for intellectual and ideological reasons following the Second World War. It had been based upon views of racial hierarchy and the white man's burden which were clearly no longer seen as valid or internationally legitimate in the wake of the failed Nazi project. Moreover, the anti-Nazi, pro-national self-determination war propaganda spread beyond Europe to their empires and their people, and it helped fuel the international rise of nationalist sentiments which led to independence movements throughout the world, including sub-Saharan Africa. In addition, newly independent nations from earlier acts of decolonization used the United Nations as a center of anticolonial sentiments, which enshrined this norms of self-determination into a significant international institution. Even in the UK and France, growingly powerful voices were questioning the need and morality of maintaining their empires, though some interests in these countries continued with a full throated defense of colonization and empire.

Moreover, Africans, who long opposed colonization and its inherent racism and discrimination, were better able to mobilize resources to resist colonization and demand more African inclusion into positions of economic and political power. The rise of African nationalism clearly impacted European colonial leaders and their calculus of how long to press for continued colonization. The early demands for African political and economic inclusion soon gave way to demands for national independence. Moreover, the first African party to demand decolonization usually became the party that would go on to rule the newly independent African nation, but as a monopoly or near monopoly party. As African nationalist movements and political parties gained momentum, as the costs of colonial rule kept rising, as the returns colonization continued to decline, as left parties gained power in France and the UK—all in the context of changed international leaders and norms—colonization quickly gave way to independence.

The relatively rapid decolonization period in the context of a weak African civil society, poverty, and low levels of literacy helped facilitate a significant concentration of both economic and political power in the hands of the new leaders.[2] Prevailing ideologies of development and economic and political nationalism legitimized these practices as well. In this context, the emerging nationalist party was the giant in the field and easily could win elections and become the ruling party in most of African nations. With their relatively high level of power on a terrain of weak opponents, African leaders who gained the mantle of power found they could hold it indefinitely, unless overthrown in a coup. Once in power, these leaders, usually without penalty from the international community, began to consolidate more and more political power into their hands: they used access to state power to solidify their hold on power, using both compellence and coercion. Many countries "naturally" formed one-party states, many used access to, or denial of, state resources to come to this conclusion, and many banned opposition parties and jailed their leaders to bring this about. Moreover, fears of civil wars and ethnic conflict also bolstered the legitimacy of one-party states or dictatorships internationally. Thus, the ideas of the time, the self-interest of the superpowers of the time, and self-interests of early African leaders reinforced these tendencies for the consolidation of political power. The one-party or no-party regime became the de facto reality for most nations of the continent.

A similar story can be told on the economic side (vis-à-vis the trends toward the concentration of economic power) following the end of WWII. Capitalism as an idea was weakened in Africa, given its association with colonization. Moreover, few actual African citizens had been allowed to own large-scale businesses (or much private property at all) under colonialism. Therefore, there was not a class or group of African citizens with either the self-interest or material resources to defend capitalism or its institutions. In fact, most property had been owned by either European or ethnic (non-black) minorities. The largest elements of the economic landscape were owned by the colonial state or by citizens of the colonizing state. The second tier was often composed of foreign-born traders and owners of small shops (such as Indians, Greeks, Lebanese et cetera). The bottom tier of the economic system comprised the indigenous Africans themselves, who engaged in the most labor-intensive activities.

In addition, the European owners of the economy, or the managers of the colonial bureaucracies who practiced active racial discrimination (e.g., color bar), found that they had few allies following independence. Therefore, they were in a difficult position when it came to defending their claims to property, especially as their claims to property were associated with the coercion of colonization. Moreover, socialism was seen by many as a potentially quick way for newly emerging states to develop. On the one hand, socialism's call for one-party rule was attractive to those trying to consolidate power. In addition, one-party rule was also useful for African elites trying to forge a sense of common identity, as was the consolidation of economic power into the hands of the people (but with the state elites in control). The resort to socialism, at least in part, also appeared to solve the problem of a missing indigenous economic business class. The relative success of the war economies of the US and UK, as well as Keynesian economics, gave credence to the idea that economic planning was a useful tool for overcoming strategic economic bottlenecks. Additionally, development economists (some running much further with Keynes's ideas) suggested that developing countries could not develop as Europe did under a free market. Moreover, intellectuals using dependency or world systems theory added support to arguments which advocated following a socialist development path. Finally, both China and the USSR appeared to be successful development role models at the time.

Also, economic nationalism, which was expressed as the desire to use state action to quickly ameliorate inequalities of economic ownership created under colonization, led many Third World leaders to pursue policies of nationalization, regardless of developmental ideology. This was seen by many as righting historic wrongs, even if it carried a socialist overtone. As mentioned elsewhere, even many nominally capitalist nations engaged in some nationalization or state creation of industries as an expression of economic nationalism.

The role of these ideas, along with American pragmatic foreign policy seeking to avoid radicalizing "moderate" socialist leaders to keep them from a firm embrace of the Soviets, gave leaders of weak states great leeway in pursuing a state-led development strategy. Openly aligning with the Soviets could result in penalties from the US, but otherwise the US was (officially) not hostile to such countries. Therefore, for example, the US did not move to reverse nationalizations of large corporations by Third World nations unless the latter were deemed communist, such as in Cuba. And America urged her allies to accept these losses.

Thus, the combination of the geopolitical interests of the great powers, the prevailing ideas of the time, the prior experience of racial discrimination and colonization, the intellectual milieu that supported or condoned state-led development, and the fear of ethnic wars or chaos, all helped reinforce the tendencies which led to the rapid consolidation of economic and political power in most states in sub-Saharan Africa. These events played themselves out usually within a decade and a half to two decades of the end of the Second World War. Not all African countries had the exact same levels of state control over the economy or one-party/military regimes, but most had one or more elements of these. The results were almost overdetermined methodologically, as many otherwise competing explanations appeared to all point in the same direction: given the international, regional, and domestic views of development ideas and political parties, the relative international autonomy of African leaders, soft African states, a weak civil society in most African states, and the intellectual legitimacy extended to state-led, one-party states and inward-oriented policies, as well as the ensuring international condoning of military coups d'état, all pointed in the direction of the concentration of so much power in the hands of so few.[3]

In the second geopolitical shift, we see the relatively rapid dissolution of the Soviet Union and the commensurate rise of the relative power of the US. At the time of this change, support for socialism, inward-oriented policies, and authoritarianism were in clear decline—even to the point of some triumphalism on the part of liberal (capitalist) democracy.[4] The presumptive champions of state socialism had quit the field of competition. Even those holding the idea of state ownership as a means of achieving national pride or goals were on the defensive as programs of privatization were becoming more common worldwide. Moreover, the relative autonomy of developing world leaders to set their own economic and foreign policy agendas became more constrained in important ways before the end of the Cold War, and this trend accelerated significantly thereafter. This was most evident in the changing nature of rising economic conditionality placed upon nations receiving additional loans or debt relief from the International Monetary Fund (IMF) and World Bank—which disproportionality impacted weaker, developing nations (of which African nations were clearly overrepresented). Moreover, it could be indirectly seen in these two institutions addressing the issue of "good governance," with its emphasis on accountability of government. This was undermining the norm of sovereignty for these nations insofar as they have to make changes to domestic political and economic rules, institutions, or policies to obtain more international aid. In addition, in 1990, the United States, France, and the United Kingdom all announced that countries not making significant changes toward "political liberalization" would receive less developmental aid. Other nations and institutions would follow suit. These changes in policies of IFIs and Western nations necessarily reduced the amount of relative autonomy of African leaders and their nations in their pursuit of gaining international sources of political and economic aid. Therefore, in this second period, we see international political, social, economic, and intellectual forces pushing for political and economic liberalization. Some of this push was out of the self-interest of the Western nations in accessing markets, while some of it was out of the belief that these policies would lead to more prosperity within African countries, especially in light of the past practices of sub-Saharan Africa during the Cold War which led to such negative outcomes.

Not only were the ideas of socialism and state involvement in the economy on the ropes internationally, but the experiment of consolidating so much economic and political power in the hands of the African political elites also gave clear evidence that state socialism and inward-oriented development policies constituted a failed approach to development in the region. In fact, as a result of the combination of inward-oriented development plans, dependence upon foreign oil supplies, and a poor record of increasing exports to earn hard currencies on the open market, many African nations suffered significant economic decline in the late 1970s and 1980s. Even oil-producing countries amassed large levels of international debt during this period. Importantly, many African countries experienced actual declines in per capita income through these decades, which necessarily reduced domestic legitimacy for these developmental approaches as well as for the leaders of these nations. Therefore, economic and political history provided significant evidence that this approach to development had not delivered on its promises of the 1960s.

Moreover, the level of debt burden, as well as debt as a percentage of exports, rose significantly in the wake of the two OPEC oil shocks. The neglect of the agricultural sector, which could have been a significant engine of growth in so many countries, exacerbated these problems. The result was even greater dependence of African elites and their societies upon Western donors and investment, and this aid was needed (or perceived to be needed) to maintain the political elites in power as well as to keep their domestic economies from imploding. So, in this second period, capitalism and democracy were seen as much more legitimate forms of organizing the economic and political systems of African states than they were in the immediate post-WWII period. This was true both internationally and regionally. There was a corresponding decrease in the legitimacy of state-led socialist development and the practice of inward-oriented development policies was shown not to to have failed as a means of escaping the expected capitalist pitfalls, such as underdevelopment.

In this second period, we again see region-wide changes in the political and economic institutions and policies of African nations in the face of these changing intellectual and material forces, though there was some variation in how "liberal" these new political and economic institutions were. This was partially a result of the potential social, political, and economic impacts of the material, intellectual, and ideational forces and self-interests swirling around and within the region and internationally. Although most international interests and rising norms appeared to militate toward political and economic liberalization, few African political elites had the same self-interests in having so much political and economic power escape their control.

Moreover, the initiation of political and economic liberalization agendas does not mean that mature democracy and capitalism emerges instantly; they have to be grown and nurtured: they cannot not just be transplanted as full-grown plants into new soil. Both capitalism and democracy require strong civil society and supporting institutions to do well, and they emerge over time: they are not just created spontaneously and instantly, despite some implicit (and sometimes explicit) ideological claims to the contrary.[5] Therefore, supporters of capitalism and democracy would be mostly doing so for ideological or intellectual reasons, and they would not likely be defending them out of short-term material self interest.

So in the second period, we see strong forces pushing both toward and against economic and political liberalization. On the one hand, many international forces and ideas were pushing in the direction of the political and economic liberalization for these nations and societies. The international and regional legitimacy was strongly in favor of the liberalization and the fragmentation of both economic and political power: as discussed previously, World Bank and IMF policies began making economic conditionality (and hence the liberalization of the economies) a requirement for debt relief or additional funding, and this trend deepened with the end of the Cold War. Also, the US and its allies had adopted the promotion of democracy and human rights as part of their foreign policy preferences, with direct links between political liberalization and aid in the early 1990s. Moreover, the legitimacy of democracy and liberal capitalism was seemingly overwhelmingly dominant right at the end of the Cold War. The Washington Consensus, as discussed previously in Chapter 5, was in full swing.

On the other hand, many aspects of African societies and economies militated against a rapid and significant liberalization of either the political or economic systems. For example, Africa may not have been ready for full-blown democracy at the end of the Cold War: African societies still suffered from low levels of civil society, low levels of wealth, relatively low levels of literacy, and low levels of economic development, as well as missing many of the other attributes many considered to be necessary for democracy to take root.[6] Many of Lipset's "social requisites" for democracy were still not in place in the region.[7] Moreover, the greatest potential beneficiaries of the changes in economic policy (private sector exporters and their employees) were quite politically weak or non-existent in many of these countries—especially in those nations which had followed strongly inward-oriented policies for several decades. In most places, exporters consisted primarily of small-scale farmers facing significant obstacles overcoming collective action costs.[8] Also many of the exporting sectors were still majority state-owned, which would be run for political power maximization, rather than economic efficiency.[9] Importantly, and linked to the prior point, few African countries had a powerful or rising capitalist class, even half a century after the end of the Second World War. The key to wealth in most countries remained in the political realm. The loss of political office was dangerous personally and could result in economic ruin as well. Moreover, any politician that allowed a political opening and lost office could potentially face charges of corruption by the new elites, either as a means to address injustices or as a means to eliminate a potential political rival from returning to power. Therefore, many of the most powerful, wealthiest, and best educated people in the region had self-interests in maintaining one-party, no-party (military), or (at the least) one-party dominant systems, in order to avoid risking all in truly competitive multiparty elections. Moreover, fighting a rear guard action against economic liberalization and keeping the most lucrative economic sectors (usually oil or mining) in state hands would help maintain the patronage system that allowed the dominant or majority party to remain in power. The leaders of African regimes had similar interests to earlier leaders: they wanted to maintain themselves in power as long as they possibly could. Therefore, the new leaders wanted the minimal amount of reform that would satisfy international donors as well as domestic social and political forces pushing for reforms, but which would allow as much as the prior patronage-based political systems to remain intact as possible.

Thus, with regional and domestic self-interest at odds, and with the combined power of American and Western European self-interests in political and economic reforms, as well as the widespread intellectual and academic support for reform, most of the region experienced a significant change in the outward appearance of their political and economic institutions. Nonetheless, the major political and economic structures were still controlled by the political elites. Reforms were implemented as a response to both international and domestic pressures, but they were implemented by reluctant reformers who wanted to keep the general arrangement of domestic power as similar to the prior structures as possible (especially for later reformers).[10] The result was massive shifts in economic policies that were potentially reversible, and some structural changes in privatization for the sectors of the economy which were losing money or which did not provide so many jobs to followers. But these were done to satisfy external constituencies and to turn the aid and investment spigots back on. Also, domestic social forces that had led to so many protests would have to be appeased enough with the level of reforms for the protests to stop. However, sectors of the economy which were creating economic resources or significant flows of foreign currency were usually either not privatized, or only done so slowly, reluctantly, and partially. In addition, the shift to the adoption of multiparty competition, especially in the latter rounds of election, rarely resulted in an immediate turnover in power from one party to another, though it had the potential to do so. Moreover, most African nations have maintained very high levels of government control and ownership of the economy and formal sector employment combined with one-party dominant systems.

Most African leaders were not able to resist changes to the one-party system: they still had to reform the systems enough to satisfy both domestic social forces and international donors in order to keep aid money flowing and to have protests stop, while remaining in political power. It was a delicate balancing act, and not all leaders taking this risk stayed in power. Bratton showed, in the early elections (1989–1994), that over a third of these founding elections resulted in a change in the chief executive (37.9%), while for the latter elections (1995–1997), only around 7% had lost power.[11] So even where the chances of electoral turnover were greatest, incumbents kept power in over 60% of the cases; however, even in loss, the leaders of the former dominant party (FDP) were likely to become the main opposition party, often later recapturing power.[12]

So the facades of power were changed, the chances of turnover and accountability rose, but most of the faces running the country often remained the same. This characterization can be seen on the political side with a region-wide shift to multiparty electoral systems, but where only nine countries became "free." Moreover, significant changes in economic policy took place, though they tended to be fiscal policies that could be reversed if the need arose.[13] And many formerly state-owned economic firms have been privatized or liquidated, though large mineral or oil exporting sectors, as well as the companies with the largest number of jobs, have tended to remain in state hands. As a rule, the less constrained the political leadership was by domestic or international forces, the less real the reforms and the more power maintained in the hands of the political elite.[14]

This point about reluctant real changes in the flow of economic and political power was illustrated in Chapter 8. The logic set out was that countries which had featured majority state ownership (MSO) of most capital-intensive industries, but which did not have or find a lucrative mining or oil exporting sector, were the most vulnerable to external pressures due to their inward-oriented policies that collapsed their exports from their comparative advantage, and which did not result in exporting of manufactures, oil, or minerals (see Chapter 8 for full logic). I found that these countries were, in fact, the ones with the largest absolute gains in political and civil rights between the two periods. Of all the countries with a two or more point gain (on the seven point scale), all but one had had majority state ownership but without a vibrant oil or mining exporting sector. Moreover, for all African countries not in this category, the average gain in rights was only 0.45, while for these particular countries, the average change was 2.95. So, it appears to be the case that international pressure was strong enough to be associated with a change to multiparty electoral regimes in nearly every regime in Africa, though the nations which were associated with the greatest real increase in political and civil rights were the countries which had featured MSO of their industries but without mining or oil (MSO-WOM). They could no longer maintain patronage systems, with their prior policy choices resulting in no real ability to export or pay back loans in international currency, especially once the international community changed its aid policies toward these nations.

Also, other variables predicted having higher levels of political and civil rights in the second period. First, prior levels of political and civil rights were a robust predictor: on average, freer countries were freer later, and more authoritarian countries were more authoritarian later, *ceteris paribus*. In addition, having been Afro-Marxist was found to be significantly and positively linked with higher levels of rights in one model, though this proved to be a less than robust finding.

The variables found to be negatively linked with later rights were civil war and Belgian colonization. Also, countries that found new mineral or oil exporting sectors in the transition period were significantly less likely to be associated with increased political and civil rights in the second period.

Nonetheless, despite the intention of elites reforming just enough to maintain international resources and gain social peace, it could turn out that the new institutions will result in the continued fragmentation of political and economic power. Over time, competitive elections may produce more accountability and freedoms than they currently provide.[15] Also, the privatizations that have taken place are unlikely to be reversed, and this may help create a bourgeois class independent of the political class. We have to remember that such a reversal is not impossible, as an example from Russia shows us: Putin renationalized key oil firms after their owners became interested in engaging in the political system (and he tossed one of the most important oligarchs in jail).[16] This is less likely to be done to non-politically threatening foreign corporations which tend to follow the doctrine of domicile.[17] Nonetheless, such actions in Africa remain unlikely because any country under programs of economic conditionality would have a very hard time getting the World Bank and IMF on board for raising money for a (re)nationalization. It would have to be a straight-up appropriation, or funds would have to be repaid out of later revenue flows. And these leaders would risk losing other sources of aid and FDI if it is seen as too aggressive.

In sum, the basic argument that significant shifts in global geopolitical power have led to later changes in African political and economic institutions and practices has been supported. The evidence is consistent with the theory, even if it is not proven beyond a doubt; nonetheless, it seems to meet a preponderance of the evidence at least. Although it is possible that simultaneous trends in the economies of Africa were so in tune that no international forces were truly at work, such a conclusion ignores so much of what people have said about the power of international aid regimes, the role of ideas in shaping preferences and agendas, the role of regional and international diffusion effects, and the presumption of so much power and international influence on the part of hegemons or great powers in the international relations literature.

GEOPOLITICAL SHIFTS IN THE NEAR TERM?

One clear conclusion that can be drawn from the above analysis is that another relatively rapid change in global geopolitical power, especially one accompanied with significant changes in the levels of legitimacy accorded to private markets and democracy, would result in another regional and nearly simultaneous shift in economic and political institutions in sub-Saharan Africa. Without such a shift, international institutions, international norms, regional institutions, and regional norms will likely continue to reinforce tendencies for more political and economic accountability. The African political elite's self-interest to exercise as much power as possible, however, will likely remain in tension or conflict with the other norms and institutions militating for the fragmentation of political and economic power.

Therefore, if no significant geopolitical shift appears in the near future, changes in the nature of the economic and political institutions of sub-Saharan Africa will be driven more by idiosyncratic domestic factors, and not likely on a continent-wide basis. Or we might see shifts of a sub-regional nature, as conflicts (and cooperation) can diffuse more likely among neighbors.[18] The tension between forces to consolidate power will play out against forces for the fragmentation of power on a country by country basis, though Western aid regimes will likely keep pressure on these countries to maintain at least a minimum level of political and economic accountability. To the degree that countries had more democracy after the transition, and more sources of societal power exist outside of state hands, then the greater the changes of maintaining these freedoms and keeping more fragments of political and economic power spread throughout society. However, to the degree that countries designed institutions only to look like electoral regimes, the more likely they are to remain as such, or even become less accountable. However, as institutions mature, and as particular politicians "age out" of the system, the built-in fragments of political and economic accountability systems may become stronger.

But we have to explore the following questions: Will African nations continue on their partial liberalization of political and economic institutions? Will such elections still be seen as merely de jure multiparty competitive systems or will they evolve over time to become de facto multiparty competitive systems? Will a new geo-political shift lead to new changes? Will the US and Europe keep an emphasis on its support for free trade, access to markets, democracy, and human rights? Such things are hard to predict, but a few rising trends are apparent.

THE WAR ON TERROR

It is likely, and apparent for some countries in sub-Saharan Africa, that being considered an important actor in the war on terror could be like allying with the US during the Cold War and lessen international pressure for increasing political and civil rights. Cooperating in opposing the rise of Islamic radical groups may become seen as a greater foreign policy need or good for the

West than the particular country's level of democracy and/or Western access to markets. In addition, countries that are seen as likely candidates for collapse and/or future terrorist havens, or ones which actively work with the US in finding and fighting terrorists, may get a pass on their level of political and economic liberalization, or level of human rights. For example, Ethiopia is an active participant in American interests in the Horn of Africa, and its government is considered to be authoritarian, but it is receiving quite high levels of American aid. In fact, in 2010, America was the largest contributor of aid to Ethiopia despite its overall low level of political and civil rights.[19] Nonetheless, it has held several rounds of elections, though they were not considered to be free and fair by most. Additionally, other countries, such as Somalia, Nigeria, Mali, and Niger, may also be in a similar situation given their regional and domestic issues vis-à-vis terrorism. So, some backslide in such countries may be condoned by Western donors and Western-backed institutions. Moreover, the recent examples of civil war and chaos in Libya and Syria may be seen as humbling for those who would otherwise pressure governments into changing too quickly.

GOOD GOVERNANCE/GOOD ECONOMIC POLICY

Within this new period, it may turn out that some leaders also get a partial pass if they govern a state that had been seen as hard to govern and are able to reduce levels of corruption and/or lead to economic growth. During the Clinton years, the leaders of Ethiopia, Eritrea, Uganda, and Rwanda were praised as being among the "new leaders" of Africa. None of these countries could have been considered to be free at the time, but their progress on economic reform seems to have been enough to garner such praise. Therefore, it appears to be the case that countries that are pursuing the "good governance" model by achieving economic growth, by allowing capitalist investment (FDI), and by following the economic policy prescriptions of the World Bank and IMF get a reprieve (or a stay) on having to achieve significant political reforms. This tendency is evident in the above countries, though the IMF did pressure Uganda to halt its war in DRC, and Museveni did finally give way to pressures to hold multiparty elections. So the pass given for these countries may be temporary or partial.

THE RISE OF CHINA

Those who view conflict as the key for understanding international relations should see China with its very large population, growing GDP, its growing nuclear capabilities, and its dynamic manufacturing sector as the next real contender to American power, though it may not become so for years, if ever.[20] China does indeed have a large and growing GDP.[21] With its large army (the largest in the world), it has significant power at home, though it is only now adopting ways of projecting power abroad. Adding to the idea of rising Chinese power, some have suggested that the post-Cold War period will be marked more by economic issues than traditional diplomatic ones.[22] They suggest that foreign policy and trade policy are indistinguishable for many countries, and that globalization will increase these tendencies—which could advantage the Chinese, especially in the developing world.

Importantly, as a sign of its rising power, China has launched a development bank meant to rival the World Bank, along with its fellow BRICS members (Brazil, Russia, India, and South Africa).[23] The BRICS countries constitute 40% of the world's population and 20% of global economic output.[24] How much these institutions are a challenge to democracy, however, may be limited by South African and Indian membership (both are democratic nations). Another Chinese-led initiative is the Asian Infrastructure Investment Bank, which the US lobbied its allies not to join, but even longtime US ally, Britain, joined the bank.[25]

China has also become a greater source of FDI and OOF (other official flows) to developing countries since the end of the Cold War. Although their influence is on the rise, it seems to be limited to developing countries which can serve as export markets of China or to those that can sell natural materials to them. A few countries may find a safe harbor in China as long as these convergent interests last. Some even suggest that a Beijing consensus could be emerging where non-democratic, but economically viable, economies are a developmental model to be emulated. Ethiopia may be one such example.

Should China become seen as equally or more powerful as the US economically, militarily, and diplomatically in a way that signals another major geopolitical change, the easy prediction is that another shift in international resources and ideas would likely result in a shakeup of African political and economic institutions. In reality, however, it is more likely that we will see a gradual rise of Chinese power and not a rapid one. Even so, power transition theorists would predict a war between the US and China when Chinese military power begins to approximate American power.[26] This would require, however, a rising and disgruntled China which felt injured vis-à-vis the international system similar to Germany and Japan just prior to WWII, or even Germany before WWI. Other ways that Chinese power could overtake American are discussed briefly, but a collapse of the American economy undermining its ability to run and fund international organizations in conjunction with a non-collapsing (or less collapsing) China could also lead to a new geopolitical shift. Given the self-interest of so many political leaders in the consolidation of power, the diminishment of external pressure, absent the rise of constraining domestic pressures, a system with an authoritarian China as coequal with the US or replacing it as hegemon would likely see the return of more traditional authoritarian politics. However, as Ikenberry points out, China's rise is within Western dominance as much as US dominance.[27] Therefore, not only would America have to decline, but so too would most of its allies. And China benefits quite a lot from the current open trading system, even if they would like to free ride as much as possible. Therefore, China is unlikely to try to completely overhaul the international system if/when it becomes so powerful. Nonetheless, many scholars see a conflict between rising China and the US as almost foregone.[28]

Limits on Chinese Challenge

Nonetheless, China has had real limits to its ability to influence the international institutions of liberal power, such as the World Bank and IMF. It was only recently granted permanent Most Favored Nation status in the WTO, in 2000.[29] Also, it has not been a significant aid donor: in 2011 it gave $2 billion in aid, compared to the US contribution of $30B the overall OECD contribution of $128B. However, one place where China may be a rival economic power to the the the US and her allies is in its levels of foreign direct investment (FDI) as well as other official flows (OOF). In 2010, it had an outflow of $68.8B in FDI compared to US $51B.[30] Of this amount, $2.1 B went to Africa, representing around 3% of its outward FDI. For comparison, American FDI to sub-Saharan Africa in 2011 was $3.1B.[31]

Also, even if China's GDP is gaining on that of the US, it is unlikely to match American per capita income anytime soon. In 2014, Chinese per capita income was $7,594, while the US's level was $ 54,630, which is over seven times as high as China's.[32] Moreover, China is no match for the US in terms of an air force or navy, though these capabilities are growing. According to Nye, China is behind the US in most major indicators of power: economic, military, and soft; and they are likely to remain so for quite some time.[33] Therefore, the Chinese threat should be seen as a longer term one.

Even with rising Chinese power, one must ask if China's rise is likely to upset the larger liberal trading regimes and general pro-democracy foreign policies of the US and its allies. First, it should be remembered that China's rise is associated with increased global free trade, even if not increased political freedom. In fact, China is now a member of the World Trade Organization (WTO). Second, China unilaterally moved away from the socialist development model, allowing foreign direct investment in the 1970s, and even allowing wholly foreign-owned firms from 1986 onwards. It might rise as a national challenge to the US over time, but it would be as an authoritarian growth model, and not as a socialist growth model. Third, Chinese prosperity is linked to peaceful trading relations, especially with the US, and the Chinese have allowed significant amounts of US FDI to enter its borders. According to one analyst of Chinese-American trade relations, "almost 60% of Chinese exports to the United States are produced by firms owned by foreign companies, many of them American."[34]

Given the above facts, Chinese interests should not truly represent an direct ideological challenge to the US and its allies. Although Chinese FDI, ODA, and OOF may have flowed to nondemocratic nations such as Sudan and others, it follows a more mercantilist logic than an anti-American or anti-Western foreign policy. How they play their hand after they are more powerful, however, is yet to be seen. Nonetheless, many thinkers point to growing US indebtedness and lack of will to raise taxes or cut spending (or both) quickening China's rise.[35] In sum, although a few African countries could find safe harbor with China, most will not be so able. Moreover, they would also have to be seen as important to China to obtain enough aid from China to offset forgone aid from the West.

Importantly, however, China's rise does not constitute a global geopolitical shift in international power as described in this work, at least not yet. And even if its rise does lead to a global geopolitical shift, this change does not currently appear to be on the path of becoming a sudden one. Should the next transition be slow, the likelihood of a rapid change in equilibrium is lower, and a likely rapid and region-wide response in sub-Saharan Africa is unlikely. Also, the learning that sweeps through a system which re-evaluates who won and lost and why would also be slow motion as well as contested. Therefore, a slow rise of China would unlikely lead to a rapid or simultaneous regional shift in political or economic institutions or worldwide learning or shifts in legitimacy. It is more likely that countries with large markets or mineral or oil exports would draw Chinese investment and aid, and these African countries would be better able to resist pressures to continue with political and economic reforms, if the substituted support from China was sufficient and domestic pressure was limited or contained. Some of the countries suggested to have been favored by China were Sudan, Zimbabwe, and Ethiopia.

However, obtaining support from China is probably not the same all or nothing proposition associated with the Cold War period: countries could decide to engage in trade and investment relations with China as well as keep the appearance of electoral democracy for Western aid to keep flowing. African leaders might diversify their aid and investment portfolios, as Ethiopia appears to have done.[36] However, where a leader does not want to risk the future to elections, and they have resources that China needs, they may have another alternative to meeting Western demands for reforms and holding risky elections. This, however, seems an unlikely path for most African states.

The countries with the largest amount of Chinese aid in the region between 2005 and 2015 (including contracts) were Nigeria at $20.7 billion, Ethiopia at $15.6 billion, South Africa at $8.9b, Guinea $7.9b, Angola $7.9b, Chad $7.3b, Kenya at $7b, and DRC $7.9b.[37] Most of these countries were energy producers, though not all investment was only about that sector. From 2003 to 2010, more than half of Chinese FDI was related to oil, though these have become more diversified since.[38] Increasing investment is also going into such things as light manufacturing, food processing, transportation, and so forth. Given Chinese trade surpluses, it is natural that they are seeking means of investing this surplus internationally. So, if the rise of China is slow, we would see a slow defection of African countries away from keeping or maintaining their more accountable systems, especially if China was one of that country's benefactors.

Also, the role of China could become a wild card, should China itself become more liberal (or destabilized). They have liberalized economically in important ways: a rising middle class is becoming apparent, and overall prosperity has been growing. Urban pressures are rising, and the go-go growth of the nation is unlikely to keep pace with past performance. One place the leaders of China could replace legitimacy conferred by economic growth may be in its own partial liberalization of its political process. Should this take place, they might still pursue a primarily neo-mercantilist foreign policy which could downplay democracy and human rights, though a more liberal China might lead in demanding human rights (or at least human dignity) in the future. I am not making such a prediction, though it would not be impossible: few predicted the end of the Cold War, and fewer still predicted mass protests in North Africa and the Middle East launching the Jasmine Revolution. China could have its own democratic/social revolution without warning.[39] It could also find itself turning inward should an attempt at pressuring the government to become more democratic fail, and should the advocates turn violent.

REVERSE THIRD WAVE/WORLD RECESSION

Huntington's book on the third wave suggested a few conditions that could lead to a reversal of the democratic tide.[40] Should the overall legitimacy of capitalism or democracy become devalued due to a collapse in global markets or in a rapid fall in power of the US or Europe, or both, we might expect to see a significant change in the institutions of Africa following from the presumed global geopolitical shift that would ensue (especially should there be a snowball/diffusion effect). Both the material and ideological bases of liberal capitalism would be weakened. In such a case, we should expect the partial democratization and liberalization of the region to weaken, and we would likely see more autarkic and authoritarian approaches to development. Only countries in the region with very strong domestic or regional support and supporters for both capitalism and democracy would likely ride out that storm.

However, for the foreseeable future, a somewhat less triumphant economic and political liberalism seems to be ascendant and still considered to be the most legitimate form of government and economic policy. Moreover, these ideas are strongly backed by countries comprising most the world's GDP: OECD countries. This embrace of liberal capitalism is not without question: the economic troubles of 2008 did send shock waves through the American and Western European economies, with part of Europe still reeling as late as 2015. Also, the Asian currency crisis of 1997 has taken some of the sheen off of the capitalism veneer.

Continued Chinese success could give some additional support for a renewed interest in a form of authoritarian developmental model, though domestic pressures in China for reform may resurface should their economic miracle start to stall. However, they could respond with greater international competition to foment nationalist sentiment at home to increase the legitimacy of the regime, or they could continue their piecemeal reform of more accountability, if not democracy.[41] China's rise has been on the back of economic reforms that contain important liberal elements, but political reforms have been minimal and multiparty elections do not appear on the near horizon. However, neither were they on the near horizon in 1988 for most of Eastern Europe.

Weak State Institutions/State Collapse

Although this analysis has highlighted the liberalization of the political and economic institutions in sub-Saharan Africa, one major theme that has been overlooked so far is the relatively weak institutions of the region, leading to the possibility of collapse or state failure.[42] According to Huntington's 1968 work, rapid change can bring about decay as well as progress, and recent events in Libya and Syria testify to this.[43] Much depends on the strength of the institutions involved in the process. Most of the African region has engaged in political and economic liberalization, though usually by reluctant ruling elites. Importantly, building strong domestic institutions was not always a priority of African leaders during the Cold War period. In fact, some African leaders have been known to intentionally undermine their own domestic institutions (e.g., party, bureaucracy, army) to keep domestic threats in the form of rising domestic political actors at bay.[44] The threat of foreign pretenders for the throne have clearly been less threatening to so many African leaders compared to potential domestic claimants. As a result, domestic institutions that are important for nation building and economic development were often neglected or intentionally weakened, as they could have become a base of support for possible opponents of the leader or the party. In fact, some have suggested the end of the Cold War, poor economic performance in Africa, and the international pressures to liberalize are as likely to lead to collapse or warlord politics in Africa as they are in more liberal societies.[45] African political and economic institutions need to be built and strengthened for real development (political or economic) of Africa to occur. But in what state do we find them now? We now look at various attempts to measure government effectiveness from recent data.

Using the World Bank index of government effectiveness for 2014, which runs from +2.5 (high) to −2.5 (low), sub-Saharan Africa has an average of −0.815, where the world average is 0.[46] In Table 9.1, the highest and lowest scoring countries in sub-Saharan Africa are listed. Unsurprisingly, nearly all the highest scoring countries were listed as "free" by Freedom House, aside from the Seychelles, which was listed as "partly free". The countries considered to have the lowest levels of government effectiveness were all "not free," aside from the Comoros (which was listed as partly free in 2013).

Another gauge of how strong African states are could be measured by the Fragile State Index. Looking at indices of failed or failing states, many in sub-Saharan Africa would fit on the weaker end of the scale. For example, in 2014, of the five countries on the highest alert [Very High Alert], all are from sub-Saharan Africa: South Sudan, Somalia, Central African Republic, Congo (DRC), and Sudan. Moreover, of the 16 countries at Alert or High Alert (including above four), ten are from sub-Saharan Africa (62.5%).[47] Table 9.2 shows which countries were in which categories: the categories from most concerning to least are these: Very High Alert, High Alert, Alert, Very High Warning, High Warning, Warning, Less Stable, Stable, Very Stable, Sustainable, and Very Sustainable. No sub-Saharan African countries were in the

Table 9.1 Index of Government Effectiveness: 2014

Best	Scores	Worst	Scores
Mauritius	0.93	Central African Republic	−1.46
Botswana	0.44	Sudan	−1.46
Seychelles	0.38	Chad	−1.49
South Africa	0.33	Eritrea	−1.51
Namibia	0.12	Comoros	−1.55
Cape Verde	0.1	South Sudan	−1.59
		Equatorial Guinea	−1.65
		DRC (Congo)	−1.66
		Somalia	−2.30

Table 9.2   Fragile States Index: 2014

Very High Alert	South Sudan / Somalia / Central African Republic / Congo (D. R.) / Sudan
High Alert	Chad / Zimbabwe / Guinea / Cote d'Ivoire / Guinea Bissau
Alert	Nigeria / Kenya / Ethiopia / Niger / Burundi / Uganda / Eritrea / Liberia Cameroon / Mauritania / Rwanda
Very High Warning	Sierra Leone / Mali / Congo (Republic) / Malawi / Burkina Faso / Togo / Angola / Djibouti / Zambia / Mozambique / Swaziland / Equatorial Guinea / Comoros / Gambia / Madagascar / Senegal / Tanzania
High Warning	Lesotho / Benin / Sao Tome / Cape Verde / Gabon / Namibia / Ghana
Warning	South Africa / Botswana / Seychelles
Less Stable	
Stable	Mauritius

last three categories. Only one was in Stable. All the rest were in Warning to Very High Alert.

Civil War, Collapsing States, and Diffusion of Disorder

Recent experience in Africa seems to confirm that the outcome of a collapsed state in the region is disorder and social chaos, as opposed to a prosperous and pacifistic Lockean state of nature. It is also clear that this disorder can spread or diffuse to neighboring nations. Recently, Kaddafi's overthrow in Libya can be linked to the loss of democracy in Mali. Many Malian Tuareg were hired as mercenaries in Libya who returned to Mali and helped destabilize the regime. Moreover, we also can see the effects of the genocide in Rwanda that led to civil war and Mobutu's overthrow.[48] With the growing number of insurgent groups in the region, such as Boko Haram in Nigeria, and the al-Qaeda in the Islamic Maghreb in North Africa, or Al-Shabaab in the Horn, countries with security concerns may become tempted to justify a power grab or a reduction of rights, citing a domestic or regional insurgency for cover. Moreover, insurgent groups could make the ordinary practice of democracy difficult or dangerous for parts of the country. This could again militate in favor of more of a police or military role in civilian affairs and justify a greater consolidation of power in the hands of the political elites.

Moreover, disorder, especially in the form of civil war or low-intensity conflicts, has particularly strong implications for economic growth. Few countries fare well economically during such times, and insofar as economic growth militates in favor of continued political liberalization, chaos and disorder are bad omens for democratic polities. Should civil wars or low-intensity conflicts emerge and diffuse, the nascent political and economic regimes that had recently liberalized might revert to privileging order over economic and political freedom.

A POSSIBLE SOURCE FOR OPTIMISM: MUTUALLY REINFORCING FRAGMENTS OF POLITICAL AND ECONOMIC ACCOUNTABILITY

Richard L. Sklar wrote of developmental democracy a few decades ago and suggested that fragments of political accountability could reinforce each other.[49] I would extend this to say that fragments of economic accountability can also reinforce fragments of political accountability (as well as vice versa).[50] Where an independent business class can fund opposition campaigns, civil society may have sources of funding to participate in politics and hold politicians accountable. In addition, an independent and privately owned press can bolster and help maintain an independent judiciary, and a powerful union can help bolster an independent press. Owners of private firms and businesses could potentially counter what historically has been a near economic monopoly of power by state leaders. Moreover, strong international legitimacy for responsible capitalism can bolster property rights for African business people, which, in turn, could help support economic growth, which could then help sustain nascent political regimes. Students of history may point out that business power can be too great, and this scholar would agree. The rise of unchecked capitalist power often emerged prior to universal franchise, strong labor movements, a strong and wealthy middle class, education for the masses, or a state willing and capable of breaking up monopolies which had allowed business interests to have disproportionate power. With the recent rise of multinational corporate power, less powerful unions, and the rise of conglomerations, a consolidation of power in the hands of a few in the private sector could be on the rise again, and this is not promising either. Democracy probably requires competing centers of autonomous power, both political and economic.

Returning to Africa, what appears to be emerging as a result of the multiparty electoral regimes, more liberal economic trade policies, and policies of privatization is a civil society that can become more vibrant and have more of a chance to affect political and economic outcomes in the region. However, these practices have to become institutionalized through repeated elections for real competition to flourish. And Lindberg has argued, practice with even flawed elections leads to the improvement in the quality of elections over time.[51] Interest groups and political parties also have to institutionalize and adapt to the needs and demands of the societies in which they find themselves. The privatization of economic resources has the potential to result in the economic empowerment of more citizens in these countries, though many of the direct (and short-term) benefactors may be international companies who may or may not have self-interest in helping promote democracy in African countries. The new owners are often the political elites that probably have more interest in political power than their newly acquired property, though this preference order could change with time. However, they probably do have incentives in predictable rule of law and lower levels of corruption, even in the short term. Indirectly, the employees working for a predominately private sector may also compose an aspect of a more vibrant civil society. Moreover, governments may be less threatened by unions which target private owners as opposed to state-owned sectors.[52] Also, as political rights become more respected, and the force of law is more widely applied, the need for lawyers and judges rises, and these groups could form another potentially strong component of domestic civil society. The rise of the NGO sectors with funding from abroad could also have strong independent effects on the civil society of the region as well as on the economies, especially if they are working toward such goals. Finally, countries with term limits are likely to see power devolve to the party away from particular leaders as they age, and possibly to other parties. In Ghana, for example, term limits on the chief executives and competitive parties have resulted in the alternation of power between two major parties on several occasions. Term limits do not guarantee such things, as other cases such as Botswana demonstrate, but it opens up the possibility more so.

For the foreseeable future, Africa will have multiparty competition in most states, dominated by one strong party (often a dominant party), and usually one strong personality at a the head of the party.[53] Countries with term limits will tend to see more alternations in power—and maybe even more alterations in party. However, a one-party dominant system with some limited rights and protections for minorities seems to be the new equilibrium for many countries. However, this represents only a partial step toward a true democracy, but it is an important step. Many of these countries are likely to stay in the electoral authoritarian camp, but powerful personalities can change what appears to be inevitable.

With rising African economic integration regionally and globally, and with increasing FDI and ODA to Africa, it remains likely that Western influence will remain strong concerning economic foreign policy making regionally. A return to inward-oriented development policies, leading with import substitution industrialization (ISI), is unlikely to reemerge in a regional (or international) wave, unless some global shutdown or closure of trade on the international level emerges.[54] Moreover, as transnational companies continue to invest in Africa, their policy preferences for openness are likely to be respected, especially as a means of drawing additional investment. The increase of bilateral investment treaties is likely to act as a source of inertia in these regards as well (see Chapter 7). Also, the ideological emphasis on the developmental superiority of an outward-oriented development regime is hard to contradict at the moment, though some of Asia's outward-driven policies were clearly dirigiste (as is China's right now, properly understood). In addition, lessons from history, and the relative small market size of most

African states, militate away from a return to ISI in protected markets. Clearly, the countries with continued majority state ownership of competitive sectors will face rising pressures either to privatize and allow competition or to keep these assets and increase protectionism. State-owned mining or oil sectors will not be under the same pressures: just having the resource creates a comparative advantage for selling these goods abroad, though as the case of Zambia shows, if very poorly run, they can be run into the ground.[55] However, such countries could refine these products before they are exported, but few state-owned sectors have ever done so.

The partial reforms may slowly deepen and even expand as the elements of society that benefit from them become more powerful, either politically or economically. The political elites still have commanding power domestically, but they are quite constrained in economic foreign policy regimes, and if they are highly aid dependent, they are also constrained somewhat politically. Some countries which are key allies in the war on terror, or who can obtain economic resources from either domestic sources (oil, mining) or from international sources that care less about political and economic reform (e.g., China), may stay as electoral authoritarian regimes or could even revert to full authoritarian systems. Even these nations still risk domestic backlash from constituents seeking to keep or expand political and economic power or rights, as well as from regional and international pressures.

Most countries in the region will probably limp along as partially flawed democracies and electoral regimes with slowly devolving power to rising economic, political, and social actors. A few countries will have leaderships that challenge the international regimes and norms, and their societies will pay high prices in forgone wealth, prosperity, and peace (as Zimbabwe has). Nonetheless, the leaders of such countries need strong coercive power to survive, as the patronage glue holding together the social peace would not likely hold with the decreases in access to international sources of resources—unless, of course, they are oil or mineral exporters who do not have to supply many public goods to extract wealth from their economies. International and domestic legitimacy in such an endeavor is quite likely to be low.

The new road oft traveled in Africa seems to be one of emerging capitalism with weakly institutionalized electoral regimes, with usually one dominant political party. External support will probably be necessary to help African economies maintain their economic growth and to keep these systems from returning to the prior roads of more authoritarian systems and inward-oriented economies.[56] As long as pressure from the combination of strong norms and international resources remain mostly in place, some externally assisted liberalization may allow domestic forces which favor democracy and some market-based economic systems to become strong enough to defend these political and economic institutions domestically.[57] Africa has returned to the threshold of the problems of nation building, capacity building, and institution building, as well as expanding economic and political opportunities. Most nations tried to develop using one-party rule and economies dominated by the political elite, but the results laid bare the problems of corruption, cronyism, and weak institutions. African leaders only had such autonomy while the great nations and superpowers were courting weaker nations during the Cold War. A system of government more accountable to more of its people with more economic power distributed outside of state hands holds out little promise for very rapid development, but perhaps it holds out promise for a slow and steady journey to empowerment and economic development. The shortcut to progress was attempted and failed; now the slow and sometimes painful journey has to be begun again. This time with more participation by more African citizens in the economic and political institutions of their nations.

NOTES

1. From Hobson, to Lenin, Baran, and Wallerstein and beyond, many have held capitalism to be the cause of colonization/imperialism. For an overview of this view, see Peter B. Evans, *Dependent Development: The Alliance of Multinational, State, and Local Capital in Brazil* [Vol 487] (Princeton: Princeton University Press, 1979).

2. For original argument, see John J. Quinn, "The Impact of State Ownership of Resources on Economic and Political Development in Sub-Saharan Africa," *Ufahamu* Vol. XXI, No 1and 2 (Winter/Spring): 60–79.

3. For issues of overdetermination, see Juan J. Lopez, "Theory Choice in Comparative Social Inquiry," *Polity* 25, 2 (Winter 1992): 267–82.

4. Francis Fukuyama, *The End of History and the Last Man* (Simon and Schuster, 2006).

5. For a critique of doing too much economic liberalization before the proper institutions are in place, see Joseph E. Stiglitz, *Globalization and its Discontents* (New York: W. W. Norton & Company, 2003).

6. For evidence of low levels of civil society, see E. Gyimah-Boadi, "Civil Society and Democratic Development," in E. Gyimah-Boadi, ed., *Democratic Reform in Africa: The Quality of Progress* (Boulder, CO: Lynne Rienner Publishers, 2004): 99–119; Michael Bratton, "Beyond the State: Civil Society and Associational Life in Africa," *World Politics* 40, (April 1990): 407–430; also John James Quinn, "Democracy and Development," in Emmanuel Nnadozie, ed., *African Economic Development* (New York: Academic Press, 2003): 231–58.

7. Seymour Martin Lipset, "Some Social Requisites of Democracy: Economic Development and Political Legitimacy," *American Political Science Review* 53 (March 1959): 69–105.

8. Mancur Olson, *The Logic of Collective Action: Public Goods and the Theory of Groups* (Cambridge, MA: Harvard University Press, 1965); Robert H. Bates,

Markets and States in Tropical Africa: the Political Basis of Agricultural Policies (Los Angeles and Berkeley, CA: University of California Press, 1981).

9. John James Quinn, *The Road oft Traveled: Development Policies and Majority State Ownership of Industry in Africa* (Westport, CT: Praeger, 2002).

10. Michael Bratton, "Second Elections in Africa," *Journal of Democracy* 9, 3 (1998): 51–66.

11. Ibid., Table 1. However, this does compare a six year period to a three year one.

12. See John Ishiyama and John James Quinn, "Phoenix from the Ashes: The Formerly Dominant Parties in New Democracies in Africa," *Party Politics* 12, 3 (May 2006): 317–40.

13. van de Walle makes this point, see Nicolas van de Walle, *African Economies and the Politics of Permanent Crisis, 1979–1999* (Cambridge: Cambridge University Press, 2001).

14. For argument about external constraints and its effects on African leaders, see John J. Quinn, "Economic Accountability: Are Constraints on Economic Decision Making a Blessing or a Curse?" *Scandinavian Journal of Development Alternatives and Area Studies* 19, no. 4 (2000): 131–84

15. Lindberg makes this point about holding de jure free and fair elections result in later de facto free and fair elections. Staffan I. Lindberg, *Democracy and Elections in Africa* (Baltimore, MD: The Johns Hopkins University Press, 2006).

16. For a discussion and background on this, see Marshall I. Goldman, "Putin and the Oligarchs," *Foreign Affairs* 83, 6 (Nov.–Dec., 2004): 33–44.

17. For doctrine of domicile, see Richard L. Sklar, *Corporate Power in an African State: The Political Impact of Multinational Mining Companies in Zambia* (Los Angeles: University of California Press, 1975).

18. For ideas on diffusion, see Steven E. Lobell and Philip Mauceri, eds., *Ethnic Conflict and International Politics: Explaining Diffusion and Escalation* (New York: Palgrave Macmillan, 2004): 111–32; also, David A. Lake and Donald Rothchild, *The International Spread of Ethnic Conflict: Fear, Diffusion, and Escalation* (Princeton: Princeton University Press, 1998). In Africa, see John James Quinn, "Diffusion and Escalation in the Great Lakes Region: the Rwandan Genocide, the Rebellion in Zaire, and Mobutu's Overthrow," in Lobell and Mauceri, *Ethnic Conflict*: 111–32.

19. John James Quinn, John Ishiyama and Marijke Breuning, "Aid, Development, and Foreign Policy under the Meles Regime," Annual Meeting of the Midwest Political Science Association, Chicago, Il. (April 11–14, 2013).

20. See especially John J. Mearsheimer, *The Tragedy of Great Power Politics* (New York: W. W. Norton & Company, 2014).

21. According to IMF data, China passed the US in 2014 using PPP, though many dispute how good Chinese data really is. See, for example, Ben Carter, "Is China's Economy Really the Largest in the World?" *Economist* (16 December 2014): http://www.bbc.com/news/magazine-30483762.

22. See Richard J. Payne and Cassandra R. Veney, "China's Post-Cold War African Policy," *Asian Survey* 38, 9 (September 1998): 867–79.

23. "A Challenge from the BRICS," *New York Times* (July 24, 2014).

24. Ibid.

25. Geoff Dyer and George Parker, "US Attacks UK's 'Constant Accommodation' with China," *Financial Times* (March 12, 2015); see also Rhys Blakely, "US rebuke on China bank," *The Times (of London)* (March 13, 2015 Friday) Edition 1.

26. See, for example, A.F.K. Organski, *World Politics* (New York: Knopf, 1958) and A.F.K. Organski and J. Kugler, *The War Ledger* (Chicago: University of Chicago Press, 1980).

27. G. John Ikenberry, "The Rise of China and the Future of the West: Can the Liberal System Survive?" *Foreign Affairs* (2008): 23–37

28. For an example of such a debate, see Ibid.

29. Adam Davidson, "Come On, China, Buy Our Stuff!" *New York Times* (January 25, 2012). http://www.nytimes.com/2012/01/29/magazine/come-on-china-buy-our-stuff.html?pagewanted=all&_r=0

30. Unless stated otherwise, data on FDI from China for this section come from BBVA Research, Economic Watch: China, (October 12, 2011): http://www.bbvaresearch.com/KETD/fbin/mult/111014_ChinaWatch_ofdi_tcm348-273161.pdf?ts=7112011. Data for US come from OECD's Aid Statistics. For more on China's aid and investment to developing countries, see Debora Brautigam, *The Dragon's Gift: The Real Story of China in Africa* (Oxford: Oxford University Press, 2010).

31. Bureau of Economic Analysis (BEA), Foreign Direct Investment database. Cited in Vivian C. Jones and Brock R. Williams, "U.S. Trade and Investment Relations with sub-Saharan Africa and the African Growth and Opportunity Act," Congressional Research Service, 7–5700, www.crs.gov, RL31772. http://www.fas.org/sgp/crs/row/RL31772.pdf

32. Word Bank, *World Development Indicators*, S.V., GDP per capita (current US$): http://data.worldbank.org/indicator/NY.GDP.PCAP.CD. Numbers rounded to nearest dollar. Accessed 7/21/ 2015.

33. Joseph S. Nye, Jr., *Is the American Century Over?* (Malden, MA: Polity, 2015).

34. Neil C. Hughes, "A Trade War with China?: The Eagle and the Dragon," *Foreign Affairs* (July/August 2005). http://www.foreignaffairs.com/articles/60825/neil-c-hughes/a-trade-war-with-china; See also J. Bradford Jensen, Dennis P. Quinn, and Stephen Weymouth, "The Influence of Firm Global Supply Chains and Foreign Currency Undervaluations on US Trade Disputes," International Organization 69 (2015): 913-947.

35. Arvind Subramanian, "The Inevitable Superpower" Why China's Dominance is a Sure Thing," *Foreign Affairs* (September/October 2011).

36. Quinn, Ishiyama, and Breuning, "Aid, Development, and Foreign Policy."

37. Data from this section comes from Heritage House, "China Global Investment Tracker" http://www.heritage.org/research/projects/china-global-investment-tracker-interactive-map

38. See Kathleen Caulderwood, "Chinese Money in Africa Directed Away From Oil, Toward Other Sectors," *International Business Times* (May 15 2014).

39. For views of China becoming democratic, see Yu Liu and Dingding Chen, "Why China will democratize," *The Washington Quarterly* 35, 1 (2012): 41–63, also Henry Rowen, "When Will the Chinese People Be Free?" *Journal of Democracy* 18, 3 (July 2007): 38–52.

40. For waves and reverse waves, see Samuel P. Huntington, *The Third Wave: Democratization in the Late Twentieth Century* (Norman, OK: University of Oklahoma Press 1991).

41. See, for example, Elizabeth J. Perry and Merle Goldman, eds., Grassroots Political Reform in Contemporary China (Cambridge, MA: Harvard University Press, 2007).

42. For background on this notion and its concerns at the end of the Cold War, see I. William Zartman, *Collapsed States: the Disintegration and Restoration of Legitimate Authority* (Boulder, CO: Lynne Rienner Publishers, 1995).

43. Samuel Huntington, *Political Order and Changing Societies* (New Haven: Yale University Press, 1968)

44. See Robert H. Jackson, and Carl G. Rosberg, "Why Africa's Weak States Persist: the Empirical and the Juridical in Statehood," *World Politics* 35, 1 (1982): 1–24; Christopher Clapham, *Africa and the International System: The Politics of State Survival* (Cambridge: Cambridge University Press, 1996); Thomas M. Callaghy, *The State-Society Struggle: Zaire in Comparative Perspective* (New York: Columbia University Press, 1984); William Reno, *Warlord Politics and African states* (Lynne Rienner Publishers, 1999) for similar arguments. Perhaps the most audacious acts of undermining the domestic society to stay in power were acts by Mobutu. Famously, under Mobutu, Kananga was the largest city in the world without electricity while the main line of the Inga-Shaba dam, which brought electricity to the copper mines in Lubumbashi, ran just outside of the town. The dam has enough electricity (potentially) to have electrified the whole country, and none was provided for the capital of one of the provinces, Kasaï-Occidental.

45. Reno, *Warlord Politics*; for general discussions on failed states see, Robert I. Rotberg, "Failed States, Collapsed States, Weak States: Causes and Indicators," *State Failure and State Weakness in a Time of Terror* (Brookings Institution Press and the World Peace Foundation, 2003): 1–25.

46. Unless stated otherwise, the data from this section comes from World Bank, *World Governance Indicators*: http://info.worldbank.org/governance/wgi/index.aspx?fileName=wgidataset.xlsx#home . accessed 4/28/ 2014.

47. State failure data taken from the Fund for Peace, 2013. http://ffp.statesindex.org/rankings-2013-sortable

48. For a summary of this and its literature, see John James Quinn, "The Nexus of the Domestic and Regional within an International Context: The Rwandan Genocide and Mobutu's Ouster," in Amy L. Freedman, ed., *Threatening the State: the Internationalization of Internal Conflicts* (Oxford: Routledge, 2014): 39–74.

49. Richard L. Sklar, "Developmental Democracy," *Comparative Studies in Society and History*, Vol. 29, No. 4 (Oct., 1987): 686–714.

50. For fragments of economic accountability see Quinn, "Economic Accountability." also Ryan Kennedy, "Fragments of Economic Accountability and Trade Policy." *Foreign Policy Analysis* 3, no. 2 (2007): 145–169.

51. Lindberg, *Democracy and Elections in Africa*

52. For diminished role of unions in post-colonial period, see William Tordoff, *Government and Politics in Africa, 3rd Edition* (Bloomington and Indianapolis: Indiana University Press, 1997), esp. p. 117.

53. See prior chapters as well as Thomas Carothers, "The End of the Transition Paradigm," *Journal of Democracy* 13, 1 (January 2002): 5–21; also Steven Levitsky and Lucan A. Way, "The Rise of Competitive Authoritarianism," *Journal of Democracy* 13.2 (2002): 51–65.

54. As Hirschman pointed out, the Second World War was one of the impulses for ISI in Latin America. See, Albert O. Hirschman, "The Political Economy of Import-Substituting Industrialization in Latin America," *The Quarterly Journal of Economics* (1968): 1–32.

55. No pun intended.

56. Quinn, "Democracy and Development."

57. Similar to idea of John W. Harbeson, "Externally Assisted Democratization: Theoretical Issues and African Realities," in John W. Harbeson and Donald Rothchild, eds., *Africa in World Politics: The African State System in Flux* (Boulder, CO: Westview Press, 2000): 235–62.

Appendix I

Minerals or oil had to constitute approximately 40% or more of export earnings for several years during the first period for a country to be coded as a significant mining or oil exporting country. The following are countries were so coded: Angola, Botswana, Cameroon, Congo-Brazzaville, Gabon, Guinea, Liberia, Mauritania, Niger, Nigeria, Sierra Leone, Togo, Zaire (DRC), and Zambia.[1]

Countries with prior majority state ownership of industries, but not a major exporter of oil or minerals, new or old, were these: Benin, Burkina Faso (Upper Volta), Cape Verde, Chad, Ethiopia, Ghana, Guinea Bissau, Madagascar, Mali, Mozambique, Sao Tome, Seychelles, Tanzania, and Uganda.[2]

Countries without major mining or oil exporting sectors or without majority state ownership during the first period were these: Burundi, Central African Republic, Comoros, Cote d'Ivoire, Djibouti, Equatorial Guinea, the Gambia, Kenya, Lesotho, Malawi, Mauritius, Rwanda, Senegal, Sudan, Swaziland, and Zimbabwe.

Countries coded as having found new oil (and revenues or strongly anticipated revenues in the second period) were these: Equatorial Guinea, Chad, and Sudan (2000).

Countries listed as having been socialist are these: Burkina Faso, Congo, Rep., Ghana, Guinea, Guinea-Bissau, Mauritius, Tanzania, and Zambia.

Afro-Marxist (former) regimes included these: Angola, Benin, Cape Verde, Ethiopia, Madagascar, Mozambique, Sao Tome and Principe, and Zimbabwe.

NOTES

1. Central Africa Republic had diamonds, but it was closer to 25% of exports, though it was as high as 40% for only one year (according to official statistics). Lesotho had diamonds, but its peak exports were 1980s, and by 1985, most had been exhausted.

2. Somalia is excluded as it broke into parts during the second period and became a collapsed state; moreover, its inclusion does not change the main findings.

Bibliography

2010 Index of Economic Freedom, Freedom House. http://www.heritage.org/index/.

Abd-el-Kader Boye. *L'acte de nationalization*. Daker: Édition Berger-Levrault, 1979: 12–24.

Acheson, Dean. *Present at the Creation*. New York: Norton, 1969.

Adda, Jacques and Marie-Claude Smoots. *La France face au Sud: le miroir brisé*. Paris: Karthala 1989.

Ade Ajayi, J. F. "Expectations of Independence." In "Black Africa: A Generation After Independence." Special issue of *Daedalus: Journal of the American Academy of Arts and Sciences* (Spring 1982).

Adedeji, Adebayo. "The *raison d'être* of indigenization." Part 1 of Chapter 2: "Historical and theoretical background." In Adebayo Adedeji, ed. *Indigenization of African Economies*. London: Hutchinson & Co. Ltd, 1981.

Adedeji, Adebayo, ed. *Indigenization of African Economies*. London: Hutchinson & Co. Ltd, 1981.

Africa South of the Sahara. London; Europa Publications Limited, Various years.

African Elections Database. http://africanelections.tripod.com/ug.html.

Ajayi, J.F. Ade and A. E. Ekoko. "Transfer of Power in Nigeria: Its Origins and Consequences." In Gifford and Louis. *Decolonization and African Independence*: 245–269.

Ake, Claude ed. *Political Economy of Nigeria*. London: Longman, 1985.

Aldrich, Robert and John Connell, eds. *France in World Politics*. New York: Routledge 1989.

Alesina, Alberto and David Dollar. "Who Gives Foreign Aid to Whom and Why?" *Journal of Economic Growth*, 5, 1 (2000): 33–63.

Alt, James E. and Kenneth A. Shepsle. *Perspectives on Positive Political Economy*. Cambridge: Cambridge University Press, 1990.

Ambrose, Stephen E. *Rise to Globalism: American Foreign Policy, 1938–1976*. New York: Penguin Books, 1971/ Revised 1976.

Amin, Samir. "Nationalism." In John Eatwell et al., eds. *The New Palgrave: Economic Development*. New York: W.W. Norton, 1989: 247–251.

Amin, Samir. *Accumulation on a World Scale* 2 Vol. New York: Monthly Review Press, 1974.

Anderson, Kym and Ernesto Valenzuela. "Estimates of Distortions to Agricultural Incentives, 1955 to 2007. World Bank, Washington DC, October, 2008.

Anderson, Lisa, ed. *Transitions to Democracy*. New York: Columbia University Press, 1999.

Appiah-Kubi, Kojo. "State-Owned Enterprises and Privatisation in Ghana." *The Journal of Modern African Studies*. Vol. 39, No. 2 (Jun., 2001): 197–229.

Arndt, H.W. *Economic Development: The History of an Idea*. Chicago: University of Chicago Press, 1987.

Arriola, Leonardo R. *Patronage Circulation and Party System Fragmentation in Africa*. Working Paper, UCLA, 2011.

Auty, R.M. "The Political Economy of Resource-Driven Growth." *European Economic Review* 45 (2001): 839–846.

Auty, R.M., ed. *Resource Abundance and Economic Development*. Oxford, UK: Oxford University Press, 2001.

Ayittey, George B. N. *Africa Betrayed*. Forward by Makaziwe Mandela. New York: St. Martin's Press, 1992.

Ayoob, Mohammed. "Inequality and Theorizing in International Relations: The Case for Subaltern Realism." *International Studies Review* 4, 3 (Autumn 2002): 27–48

Ayoob, Mohammed. *The Third World Security Predicament*. Boulder, CO: Lynne Rienner Publishers, 1995.

Azam, Jean Paul, Bruno Biais, and Magueye Dia. *Privatization versus Regulation in Developing Economies: The Case of West African Banks*. Working Paper Number 315 (February 2000). http://wdi.umich.edu/files/publications/workingpapers/wp315.pdf

Babarinde, Femi. "Regionalism and Economic Development." In *African Economic Development*. Emmanuel Nnadozie, ed. New York: Academic Press, 2003: 473–498

Bagchi, Amiya Kumar. "Development Planning." In John Eatwell et al., eds. *The New Palgrave: Economic Development*. New York: W.W. Norton, 1989: 98–108.

Baker, Bruce. "The Class of 1990: How Have the Autocratic Leaders of Sub-Saharan Africa Fared?" *Third World Quarterly* 19, 1 (1998): 115–127.

Balassa, Bela. "Exports and Economic Growth: Further Evidence." *Journal of Development Economics* 5 (June 1978): 181–189.

Balassa, Bela. "Exports, Policy Choices, and Economic Growth in Developing Countries after the 1973 Oil Shock." *Journal of Developing Economics* 18 (1985): 23–35.

Bamfo, Napoleon. "Term Limit and Political Incumbency in Africa: Implications of Staying in Power Too Long with References to the Cases of Kenya, Malawi, and Zambia." *African & Asian Studies* 4, 3 (2005): 327–355.

Barad, Robert. "Privatization of State-Owned Enterprises: The Togolese Experience." In Grosh and Mukandala. *State-Owned Enterprises*: 175–196.

Barad, Tobert. "Privatization of State-Owned Enterprises: The Togolese Experience." In Grosh and Mukandala, *State-Owned Enterprises*.

Baradat, Leon P. *Political Ideologies: Their Origins and Impact 9th edition*. Upper Saddle River: Pearson Education, 2009.

Baran, Paul A. *Political Economy of Growth*. New York: Monthly Review Press, 1957.

Barkan, Joel D. "Legislatures on the Rise?" *Journal of Democracy* 19, 2 (2008) 124–137.

Barkan, Joel D. "Regime Change in Africa." *Journal of Democracy* 10, 2 (1999) 165–170.

Barraclough, Geoffrey. *An Introduction to Contemporary History*. New York: Penguin Books, 1978.

Barro, Robert J. "The Determinants of Democracy." *Journal of Political Economy* 107, 6 (1999): 158–183.

Basedau, Matthais, Matthijs Bogaards, Christof Harmann and Peter Niesen. "Ethnic Party Bans In Africa: A Research Agenda." *German Law Journal* 8, 6 (2007): 617–634.

Bates, Robert H. "The Impulse to Reform in Africa." In Widner, ed. *Economic Change*: 13–28.

Bates, Robert H. *Markets and States in Tropical Africa: the Political Basis of Agricultural Policies*. Los Angeles and Berkeley, CA: University of California Press, 1981.

Bayart, Jean-François. *The State in Africa: The Politics of the Belly*. Translated by Mary Harper et al. New York: Longman, 1993.

BBC News. "World Bank: Africa held back by land ownership confusion." (23 July 2013). http://www.bbc.com/news/business-23421548

Becker, David G. and Richard L. Sklar. "Why Postimperialism?" In David Becker et al., eds. *Postimperialism: International Capitalism and Development in the Late Twentieth Century*. Boulder: Lynne Rienner Publishers, 1978: 1–18.

Bender, Gerald J. *Angola under the Portuguese: The Myth and the Reality*. Berkeley: University of California Press, 1978.

Bennell, Paul. "Privatizing in Sub-Saharan Africa: Progress and Prospects during the 1990s." *World Development* 25, 11 (1997): 1785–1803.

Berg, Elliot J., and Jeffrey Butler. "Trade Unions." In Coleman and Rosberg, *Political Parties*: 340–381.

Bernard, A.B., J.B. Jensen, and P.K. Schott. "Importers, Exporters and Multinationals: A Portrait of the Firms in the U.S. that Trade Goods." *NBER Working Paper No. 11404* (June 2005).

Beveridge, Andrew A. and Anthony R. Oberschall. *African Businessmen and Development in Zambia*. Princeton, NJ: Princeton University Press, 1979.

Bienen, Henry and Jeffrey Herbst. "The Relationship between Political and Economic Reform in Africa." *Comparative Politics* 29, 1 (Oct. 1996): 23–42.

Biersteker, Thomas J. "Indigenization and the Nigerian Bourgeoisie: Dependent Development in an African Context." In Lubeck, ed. *The African Bourgeoisie*: 255–262.

Biersteker, Thomas J. *Multinationals, the State and Control of the Nigerian Economy.* Princeton, NJ: Princeton University Press, 1987.

Birdsall, Nancy and John Nellis. "Winners and Losers: Assessing the Distributional Impact of Privatization." Center for Global Development. Working Paper No 6 (May 2002).

Blonigen, Bruce A. "Foreign Direct Investment Behavior of Multinational Corporations." *NBER Reporter: Research Summary* (Winter 2006).

Bogaards, Matthijs. "Counting Parties and Identifying Dominant Party Systems in Africa." *European Journal of Political Research* 43 (2004): 173–197.

Boix, Carles and Susan C. Stokes. "Endogenous Democratization." *World Politics* 55, 4 (2003): 517–549.

Bollen, Kenneth and Robert W. Jackman. "Political Democracy and the Size Distribution of Income." *American Sociological Review* 50, 4 (August 1985): 438–457.

Bolton, Dianne. *Nationalization—A Road to Socialism?: The Lessons of Tanzania.* London: Zed Books Ltd., 1985.

Boone, Catherine. "Accumulating Wealth, Consolidating Power: Rentierism in Senegal." In Bruce J. Berman and Colin Leys, eds. *African Capitalists in African Development.* Boulder, CO: Lynne Rienner Publishers, 1994.

Boutros-Ghali, Boutros. *An Agenda for Peace: Preventive Diplomacy, Peacemaking and Peacekeeping.* New York: United Nations, 1992.

Bragança, Aquino de with Basil Davidson. "Independence without Decolonization: Mozambique." In Gifford and Louis. *Decolonization and African Independence*: 427–444.

Bratton, Michael, and Eric C. C. Chang. "State Building and Democratization in Sub-Saharan Africa: Forwards, Backwards, or Together?" *Comparative Political Studies* 39, 9 (November 2006): 1059–1083.

Bratton, Michael, and Nicolas van de Walle. *Democratic Experiments in Africa: Regime Transitions in Comparative Perspective.* Cambridge: Cambridge University Press, 1997.

Bratton, Michael, and Nicolas van de Walle. "Toward Governance in Africa: Popular Demands and State Responses." In Goran Hyden and Michael Bratton, eds. *Governance and Politics in Africa.* Boulder, CO: Lynne Rienner Publishers, 1992: 27–56.

Bratton, Michael. "Beyond the State: Civil Society and Associational Life in Africa." *World Politics* 40 (April 1990): 407–430.

Bratton, Michael. "Civil Society and Political Transition in Africa." *Institute for Development Research Reports* 11, 6 (1994).

Bratton, Michael. "Second Elections in Africa." *Journal of Democracy* 9, 3 (1998).

Brautigam, Debora. *The Dragon's Gift: The Real Story of China in Africa.* Oxford: Oxford University Press, 2010.

Brinks, Daniel, and Michael Coppedge. "Diffusion Is No Illusion: Neighbor Emulation in the Third Wave of Democracy." *Comparative Political Studies* 39, 4 (May 2006): 463–489.

Brooks, Stephen G., and William C. Wohlforth. "American Primacy in Perspective." *Foreign Affairs* (July/August 2002).

Brown, Stephen. "Authoritarian Leaders and Multiparty Elections in Africa: How Foreign Donors Help to Keep Kenya's Daniel Arap Moi in Power Author." *Third World Quarterly* 22, 5 (Oct., 2001): 725–739.

Brown, Stephen. "Foreign Aid and Democracy Promotion: Lessons from Africa." *The European Journal of Development Research* 17, 2 (June 2005): 179–198.

Brune, Nancy, Geoffrey Garrett, and Bruce Kogut. "The International Monetary Fund and the Global Spread of Privatization." *IMF Staff Papers.* Vol. 51, No. 2 (2004): 195–219.

Buchs, Thierry D. "Privatization in Sub-Saharan Africa: Some Lessons from Experiences to Date." *International Finance Corporation*, mimeo, 2003. http://www.nioclibrary.com/privatization/e025.pdf

Bunce, Valarie. "Rethinking Recent Democratization: Lessons from the Postcommunist Experience. *World Politics* 55, 2 (2003): 167–192.

Byamugisha, Frank F. K. *Securing Africa's Land for Shared Prosperity: A Program to Scale up Reforms and Investments.* Washington D.C.: World Bank and Agence Française de Développement, 2013.

Callaghy, Thomas M. "Africa and the World Political Economy: More Caught between a Rock and a Hard Place." In Harbeson and Rothchild. *Africa in World Politics:* 43–82.

Callaghy, Thomas M. "Africa and the World Political Economy: Still Caught between a Rock and a Hard Place." In Harbeson and Rothchild. *Africa in World Politics:* 39–71.

Callaghy, Thomas M. and John Ravenhill, eds. *Hemmed In: Responses to Africa's Economic Decline.* New York: Columbia University Press, 1993.

Callaghy, Thomas M. *The State-Society Struggle: Zaire in Comparative Perspective.* New York: Columbia University Press, 1984.

Callinicos, Alex. "Whither Marxism?" *Economic and Political Weekly* (1996): PE9-PE17.

Campos, Alicia. "The Decolonization of Equatorial Guinea: The Relevance of the International Factor." *The Journal of African History* 44, 1 (2003): 95–116

Carats as Carrots in Botswana." *The Southern African Economist* (February/March 1988).

Cardoso, Fernando Henrique and Enzo Faletto. *Dependency and Development in Latin America.* Translated by Marjorie Mattingly Urquidi. Los Angeles: University of California Press, 1971.

Carothers, Thomas. "The End of the Transition Paradigm." *Journal of Democracy* 13, 1 (January 2002): 5–21.

Carter, Gwendolen M. and Patrick O'Meara, eds. *African Independence: The First Twenty-Five Years.* Bloomington: Indiana University Press, 1986.

Caves, Richard E. and Ronald W. Jones. *World Trade and Payments: an Introduction.* Boston: Little, Brown, 1985.

Cerny, Philip G. "Globalization and the Changing Logic of Collective Action." *International Organization* Vol. 49, No. 4 (Autumn 1995): 595–625.

Chabal, Patrick. "The Quest for Good Government and Development in Africa: Is NEPAD the Answer? *International Affairs* Vol. 78, No. 3 (Jul., 2002): 447–462.

Chafer, Tony. *The End of Empire in French West Africa: France's Successful Decolonization?* New York: Berg, 2002.

Chazan, Naomi et al. *Politics and Society in Contemporary Africa.* Boulder, CO: Lynne Rienner Publishers, 1988.

Checkel, Jeffrey T. "The Constructivist Turn in International Relation Theory." *World Politics* 50, 2 (Jan. 1998): 324–348.

Chege, Sam. "Donors Shift More Aid to NGOs: But Cooperation Between Governments and NGOs is Critical for Greater Effectiveness." *African Recovery* http:// www.un.org/ecosocdev/geninfo/afrec/vol13no1/aid2ngo.htm

Chenery, Hollis. "Comparative Advantage and Development Policy." *American Economic Review* 51, 1 (March 1961): 18–51.

CIA World Factbook various countries, various years. https://www.cia.gov/library/ publications/the-world-factbook/

Clapham, Christopher. "Sovereignty and the Third World State." *Political Studies* 47, 3, Special Issue (1999): 522–537.

Clapham, Christopher. *Africa and the International System: The Politics of State Survival.* Cambridge: Cambridge University Press, 1996.

Clark, John F. "The Decline of the African Military Coup." *The Journal of Democracy* 18, 3 (2007): 141–155.

Clarke, George R. G. "Why Don't African Manufacturing Enterprises Export More? The Role of Trade Policy." *Infrastructure Quality and Enterprise Characteristics* (October 2004).

Cobbe, James H. *Governments and Mining Companies in Developing Countries.* Boulder: Westview Press, 1979.

Coleman, James S. *Nigeria: Background to Nationalism.* Los Angeles: University of California Press, 1958.

Coleman James S. and Carl G. Rosberg, eds. *Political Parties and National Integration in Tropical Africa.* Berkeley: University of California Press, 1964.

Collier, Berins. *Regimes in Tropical Africa: Changing Forms of Supremacy, 1945–1975.* Berkeley: University of California Press, 1982.

Collier, Paul. "Implication of Ethnic Diversity." In Emmanuel Nnadozie, ed. *African Economic Development.* New York: Academic Press, 2003: 149–179.

Collier, Paul. "Learning from Failure: The International Financial Institutions as Agencies of Restraint in Africa." In Andreas Schedler et al., eds. *The Self-Restraining State: Power and Accountability in New Democracies* (Boulder, CO: Lynne Rienner Publishers, 1999): 313–330.

Collier, Paul, and David Dollar. *Development Effectiveness: What Have we Learnt?* Washington, DC: World Bank, 2001.

Collier, Paul and Anke Hoeffler. "On the Incidence of Civil War in Africa." *The Journal of Conflict Resolution* 46, 1 (February 2002): 13–28.

Collins, Paul. "The State and Industrial Capitalism." *Development and Change* 14, 3 (July 1983).

Columbia Encyclopedia, 5th ed., S.V. "Atlantic Charter." New York: Columbia University Press, 1993.

Cook, Paul, and Colin H. Kirkpatrick. "Privatisation in Less Developed Countries: An Overview." In Cook and Kirkpatrick. *Privatisation in Less Developed Countries.*

Cook, Paul, and Colin H. Kirkpatrick, eds. *Privatisation in Less Developed Countries*. London: Harvester Wheatsheaf. 1988.

Correlates of War database, intra-war. http://www.correlatesofwar.org/cow2%20 data/WarData/IntraState/Intra-State%20War%20Format%20(V%203-0).htm

Craig, John. "Privatisation and Indigenous Ownership: Evidence from Africa." *Annals of Public and Cooperative Economics* 73, 4 (2002): 559–576.

Cumming, Gordon. "French Development Assistance to Africa." *African Affairs* 94, 376 (July 1995): 383–398.

Cumming, Gordon. *Aid to Africa: French and British Policies from the Cold War to the New Millennium* Aldershot: Ashgate, 2001.

Daniels, Robert V. *The End of Communist Revolution*. London: Routledge, 1993.

David-Barrett, Liz, and Ken Okamura. "The Transparency Paradox: Why do Corrupt Countries Join EITI?" *European Research Centre for Anti-Corruption and State–Building Working* Paper No. 38 (November 2013). http://eiti.org/files/The-Transparency-Paradox.-Why-do-Corrupt-Countries-Join-EITI1.pdf

Davidson, Adam. "Come On, China, Buy Our Stuff!" *New York Times* (January 25, 2012). http://www.nytimes.com/2012/01/29/magazine/come-on-china-buy-our-stuff.html?pagewanted=all&_r=0

Davidson, Basil. *The Black Man's Burden: Africa and the Curse of the Nation-State*. New York: Times Books, 1992.

de Mesquita, Bruce Bueno, Alastair Smith, Randolph M. Siverson, and James D. Morrow. *The Logic of Political Survival*. Cambridge: The MIT Press, 2003.

Decalo, Samuel. *Coups and Army Rule in Africa*. New Haven: Yale University Press, 1976.

Deng, Francis M. "Reconciling Sovereignty with Responsibility: A Basis for International Humanitarian Action." In Harbeson and Rothchild: 353–378.

Deng, Francis Mading. "State Collapse: The Humanitarian Challenge to the United Nations." In Zartman. *Collapsed States:* 207–219.

Deng, Francis, Sadikiel Kimaro, Terrence Lyons, Donald Rothchild, and I. William Zartman. *Sovereignty as Responsibility*. The Brookings Institution, Washington D.C., 1996.

Diamond, Larry Jay. "The Rule of Law versus the Big Man." *The Journal of Democracy* 19, 2 (2008): 138–149.

Diamond, Larry. "Class Formation and the Swollen State." *The Journal of Modern African Studies* 25, 4 (1987): 567–590.

Diamond, Larry. "Nigeria: Pluralism, Statism, and the Struggle for Democracy." In Diamond et al., eds. *Democracy in Developing Countries: Africa* Vol 2. Boulder, CO: Lynne Rienner Publishers, 1988: 33–92.

Diamond, Larry. "Is the Third Wave Over?" *Journal of Democracy* 7, 3 (1996): 20–37.

Diamond, Larry. "Thinking About Hybrid Regimes." *Journal of Democracy* 13 2 (2002): 21–36.

Dollar, David, and J. Svensson. "What Explains the Success or Failure of Structural Adjustment Programs?" *Policy Research Working Paper 1938*. Washington, DC: World Bank, 1998.

Dollar, David. "Outward-Oriented Developing Economies Really do Grow More Rapidly: Evidence from 95 LDCs, 1976–1985." *Economic Development and Cultural Change* (1992): 523–544.

Doornbos, Martin. "'Good Governance:' The Metamorphosis of a Policy Metaphor," *Journal of International Affairs* 57, 1 (Fall 2003): 3–17.

Dos Santos, Theotonio. "The Structure of Dependence." In K.T. Fann and Donald C. Hodges, eds. *Readings in U.S. Imperialism.* Boston: Porter Sargent, 1971: 225–236.

Doyle, Michael W. "Liberalism and World Politics." *The American Political Science Review* 80, 4 (Dec., 1986): 1151–1169.

Dreher Axel. "Does Globalization Affect Growth? Empirical Evidence from a new Index." *Applied Economics* 38, 10 (2006): 1091–1110;

Dreher, Axel, Noel Gaston and Pim Martens, 2008. *Measuring Globalization—Gauging its Consequence.* New York: Springer, 2008.

Dugger, Celia W. "Angola Moves to Make President Stronger." *The New York Times* (January 22, 2010) Section A; Column 0; Foreign Desk; Pg. 9.

Dugger, Celia W. "Governing Party in Angola Wins Election in a Landslide, Official Results Show." *The New York Times* (September 10, 2008).

Dunn, Kevin C. "Tales from the Dark Side: Africa's Challenge to International Relations Theory." *Journal of Third World Studies* 17 (2000): 61–90.

Dunn, Kevin C., and Timothy M. Shaw. *Africa's Challenge to International Relations Theory.* London: Palgrave Macmillan, 2001.

Dunning, Thad. "Conditioning the Effects of Aid: Cold War Politics, Donor Credibility, and Democracy in Africa." *International Organization* Vol. 58, No. 2 (Spring, 2004): 409–423.

East, Maurice A. "Size and Foreign Policy Behavior: A Test of Two Models." *World Politics* 25, 4 (1973): 556–576.

Easterly, William and Ross Levine. "Africa's Growth Tragedy: Policies and Ethnic Divisions." *Quarterly Journal of Economics* 112, 4 (November 1997): 1203–1250.

Easterly, William. "What Did Structural Adjustment Adjust? The Association of Policies and Growth with Repeated IMF and World Bank Adjustment Loans." *Journal of Development Economics* 76 (2005): 1–22.

Economic Commission for Africa. *Rapport sur la gourvernance ien Afrique II 2009.* Addis Ababa: UNECA, 2009.

Edogun, Cliff. "The Structure of State Capitalism in the Nigerian petroleum industry." In Ake, *Political Economy of Nigeria.*

Elkink, Johan A. "The International Diffusion of Democracy." *Comparative Political Studies* 44, 12 (2011): 1651–1674.

Elkins, Zachary, Andrew T. Guzman, and Beth Simmons. "Competing for Capital: The Diffusion of Bilateral Investment Treaties, 1960–2000." *International Organization* 60 (Fall 2006): 811–846.

Emerson, Rupert. "Colonialism, Political Development, and the UN." *International Organization* 19, 3 (Summer, 1965): 484–503.

Emmanuel, Nikolas. "Undermining Cooperation: Donor-Patrons and the Failure of Political Conditionality." *Democratization* 17, 5 (2010): 856–877.

Englebert, Pierre. *State Legitimacy and Development in Africa*. Boulder, CO: Lynne Rienner Publishers, 2000.

Evans, Peter B. *Dependent Development: The Alliance of Multinational, State, and Local Capital in Brazil*. [Vol. 487] Princeton: Princeton University Press, 1979.

Ezeife, Emeka. "Nigeria." In Adedeji. *Indigenization of African Economies*: 164–185.

Fallon, Peter R. and Luiz A. Pereira da Silva. In David L. Lindauer, Barbara Nunberg, eds. *Rehabilitating Government: Pay and Employment Reform in Africa*. Washington, DC: World Bank, 1994: 82–102.

Fan, Shenggen, and Anuja Saurkar. "Public Spending in Developing Countries: Trends, Determination, and Impact." EPTD Discussion Paper 99. Washington, DC: International Food Policy Research Institute, 2003.

Fatton Jr., Robert. *Predatory Rule: State and Civil Society in Africa*. Boulder, CO: Lynne Rienner Publishers, 1992.

Fieldhouse, D.K. "Arrested Development in Anglophone Black Africa?" In Gifford and Louis. *Decolonization and African Independence*: 135–158.

Fieldhouse, D.K. *Black Africa 1945–1980: Economic Decolonization & Arrested Development*. Boston: Unwin Hyman, 1986.

Finer, S.E. *Man on Horseback: The Role of the Military in Politics*. New York: Frederick A. Praeger Publishers, 1962: 35–47.

Finnemore, Martha and Kathryn Sikkink. *"International Norm Dynamics and Political Change." International Organization 52*, 4 (1998): 887–917.

First, Ruth. *Power in Africa*. New York: Pantheon Books, 1970.

Fish, M. Steven, and Matthew Kroenig. *The Handbook of National Legislatures: A Global Survey*. New York: Cambridge University Press, 2009.

Foley, Michael W., and Bob Edwards. "The Paradox of Civil Society." *The Journal of Democracy* 7, 3 (July 1996): 38–52.

Forrest, Tom. *Politics and Economic Development in Nigeria*. Boulder, CO: Westview Press, 1993.

Frank, André Gunder. *Capitalism and Underdevelopment in Latin America*. New York: Monthly Review Press, 1967.

Freedom House. www.freedomhouse.org.

Fuchs, Jean-Paul. *Pour une politique de développement efficace, maîtrisée, et transparente: Rapport au Premier ministre*. Paris: La documentation Française (1995).

Fukuyama, Francis. *The End of History and the Last Man*. New York: Free Press, 1992.

Gaddis, John Lewis. "International Relations Theory and the End of the Cold War." *International Security* 17, 3 (Winter, 1992–1993): 5–58.

Geddes, Barbara. "How the Approach You Choose Affects the Answers You Get: Rational Choice and its Uses in Comparative Politics." *Paradigms and Sand Castles: Theory Building and Research Design in Comparative Politics*. Ann Arbor: University of Michigan Press, 2003: Chapter 5.

Geddes, Barbara. "What Do We Know about Democratization after 20 Years? *Annual Review of Political Science* 2 (1999): 115–144.

George R, G. Clarke, Robert Cull, and Mary Shirley. "Empirical Studies." In G. Caprio, J. Fiechter, R. Litan, and M. Pomerleano, eds. *The Future of*

State-Owned Financial Institutions. Washington, DC: Brookings Institution Press, 2004: 280–281.

Gerschenkron, Alexander. *Economic Backwardness in Historical Perspective*. Cambridge, MA: Harvard University Press, 1962.

Gertzel, Cherry, Carolyn Baylies, and Morris Szeftel. "Introduction: The Making of the One-Party state." In Cherry Gertzel, Carolyn Baylies, and Morris Szeftel, eds. *The Dynamics of the One-Party State in Zambia* Manchester: Manchester University Press, 1984.

Gertzel, Cherry, and Morris Szeftel. "Politics in an African Urban Setting: The Role of the Copperbelt in the Transition to the One-Party State 1964–1973." In Cherry Gertzel, Carolyn Baylies, and Morris Szeftel, eds. *The Dynamics of the One-Party State in Zambia*. Manchester: Manchester University Press, 1984.

Gettleman, Jeffrey. "After Years of Struggle, South Sudan Becomes a New Nation." *New York Times* (July 9, 2011): http://www.nytimes.com/2011/07/10/world/africa/10sudan.html?pagewanted=all

Gifford, Prosser and Wm. Roger Louis, eds. *Decolonization and African Independence: The Transfer of Power, 1960–1980*. New Haven: Yale University Press, 1988.

Gifford, Prosser, and Wm. Roger Louis, eds. *The Transfer of Power in Africa: Decolonization 1940–1960*. New Haven: Yale University Press, 1982.

Gilpin, Robert. *Global Political Economy: Understanding the International Economic Order*. Princeton: Princeton University Press, 2001.

Gilpin, Robert. *The Political Economy of International Relations*. Princeton, NJ: Princeton University Press, 1987.

Gilpin, Robert. *U.S. Power and the Multinational Corporation: The Political Economy of Foreign Direct Investment*. New York: Basic Books, 1975

Githu, M. "Kenya's Opposition and the Crisis of Governance." *Issue: A Journal of Opinion* 21, 1–2 (1993).

Gladwell, Malcolm. *The Tipping Point: How Little Things Can Make a Big Difference*. London: Little Brown, and Co, 2000.

Gleditsch, Kristian Skrede, and Michael D. Ward. "Diffusion and the International Context of Democratization." *International Organization* 60 (2006): 911–933.

Goldman, Marshall I. "Putin and the Oligarchs." *Foreign Affairs* 83, 6 (Nov.-Dec., 2004): 33–44.

Goldsmith, Arthur A. "Donors, Dictators and Democrats in Africa." *Journal of Modern African Studies* 39, 3 (20001): 41–436.

Goldstein, Judith and Robert O. Keohane, eds. *Ideas and Foreign Policy*. Ithaca, NY: Cornell University Press, 1993.

Goldstein, Judith, "Ideas, institutions, and American Trade Policy." In G. John Ikenberry, David A. Lake, and Michael Mastanduno, eds. *The State and American Foreign Economic Policy*. Ithaca, NY: Cornell University Press, 1988: 179–218.

Gordon, David F. "Debt, Conditionality, and Reform: The International Relations of Economic Restructuring in Sub-Saharan Africa." In Callaghy and Ravenhill, *Hemmed In*: 90–129.

Gourevitch, Peter Alexis. *Politics in Hard Times: Comparative Responses to International Economic Crises*. Ithaca, NY: Cornell University Press, 1986.

Gourevitch, Peter Alexis. "Breaking with Orthodoxy: The Politics of Economic Policy Responses to the Depression of the 1930s." *International Organization* 38, 1 (1984): 95–129.

Gow, Bonar A. "Madagascar." In Michael Crowder. *The Cambridge History of Africa* Vol. 8, 1940–1975. Cambridge: Cambridge University Press, 1984: 674–697.

Gowa, Joanne, and Raymond Hicks. "The Most-Favored Nation Rule in Principle and Practice: Discrimination in the GATT." *Review of International Organization* 7 (2012): 247–266.

Gran, Guy. *Zaire: The Political Economy of Underdevelopment*. New York: Praeger, 1979.

Greene, Kenneth F. *Why Dominant Parties Lose: Mexico's Democratization in Comparative Perspective*. New York: Cambridge University Press, 2007.

Grosh, Barbara and Rwekaza S. Mukandala, eds. *State-Owned Enterprises in Africa*. Boulder, CO: Lynne Rienner Publishers, 1994.

Grosh, Barbara. "Though the Structural Adjustment Minefield: Politics in an Era of Economic Liberalization." In Widner, ed. *Economic Change*: 29–46.

Gunitsky, Seva. "From Shocks to Waves: Hegemonic Transitions and Democratization in the Twentieth Century." *International Organization* 68, 3 (June 2014): 1–37.

Gwartney, James, Robert Lawson, and Walter Block. *Economic Freedoms of the World 1975—1995*. Canada: Fraser Institute, 1996.

Gyimah-Boadi, E. "Civil Society and Democratic Development." In Gyimah-Boadi, ed. *Democraatic Reform*; 99–119.

Gyimah-Boadi, E. "Civil Society In Africa." *Journal of Democracy* 7, 2 (1996): 118–132.

Gyimah-Boadi, E., ed. *Democratic Reform in Africa: The Quality of Progress*. Boulder, CO: Lynne Rienner Publishers, 2004.

Haas, Ernst B. *When Knowledge is Power: Three Models of Change in International Organizations*. Los Angeles: University of California Press, 1990.

Haggard, Stephan, and Robert R. Kaufman. "Economic Adjustment in New Democracies." In Joan M. Nelson et al., eds. *Fragile Coalitions: The Politics of Economic Adjustment*. New Brunswick, N.J.: Transaction Books, 1989: 57–78

Haggard, Stephan and Robert R. Kaufman. *The Political Economy of Democratic Transitions*. Princeton: Princeton University Press, 1995.

Haggard, Stephan, and Steven B. Webb. "What Do We Know about the Political Economy of Economic Policy Reform?" *The World Bank Research Observer* 8, 2 (July 1993): 143–168.

Hall, Peter. "Policy Paradigms, Social Learning, and the State: The Case of Economic Policymaking in Britain." *Comparative Politics* 25, 3 (1993): 275–296.

Hall, Peter A., ed. *The Political Power of Economic Ideas: Keynesianism Across Nations*. Princeton: Princeton University Press, 1989.

Hall, Peter A., and Rosemary C.R. Taylor. "Political Science and the Three Institutionalisms." *Political Studies* XLIV (1996): 936–957.

Handbook of Trade Control Measures of Developing Countries: A Statistical Analysis of Trade Control Measures of Developing Countries 1987. Geneva: United Nations Conference on Trade and Development, 1987.

Hanna, William John. "Students." In Coleman and Rosberg eds. *Political Parties*, pp. 413–443.

Hanson, James A. "The Transformation of State-Owned Bank." In Gerard Caprio, Jonathan L. Fiechter, Robert E. Litan, and Michael Pomerleano, eds. *The Future of State-Owned Financial Institutions*. Washington, DC: Brookings Institution Press, 2004.

Harbeson, John W. "Externally Assisted Democratization: Theoretical Issues and African Realities." In Harbeson and Rothchild. *Africa in World Politics*: 235–262.

Harbeson, John W. and Donald Rothchild, eds. *Africa in World Politics: The African State System in Flux*. Boulder, CO: Westview Press, 2000.

Harbeson, John W. and Donald Rothchild, eds. *Africa in World Politics: Reforming Political Order*. Boulder, CO: Westview, 2009.

Harbeson, John W., Donald Rothchild, and Naomi Chazan, eds. *Civil Society and the State in Africa*. Boulder, CO: Lynne Rienner Publishers, 1994.

Harbeson, John W. "Promising Democratization Trajectories in Africa's Weak States." In Harbeson and Rothchild. *Africa in World Politics*.

Hargreaves, John D. *Decolonization in Africa*. New York: Longman, 1988.

Heilbrunn, John R. "Social Origins of National Conferences in Benin and Togo." *The Journal of Modern African Studies* 31, 2 (June 1993): 277–299.

Heller, Peter S. and Alan A. Tait. "Government Employment and Pay: Some International Comparisons." Occasional Paper 24. Washington, D.C.: International Monetary Fund, October 1983.

Herbst, Jeffrey. "Political Liberalization in Africa after Ten Years." *Comparative Politics* 33 (April 2001): 357–375.

Herbst, Jeffrey. "The Fall of Afro-Marxism." *Journal of Democracy* 1, 3 (Summer 1990): 92–101.

Herbst, Jeffrey. *States and Power in Africa: Comparative Lessons in Authority and Control*. Princeton: Princeton University Press, 2000.

Jeffery Herbst. "Western and African Peacekeepers: Motives and Opportunities." In Harbeson and Rothchild. *Africa in World Politics*: 308–323.

Herszenhorn, David M. "In Crimea, Russia Moved to Throw Off the Cloak of Defeat." *New York Times* (March 24, 2014): A9. http://www.nytimes.com/2014/03/25/world/europe/ukraine.html

Himbara, David. *Kenyan Capitalist, the State, and Development*. Boulder, CO: Lynne Rienner Publishers, 1994.

Hirschman, Albert O. *Essays in Trespassing: Economics to Politics and Beyond*. Cambridge: Cambridge University Press, 1981.

Hirschman, Albert O. *Exit, Voice, and Loyalty: Responses to Decline in Firms, Organizations, and States*. Cambridge: Harvard University Press, 1970.

Hirschman, Albert O. *The Strategies of Economic Development*. New Haven: Yale University Press, 1958.

Hodder-Williams, Richard. *An Introduction to the Politics of Tropical Africa*. London: George Allen & Unwin, 1984.

Hodgkin, Thomas. *Nationalism in Colonial Africa*. New York: New York University Press, 1957.

Hoffmann, Stanley. "The Debate About Intervention." In Phil Williams, Donald, M. Goldstein, and Jay M. Sharfitz, eds. *Classic Readings and Contemporary Debates in International Relations.* Belmont, CA: Thomas Wadsworth, 2006: 667–674.

Holm, John. "Botswana: A Paternalistic Democracy." In Diamond et al., eds. *Democracy in Developing Countries* Vol 2. Boulder, CO: Lynne Rienner Publishers, 1988.

Holman, Michael. "Welcome to the Aid Business." *Open Democracy* (June 2005). http://www.globalpolicy.org/component/content/article/176/31419.html

Hook, Steven W. *National Interest and Foreign Aid.* Boulder, CO: Lynne Rienner Publishers, 1995.

Hoover, Kenneth R. "The Rise of Conservative Capitalism: Ideological Tensions within the Reagan and Thatcher Governments." *Comparative Studies in Society and History* 29, 2 (1987): 245–268.

Hopf, Ted. "The Promise of Constructivism in International Relations Theory." *International Security* 23, 1 (Summer, 1998): 171–200

Hughes, Neil C. "A Trade War with China?: The Eagle and the Dragon." *Foreign Affairs* (July/August 2005). http://www.foreignaffairs.com/articles/60825/neil-c-hughes/a-trade-war-with-china

Huntington, Samuel P. *The Third Wave: Democratization in the Late Twentieth Century.* Norman, OK: University of Oklahoma Press 1991.

Huntington, Samuel P. *The Clash of Civilizations and the Remaking of the World Order.* New York: Simon and Shuster, 1996.

Huntington, Samuel. "The Lonely Superpower." *Foreign Affairs* (March/April 1999).

Huntington, Samuel. *Political Order in Changing Societies.* New Haven: Yale University Press, 1968.

Hyden, Goran. *African Politics in Comparative Perspective.* Cambridge: Cambridge University Press 2006.

Hyden, Goran and Michael Bratton, eds. *Governance and Politics in Africa.* Boulder, CO: Lynne Rienner Publishers, 1992.

Ikenberry, G. John. "The International Spread of Privatization Policies: Inducements, Learning and 'Policy Bandwagoning.'" In Ezra Suleiman and John Waterbury, eds. *The Political Economy of Public Sector Reform and Privatization.* Boulder, Co.: Westview Press, 1990: 88–110.

Ikenberry, G. John. "The Rise of China and the Future of the West: Can the Liberal System Survive?" *Foreign Affairs* (2008): 23–37.

IMF Factsheet, "Debt Relief Under the Heavily Indebted Poor Countries (HIPC)." December 2011. http://www.imf.org/external/np/exr/facts/hipc.htm

International Monetary Fund, *World Economic and Financial Surveys: Regional Economic Outlook: Sub-Saharan Africa* Washington, DC: International Monetary Fund, 2012.

IMF World Economic Outlook Database. http://www.imf.org/external/pubs/ft/weo/2014/01/weodata/index.aspx

Investment Promotion Network at Pananet at www.ipanet.com.

Ishiyama, John and John James Quinn. "Phoenix from the Ashes: The Formerly Dominant Parties in New Democracies in Africa." *Party Politics* 12, 3 (May 2006): 317–340.

Jackman, Robert W. "On the Relationship of Economic Development to Political Performance." *American Journal of Political Science* 17 (1973): 611–621.

Jackson, Robert H. and Carl G. Rosberg, *Personal Rule in Black Africa: Prince, Auto-crat, Prophet, Tyrant.* Los Angeles: University of California Press, 1982.

Jackson, Robert H., and Carl G. Rosberg. "The Marginality of African States." In Carter and O'Meara. *African Independence*: 45–70.

Jackson, Robert H., and Carl G. Rosberg. "Why Africa's Weak States Persist: The Empirical and the Juridical in Statehood." *World Politics* 35, 1 (1982): 1–24.

Jackson, Robert H. *Quasi-states: Sovereignty, International Relations, and the Third World.* Cambridge: Cambridge University Press, 1990.

Jaycox, Edward V.K. "Structural Adjustment in sub-Saharan Africa: The World Bank's Perspective." *Issue: A Journal of Opinion*, Vol. 18, No. 1 (Winter, 1989): 36–40.

Jensen, J. Bradford, Dennis P. Quinn, and Stephen Weymouth. "The Influence of Firm Global Supply Chains and Foreign Currency Undervaluations on US Trade Disputes." International Organization, 69 (2015), pp 913-947 doi:10.1017/S0020818315000247

Jensen, Nathan, and Leonard Wantchekon. "Resource Wealth and Political Regimes in Africa." *Comparative Political Studies* 37 (September 2004) 816–841.

John Ravenhill, ed. *Africa in Economic Crisis.* New York: Columbia University Press.

Johnson, Harry G. "A Theoretical Model of Economic Nationalism in New and Developing State." *Political Science Quarterly* 80, 2 (June 1965): 169–185.

Johnson, John J., ed. *The Role of the Military in Underdeveloped Countries.* Princeton: Princeton University Press, 1962.

Jones, Vivian C., and Brock R. Williams. "U.S. Trade and Investment Relations with sub-Saharan Africa and the African Growth and Opportunity Act." Congressional Research Service, 7–5700, www.crs.gov, RL31772. http://www.fas.org/sgp/crs/row/RL31772.pdf

Joseph, Richard. "Africa, 1990–1997: From Abertura to Closure." *Journal of Democracy* 9, 2 (1998): 3–7.

Joseph, Richard. "Democratization in Africa after 1989: Comparative and Theoretical Perspectives." *Comparative Politics* 29, 3, (Apr., 1997): 363–382

Joseph, Richard. "The Reconfiguration of Power in Late Twentieth-Century Africa." In Joseph. *State, Conflict, and Democracy*: 57–82.

Joseph, Richard, ed. *State, Conflict, and Democracy in Africa.* Boulder, CO: Lynne Rienner Publishers, 1999.

Kabongo, Ilunga. "The Catastrophe of Belgian Decolonization." In Gifford and Louis. *Decolonization and African Independence*: 381–400.

Kahler, Miles. *Decolonization in Britain and France: The Domestic Consequences of International Relations.* Princeton: Princeton University Press, 1984.

Karl, Terry Lynn. *The Paradox of Plenty: Oil Booms and Petro-States.* Berkeley: University of California, 1997.

Kavanagh, Michael J. "Gecamines of Congo Will Seek Profit from Takeovers, Audits." *Bloomberg* (October 6, 2011). http://www.bloomberg.com/news/2011–10–06/gecamines-of-congo-will-seek-profit-from-takeovers-audits-1-.html

Kayizzi-Mugerwa, Steve. "Privatization in sub-Saharan Africa: On Factors Impacting Implementation." WIDER Discussion Paper 12 (UNU-WIDER, 2012).

Keller, Edmond. "Decolonization, Independence and Beyond." In Phyllis M. Martin and Patrick O'Meara, eds. *Africa* 2nd Ed. Bloomington, IN: Indiana University Press, 1986.

Keller, Edmond J. "Reexamining Sovereign States in Africa." *International Studies Review* 4, 1 (Spring, 2002), pp. 197–200.

Keller, Edmond J. and Donald Rothchild, eds. *Afro-Marxist Regimes: Ideology and Public Policy*. Boulder, CO: Lynne Rienner Publisher, 1987.

Kennedy, Paul. *African Capitalism: The Struggle for Ascendancy*. Cambridge: Cambridge University Press, 1988.

Kennedy, Ryan. "The Contradiction of Modernization: A Conditional Model of Endogenous Democratization." *The Journal of Politics* 72, 3 (July 2010): 785–798.

Keohane, Robert O. *After Hegemony: Cooperation and Discord in the World Political Economy*. Princeton, NJ: Princeton University Press, 1984.

Keohane, Robert O., and Joseph S. Nye. *Power and Interdependence*. Boston: Little, Brown, 1977.

Khadiagala, Gilbert, and Terrence Lyons. "Foreign Policy Making in Africa: An Introduction." In Gilbert M. Khadiagala and Terrence Lyons, eds. *African Foreign Policies: Power and Process*. Boulder, CO: Lynne Rienner Publishers, 2001: 1–13

Kherallah, Mylène, Christopher Delgado, Eleni Gabre-Madhin, Nicholas Minot, and Michael Johnson. *The Road Half Traveled: Agricultural Market Reform in Sub-Saharan Africa*. Washington, D.C.: International Food Policy Research Institute, 2000.

Kholi, Atul. "Democracy and Development." In John P. Lewis and Valeriana Kallab, eds. *Development Strategies Reconsidered*. New Brunswick, N.J.: Transaction Books, 1986.

Killick, Tony. *Development Economics in Actions: A Study of Economic Policies in Ghana*. London: Heinemann, 1978.

Kindleberger, Charles P. "Dominance and Leadership in the International Economy: Exploitation, Public Goods, and Free Rides." *International Studies Quarterly* 25 (June 1981).

Kindleberger, Charles P. *The World in Depression, 1929–1939*. Berkeley: University of California Press, 1973.

Kinsella, David, Bruce Russett, and Harvey Starr. *World Politics: The Menu for Choice* (Boston: Wadsworth, 2013).

KOF Index of Globalization. http://globalization.kof.ethz.ch/

Krasner, Stephen D. "State Power and the Structure of Foreign Trade." *World Politics* 28 (April 1976): 317–347.

Krasner, Stephen D. *Defending the National Interest: Raw Materials Investments and U.S. Foreign Policy*. Princeton: Princeton University Press, 1978.

Krasner, Stephen D., ed. *International Regimes*. Ithaca: Cornell University Press, 1983.

Krasner, Stephen D. "Sovereignty: An Institutional Perspective." *Comparative Political Studies* 21, 1 (1988): 66–94.

Krasner, Stephen D. "Structural Causes and Regime Consequences: Regimes as Intervening Variables." In Krasner, ed. *International Regimes*: 1–21.

Krasner, Stephen D. *Structural Conflict: The Third World Against Global Liberalism.* Berkeley & Los Angeles: University of California, 1985.

Krauthammer, Charles. "The Unipolar Moment." *Foreign Affairs—America and the World*, 1990, Special Issue, 70, 1 (1990/91): 25–33.

Krueger, Anne O. *Foreign Trade Regimes and Economic Development: Liberalization Attempts and Consequences* Vol X. Ballinger Publishing Company: Cambridge Mass., 1978.

Krueger, Anne O. "The Political Economy of the Rent-Seeking Society." *The American Economic Review* 60, 3 (June 1974): 291–303.

Krueger, Anne O. "Trade Policy as an Input to Development." *American Economic Association* 70, 2 (May 1980): 288–292.

Krueger, Anne O. "Virtuous and Vicious Circles in Economic Development." *American Economic Review* 83, 1–2 (May 1993): 351–355.

Kuenzi, Michelle and Gina Lambright. "Party System Institutionalization in 30 African Countries." *Party Politics* 7, 4 (July 2001): 437–468.

Kunz, Frank A. "Civil Society in Africa." *The Journal of Modern African Studies* 33, 1 (March 1995): 181–187.

Kuznets, Simon. *Postwar Economic Growth*. Cambridge, MA: Harvard University Press, 1964.

Lairson, Thomas D, and David Skidmore. *International Political Economy: The Struggle for Power and Wealth, 2nd Edition*. Belmont, CA: Thomson-Wadsworth: 325–362.

Lake, David. "Escape the State of Nature: Authority and Hierarchy in World Politics." *International Security* 32, 1 (2007): 47–79.

Lake, David. "Leadership, Hegemony, and the International Economy." *International Studies Quarterly* 37 (Winter 1993–94): 459–489.

Lake, David A. *Power Protection, and Free Trade: International Sources of U.S. Commercial Strategy, 1887–1939.* Ithaca, NY: Cornell University Press, 1988.

Lake, David A. and Donald Rothchild. *The International Spread of Ethnic Conflict: Fear, Diffusion, and Escalation.* Princeton: Princeton University Press, 1998.

Lal, Deepak. *The Poverty of "Development Economics.* Cambridge Mass.: Harvard University Press, 1985.

Lancaster, Carol. "Africa in World Affairs." In Harbeson and Rothchild, *Africa in World Politics*, pp. 208–234.

Lancaster, Carol. *Aid to Africa So Much To Do, So Little Done.* Chicago: University of Chicago Press, 1999.

Lancaster, Carol. "Economic Restructuring in Sub-Saharan Africa." *Current History: Africa 1989* (May 1989).

Lancaster, Carol. *Foreign aid: Diplomacy, development, domestic politics.* University of Chicago Press, 2008.

Larson, Deborah Welch. *Origins of Containment: A Psychological Explanation.* Princeton: Princeton University Press, 1989.

Layne, Christopher. "The Waning of U.S. Hegemony—Myth or Reality? A Review Essay." *International Security* 34, 1 (Summer 2009): 147–172.

Leibenstein, Harvey. *Economic Backwardness and Economic Growth.* New York: Wiley, 1957.

Lemarchand, Rene. "The CIA in Africa: How Central, How Intelligent?" *Journal of Modern African Studies* 14, 3 (1976): 401–426.

Lemke, Douglas. "African Lessons for International Relations Research." *World Politics* 56, 1 (2003): 114–138.

Lemke, Douglas. *Regions of War and Peace.* Cambridge: Cambridge University Press, 2002.

Levi, Margaret. "A Model, A Method, and A Map: Rational Choice in Comparative and Historical Analysis." In Mark Irving Lichbach and Alan S. Zuckerman, eds. *Comparative Politics: Rationality, Culture, and Structure.* Cambridge: Cambridge University Press, 1997.

Le Vine, Victor T. "African Patrimonial Regimes in Comparative Perspective." *The Journal of Modern African Studies* 18, 4 (Dec., 1980): 657–673.

Levitsky, Steven, and Lucan A. Way. "Linkage versus Leverage. Rethinking the International Dimension of Regime Change." *Comparative Politics* 38, 4 (July 2006): 379–400.

Levitsky, Steven, and Lucan A. Way. "Rethinking the International Dimension of Regime Change." *Comparative Politics* 38, 4 (July 2006): 379–400.

Levitsky, Steven, and Lucan A. Way. "The Rise of Competitive Authoritarianism." *Journal of Democracy* 13.2 (2002) 51–65.

Lewis, Peter M. "Economic Reform and Political Transition in Africa: The Quest for a Politics of Development." *World Politics* 49, 1 (1996): 92–129.

Leys, Colin. "African Economic Development in Theory and Practice." In "Black Africa." Special Issue of *Dædalus.*

Leys, Colin. *Underdevelopment in Kenya: The Political Economy of Neo-Colonialism 1964–1971.* Berkeley: University of California Press, 1975.

Liebenow, J. Gus. "The Military Factor in African Politics: A Twenty-Five-Year Perspective." In Carter and O'Meara. *African Independence*: 126–159.

Liebenow, J. Gus. *African Politics: Crises and Challenges.* Bloomington: Indiana University Press, 1986.

Lienert, Ian, and Jitendra Modi. "A Decade of Civil Service Reform in Sub-Saharan Africa." *IMF Working Paper* A Decade of Civil Service Reform in Sub-Saharan Africa—WP/97/179 (December 1997): 1–47

Lijphart, Arend. "Comparative Politics and Comparative Method." *American Political Science Review* 65 (1971): 682–693.

Lijphart, Arend. *Patterns of Democracy: Government Forms and Performance in Thirty-Six Countries.* New Haven: Yale University Press, 1999.

Lindberg, Staffan I. *Democracy and Elections in Africa.* Baltimore, MD: The Johns Hopkins University Press, 2006.

Lindblom, Charles E. *Politics and Markets: The World's Political-Economic Systems.* New York: Basic Books, Inc., 1977.

Lipset, Seymour Martin. "Some Social Requisites of Democracy: Economic Development and Political Legitimacy." *American Political Science Review* 53 (March, 1959): 69–105.

Little, I.M.D. *Economic Development: Theory Policy and International Relations.* New York: Basic Books, 1982.

Lofchie, Michael F. "The New Political Economy in Africa." In David E. Apter and Carl G. Rosberg, eds. *Political Development and the New Realism in Sub-Saharan Africa*. Charlottesville: University of Virginia Press, 1994: 160–165.

Lofchie, Michael. *The Policy Factor: Agricultural Performance in Kenya and Tanzania*. Boulder, CO: Lynne Rienner Publishers, 1989.

Lofchie, Michael F. "The Uganda Coup—Class Action by the Military." *Journal of Modern African Studies* 10 (1972): 19–35.

Lopez, Juan J. "Theory Choice in Comparative Social Inquiry." *Polity* 25, 2 (Winter 1992): 267—282.

Louis, William Roger. "Libyan Independence, 1951: The Creation of a Client State." In Gifford and Louis. *Decolonization and African Independence*: 159–184.

Louis, William Roger and Ronald Robinson. "The United States and the Liquidation of British Empire in Tropical Africa, 1941–1951." In Gifford and Louis. *The Transfer of Power in Africa*: 31–56.

Low, Anthony. "The End of the British Empire in Africa." In Gifford and Louis. *Decolonization and African Independence*: 33–72.

Lubeck, Paul M., ed. *The African Bourgeoisie: Capitalist Development in Nigeria, Kenya, and the Ivory Coast*. Boulder, CO: Lynne Rienner Publishers, 1987.

Luckham, Robin. "French Militarism in Africa." *Review of African Political Economy* 24 (May-August, 1982): 55–84.

Luckham, Robin. "The Military, Militarization and Democratization in Africa: A Survey of Literature and Issues." *African Studies Review* 37, 2 (September 1994): 13–76.

Maizels, Alfred and Machiko K. Nissanke. "Motivations for Aid to Developing Countries." *World Development* 12, 9 (1994): 879–900.

Mamdani, Mahmood. *When Victims Become Killers: Colonialism, Nativism, and the Genocide in Rwanda*. Princeton: Princeton University Press, 2001.

Manji, Firoze, and Carl O'Coill. "The Missionary Position: NGOs and Development in Africa." *International Affairs* 78, 3 (2002): 567–83.

Maoz, Zeev, and Bruce Russett. "Normative and Structural Causes of Democratic Peace, 1946–1986." *The American Political Science Review* 87, 3 (Sep., 1993): 624–638.

Marcum, John A. "The People's Republic of Angola: a Radical Vision Frustrated." In Edmond J. Keller and Donald Rothchild, eds. *Afro-Marxist Regimes: Ideology and Public Policy*. Boulder, CO: Lynne Rienner Publisher, 1987: 68–71.

Marshall, Monty G. and Donna Ramsey Marshall. Center for Systemic Peace. July 30, 2010. http://www.systemicpeace.org/inscr/inscr.htm

Martin Fransman, ed. *Industry and Accumulation in Africa*. London: Heinemann, 1982.

Marx, Karl. "Critique of the Gotha Program." In Robert C. Tucker, ed. *The Marx-Engels Reader* 2nd Edition. New York: W.W. Norton & Company, 1978.

M'Bokolo, Elikia. "French Colonial Policy in Equatorial Africa." In Gifford and Louis. *The Transfer of Power in Africa*: 173–210.

McGowan, Patrick J. "African military coups d'état, 1956–2001: frequency, trends and distribution." *Journal of Modern African Studies*, 41, 3 (2003), pp. 339–370.

McGowan, Patrick, and Thomas H. Johnson. "Military Coups d'état and Underdevelopment." *Journal of Modern African Studies* 22, 4 (1984).

McHenry, Jr., Dean E. "Federalism in Africa: Is it a Solution to, or a Cause of, Ethnic Problems?" Presented at the Annual Meeting of the African Studies Association in Columbus, Ohio, November 1997.

McHenry, Donald F. "The United Nations: Its Role in Decolonization." In Carter and O'Meara. *African Independence*: 31–44.

McKinlay, R.D. "The Aid Relationship: A Foreign Policy Model and Interpretation of the Distributions of Official Bilateral Economic Aid of the United States, the United Kingdom, France, and Germany, 1960–1970." *Comparative Political Studies* 11, 4 (1979): 411–463.

McMillan, Margaret. "Why Kill The Golden Goose? A Political-Economy Model of Export Taxation." *The Review of Economics and Statistics* (February 2001): 83, 1: 170–184.

Mearsheimer, John J. "Realism, the Real World, and the Academy." *Realism and Institutionalism in International Studies* (2002): 23–33.

Mearsheimer, John J. *The Tragedy of Great Power Politics*. New York: W. W. Norton & Company, 2014.

Megginson, William. "Privatization." *Foreign Policy*, No. 118 (Spring, 2000): 14–27.

Megginson, William L. and Jeffry N. Netter. "From State to Market: A Survey of Empirical Studies on Privatization." *Journal of Economic Literature* 39, 2 (June 2001): 321–389, p. 380.

Meier, Gerald M. "The Formative Period." In Gerald M. Meier and Dudley Seers, eds. *Pioneers in Development*. Washington D.C.: Oxford University Press for World Bank, 1984.

Meier, Gerald M., and William F. Steel. *Industrial Adjustment in Sub-Saharan Africa*. London: Oxford University Press, 1989.

Meier, Gerald M., and Joseph E. Stiglitz, eds. *Frontiers of Development Economics: The future in Perspective*. New York: Oxford University Press, 2001.

Michael Lipton. *Why Poor People Stay Poor: Urban Bias in World Development*. Cambridge, MA: Harvard University Press, 1976.

Midlarsky, Manu I. "Democracy and Islam: Implications for Civilizational Conflict and the Democratic Peace." *International Studies Quarterly* 42 (1998): 485–511.

Milne, R.S. *Politics in Ethnically Bipolar States: Guyana, Malaysia, Fiji*. Vancouver: University of British Columbia Press, 1981.

Moehler, Devra C., and Staffan I. Lindberg. "Narrowing the Legitimacy Gap: Turnovers as a Cause of Democratic Consolidation." *The Journal of Politics* 71, 4 (Oct., 2009): 1448–1466.

Moore Jr., Barrington. *Social Origins of Dictatorship and Democracy: Lord and Peasant in the Making of the Modern World*. Boston: Beacon Press, 1966.

Morganthau, Hans. "A Political Theory of Foreign Aid." *American Political Science Review* 56, 2 (1962): 301–309.

Morgenthau, Hans J. *Politics Among Nations: The Struggle for Power and Peace, Fifth Edition, Revised*. New York: Alfred A. Knopf, 1978.

Morgenthau, Ruth Schachter. *Political Parties in French-Speaking West Africa*. Oxford: Clarendon Press, 1964.

Morgenthau, Ruth Schachter. *Political Parties in French-Speaking West Africa.* Oxford: Clarendon Press, 1964.

Morgenthau, Ruth Schachter, and Lucy Creevey Behrman. "French-Speaking Tropical Africa." In Michael Crowder, ed. *The Cambridge History of Africa Vol. 8 from c. 1940 to c. 1975.* Cambridge: Cambridge University Press, 1984.

Moroff, Anika. "Ethnic Party Bans in East Africa from a Comparative Perspective." *GIGA Research Programme: Violence and Security* No 129 (April 2010).

Morse, Chandler. "The Economics of African Socialism." In William H. Friedland and Carl G. Rosberg, ed. *African Socialism.* Stanford, CA: Stanford University Press, 1964: 35–52.

Mosely, Paul, Turan Subasat, and John Weeks. "Assessing Adjustment in Africa." *World Politics* 23 (1995): 1459–1473.

Mosley, Paul. "Privatization, Policy-Based Lending and World Bank Behavior." In Paul Cook and Kirkpatrick, *Privatisation in Less Developed Countries.*

Moss, Todd, David Roodman, and Scott Standley. "The Global War on Terror and U.S. Development Assistance: USAID allocation by country, 1998–2005." *Center for Global Development* Working Paper 62 (July 2005).

Myrdal, Gunner. *Economic Theory and Under-Developed Regimes.* London: Methuen, 1957.

NATO homepage. http://www.nato.int/cps/en/natolive/nato_countries.htm

Nellis, John R. "Public Enterprises in Sub-Saharan Africa." In Grosh and Mukandala, *State-Owned Enterprises.*

Nellis, John. "Privatization in Africa: What has Happened? What is to Be Done?" In Gerard Roland, ed. *Privatization: Successes and Failures.* New York: Columbia University Press, 2008: 109–135.

Nellis, John. Privatization in Africa: What Has happened? What is to Be Done? Fondzione Eni Enrico Matte. (October 2005).

Nelson, Joan M. *Economic Crisis and Policy Choice: The Politics of Adjustment in the Third World.* Princeton: Princeton University Press, 1990.

NEPAD webpage http://www.nepad.org/economicandcorporategovernance/african-peer-review-mechanism/about

Newbury, Catharine. *The Cohesion of Oppression: Clientship and Ethnicity in Rwanda, 186–1960.* New York: Columbia University Press, 1988.

Nkrumah, Kwame. *Neo-Colonialism: The Last Stage of Imperialism.* New York: International Publishers, 1965.

North, Douglass C. *Institutions, Institutional Change and Economic Performance.* Cambridge: Cambridge University Press, 1990.

North, Douglass C. *Structure and Change in Economic History.* New York: W. W. Norton & Co., 1981.

Nossiter, Adam. "U.S. Engages With an Iron Leader in Equatorial Guinea." *New York Times,* May 30, 2011.

Nurske, Ragnar. *Problems of Capital Formation in Underdeveloped Countries.* Oxford: Blackwell, 1953.

Nye, Joseph S. *Is the American Century Over?(Global Futures).* Malden, MA: Polity Press, 2015.

Nye, Joseph S. "Limits of American Power." *Political Science Quarterly* 117, 4 (2002/2003).

Nye, Joseph S. "Soft Power." *Foreign policy* 80 (1990): 153–171.

O'Donnell, Guillermo, and Philippe C. Schmitter. *Transitions from Authoritarian Rule: Tentative Conclusions About Uncertain Democracies.* Baltimore: Johns Hopkins University Press, 1986.

O'Loughlin, John, Michael D. Ward, Corey L. Lofdahl, Jordin S. Cohen, David S. Brown, David Reilly, Kristian S. Gleditsch, and Michael Shin. "The Diffusion of Democracy, 1946–1994." *Annals of the Association of American Geographers* 88, 4 (1998): 545–574.

Ocheje, Paul. "The Extractive Industries Transparency Initiative (EITI): Voluntary codes of conduct, poverty and accountability in Africa." *Journal of Sustainable Development in Africa* 8, no. 3 (2006): 222–39. http://www.jsd-africa.com/Jsda/Fall2006/PDF/Arc_the%20Extractive%20Industries%20Transparency%20Initiative.pdf

O'Donnell, Guillermo A. "Horizontal Accountability in New Democracies." *Journal of Democracy* 9, 3 (1998): 112–116.

O'Donnell, Guillermo A. *Modernization and Bureaucratic-Authoritarianism: Studies in South American Politics.* Berkeley: Institute of International Studies/University of California, 1973, 1979.

OECD, *Development Co-operation: Effort and Policies of the Members of the Development Assistance Committee.* OECD, 1998.

Ogot, Bethwell A., and Tiyambe Zeleza. "Kenya: The Road to Independence and After." In Gifford and Louis. *Decolonization and African Independence*: 401–426.

Olsen, Gorm Rye. "Europe and the Promotion of Democracy in Post Cold War Africa: How Serious is Europe and For What Reason." *African Affairs* 97 (1998): 343–367.

Olson, Mancur. *The Logic of Collective Action: Public Goods and the Theory of Groups.* Cambridge: Harvard University Press, 1965.

Olson, Mancur. *The Rise and Decline of Nations: Economic Growth, Stagflation, and Social Rigidities.* New Haven, CT: Yale University Press, 1984.

O'Neil, Patrick H. "Revolution from Within: Analysis, Transitions from Authoritarianism, and the Case of Hungary." *World Politics* 48, 4 (1996): 579–603.

Organski A.F.K. and J. Kugler. *The War Ledger.* Chicago: University of Chicago Press, 1980.

Organski, A.F.K. *World Politics.* New York: Knopf, 1958.

Ottaway, Marina. "African Democratisation and the Leninist Option." *Journal of Modern African Studies* 35, 1 (March 1997): 1–15.

Ottaway, Marina. "From Political Opening to Democracy." In Marina Ottaway ed. *Democracy in Africa: The Hard Road Ahead.* Boulder: Lynne Rienner Publishers 1997: 1–15.

"Overpricing Zambia's Family Silver." *The Economist* 347, 8067 (May 9, 1998).

Overseas Development Institute, "NGOs and Official Donors." Briefing paper 4 (August 1995).

Owen, IV., John M. "Iraq and the Democratic Peace." *Foreign Affairs* (Nov. /Dec. 2005);

Panther-Brick, Keith. "Independence, French Style." In Gifford and Louis. *Decolonization and African Independence*: 78–95.

Paul, Thazha V. "Soft Balancing in the Age of US Primacy." *International Security* 30, 1 (2005): 46–71.

Payne, Richard J. and Cassandra R. Veney, "China's Post-Cold War African Policy." *Asian Survey* 38, 9 (September 1998): 867–879.

Peemans, Jean-Philippe. "Accumulation and Underdevelopment in Zaire: General Aspects in Relation to the Evolution of the Agrarian Crisis." In Nzongola-Ntalaja, ed. *The Crisis in Zaire: Myths and* Realities. Trenton, NJ: Africa World Press, Inc., 1986.

Person, Yves. "French West Africa and Decolonization." In Gifford and Louis. *The Transfer of Power in Africa*: 141–172.

Piccone, Theodore J. *International Mechanisms for Protecting Democracy*. Washington, D.C.: Democracy Coalition Project, 2004.

Pick's Currency Yearbook. New York: Pick Publication Corporation, Various years.

Pitcher, Anne, Mary H. Moran, and Michael Johnston. "Rethinking Patrimonialism and Neopatrimonialism in Africa." *African Studies Review* Volume 52, Number 1 (April 2009): 125–156.

"Political Regimes and Regime Transitions in Africa, 1910 [sic (1989)]–1994." Michigan, Ann Arbor: ICPSR –producer, 1997. South African Data Archive- distributor, 2000.

Posen, Adam S. "Fleeting Equality: The Relative Size of the U.S. and EU Economies to 2020." Brooking Institution, U.S.-Europe Analysis, Number 8 (September 2004).

Posner, Daniel N., and Daniel J. Young. "The Institutionalization of Political Power in Africa." *Journal of Democracy* 18, 3 (2007) 126–140.

Prebisch, R. *The Economic Development of Latin America and its Principal Problems*. New York: United Nations, 1950.

Prempeh, H. Kwasi. "Presidents Untamed." *Journal of Democracy* 19, 2 (2008): 109–123.

Prichett, Lant. "Measuring Outward Orientation in Developing Countries: Can it be Done?" *World Bank Working Paper*. Washington, D.C.: The World Bank, 1991.

Prunier, Gérard. *The Rwanda Crisis: History of a Genocide*. Columbia University Press, 1995.

Przeworski, Adam. *Democracy and the Market: Political and Economic Reforms in Eastern Europe and Latin America*. Cambridge: Cambridge University Press, 1991.

Przeworski, Adam, Michael Alvarez, José Antonio Cheibub & Fernando Limongi. "What Makes Democracies Endure." *Journal of Democracy* 7, 1 (1996): 39–55.

Przeworski, Adam and Fernando Limongi. "Modernization: Theories and Facts." *World Politics* 49 (January 1997): 155–83.

Przeworski, Adam and Henry Teune. *The Logic of Comparative Social Inquiry*. New York: John Wiley, 1970.

Putnam, Robert D. "Diplomacy and Domestic Politics: The Logic of Two-Level Games." *International Organization* 42, 3 (Summer 1988): 427–460.

Quinn, Dennis P. *Restructuring the Automobile Industry: A Study of Firms and States in Modern Capitalism.* New York: Columbia University Press, 1988.

Quinn, Dennis P., and A. Maria Toyoda. "Ideology and Voter Preferences as Determinants of Financial Globalization." *American Journal of Political Science* 51, 2 (2007): 344–363, eds., In Beth Simmons, Frank Dobbin, and Geoff Garrett, eds. *The Global Diffusion of Neoliberalism.* Cambridge University Press.

Quinn, John J. "The Impact of State Ownership of Resources on Economic and Political Development in Sub-Saharan Africa." *Ufahamu* Vol. XXI, No 1and 2 (Winter/Spring 1993): 60–79.

Quinn, John J. "The Managerial Bourgeoisie: Capital Accumulation, Development and Democracy." In David G. Becker and Richard L. Sklar, eds. *Postimperialism and World Politics.* Westport, CT: Praeger, 1999: 219–252.

Quinn, John James. "African Foreign Policies." In Robert Denemark et. al., eds. *The International Studies Compendium Project.* Oxford: Wiley-Blackwell, 2010: 24–46.

Quinn, John James. "Democracy and Development." In Emmanuel Nnadozie, ed. *African Economic Development.* New York: Academic Press, 2003: 231–258.

Quinn, John James. "Diffusion and Escalation in the Great Lakes Region: the Rwandan Genocide, the Rebellion in Zaire, and Mobutu's Overthrow." In Steven E. Lobell and Philip Mauceri, eds. *Ethnic conflict and international politics: explaining diffusion and escalation.* New York: Palgrave Macmillan, 2004: 111–132.

Quinn, John James. "Economic Accountability: Are Constraints on Economic Decision Making a Blessing or a Curse?" *Scandinavian Journal of Development Alternatives and Area Studies* 19, 4 (December 2000): 131–169.

Quinn, John James. "The Effects of Majority State Ownership of Significant Economic Sectors on Corruption: A Cross-Regional Comparison." *International Interactions* 34, 1 (2008): 81–128.

Quinn, John James. "The Nexus of the Domestic and Regional within an International Context: The Rwandan Genocide and Mobutu's Ouster." In Amy L. Freedman, ed. *Threatening the State: the Internationalization of Internal Conflicts.* Oxford: Routledge, 2014: 39–74.

Quinn, John James. *The Road oft Traveled: Development Policies and Majority State Ownership of Industry in Africa.* Westport, CT: Praeger, 2002.

Quinn, John James. "When You Cannot Find the Perfect Match: Using the Accumulated Most Similar Design Case Study." *Journal of Political Science Education* 5, 3 (July-September 2009): 250–267.

Quinn, John James. "W(h)ither the State (System)?" *International Politics* 38, 3 (2001): 437–446.

Quinn, John James, John Ishiyama and Marijke Breuning, "Aid, Development, and Foreign Policy under the Meles Regime," Annual Meeting of the Midwest Political Science Association. April 11–14, 2013. Chicago, Il.

Quinn, John James and David J. Simon. "Plus ça change, . . . : The Allocation of French ODA to Africa During and After the Cold War." *International Interactions* 32 (2006): 295–318.

Radetzki, Marian. *State Mineral Enterprises: An Investigation into Their Impact on International Mineral Markets.* Washington, D.C.: Resources for the Future, 1985.

Rakner, Lise and Nicolas van de Walle. "Opposition Weakness in Africa." *Journal of Democracy* 20, 3 (July 2009): 108–121, p. 110.

Ramachandran, Vijaya, Alan Gelb, Manju Kedia Shah. *Africa's Private Sector: What's Wrong with the Business Environment and What to Do About It.* Washington, DC: Center for Global Development, 2009.

Ramamurtri, Ravi. "The Search for Remedies." In Ravi Ramamurtri and Raymond Vernon, eds. *Privatization and Control of State-Owned Enterprises.* Washington, D.C: The World Bank, 1991: 7–28, 15.

Ran, Rati. "Exports and Economic Growth in Developing Countries: Evidence from Time Series and Cross Section Data." *Economic development and Cultural Change* 31 (October 1987): 51–73.

Randall, Vicky, and Robin Theobald, *Political Change and Underdevelopment: A Critical Introduction to Third World Politics.* Durham, NC: Duke University Press, 1985.

Rapley, John. *Ivoirien Capitalism: African Entrepreneurs in Côte d'Ivoire.* Boulder, CO: Lynne Rienner Publishers, 1993.

Rapley, John. "The Ivoirien Bourgeoisie." In Bruce J. Berman and Colin Leys, eds. *African Capitalists in African Development.* Boulder, CO: Lynne Rienner Publishers, 1994.

Rapley, John. *Understanding Development: Theory and Practice in the Third World, 3rd Edition.* Boulder, CO: Lynne Rienner Publications, 2007.

Ravenhill, John. "Africa's Continuing Crises: The Elusiveness of Development." In John Ravenhill, ed. *Africa in Economic Crisis.* New York: Columbia University Press, 1986: 1–43.

Reno, William. "Africa's Weak States, Nonstate Actors, and the Privatization of Interstate Relations." In John Harbeson and Donald Rothschild, eds. *Africa in World Politics: the African State System in Flux.* Boulder: West View Press, 2000: 286–307.

Reno, William. *Warlord Politics.* Boulder, CO: Lynne Rienner Publishers, 1998.

Reno, William. *Warlord politics and African states.* Lynne Rienner Publishers, 1999.

Reuters. "FACTBOX-Africa's presidents prolong their rule." Fri Aug 7, 2009 8:09am. http://www.reuters.com/article/idUSL7120283.

Riddell, J. Barry. "Things Fall Apart Again: Structural Adjustment Programmes in Sub-Saharan Africa." *The Journal of Modern African Studies* 30, 1 (Mar., 1992): 53–68.

Rimmer, Douglas, ed. *Action in Africa: The Experience of People Involved in Government Business & Aid.* Portsmouth, N.H.: Heinemann, 1993.

Robinson, Pearl T. "The National Conference Phenomenon in Francophone Africa." *Comparative Studies in Society and History* 36, 3 (July 1994): 575–610.

Rodman, Kenneth A. *Sanctity Versus Sovereignty: The United States and the Nationalization of Natural Resource Investments.* New York: Columbia University Press, 1988.

Rogowski, Ronald. *Commerce and Coalitions: How Trade Affects Domestic Political Alignments*. Princeton: Princeton University Press, 1989.

Rood, Leslie L. "Nationalisation and Indigenisation in Africa." *Journal of Modern African Studies* 14, 2 (1976): 427–447.

Rose, Richard. "Democracy and Enlarging the European Union Eastwards." *Journal of Common Market Studies* 33, 3 (September 1995): 427–450.

Rosecrance, Richard. *The Rise of the Trading State: Commerce and Conquest in the Modern World*. New York: Basic Books, 1986.

Ross E. Burkhart, and Michael S. Lewis-Beck. "Comparative Democracy: The Economic Development Thesis." *The American Political Science Review* 88, 4 (Dec., 1994): 903–910.

Ross, Michael. "Does Oil Hinder Democracy?" *World Politics* 53, 3 (2001): 325–361.

Ross, Michael. "The Political Economy of the Resource Curse." *World Politics* 51 (1999): 297–322.

Ross, Will. "Cameroon Makes Way for a King." BBC News, Friday, 11 April 2008.

Rostow, W.W. *The Stages of Economic Growth: A Non-Communist Manifesto*. New York: Cambridge University Press, 1960.

Rotberg, Robert I. "Failed States, Collapsed States, Weak States: Causes and Indicators." *State Failure and State Weakness in a Time of Terror*. Brookings Institution Press and the World Peace Foundation, 2003: 1–25.

Rotberg, Robert I., and Rachel M. Gisselquist. *"2009 Index of African Governance Data Set."* downloaded from http://www.nber.org/data/iag.html

Ruggie, John Gerard. "What Makes the World Hang Together?" Neoutilitarianism and the Social Constructivist Challenge. *International Organization* 52 (1998): 855–885.

Russett, Bruce. "Bushwhacking the Democratic Peace." *International Studies Perspectives* 6 (2005): 395–408.

Rustow, Dankwart. "Transitions to Democracy: Toward a Dynamic Model." *Comparative Politics* 2, 3 (April 1970): 337–363.

Sachs, Jeffrey D. "Conditionality, Debt Relief, and the Developing Country Debt Crisis." In Sachs, ed. *Developing Country Debt*: 275–284.

Sachs, Jeffrey, *Developing Country Debt*.

Sachs, Jeffrey D. "External Debt and Macroeconomic Performance in Latin America and East Asia." Brookings Papers on Economic Activity 2 (1985): 523–64, quote on 525.

Sachs, Jeffrey D. and Andrew M. Warner. "Fundamental Sources of Long-Run Growth." *American Economic Review* 87, 2 (1997).

Sachs, Jeffrey D. and Andrew M. Warner. "Natural Resource Abundance and Economic Growth" *NBER*, December 1995.

Sachs, Jeffrey. "Introduction." In J. Sachs, ed. *Developing Country Debt and the World Economy National Bureau of Economic Research*. Chicago: University of Chicago Press, 1989: 275–284.

Sandbrook, Richard. "Patrons, Clients and Factions: New Dimensions of Conflict Analysis in Africa." *Canadian Journal of Political Science* Vol. V, No 1 (March 1972).

Sandbrook, Richard. *The Politics of Africa's Economic Recovery*. Cambridge: Cambridge University Press, 1993.

Sartori, Giovanni. "Rethinking Democracy: Bad Polity and Bad Politics." *International Social Science Journal* 129 (August 1991): 437–451.

Sautman, Barry and Yan Hairong. "Trade, Investment, Power and the China-in-Africa Discourse." *The Asia-Pacific Journal* http://japanfocus.org/-Yan-Hairong/3278/article.pdf

Schatz, Sayre P. *Nigerian Capitalism*. Berkeley: University of California Press, 1977.

Schatz, Sayre P. "Pirate Capitalism and the Inert Economy of Nigeria." *The Journal of Modern African Studies* 22, 1 (1984): 45–57.

Schatzberg, Michael. "Zaire." In Timothy Shaw and Olajide Aluko, eds. *The Political Economy of African Foreign Policy*. Aldershot, UK: Gower, 1984: 283–318.

Schmitt, David E. "Bicommunalism in Northern Ireland." *Publius: The Journal of Federalism* 18 (Spring 1988).

Schraeder, Peter J. *African Politics and Society: A Mosaic in Transformation* 2nd Edition. Belmont, CA: Thompson, Wadsworth, 2004.

Schraeder, Peter J. "Foreign-Aid Posturing in Francophone Africa." In Steven W. Hook, ed. *Foreign Aid Toward the Millennium*. Boulder, CO: Lynne Rienner Publishers, 1996: 173–190.

Schraeder, Peter J., Steven W. Hook, and Bruce Taylor. "Clarifying the Foreign Aid Puzzle: A Comparison of American, Japanese, French, and Swedish Aid Flows." *World Politics*, 50, 2 (1998): 294–323.

"Selling the Family Copper." *The Economist* 353, 814 (November 6, 1999).

Shafer, D. Michael. "Capturing the Mineral Multinationals: Advantage or Disadvantage." *International Organization* 37, 1 (Winter 1983): 93–119.

Shepherd, Andrew W., and Stefano Farolfi. *Export Crop Liberalization in Africa: A Review*. Rome: Food and Agriculture Organization of the United Nations, 1999.

Shields, Joseph, and Jonathan Elist. "The Key to Unlocking Africa's Multi-Billion Dollar Agriculture Opportunity: Great Managers." http://africa.harvard.edu/apj/the-key-to-unlocking-africas-multi-billion-dollar-agriculture-opportunity-great-managers/

Shively, W. Phillips. *Power and Choice: An Introduction to Political Science* 14th edition. New York: McGraw-Hill Education, 2014.

Sigmund, Paul E., ed. *The Ideologies of the Developing Nations* 2nd Edition. New York: Praeger Publishers, 1972.

Singer, H. "The Distribution of Gains Between Investing and Borrowing Countries." *American Economic Review* 40 (May 1950): 473–485.

Sklar, Richard L. "The Colonial Imprint on African Political Thought." In Carter and O'Meara Eds., *African Independence*, pp. 1–31.

Sklar, Richard L. *Corporate Power in an African State: The Political Impact of Multinational Mining Companies in Zambia*. Los Angeles: University of California Press, 1975.

Sklar, Richard L. "Democracy in Africa." *African Studies Review* 26, 3/4 (September-December 1983).

Sklar, Richard L. "Developmental Democracy." *Comparative Studies in Society and History* 29, 4 (October 1987): 686–714.

Sklar, Richard L. "The Nature of Class Domination in Africa." *The Journal of Modern African Studies* 17, 4 (1979), p. 531.

Sklar, Richard L. *Nigerian Political Power: Power in an Emergent African Nation.* Princeton: Princeton University Press, 1963.

Sklar, Richard L. "Postimperialism: A Class Analysis of Multinational Corporate Expansion." In David G. Becker et al., eds. *Postimperialism: International Capitalism and Development in the Late Twentieth Century.* Boulder, Co.: Lynne Rienner Publishers, 1987: 19–40.

Sklar, Richard L. "Postimperialism: Concepts and Implications." In David G. Becker and Richard L. Sklar, eds. *Postimperialism and World Politics.* Westport, CT: Praeger, 1999: 11–36.

Sklar Richard L. and C.S. Whitaker, Jr. "Nigeria." In Coleman and Rosberg. *Political Parties*: 597–654.

Skocpol, Theda. "Bringing the State Back In: Strategies of Analysis in Current Research." In Peter B. Evans, Dietrich Rueschemeyer, and Theda Skocpol, eds. *Brining the State Back In.* Cambridge: Cambridge University Press, 1985: 3–43.

Skocpol, Theda. *States and Social Revolutions: A Comparative Analysis of France, Russia and China.* Cambridge University Press, 1979.

Smith, David. "Mugabe and Allies Own 40% of Land Seized from White Farmers—Inquiry" *The Guardian* (Tuesday 30 November 2010 13.59 EST).

Smith, Tony. "Patterns in the Transfer of Power: A Comparative Study of French and British Decolonization." In Gifford and Louis. *The Transfer of Power in Africa*: 87–116.

Smith, Tony. "Requiem or New Agenda for Third World Studies?" *World Politics* 37, 4 (July 1985) 532–561.

Snidal, Duncan. "Limits of Hegemonic Stability Theory." *International Organization* 39 (August 1985): 579–614.

Southall, Roger. "The Centralization and Fragmentation of South Africa's Dominant Party System." *African Affairs* (1998), 97, 443–469.

Spero, Joan E. and Jeffrey A. Hart. *The Politics of International Economic Relations* 7th Edition. Stamford, CT: Cengage, 2003.

Stacy, Helen. "Relational Sovereignty." *Stanford Law Review* 55, 5 (May, 2003): 2029–2059.

Stanley, Charles E. *A History of Economic Thought: From Aristotle to Arrow.* Cambridge, MA: Blackwell, 1989: 222–240.

Starr, Harvey. "Democratic Dominoes: Diffusion Approaches to the Spread of Democracy in the International System." *The Journal of Conflict Resolution* Vol. 35, No. 2 (Jun., 1991): 356–381.

Starr, Harvey and H., C. Lindborg, C. "Democratic Dominoes Revisited: The Hazards of Governmental Transitions, 1974–1996." *Journal of Conflict Resolution* 47, 4, (2003): 490–519.

Statistics of Sanctioned Posts in the Public Services of Nigeria, prepared by the Chief Statistician, Lagos. Comparative Tables 1960–1961 to 1965–1966.

Stengers, Jean. "Precipitous Decolonization: The Belgian Congo." In Gifford and Louis. *The Transfer of Power in Africa*: 305–336.

Stepan, Alfred, and Cindy Skach. "Constitutional Frameworks and Democratic Consolidation: Parliamentarianism versus Presidentialism." *World Politics* 46 (October 1993): 1–22

Stevens, P. "Resource Impact: Curse or Blessing? A Literature Survey." *Journal of Energy Literature* 9, 1 (2003): 1–42.

Stiglitz, Joseph E. *Globalization and its Discontents*. New York: W. W. Norton & Company, 2003.

Sturman, Kathryn. "Niger: Who Needs Presidential Term Limits?" *All Africa.com* (17 August 2009).

Subramanian, Arvind. "'The Inevitable Superpower' Why China's Dominance is a Sure Thing." *Foreign Affairs* (September/October 2011).

Subramanian, Arvind and Shang-Jin Wei. "The WTO Promotes Trade, Strongly but Unevenly." *Journal of International Economics* 72, 1 (2007): 151–175.

Suleiman, Ezra N., and John Waterbury. "Introduction: Analyzing Privatization in Industrial and Developing Countries." In Ezra N. Suleiman and John Waterbury, eds. *The Political Economy of Public Sector Reform and Privatization*. Boulder, CO: Westview Press, 1990: 1–21.

Sutton, F.X. "Planning and Rationality in the Newly Independent State in Africa." *Economic and Cultural Change* 10 (Oct-July 1961–1962).

Swainson, Nicola. "Indigenous Capitalism in Postcolonial Kenya." In Lubeck, ed. *The African Bourgeoisie*.

Tangri, Roger. *The Politics of Patronage in Africa: Parastatals, Privatization, & Private Enterprise*. Trenton, NJ: Africa World Press,1999.

Tangri, Roger and Andrew Mwenda. "Corruption and Cronyism in Uganda's privatization in the 1990s." *African Affairs* 100 (2001): 117–133.

Taylor, Charles Lewis, and Michael C. Hudson. *World Handbook of Political and Social Indicators* 2nd Edition (New Haven: Yale University Press, 1982).

Taylor, Ian. "China's Foreign Policy towards Africa in the 1990s," *Journal of Modern African Studies* 36, 3 (1998): 443–460.

The South African Data Archive (ICPSR). International-University Consortium for Political and Social Research (ICPSR).

The World Bank: World Development Indicators Database. World Bank http://siteresources.worldbank.org/DATASTATISTICS/Resources/GDP.pdf.

Thomas, Scott. "The Politics and Economics of Central and Eastern Europe." In *Columbia Journal of World Business* Volume XXVIII, No. 1 (Spring 1993): 168–179.

Tordoff, William. *Government and Politics in Africa*. Bloomington: Indiana University Press, 1984.

Tordoff, William. *Government and Politics in Africa* 2nd Edition. Bloomington: Indiana University Press, 1993.

Tull, Denis M. China's Engagement in Africa: Scope, Significance and Consequences." *Journal of Modern African Studies*, 44, 3 (2006), pp. 459–479.

Turner, Thomas. "Congo-Kinshasa Leans toward Federalism." *Federations Magazine* (October/November 2007): 4–5. http://www.forumfed.org/en/products/magazine/vol7_num1/congo.php.

Tyler, William G. "Growth and Export Expansion in Developing Countries." *Journal of Developmental Economics* 9 (1981): 121–138.

U.N. *Human Development Report, 2009: Overcoming barriers: Human mobility and development*. New York: United Nations Development Programme, 2009.

U.N. Secretary General. *Permanent Sovereignty Over Natural Resource*, A/9716 (Supplement to E/5425), 20 September 1974.

UNCTAD. *Bilateral Investment Treaties 1959–1999*. New York: United Nations, 2000. http://www.unctad.org/Templates/Page.asp?intItemID=2344&lang=1

UNCTAD. *Handbook of Trade Control Measures of Developing Countries: A Statistical Analysis of Trade Control Measures of Developing Countries 1987*. Geneva: United Nations Conference on Trade and Development, 1987.

UNCTAD. *World Investment Report: Transnational Corporations, Agricultural Development, and Agriculture*. Geneva: United Nations, 2009.

UNCTADstat. http://unctadstat.unctad.org/TableViewer/dimView.aspx

USAID Support for NGO Capacity-Building: Approaches, Examples, Mechanisms. Washington, DC: Office of Private and Voluntary Cooperation, USAID, July 1998.

van de Walle, Nicolas. *African Economies and the Politics of Permanent Crisis, 1979–1999*. Cambridge: Cambridge University Press, 2001.

van de Walle, Nicolas. "Elections without Democracy: Africa's Range of Regimes." *Journal of Democracy* 13, 2 (April 2002): 66–80.

van de Walle, Nicolas. "Neopatrimonialism and Democracy in Africa, with an Illustration from Cameroon." In Widner, ed. *Economic Change*: 129–157.

van de Walle, Nicolas. "The Politics of Public Enterprise Reform in Cameroon." In Grosh and Mukandala. *State-Owned Enterprises*: 151–174.

van de Walle, Nicholas. "Presidentialism and Clientism in Africa's Emerging Party Systems." *The Journal of Modern African Studies* 41, no. 2 (June 2003): 297–322.

van de Walle N. and K. S. Butler. "Political parties and party systems in Africa's illiberal democracies." *Cambridge Review of International Studies* 13, 1 (1999): 14–28.

Vansina, Jan. "Mwasi's Trials." In "Black Africa." Special issue of *Daedalus*: 49–70.

Wade, Robert. *Governing the Market: Economic Theory and the Role of Government in East Asian Industrialization*. Princeton: Princeton University Press, 1990.

Wallerstein, Immanuel. "Voluntary Associations." In Coleman and Rosberg, *Political Parties*: 318–339.

Wallerstein, Immanuel. *The Modern World System*. New York: Academic Press, 1974.

Waltz, Kenneth. *Theory of International Relations*. Reading, MA: Addison-Wesley Publishing Company, 1979.

Warren, Bill. *Imperialism: Pioneer of Capitalism*. London: Verso, 1980.

Weber, Max. "The Three Types of Legitimate Rule" *Berkeley Publications in Society and Institutions* 4, 1 (1958): 1–11. Translated by Hans Gerth.

Welch Jr., Claude E. "The African Military and Political Development." In Henry Bienen, ed. *The Military and Modernization*. Chicago: Aldine, Atherton, 1971.

Welch Jr., Claude E. *Soldier and State in Africa*. Evanston, IL: Northwestern University Press, 1970.

Wendt, Alexander. "Anarchy Is What States Make of It: The Social Construction of Power Politics." *International Organization* 46, 2 (Spring 1992): 391–425.

White, Oliver Campbell, and Anita Bhatia, *Privatization in Africa*. Washington, DC: The World Bank, 1998.

Widner, Jennifer, ed. *Economic Change and Political Liberalization in Sub-Saharan Africa*. Baltimore: Johns Hopkins University Press, 1994.

Widner, Jennifer. "Political Reform in Anglophone and Francophone African Countries." In Widner, ed. *Economic Change*: 49–79.

Williams, David. "Aid and Sovereignty: Quasi-States and the International Financial Institutions." *Review of International Studies* 26, 4 (2000): 557–573.

Williams, Paul D. "From Non-Intervention to Non-Indifference: The Origins and the Development of the African Union's Security Culture." *African Affairs* 106, 423 (March 2007): 253–279.

Williamson, John. "Democracy and the 'Washington Consensus.'" *World Development* 21, 8 (1993): 1329–1336.

Williamson, John. "What Should the World Bank Think About the Washington Consensus?" *The World Bank Research Observer* 15, 2 (August 2000): 251–264.

Williamson, Oliver E. *The Economic Institutions of Capitalism: Firms, Markets, Relational Contracting*. New York: The Free Press, 1985.

Wilson, Ernie. "French Support for Structural Adjustment Programs in Africa." *World Politics* 21, 3 (1993): 331–347.

Wines, Michael. "Zimbabwe: Mugabe To Pursue Nationalization." *The New York Times*, Section A; Column 0, Pg. 7 (July 25, 2007).

Wohlforth, William C. "Realism and the End of the Cold War." *International Security* 19, 3 (Winter, 1994–1995): 91–129.

Wohlforth, William C. "The Stability of a Unipolar World." *International Security* 24, 1 (1999): 5–41.

World Bank. *Accelerated Development in Sub-Saharan Africa*. Washington, DC: World Bank, 1981.

World Bank. *Adjustment in Africa: Reforms, Results, and the Road Ahead*. Washington, D.C.: The World Bank, 1994.

World Bank. *African Development Indicators*, 1992. Washington D.C: World Bank.

World Bank. *Bureaucrats in Business: The Economics and Politics of Government Ownership*. Washington, DC: World Bank, 1995.

World Bank. *Governance and Development*. Washington, DC: World Bank, 1992.

World Bank. *Sub-Saharan Africa: From Crisis to Sustainable Growth*. Washington, DC: World Bank, 1989.

World Bank. *World Development Indicators*. http://data.worldbank.org/data-catalog/world-development-indicators

World Bank. *World Development Report 1983*. Washington, DC: World Bank, 1983.

World Bank. *World Development Report 1987*. Washington, D.C.: World Bank, 1987.

World Bank. *World Development Report 1989*. Washington DC: World Bank, 1989.

World Bank. *World Development Report 1982*. Washington DC: World Bank, 1992.

World Bank. *World Development Report 1997*. Washington, DC: World Bank, 1997.

World Currency Yearbook. Brooklyn, NY: International Currency Analysis, Inc., Various years.

World Economic Outlook Database, April 2010. IMF. http://www.imf.org/external/pubs/ft/weo/2010/01/weodata/index.aspx.

Wright, Stephen, ed. *African Foreign Policies.* Boulder: Westview, 1999.

Yang, Yongzheng and Sanjeev Gupta. "Regional Trade Arrangements in Africa: Past Performance and the Way Forward." *IMF Working Paper.* Washington, DC: International Monetary Fund, 2005.

Young, Crawford. *The African Colonial State in Comparative Perspective.* New Haven: Yale University Press, 1994.

Young, Crawford. *Ideology and Development in Africa.* New Haven: Yale University Press, 1982.

Young, Crawford. *Politics in the Congo: Decolonization and Independence.* Princeton: Princeton University Press, 1965.

Young, Crawford. "The Third Wave of Democratization in Africa: Ambiguities and Contradictions." In Joseph. *State, Conflict, and Democracy*: 15–38.

Young, Crawford. "Zaire, Rwanda and Burundi." In Michael Crowder, ed. *The Cambridge History of Africa,* Vol. 8 1940–1975. Cambridge: Cambridge University Press, 1984: 698–754.

Young, Crawford and Thomas Turner. *The Rise and Decline of the Zairian State.* Madison, WI: University of Wisconsin Press, 1985.

Young, Oran R. "Regime dynamics: the rise and fall of international regimes." *International Organization* 36, no. 02 (1982): 277–297.

Young, Peter. "Privatization around the World." *Proceedings of the Academy of Political Science,* Vol. 36, No. 3, Prospects for Privatization (1987), pp. 190–206.

Zartman, I. William. "Africa as a Subordinate State System in International Relations." *International Organization* 21, 3 (1967): 545–564

Zartman, I. William, ed., *Collapsed States: the Disintegration and Restoration of Legitimate Authority.* Boulder, CO: Lynne Rienner Publishers, 1995.

Zartman, I. William. *The Political Economy of Nigeria.* New York: Praeger Publishers, 1983.

Zolberg, Aristide. "Military Intervention in the New States of Tropical Africa: Elements of Comparative Analysis." In Henry Bienen, ed., *The Military Intervenes: Case Studies in Political Development.* New York: Russell Sage Foundation, 1968: 71–102.

Zolberg, Aristide. "The Military Decade in Africa." *World Politics* 25, 2, pp. 309–331.

Zolberg, Aristide. *Creating Political Order: The Party-States of West Africa.* Chicago: Rand McNally & Company, 1966.

Zolberg, Aristide. *One Party Government in the Ivory Coast.* Princeton: Princeton University Press, 1964.

Index*

---

* only scholars named in text are in index/others in Bibliography and/ or endnotes

About the Author

John James Quinn (Ph.D., University of California, Los Angeles) is Professor of Political Science at Truman State University where he teaches and writes on issues of African development and democratization as well as international relations, comparative politics, methodology, and international political economy. His African experiences include being a Peace Corp Volunteer in Zaire (now the Democratic Republic of the Congo) as well as a visiting professor at the University of Ghana-Legon. His articles have appeared in such journal as *International Interactions*, *Party Politics*, *International Politics*, and *Journal of Political Science Education* as well as in edited books and other volumes. His primary research interest links majority state ownership of economic sectors to subsequent political, economic, and social outcomes. He has also written on the diffusion of the Rwandan genocide leading to Mobutu's ouster, the determinates of French ODA to Africa (during and after Cold War), the links between democracy and development in Africa, causes of corruption cross nationally, African foreign policies, and the types of political parties that emerged in Africa following the recent multiparty elections. He is also author of *The Road oft Traveled: Development Polices and Majority State Ownership of Industry in Africa.*